The Global Indie Author:

How anyone can self-publish in the U.S. and worldwide markets

By M. A. Demers

Egghead
Books

Published by Egghead Books, Canada

www.mademers.com
www.eggheadbooks.com

Published by Egghead Books, 2011

Cover design and photography by Michelle A. Demers

Library and Archives Canada Cataloguing in Publication

Demers, M. A., 1964-
    The global indie author : how anyone can self-publish in the U.S. and worldwide markets / by M. A. Demers.

Includes bibliographical references.
Issued also in electronic formats.
ISBN 978-0-9868914-4-1

    1. Self-publishing. I. Title.

Z285.5.D46 2011   070.5'93   C2011-907026-X

Contents

Preface

There is no one right way to publish a book but there is one wrong way: uninformed.

This is a truly exciting time to be an indie writer. For the first time in history, self-publishing, in particular ebook publishing, has the real potential to liberate writers the way iTunes and YouTube have liberated musicians and videographers. Never before has there been this great an opportunity to be heard and read, and to build a global audience. But self-publishing is also the new Wild West, full of promise and snake oil in equal measure. And as the industry grows so too does the debate over its merits, with both sides of the argument inhabited by many with an agenda: you will find a plethora of articles and blogs written by industry insiders who wish to maintain the status quo, or by evangelical self-publishing gurus who preach the ease and freedom of indie publishing because easy is attractive and easy sells. Neither side is being completely truthful, and neither extreme is the whole picture. *The Global Indie Author* separates the truth from the rhetoric and provides you with the information you need to create an indie publishing plan that is realistic and achievable.

Another deficiency this manual corrects is the lack of information for the non-American writer who wants to tap into the U.S. market, or for the American writer who wants to distribute globally. Amazon, Barnes & Noble, major book wholesalers such as Ingram and Baker & Taylor, and large print-on-demand companies such as CreateSpace and Lightning Source are all American and so for the non-American self-publisher—and I shall lump us all together under the moniker "foreign" for ease of use—issues will quickly emerge: some U.S. retailers will deny you an account, tax laws will require paperwork, international banking must be contended with, and company reps will all too often provide incorrect information either because they assume you are American or because they do not know the answers to your questions and do not wish to appear unknowledgeable. None of these problems are insurmountable and some are avoidable altogether if the foreign author is forewarned and prepared. And whether foreign or American, every author who sells globally through the major retail players like Amazon, Apple, or Kobo must learn about foreign income and sales tax laws; how copyright, trademark, and libel laws operate both at home and internationally; and how the ISBN system works. *The Global Indie Author* thus looks at self-publishing from an international perspective, providing information for Americans and foreigners alike (though with an English-market emphasis).

You can approach self-publishing, and this manual, in a number of ways. The first is for those who want to get their ebook to market with a minimum of fuss, either because you want to test the waters before plunging in deeper or perhaps the idea of learning new software or managing your own book distribution does not appeal to you. Rather than investing your time and energy learning the messy details, you can make a financial investment and focus on your writing. Part I shows you how to get your book onto Amazon's Kindle in ten easy steps, and then how to expand further afield through retail programs such as Barnes & Noble's PubIt!.

For those without the means or inclination to pay others, or who are keen to learn the details of the business and/or its technology, the remainder of this manual provides in-depth knowledge of every aspect of self-publishing and illustrates the pros and cons of the various options you will be able to choose from as you progress. Whether you intend to publish only to Kindle, to widen your horizons into ePubs, or widen them further still and tackle print, you will find the detailed information you need to produce a professional quality book and to distribute it to your best advantage.

You can also compromise between these approaches by tackling the manual in smaller bites, perhaps by first learning how to format your Word manuscript for Kindle while contracting out other tasks such as cover design and the more difficult ePub conversion. Rather than try to digest what is *a lot* of detail, and which can seem daunting if read all at once, you can reference different chapters as questions or problems arise and you need more information. Feel free to learn at your own pace.

Most chapters end with a list of useful links, live as at time of writing. Links include articles of interest, websites such as Kindle Direct Publishing where you will open your account, indie publishing forums, various national ISBN agencies, software downloads, and necessary evils like the IRS.

The more you learn the more you will discover that knowledge can open unexpected doors, and will increase your options and provide greater control. The process of self-publishing my first novel, *Baby Jane*, was a baptism of fire because I did not have a manual like this one and had to learn as I went along. My ignorance meant mistakes were made and delays incurred. My objective in writing this manual is to avail other indie writers of the information that I would have benefitted immensely from, information that will help you avoid potential pitfalls *before* you put a lot of time, effort, and money into your book only to have the momentum you created reversed by later setbacks. *The Global Indie Author* also reveals secrets and strategies the industry players would rather you did not know so they can lock you into unfavourable contracts, take your money before you run into problems and start asking questions, or convince you that what is really good for them is good for you.

The journey into indie publishing can be both exhilarating and frustrating. The trick is to ride the wave of exhilaration and take the frustrations in stride, and to remember that traditionally published authors also experience frustrations, just different ones. You will find, too, that with each new project your knowledge and confidence as a self-publisher will grow. Welcome to the world of indie publishing.

Introduction

How Did We Get Here?

In the past, particularly in the nineteenth and early twentieth centuries, it was not uncommon for legitimate authors to publish their own books because doing so offered greater control and profits. Lewis Carroll self-published *Alice's Adventures in Wonderland* and most of his subsequent works; some other famous authors to self-publish were Mark Twain, Zane Grey, Edgar Rice Burroughs, Virginia Woolf, George Bernard Shaw, Beatrix Potter, Edgar Allan Poe, Rudyard Kipling, Henry David Thoreau, Walt Whitman, and Anaïs Nin. Then as now, they were able to do so because they had the financial means. Authors without the means were forced to solicit the attention of established publishers, while others formed writers' collectives and pooled their resources to publish each other. Some of these writers' collectives went on to become prestigious publishing houses.

Commercial changes in the latter part of the twentieth century changed the dynamics of the publishing industry. Wholesale distribution, creation of the ISBN system in 1966, the rise of powerful publishing houses and literary agencies, elitist book reviewers and so on created a culture whereby an author either published through an established house or self-published under the stigma of assumed rejection. Self-publishing became known by the derogatory term "vanity press," its very name serving to reinforce the idea that only publishers were qualified to decide what and whom was worthy of publication, and any writer who dared to challenge this assumption by self-publishing could be dismissed as delusional or worse, a narcissist. So successful was the publishers' rise to prominence that the prejudice against the self-published writer became automatic and systemic: distributors would not distribute, booksellers would not carry stock, libraries ignored you, government literary grants were not open to the self-published and most literary awards were also closed, professional reviewers wouldn't give your book the time of day, and so on.

In this culture of beggars and choosers, writers lost what little power they had to begin with (which was never much). Sure, if you became a Stephen King your publisher had no illusions as to who called the shots, but literary megastars are few; the masses, to borrow from Thoreau, live lives of quiet desperation. Abuses abound, and most published writers have more than one horror story to tell, even those who don't work in that genre.

Still, some writers persevered, and a few used self-publishing to gain the attention of publishers. John Grisham, James Redfield, Gertrude Stein, Deepak Chopra, Tom Clancy, Stephen Crane, and Margaret Atwood, to name but a few, self-published then went on to literary success.

With the move toward media consolidation that began in earnest in the 1990s, in an ironic twist of fortune the publishers themselves came under attack. Retail channels became majority controlled by a small oligarchy, and their power forced many small bookstores into failure and more than one publisher into bankruptcy.[1] Publishers found their profit margins shrinking as retail giants demanded ever larger discounts, and the industry practice of accepting unsold stock for return and refund began to backfire immensely when the retailers began a habit of over-ordering a title then returning, on average, 25-50% of stock, saddling the publisher with the manufacturing bill and a warehouse full of depreciating assets. Publishers tried to fight back by consolidating as well, with large houses gobbling up smaller imprints only to empty them of editorial staff and release bottom-earning authors from the roster. Large publishers became leaner and meaner, small publishers tried (often in vain) to stay afloat, and the result was an industry now firmly divided between publishers who treat books solely as a business and those few remaining altruists who still believe in nurturing culture.

The effect of this on writers has been dramatic and profound. The use of sales trackers like BookNet, Nielsen BookScan, and BookTrack encourages publishers to abandon talented but poorly-selling new authors instead of nurturing them as publishers would have done in the past, or to drop established authors whose last work did not meet sales expectations.[2] Some publishers refuse to publish a client's latest work if its style or content strays from the author's proven formula,[3] while other authors find themselves and their books adrift when a publisher goes bankrupt or terminates an imprint.[4] Staff cuts have resulted in fewer editors who are nevertheless expected to maintain the publisher's annual publication quotas, and who thus have less time to help an author fix a manuscript's weaknesses. One consequence of this is that more and more editorial burden is now placed upon the literary agency, which in turn is one reason why most publishers who once welcomed unsolicited manuscripts now demand submissions through agencies, the very agencies that have become increasingly difficult to penetrate by an unproven author. And even if an author manages to find an agent and a publisher, smaller advertising budgets mean fewer resources devoted to promoting your work. Instead there is an expectation that authors will do a great deal of the promotional work themselves and at their own expense, yet these same authors are not receiving a greater portion of royalties than in the past. And those royalties are small: the author's cut is around 15% of the cover price on hardcovers, 10% or less on paperbacks, and 17.5% or less on ebook sales.

The pressures now placed on publishers has had a negative effect on creativity as well. Sales and marketing personnel are becoming increasingly more influential and are imposing themselves upon the editorial departments, meaning that commercial considerations are often dictating editorial decisions. What this means for authors is that sales people, who usually have little if any literary or editorial background, are dictating changes to your manuscript. And if you think going to a smaller, more literary press is the solution, think again: government grants and protectionist policies that support small literary presses are under threat by governments that simply do not see the value anymore in their nations' literary development, or which do not read books.

The result is that most traditional publishing—now called "legacy publishing"—has become like Hollywood: only safe, already-been-done stories (and a plethora of franchises) are deemed commercially viable, and if a trend develops publishers jump on the bandwagon instead of nurturing new ideas; you are only as good as your last project; writers exist in an absurd Catch-22 situation whereby you need an agent to get published but you usually need a publishing credit to get an agent (or a referral from an existing client); politics abound; the money people are making creative decisions they are not qualified to make; independent publishers must rely heavily on ever-diminishing government and private foundation grants to get projects made only to discover limited access to the retail market; and cultural protectionist policies, where they exist at all, are crumbling under the weight of big business lobbyists.

This is not to ignore the history of commercial fare that has always existed and its importance to the industry. Mystery, romance, and suspense novels have always lived alongside great literature, and great literature has never been the backbone of the market: for every *Ulysses* there are a million Harlequin Romances or their male-audience equivalents, the penny Western or action-adventure. Literary fiction gets the accolades but genre fiction—and the quiet world of non-fiction, especially academia—keeps the lights on. More than one "serious" writer has earned a living writing commercial fare under a *nom de plume* because literary fiction rarely pays the bills. But at least there *was* an outlet for one's literary aspirations, an outlet that is shrinking at an alarming rate.

Scarier still are the increasingly suspect business practices of some literary agencies and publishing houses. Contracts that contain draconian clauses to the disadvantage of the writer; agencies that will not promote one writer if their work conflicts with the success of another, more valuable, client; massaging of sales figures and other creative accounting practices; agents who have forgotten whom they work for and instead collude with publishers ... the list goes on. And some agencies are now becoming publishers despite the obvious conflict of interest, while others are developing new business strategies such as offering creative writing courses that promise representation to "exceptional students,"[5] a practice critics say is merely a backdoor way to charge an upfront fee for a service (the development of a manuscript) the agency previously provided as a contractual obligation to its clients.

And if you are a writer of English-language books but you are not American or British, the situation worsens. We Canadians, for example, have a poor track record of supporting our compatriots yet gobble up foreign fare, the result of which is that "Canadian bookstore[s] and library shelves are filled by about 80-per-cent foreign-written and -published books ... promoted by U.S. television programs and magazines such as *60 Minutes* and People, which have, respectively, more viewers in Canada than *the fifth estate* and more readers than Maclean's."[6] Australia, which, like Canada, has struggled to create a culture independent of the U.S. and the UK, boasts a 60% market penetration by home-grown fare but government legislation and support programs that led to this market penetration are now under threat.[7]

And Where Are We Going?

New technologies are challenging the fundamental principles of the industry. The first major development was the broad adoption of the digital printing press, which can print one book for the same price per unit it prints a thousand, and the resultant print-on-demand (POD) business model of book selling: books must no longer be printed in advance with the hope of sales but can be printed only as books are ordered by the retailer or online consumer, significantly reducing the risk to the publisher (at least in theory, if not always in practice). But the POD model has also resulted in a new breed of vanity publishers—now calling themselves "author services" companies—that have capitalized on this growing market by luring writers in with the promise of legitimacy: possible national distribution through regular sales channels. The key word is "possible," the pitch a brilliant bit of capitalism: sell a dream, make no promises, incur no costs of your own to print, distribute, and market, make a fortune off the author, then take a cut of sales if and when they happen.

The second and more significant technological change was the advent of electronic book publishing. Due to the lower retail cost of ebooks, along with their embrace by Amazon— the lion of online book sales—ebooks exploded into popular culture, taking the publishing world by surprise with their phenomenally rapid growth. According to the Association of American Publishers, "For the year to date (January/February 2011 vs January/February 2010) ... e-Books grew 169.4% to $164.1M while the combined categories of print books fell 24.8% to $441.7M."[8] This suggests a print to ebook ratio of 2.69:1, but what is hidden in that figure is that, since ebooks sell at a lower price point than physical books, the number of ebooks sold is even more impressive than the dollar figures suggest. Sales of paperbacks still dominate the industry overall, but the upward trend of ebooks cannot be ignored. And the continued introduction of new players into the market, most significantly Barnes & Noble (Nook Books), Sony (eReader Bookstore), Apple (iBookstore), and Kobo (majority owned by Indigo Books and Music), is a clear indication these global players see a future and a fortune in the ebook format.

But just as with print-on-demand, the lucrative sums possible through ebooks have attracted opportunists. These include the author services companies whose contracts include an automatic e-publishing rights clause (taking 50% of your royalties), ebook aggregators[9] who sell you a way past the gatekeepers, and literary agency contracts that assign your ebook publishing rights to themselves, effectively making the agency your ebook publisher, which will impact whether another publisher will be interested in buying the print rights to your book knowing that a significant revenue stream (ebook sales) is unavailable.

When Amazon opened its Kindle sales channel to self-publishers, the result was a profound paradigm shift in the publishing world. New writers found in the Kindle format a financially viable way to bypass the gatekeepers yet still reach a global audience: a writer can now, with the power of the Internet and social networking, market themselves if they are willing to put in the time and effort; and English-language writers of any nationality, if they take appropriate steps, can compete side by side with American and British authors. Established authors see an opportunity to earn higher royalties by no longer paying their publisher and agent a cut, instead capitalizing on existing fame to connect directly with a ready-built audience. And as the stigma of self-publishing is lifted by more and more success stories, and by the decision by some famous authors to defect over to self-publishing, mainstream book reviewers might rethink their position on lumping us all together as publisher rejects who wouldn't take no for an answer.

This is not to say that legacy publishing has nothing at all to offer you, and I do not wish to add to the rhetoric by suggesting this. The author fortunate enough to connect with the right people will benefit from editorial development and a publisher who takes on the financial risk of designing, printing, distributing, and marketing your book. Their knowledge of how to work the distribution and retail channels can be formidable, their mailing and subscription lists enviable. A legacy publisher also provides instant credibility to a new writer—your work has been vetted and critiqued—and access to professional reviewers, which helps you compete with the thousands of established writers vying for the same audience's attention. What has changed is the ability of self-publishing to act as a stepping stone to traditional publishing: what was previously derided is now seen as a viable strategy for attracting the attention of industry professionals. Some have called self-publishing platforms "the new in-box" for agents and editors, and some editors now suggest self-publishing as a first step for authors because "'It's a good way to build a brand.'"[10]

Self-publishing offers more control, higher profit margins, total creative freedom, and your book will reach the market much faster. The beauty, too, is that if you have a great manuscript it will eventually find its audience and attract the attention of the industry. When that happens you will know then if you want to stay solo, sign on with a publisher, or find a balance between the two. But most important of all, it will be *your choice*.

Shared Concerns

What is often missing in the debate between legacy publishing and self-publishing are the shared concerns of both. Legacy publishers will often point to the time the indie author has to spend marketing their work, time that could be spent writing while one's agent and publisher handle sales. But while it is true that the indie author has to spend more time on marketing unless they can afford to hire that out, the bigger truth is that *all* writers must spend time away from developing their craft to promote it. There are book signings, tours, readings, interviews, and now blogging and social networking, all unpaid and all of which means less time for writing. And the upward trend in publishing houses is for the author to do more and more of the marketing themselves, so what is the difference?

Another argument made against self-publishing is that the indie author must trust reported sales figures, whether by a retailer like Amazon or one's aggregator or distributor. How do you know they are not fudging the figures? And you can forget about auditing them: the expense is prohibitive. But the same holds true for legacy published authors: tales of creative accounting abound in the legacy world just as much as they do in the indie world. And while it might be cheaper to audit your agent or publisher, you will need to find new ones first because suing one's agent or publisher is professional suicide for anyone without a bestseller.

Legacy publishers will emphasize the risk they take to publish and market your work, and the advance they pay knowing it may never be recouped. This is valid. Yet no one points to the time the author spent writing the manuscript in the first place, time that may never be remunerated, as well as hard costs for research, especially for non-fiction writers. And a publisher's advance is merely a loan, payable against future royalties, the terms of which are more beneficial to the publisher until the advance has been repaid. It is by no means free money.

All authors must also deal with international banking, exchange rates, and tax laws. If you publish globally, if your publisher is in a different country from your own, you will have to deal with royalty tax laws in the various jurisdictions your work is sold in, you will win or lose on currency exchanges, and you will benefit from setting up international accounts. Much of the accounting might be dealt with by the publisher but that does not mean the legacy-published author is unaffected.

And lastly, competition for readers is fierce but it is fierce for everyone. In the two largest English-language markets, the U.S. and the UK, print titles legacy published in 2010, in all categories, exceeded 300,000 in the U.S.[11] and over 150,000 in the UK.[12] Canada and Australia combined publish around 20,000 books annually.[13] New Zealand adds another 2000 titles and South Africa some 2500 English-language titles.[14] How many become the bestsellers that make the news? How many *Da Vinci Code*s or *Harry Potter*s are there among the almost half-million annual titles? How many will even sell enough to earn the writer the "luxury" of not having a day job? Legacy publishing is no more a guarantee of success than is indie publishing. There are failures and successes on both sides, which is what makes legacy publishers nervous and indie publishing increasingly attractive.

Why Did I Do It?

Why did I choose to self-publish? In my case it was the intersection of several factors. The first was the impact of the 2008 recession on my then main source of income, the film industry, and the subsequent need for me to reassess my career. I decided to take advantage of some savings I had and pursue a long-shelved goal of writing a novel. But when I began talking at various writers' events about the book I was working on, it quickly became apparent that there was little support for genre fiction in Canada and that I would likely need to look abroad for representation and publication. Yet when I began pitching my novel to American agents and publishers, the first question asked was, "Are you married to the location?"—the assumption being that a book set in Canada would not appeal *at all* to a U.S. audience. I learned very fast that I would likely spend a great deal of time trying to find that elusive literary agent, who would then spend an exorbitant amount of time trying to find that elusive publisher, who would then force changes to my story to meet the demands of the sales department. Why bother when I could spend the same amount of time navigating the world of self-publishing, time and effort that might result in actual sales and not just the promise of them after I signed on the dotted line? And at least I would not have to worry about being screwed by my agent and/or publisher, or the effect my BookNet figures might have on the publication of my second book if sales of my first book were not spectacular.

In the meantime the negative changes to the publishing industry were beginning to make headlines while the self-publishing industry was getting comparable positive press, promising a revolution for writers. Self-publishing offered quicker access to the potentially lucrative U.S., UK, and other global markets. I'd had some luck in acquiring the financial resources to fund my own self-publishing experiment, I am comfortable with technology, and I possess the artistic abilities to design the cover and marketing materials (I am also a fine art photographer and have some graphic design background). I am also chronically impatient, and my impatience was buoyed by self-publishing success stories.

My experience of having worked as a writer in the film industry for the past fifteen years and having been subjected to abuse was also a factor: when my research revealed how legacy publishing had gone the way of Hollywood, I felt I would be trading one abuser for another. I know from experience that success equals power, and so if my book does well and Hollywood comes knocking, I will be in a position to protect my rights.

So while, yes, I wanted, absolutely, the affirmation of a legacy publisher, and while, yes, I would rather not be burdened with printing and distribution and marketing because that is time I could spend writing, in the end the promise of freedom and control was very alluring.

I have been a professional writer for a long time. I have written screenplays and project proposals, articles and editorials, short works of fiction and creative non-fiction, numerous Hollywood movie production notes, and I regularly blog; and I have benefitted from the luxury of peer review throughout this time. So I was confident in my abilities, made good use of editorial feedback—*Baby Jane* went through four drafts before I felt it was good enough to release—and I was capable of producing a quality cover. I did not feel that self-publishing was my only option, I felt that self-publishing was my practical option.

Having now gone through the process, would I do it again? I just did.

Useful Links

Geist article on the BookNet dictatorship.
http://www.geist.com/opinion/booknet-dictatorship

Wikipedia article on Nielsen BookScan.
http://en.wikipedia.org/wiki/Nielsen_BookScan

Toronto Life article on the erosion of CanLit protection policies.
http://www.torontolife.com/daily/hype/shelf-life/2011/01/04/chapters-indigo-versus-canadian-publishers-a-battle-looms-over-the-fate-of-canlit/

Very interesting blog about the publishing industry, by award-winning writer Kristine Kathryn Rusch.
http://kriswrites.com

Guardian article on Kindle success of UK mystery writer Stephen Leather, who self-published novellas that his legacy publisher had rejected because they were in a different genre and format from his bestselling works.
http://www.guardian.co.uk/technology/2011/feb/27/kindle-ebooks-amazon-stephen-leather?INTCMP=SRCH\

The Star article on the success of indie writer Amanda Hocking.
http://www.thestar.com/entertainment/books/article/948078--how-a-failed-author-made-2-million-from-e-books

Forbes article on the positive change in attitude of agents toward self-published authors.
http://www.forbes.com/sites/booked/2010/10/01/literary-agents-open-the-door-to-self-published-writers/

Association of American Publishers 14 April 2011 press release, "E-Books Rank as #1 Format among All Trade Categories for the Month."
http://www.publishers.org/press/30/

Bowker press release on number of new titles in both legacy publishing and self-publishing for 2010.
http://www.bowker.com/index.php/press-releases/633-print-isnt-dead-says-bowkers-annual-book-production-report

Interesting blog entry by a U.S. literary agent on what constitutes a publishing success from the perspective of the publisher.
http://askaliteraryagent.blogspot.com/2009/09/how-many-copies-must-book-sell-to-be.html

The Writer Magazine article on Curtis Brown agency's new writing school.
http://www.writermag.com/en/Articles/2011/02/A%20major%20literary%20agency%20
will%20open%20its%20own%20creative%20writing%20school.aspx

The Bookseller.com article on the move by Ed Victor Literary Agency to set up its own publishing imprint, Bedford Square Books.
http://www.thebookseller.com/news/ed-victor-sets-publishing-imprint.html

The Bookseller.com article on literary agents Curtis Brown and Blake Friedman's plans to move into publishing.
http://www.thebookseller.com/news/more-agents-explore-publishing-models.html

A funny take on manuscript rejection from writer Ruth Harris.
http://annerallen.blogspot.com/2011/05/what-it-really-means-when-your-book.html

Article about scam books on Amazon's Kindle.
http://www.reuters.com/article/2011/06/16/us-amazon-kindle-spam-idUSTRE75F68620110616

An author discusses her discovery of pirated ebooks sold on Kindle.
http://selfpubauthors.wordpress.com/2011/06/20/a-case-of-copyright-infringement-a-true-story/

PART I

The Quick and Easy Way to Self-Publish

Part I is primarily for those who want to get their book to Kindle in the fastest and easiest way possible. For the author with a manuscript and some spare cash, you can get your book published quickly for a modest investment. For those with a bit more money, you can hire an experienced editor and cover designer to create a professional quality book. For the first-time indie author, publishing quickly and only to Kindle can also be a great way to get your feet wet with minimal frustration.

In this first section we also explore the easiest road to expanding your distribution to include the ePub format. As with the Kindle, you can make a moderate investment and hire a professional to convert your manuscript to ePub and contract with an aggregator to distribute it. U.S. residents can also publish directly to Barnes & Noble's PubIt! program, which will convert your manuscript to ePub without cost.

By following these ten steps you can get your book onto Kindle in less than a month. Doing so will involve some professional assistance; while your book is out for formatting or you are awaiting your cover design, you can use the time to learn about marketing (Chapter 17) and getting paid (Chapter 18).

1/ To Kindle in Ten Steps

Step 1. Edit Your Manuscript

Before you do anything else with your manuscript, do a thorough grammar and spell check. The number one reviewer complaint of many self-published books is that they are full of grammatical and spelling errors. If grammar is not your strong point, consider hiring a professional proofreader to correct your sentence structure and punctuation. Many editors belong to professional organizations; contact these organizations for a list of editors in your area. You can also find an editor by posting a query on any of the indie publishing forums: many editors lurk there looking for work, and other writers will make recommendations. Fees range widely; expect to pay anywhere from $.005 per word up to $.0175 per word. For a typical 90,000-word novel, this amounts to a fee anywhere between $450.00 and $1575.00. Note that this will be for proofing only; it will not include manuscript development.

Step 2. Perform Basic Errors & Omissions Research

If your book is entirely a product of your imagination, does not make use—either in the text or on the cover—of any trademarks or copyrighted matter, and does not contain any characters based on real people, chances are you are good to go. But if your book does contain trademarks or copyrighted matter, is non-fiction of any kind, or contains characters based on real people, you should learn the basics of copyright, trademarks, and libel laws and make any necessary changes to your manuscript. To learn about the laws and risks as they apply to publishing, read Chapter 4: Errors & Omissions.

Step 3. Acquire Your Book Cover

Every book needs a cover. If you cannot create one yourself you will need to hire a graphic designer. There are a number of designers out there who offer cheap ebook cover design, some for as little as $35.00. You can find these graphic designers by searching for "ebook cover design," or by posting queries on the various indie writer forums (see this chapter's Useful Links).

A cover design for under $100.00 is considered ridiculously cheap, and as with most things in life you get what you pay for. For the first-time indie author, however, this low-cost option is likely the most attractive and obviously most affordable. Note that low-cost design will not give you control over the cover picture if the designer buys it from a stock image agency. Even if the designer gives you copyright of the cover itself, control of the image will be retained by the designer unless s/he uses a public domain or Creative Commons image. But for under $100.00 you will likely not care. (Creative Common images are free pictures, posted on the web, that image creators have made available for use in exchange for a proper credit, licensed under the Creative Commons Licence.)

You will need your cover created in portrait style and the title must be legible when the image is reduced to its thumbnail size, which is the tiny image you see when you first search through a retailer's online catalogue.

If you have a cover image made that is portrait style, no larger than 800 pixels wide, between 1040 and 1200 pixels tall, has a width-to-height ratio of between 1:1.3 and 1:1.5 (e.g., 800 x 1200 pixels = a ratio of 1:1.5), saved at 72 ppi and in the ideal sRGB color space, your cover will meet or exceed the minimum requirements of all ebook retailers including Kindle. This cover image will also work when embedded into your Word document, so you can use the same file for both your ebook cover and your product image (what Amazon calls your "cover image") for use on the Kindle website. To reiterate, your cover should be:

- no greater than 800 pixels wide;

- between 1040 and 1200 pixels tall;

- 72 ppi resolution; and

- in the sRGB color space.

Your designer should also provide you with JPEGs in relevant sizes for marketing emails, to add to a blog, or to submit to a reviewer. For example:

- 300 x 450 pixels, 72 ppi: medium-sized image for marketing email and blogs; and

- 100 x 150 pixels, 72 ppi: thumbnail for use in a digital signature or blog.

One word of warning: the 800 x 1200, 72 ppi file will not be of sufficient quality to create a print version of your book or marketing materials such as bookmarks or postcards. If you think that later you might like to add any of those, pay extra and have a larger, print-quality file made that you can keep in reserve.

Step 4. Format Your Manuscript

While your cover is being designed, the next step for you is to format your manuscript to adhere to ebook requirements. Ebooks require different formatting than print books because ebooks have resizable text which simply flows to more and more "pages" as the reader increases the font size. Also, each reading device differs in its screen size so you cannot design to a specific device. Fig. 1 illustrates the same ebook viewed at different font sizes.

Consequently, there are no set pages or page numbers in ebooks, no header or footer information. Ebooks are also more restrictive in your choice of fonts, for example, or how you format your paragraphs. Ebooks cannot make use of tables, columns or sidebars unless these are first converted to images, and text boxes or graphics with text wrapped around them are not recommended.

Ebook formatting is the most common cause of headaches for the novice indie publisher. However, the grief comes from not learning in advance how to format properly; your ebook

Fig. 1

then looks terrible on the reading devices or incurs various display errors. It will take you less time to learn how to format *before* you submit your book rather than trying to fix problems later. Failing that, you can hire a professional.

Hiring a Professional Formatter/ Convertor

You can produce your manuscript in any word processor then save as a Word document and send it to a professional formatting and conversion company. These companies will format your manuscript to ensure a smooth conversion to the Kindle. They will ensure, for example, that your table of contents is properly created and bookmarked, that your chapter headings are formatted correctly for best results, and the formatter will embed your cover and optimize any interior images. The Kindle Direct Publishing website provides a list of conversion service providers; you can find even more by searching online for "ebook conversion services" or by asking for recommendations from others on the indie publishing forums. Rates for a typical novel of 90,000 words will range anywhere from $75.00 to $300.00.

If you contract out the formatting, bear in mind that some companies will convert to both the Kindle (mobi) and ePub format for the same price, while others will charge less for one format only. Before you make that call, then, read the next chapter and decide if you will likely want to expand beyond Kindle; if so, have the ePub done at the same time as your mobi

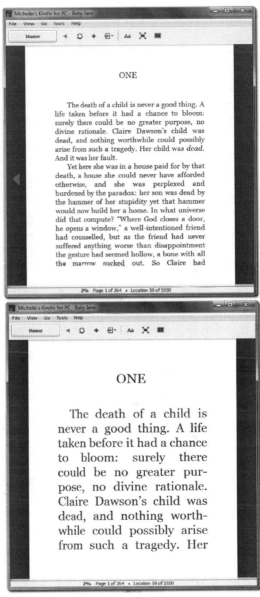

file. Also, if contracting out you must send your JPEG cover with your manuscript, in which case you need to wait for your cover to come back from the graphic designer before proceeding.

When using a formatter, they will not add your title or copyright text; you still have to add this to your manuscript yourself. The formatter will only add your table of contents for you.

Do-it-Yourself Formatting Basics

If your book has a simple structure, it is quite easy to format your Word document yourself for upload to Kindle. What follows is a step-by-step guide of how to format your manuscript. This section will not explain *why* you have to format this way, only how. For the why of it all, you will need to read Chapter 11: Manuscript Formatting for eBooks.

This simplified formatting only works where the body of your book has paragraphs with an indented first line, no breaks (blank space) between paragraphs, and uses only heading styles with a chapter break before each heading—in other words, a typical novel or creative non-fiction book. If you follow these basic guidelines your book should work, and if you still end up using a professional formatter they may reduce the fee because your manuscript will require less work to make it functional. If, however, your book structure is more complicated, you will need either to learn more about formatting or contract out.

I highly recommend that you read this section in front of your computer with Word open. This way you do not have to learn in the abstract; instead you can immediately try out the formatting instructions as you go along.

To format your manuscript, you need to:

Set your document to letter size (8.5" x 11"), portrait orientation, with all margins set to .5", and applied to the whole document. Do not split your document into sections that are formatted differently.

Set your view to Print Layout.

Turn off paragraph auto-formatting. Tools > Options > Edit tab > uncheck "Keep track of formatting." (In Word 2007+, select the Office icon > Word Options > Advanced > uncheck "Keep track of formatting.")

Do not use headers or footers. If your document contains these, remove them from your manuscript.

Use only the following fonts in your document: Arial (Regular only, not Black), Courier New, Georgia, Tahoma, Times New Roman, Trebuchet MS, and Verdana. Do not use Dingbats or Webdings. Do not use any font larger than 18 points or smaller than 10 points.

Use only the following text effects: italics, bold, underline, superscript, subscript, and strike-through. All other text effects cannot be read and will be converted to regular text. This includes text effects like all caps and small caps.

Use the Normal paragraph style for the body of your manuscript. In Word, the default Normal style is defined using the default font and font size, set to "regular"; paragraph alignment set to "left," all indents and Before/After spacing set to "0" and line spacing at "single"; your default dictionary; and widow/orphan control. Of these attributes, it is recommended that you only modify the font and default dictionary of the Normal paragraph.

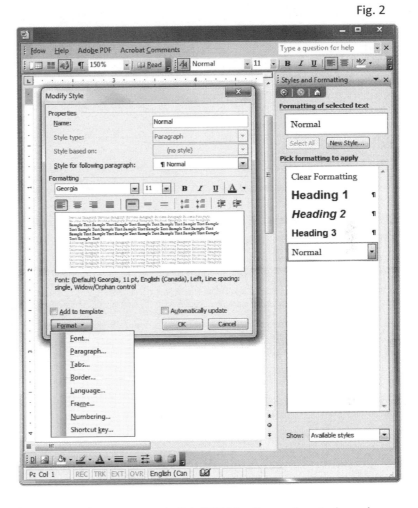

Fig. 2

To modify the Normal paragraph, select Format > Styles and Formatting (in Word 2007+, select the Styles submenu; in Mac select Format > Styles). In the right-hand list of styles that will appear you will see the style "Normal." Click on the ¶ symbol; it will change to an arrow. Click on the arrow and select "Modify" from the drop-down menu that appears. (Mac users: "Modify" is in the same dialogue box.)

Select Format > Language. Choose your language and click "OK." In the main window choose your default font and size and click "OK." You will get a warning message about affecting all future documents made using the Normal template; click "Yes." Fig. 2 (cropped to fit) shows modifications of the Normal style.

Leave paragraph alignment at the default value of "left." Most ereaders give the user the option to force paragraphs to justify, so leaving it at the default value leaves the option open for the user to have paragraphs unjustified.

Do not use tabs. Use paragraph formatting to add a first line indent. If you are working with a document like a novel where the first line of every paragraph is indented, it is easier to create and use a new paragraph style that incorporates a first line indent. I have found that a first line indent of .3" looks good on the Kindle.

Use only the default single line spacing. Any other line spacing value will be converted to single.

Do not change the right or left paragraph indentation. Leave at the default value of "0."

Do not insert blank lines of text between paragraphs by using the carriage return. If you need to have blank lines, use the Before/After spacing option under Format > Paragraph.

Do not use hanging paragraphs.

Do not use carriage returns to break up lines of text so they appear more pleasing to the eye on the page. These carriage returns will cause problems when the text is resized on the Kindle.

Do not use hyphenation to create more pleasing paragraph alignment. Use hyphens only where the word itself is hyphenated, as in "self-publishing."

Use page breaks, not carriage returns, to force text to start on a new page, such as at the end of your chapters or after the title or copyright page. If you do not use page breaks your pages will run one into the other. To insert a page break, click Insert > Break > Page break (Word 2007+: Insert tab > Pages > Page Break). Better still, wherever you need a page break, modify the first paragraph *after* the point where you need a page break to automatically include a page break: Format > Paragraph > Line and Page Breaks tab > check "Page break before." This is actually more stable than inserting a page break marker.

Do not use Word's automatic bullets and lists. Create these manually instead using numbers or asterisks and paragraph formatting.

Do not use text columns, frames, or tables.

Clean out spaces before carriage returns. Since a space is required between a period and the start of the next sentence, many of us have a habit of adding in that space when we come to the end of a paragraph and before we hit "Enter." These spaces are read as characters of text and so they can cause odd text alignment. You can check for unnecessary spaces by clicking on the Show/Hide icon (¶) on your toolbar to view hidden characters, then delete these redundant spaces.

Do not use character spacing, for example to increase the distance between points of an ellipsis ("…"). Word's Autocorrect automatically increases the space between the dots of an ellipsis but this will not translate into the Kindle. If you use an ellipsis, do not put spaces between the points (". . .") as one would in a print manuscript because each point will be read as an independent character and so your ellipsis might end up divided between lines of text.

To use ellipses, I elect to format the text using a space between the text and the ellipsis, then no spaces between the points of the ellipsis, then if text resumes another space between the ellipsis and the text ("text ... text").

If using an en dash ("–") or em dash ("—"), do not leave a space between the preceding text and the dash, or after it. Doing so can create odd text alignment. ("Text—text" not "text — text.")

Use the style "Heading 1" for your chapter headings and "Heading 2" for the titles of your ancillary pages (more on those in a minute); do not use a heading style for subsections. If necessary, modify Heading 1 and 2 to use one of the aforementioned fonts and to center the text if so desired. If you like, you can also increase the spacing between your heading and the body text by using the Before/After option under paragraph formatting. You modify heading styles the same way you modified the Normal style.

Fig. 3

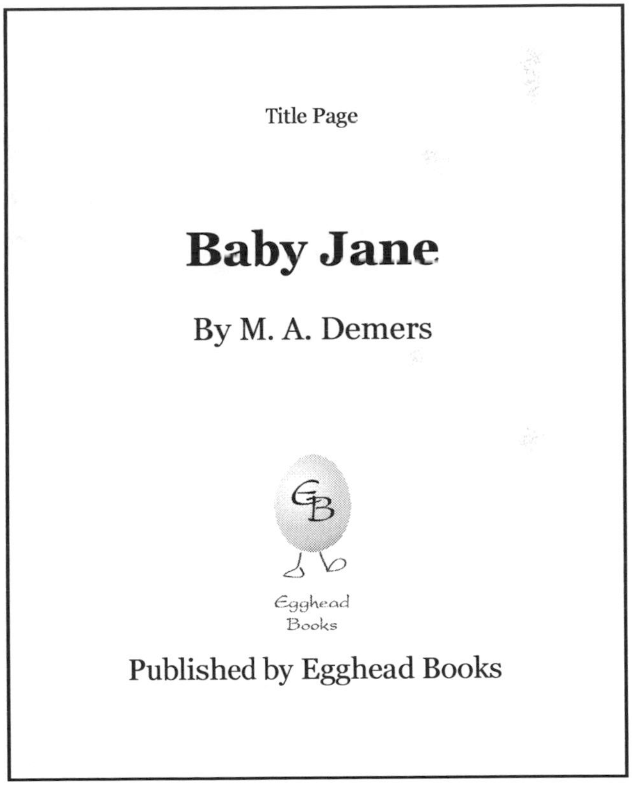

Title Page

Baby Jane

By M. A. Demers

Egghead
Books

Published by Egghead Books

When your manuscript is finished, remove all unused styles from your document. Go back into Styles and Formatting. At the bottom you will see "Show" and a drop-down menu. Select "Available styles" and delete any styles no longer in use. Next select "Available Formatting" and delete any formatting that is no longer in use. (Note: some styles, for example Normal, cannot be deleted. Do not worry about them.)

Add a Title Page

Your title page will be the first page of your document after your cover. The title page *must* contain the title, including any subtitle, and the names of anyone else accredited, for example, the illustrator if the work is a picture book, the editor if it is a compilation, or the translator if the original is in another language. It must contain any edition number, and it must contain the name and/or logo of the publisher (you).

You will need to indicate this page later in your table of contents. The easiest way (though not the prettiest) is to place a small title at the top of the page using Heading 2. To make the heading less obtrusive, you will want to format Heading 2 to be minimized in relation to the title page. My suggestion would be to use your default font, not bolded or italicized, and two to three points smaller than your body text. For example, if your main text is 12 points, modify Heading 2 to be 10 points.

Using this modified Heading 2, type in "Title Page" (no quotation marks). To separate it from your title, select Format > Paragraph and in the Spacing section set the After value to 30 points. Fig. 3 is an example of a title page using this simplified method.

Add Your Copyright Page

The copyright page always follows the title page. As with your title page, you will need a title for your copyright page that will later be included in your table of contents. Using Heading 2 again, type in "Copyright Information" (no quotation marks). Select Format > Paragraph and in the Spacing section set the After value to 24 points.

In a new paragraph, enter your copyright declaration on a single line. The declaration should take the form "Copyright © [year] [your name or pen name]" (no quotation marks).

This is followed on the next line by publisher information. If you have created your own publisher's imprint you can use this as your publisher information. If you have not created an imprint you can write "Published by the author."

The copyright notice is usually next. You can create your own or you can use the following standard text:

> All rights reserved under International and Pan-American Copyright Conventions. No part of this book may be reproduced in any form or by any electronic or mechanical means, including information storage and retrieval systems, without permission in writing from the author, except by reviewer, who may quote brief passages in a review.

If your book is a work of fiction, it should contain the following declaration:

> This is a work of fiction. Names, characters, places and incidents either are the product of the author's imagination or used fictitiously. Any resemblance to actual persons, living or dead, events or locales is entirely coincidental.

If you use trademarks in your work you can add an optional separate paragraph for this as well. Each trademark should be listed along with its registered owner, followed by a declaration that you are using these trademarks with or without permission, as the case may be. For example:

> BMW is a registered trademark of Bayerische Motoren Werke AG. Mercedes is a

registered trademark of Mercedes-Benz, a division of Daimler AG. Trademarks are used without permission. Use of the trademark is not authorized by, associated with or sponsored by the trademark owner.

If you use any copyrighted passages in your book with permission of the author(s) or their publisher(s), you should add a paragraph for them as well. For example:

> Excerpt from "Flights of Fancy" from *Flights of Fancy and other poems* by Fake Poet. ©1995 Fake Poet. Reprinted by permission of Fake Poet's Publisher.

This is then followed by the book's ISBN information, if applicable (see Step 5). If you do not have an ISBN you will omit this section.

If you have your own ISBN, some registries require they be identified along with the number. In the U.S. it is not required to put Bowker on your copyright page, only the Library of Congress if you have an LoC number or if you used their Cataloguing in Publication pre-registration option. This you will not have done so you do not have to worry about it.

In addition to the ISBN you have the option to add the author's full name and year of birth, using the convention "[last name], [first name], [year of birth]—[year of death, if applicable]." A blank space after the em dash indicates the author is still alive. This is then followed by the book title and author's name as it appears on the title page, followed by the edition. For example:

> Library and Archives Canada
> Demers, Michelle A, 1964—
> Baby Jane / M. A. Demers — Kindle edition.
> ISBN 978-0-9868914-0-3

And finally, you should credit the cover image creator or stock agency (as dictated by the sales contract) and the cover designer. For example:

> Cover image by Jane Photographer/Getty Images.
>
> Cover design by Joe Designer.

Put this all together, then, and the copyright page for the Kindle version of *Baby Jane* looks like Fig. 4.

Acknowledgements or Dedication Page

If you wish to acknowledge anyone who assisted in the creation of your book, or you wish to dedicate it to someone special, you can do so on a separate page after the copyright page. Most people will be flattered to be included here but you should always check beforehand in case anyone wishes to be excluded.

Fig. 4

If you add this page, use Heading 2 again to ensure you have an entry for your table of contents. Type in "Acknowledgements" (no quotation marks) at the top of the page. Select Format > Paragraph and in the Spacing section set the After value to 24 points.

Table of Contents

While a table of contents is technically optional, the trend is for ebooks to include them because it is easier for the reader to navigate around the book. Kindle prefers as well that you include in your table of contents an entry for your title page, copyright page, and acknowledgements (if applicable). This is why we added the titles in.

The table of contents is inserted after your title, copyright, and acknowledgements pages. Do not place it at the end of your document; if you do, Kindle will reject your book.

To create your table of contents, first insert a page break before the start of your first chapter to create a blank page. At the top of this new blank page, type in the title ("Table of Contents" or "Contents"—whatever is appropriate). Do not use a heading style for this title; use your Normal paragraph.

On the next line select Insert > Reference > Index and Tables (Word 2007+: References > Table of Contents > Insert Table of Contents). In the Index and Tables dialogue box, click on the Table of Contents tab. Uncheck boxes "Show page numbers" and "Right align page numbers." Check "Use hyperlinks instead of page numbers" if it is not already checked (Fig. 5).

In the same dialogue box, click on "Options." In the box that next appears, check "Styles." Uncheck "Outline levels" and "Table entry fields." Set the "TOC levels" to a value of "1" for all headings that

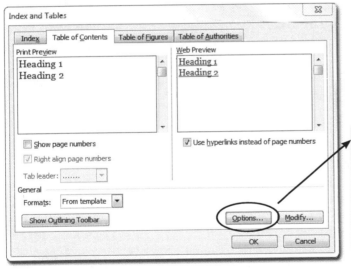

Fig. 5

have a checkmark beside them (in this case, Heading 1 and Heading 2 will have checkmarks because those are the only headings you will have used). Click "OK." The table of contents will now be automatically created.

Embed Your Cover

Fig. 6

Go to the beginning of your document and add a page break to create a blank page in which you will embed your cover.

Place your cursor at the top of the blank page. Set the paragraph alignment to center. Select Insert > Picture > From File. Navigate to the folder where your cover/product JPEG image is stored and select it. Click "Insert."

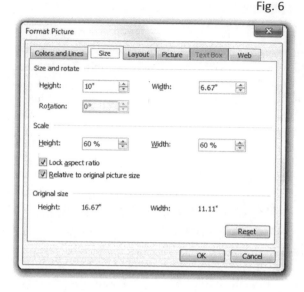

Once it is imported, click on the picture and select Format > Picture. Click on the Layout tab. Select "In Line With Text." (In Word 2007+, when you click on an image the Format toolbar comes up automatically. In the Arrange menu, click on Text Wrapping and select "In line with text." Mac users: When you click on an image the Format toolbar comes up automatically. In the Arrange menu, click on Wrap Text and select "In line with text.")

In the same Format > Picture dialogue box, click on the Size tab. If your margins are set to .5" as recommended, and if your cover image is between 1024 and 1200 pixels high and 72 ppi as recommended, in the Size dialogue box the height will have a value of 10" and the height and width scale will be a value between 60% and 68% (Fig. 6).

Menu Markers

Kindle books require hidden bookmarks be added to your Word document so that the Kindle menu options Go to Cover, Beginning, and Table of Contents will work.

Fig.7

First, click on your cover image. With the image still selected, go to your toolbar and click on Insert > Bookmark. Under "Bookmark name," change the default name to "cover"; do not use quotation marks or uppercase letters. (In Word 2007+ there is no default title, just a blank box). Click on "Add" (Fig. 7).

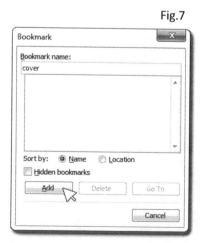

Also, as noted in the instructions, you need to click *on* the image and then place the bookmark. If you click above the image the bookmark will get pushed back and the ereader will create a blank page before your cover; placing the bookmark below or beside the cover image will result in a blank page after your cover. Either way, the reading device will point to the blank page as your cover because the bookmark says it is.

For your table of contents marker, place your cursor in front of your table of contents title. Select Insert > Bookmark. In the dialogue box name it "TOC" (no quotation marks but all uppercase). Click on "Add."

To add a Go to Beginning function, choose where you want your book to open when the reader first opens it on Kindle. This is usually your title page though some prefer the first chapter. Wherever you choose, place your cursor at the top left-hand margin of the page and select Insert > Bookmark. Type in "Start" (no quotation marks). Click "Add."

Step 5. Assign Your ISBN (optional)

An International Standard Book Number is not legally required to publish a book. Kindle does not require that a book have an ISBN assigned; instead, Kindle assigns its own internal cataloguing number, an ASIN.

If you decide you want to acquire and assign an ISBN to your Kindle book, you must do this *before* you upload to Kindle and before you send your manuscript out to be formatted and converted, as you will need to add your ISBN information to your copyright page as outlined in Step 4.

For an explanation of the pros and cons of using your own ISBN, see Chapter 7: ISBNs and Other Book Identifiers.

Step 6. Choose Your BISAC Categories

When you upload a file to Kindle you will be asked to select your book's categories, and will be allowed up to two selections. These categories are known as BISAC (Book Industry Standards and Communications) categories, and are used by booksellers and consumers to determine the primary subject or genre of a book. Each category is represented by a mixed alphabetical and numerical code and an explanatory title. There are numerous main, or "parent," categories and even more subcategories. The parent category Fiction, for example, has over ninety subcategories, of which are included the following, chosen at random:

FIC002000 FICTION / Action & Adventure

FIC009000 FICTION / Fantasy / General

FIC022000 FICTION / Mystery & Detective / General

Many of these subcategories in turn have secondary subcategories to further differentiate. For example, FIC009000 Fiction / Fantasy includes the following subcategories:

FIC009030 FICTION / Fantasy / Historical

FIC009050 FICTION / Fantasy / Paranormal

Unfortunately, while Kindle asks you to choose from among the full complement of BISAC categories, it does not use them all in its catalogue. If you assign a category Kindle does not use, it assigns your book to the nearest category to the BISAC category you selected. For example, you can choose for your vampire novel the category Fiction / Occult & Supernatural but Kindle does not include this category in its catalogue. Instead, such books will be found in fantasy or in science fiction, or can end up unclassified. As you can imagine, the results can be unpredictable.

So what is the best way to choose your categories? My advice is to first investigate the different categories used by Kindle and select those categories that best classify your book. Then visit the BISAC website (see this chapter's Useful Links) and pick the two that match or most closely match the categories available on Kindle. Make a note of these so when you upload to Kindle and select your categories the results will be more predictable and accurate.

If despite everything your book ends up in the wrong category, you have the option to email Kindle support (accessible from your publisher's dashboard) and ask for your categories to be manually assigned. When making your request, use the full catalogue string. For example, ask for Kindle Store > Kindle eBooks > Fiction > Fantasy > Historical, not Fiction > Fantasy > Historical.

Step 7. Decide Upon Digital Rights Management

Digital rights management (DRM) technology attempts to prevent the unlawful copying or printing of ebooks for sharing and/or selling. When you upload to Kindle you will be asked to enable DRM or not, and your decision is irreversible, so it behooves you to learn about DRM before you upload to Kindle. DRM is a very contentious issue and you will hear a lot of debate both for and against its use. If you are unfamiliar with the issues and arguments, read Chapter 6: Digital Rights Management so you can make an informed choice.

Step 8. Decide Upon a Price and Royalty

How you price your Kindle book determines the royalty level you will be paid. Currently, Amazon pays 35% of the sale price for ebooks priced less than $2.99 or more than $9.99 (all prices are in U.S. dollars). For ebooks priced between $2.99 and $9.99, Amazon pays 70% but charges you a delivery fee of $0.15 per megabyte, which is deducted before the royalty is calculated. Alternatively, you can choose the 35% royalty for any price point and not be subject to a delivery fee.

The 70% royalty only applies to sales in the U.S., Canada, the UK, Austria, Guernsey, Isle of Man, Jersey, Germany, Lichtenstein, Luxembourg, Switzerland, France, Monaco, and Belgium. Sales to other jurisdictions are paid at 35%. Note that since the list price in the UK includes its

Value Added Tax (VAT), the royalty is paid on the list price less VAT (otherwise Amazon would be paying you a royalty on the sales tax).

Kindle Worldwide Sales

Amazon currently sells its Kindle books through four sites, the U.S., the UK, Germany, and France. Each site serves specific geographical areas, meaning a consumer in North America usually cannot purchase from the UK site and vice versa. The Kindle device ships to over 100 countries but from the U.S. only, and the free Kindle apps are available for download in most countries. Kindle books currently support English, French, German, Spanish, Portuguese, and Italian languages only.

Ebooks are delivered via 3G and Wi-Fi networks through Amazon's Whispernet network, which is built on partnerships with companies like AT&T. Users must thus have access to a Whispernet partner network and in some areas users are subject to a hefty 3G network download fee, which increases the cost of ebooks. Once the ebook is downloaded, however, wireless access is not necessary except to sync across Kindle devices using its WhisperSync utility.

If you possess worldwide rights then Amazon places your books on all its Kindle sites, providing you with immediate access to a truly global market. If you do not possess worldwide rights, or if you choose not to distribute to certain countries, books not available in a geographical area are either not listed when the user accesses the Kindle site or are indicated as "Not Available in Your Area."

When Amazon sells your book on its UK or Continental Europe sites, in pounds sterling and euros, respectively, it does so at a price converted from the U.S. price you set or you can opt to set individual prices for each jurisdiction. Authors in the UK, Germany and France who set up accounts there will have their books converted to other currencies in the same way. If the ebook is subject to sales tax it will be included in the list price or added at point of sale, depending on the rules of the sales jurisdiction.

Step 9. Open Your Kindle Account

Kindle Direct Publishing allows anyone anywhere in the world who is of majority age to open an account. To create a Kindle account, visit its account page (see Useful Links). If you already have an Amazon.com consumer account you can log in using the same email address and password. If you have a consumer account with another Amazon site (like Canada or the UK), your consumer account cannot be used for Kindle; it must be an Amazon U.S. account.

Once you have created your account, you will land on your publisher's dashboard page. A pop-up window will ask you to accept Kindle's Terms of Service. Read and click "Agree." Once you have done this you will be assigned a publisher account number, which will appear on your dashboard and in your account details.

On the upper-right bar of your dashboard you will see your name and "Account." Click on this to be taken to your account details. You have the option to open the account in your personal name or a company name. If you are publishing under a pen name, do *not* use your pen name to open the account; you must use your real name. If you are signing on using a company name and your company is a partnership or incorporated, you may need to assign to the company the proceeds from your copyright in order for Amazon to pay royalties arising from copyright held by you, the author. You should seek legal advice before proceeding.

If you are a sole proprietor, unless you have a bank account in the name of your proprietorship, my advice is to sign up either under your personal name or as your name doing business as your proprietorship (e.g., Michelle A. Demers dba Egghead Books). This ensures both your personal name and sole proprietorship are linked to your account.

Amazon pays 60 days after the month in which a sale is made. Payment is made either by electronic funds transfer (EFT) or by cheque, depending on where the sale was made and whether or not the author has the relevant bank account. Sales in the three currencies can be converted to U.S. dollars; sales in euros can be converted to either U.S. dollars or pounds sterling. To summarize, this is from Amazon's website:

Receive Amazon.com payments via:

- Electronic funds transfer in USD ($) to your US bank account
- Check in USD ($)

Receive Amazon.co.uk payments via:

- Electronic funds transfer in USD ($) to your US bank account
- Electronic funds transfer in GBP (£) to your UK bank account
- Paper cheque in GBP (£)

Receive Amazon.de payments via:

- Electronic funds transfer in USD ($) to your US bank account
- Electronic funds transfer in GBP (£) to your UK bank account
- Electronic funds transfer in EUR (€) to your EUR denominated bank account
- Paper check in EUR (€)[15]

For electronic funds transfer, royalties due must be a minimum of $10.00/£10.00/€10,00 or more; if by cheque, there is a minimum royalty balance of $100.00/£100.00/€100,00. (At time of writing, Amazon had not yet updated its website to include information on Amazon.fr.)

In other words, the simplest and fastest way to be paid is to have a U.S. bank account and have all sales converted to that currency and paid into the U.S. account by EFT. For authors in the UK, the most expedient method is to have your sterling and euro sales paid directly into your UK account and accept paper cheques for your USD sales, or open a U.S. bank account for the latter and transfer funds home as and when you wish. For Continental Europeans, you can have your euro sales paid into your bank account but will have to accept paper cheques for your sterling and USD sales unless you open UK and/or U.S. bank accounts. All other authors must accept paper cheques or open bank accounts in the U.S. and/or UK, and/or open a euro account at home.

On your account page, the default payment method is by cheque. If you wish to be paid by EFT, for each sale currency you must select your payment currency and provide the relevant bank account details.

Non-U.S. residents will be subject to a 30% withholding tax for sales made from the U.S. site. Foreign authors can reduce the amount of withholding tax if they acquire a U.S. tax identification number and are living in a country that has signed a tax treaty with the U.S. To find out more about this, see Chapter 18: Getting Paid.

There is no withholding tax on UK or Euro sales for any authors.

Step 10. Upload Your Book

On your publisher's dashboard, click "Add a new title." This will open a window where you will input your book's data (Fig. 8).

1. Enter Your Book Details

Enter the book's title. If it has a subtitle, the format is [book title]: [subtitle]. If the book is part of a series, a trilogy for example, input the name of the series and which book this title is in the series, for example "Volume 1" or "Book 3" or perhaps just "III."

The edition number is optional but if you later update to a second edition this needs to be inputted. If you are using an ISBN you can also input "Kindle" here because "Kindle" is an edition.

"Description" is your book's synopsis. A synopsis is essential to sell your book so you need to write one and to write a good one. You can enter a description of between 30 and 4000 characters in length. See the section "Write a Great Book Description" in Chapter 17: Marketing Your Book for guidelines and restrictions.

The book contributors are you, the author(s), but also if applicable the book's illustrator, translator, editor (if a compilation), photographer, or the author of a guest introduction/ forward or epilogue. You do not put in the name of a proofreader or copyeditor here, or the book designer; the first two are not credited anywhere and the designer is credited on the copyright page.

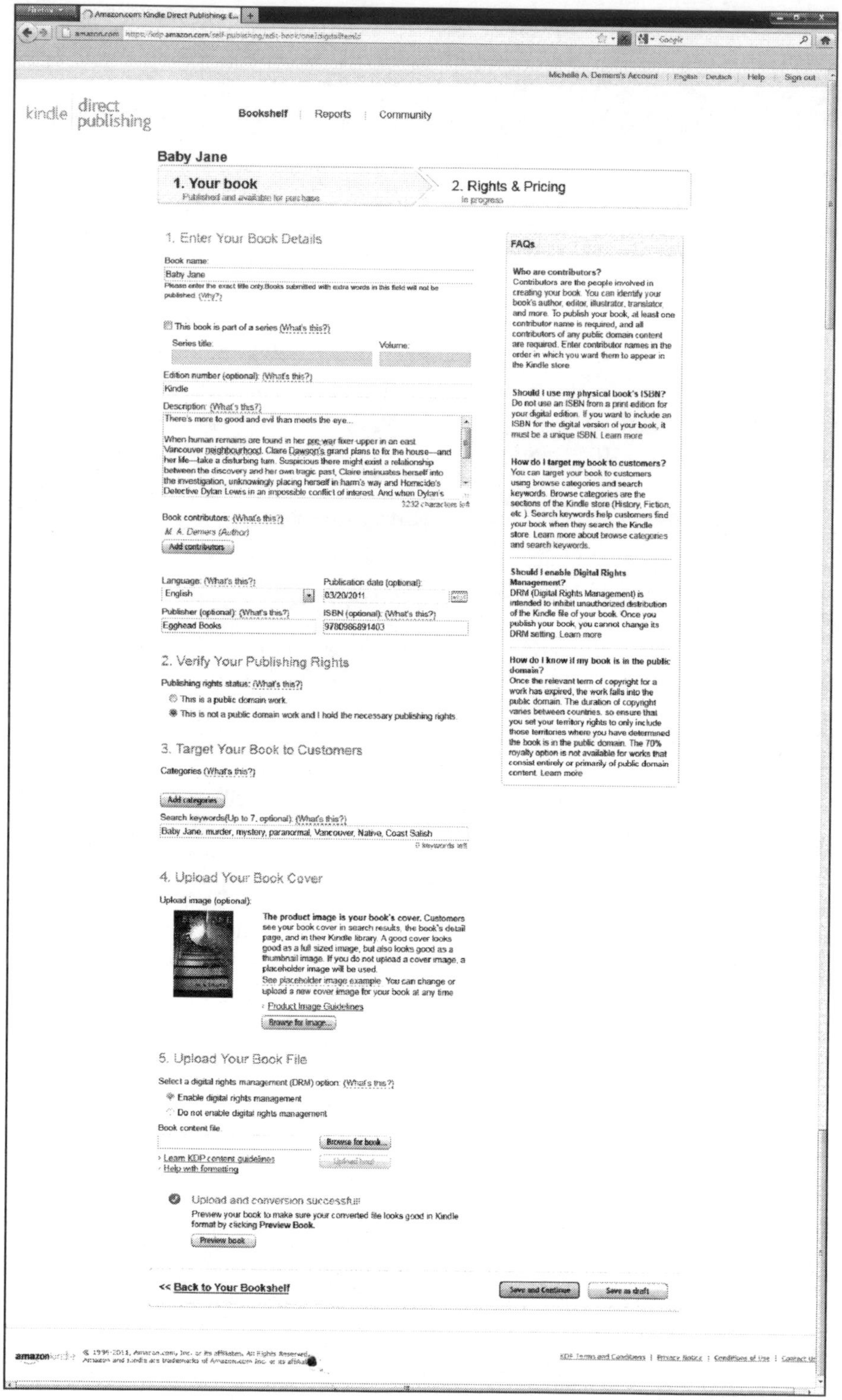

Michelle A. Demers's Account | English | Deutsch | Help | Sign out
kindle direct publishing
Bookshelf | Reports | Community
Baby Jane
1. Your book
Published and available for purchase
2. Rights & Pricing
In progress
1. Enter Your Book Details
Book name:
Baby Jane
Please enter the exact title only. Books submitted with extra words in this field will not be published. (Why?)
This book is part of a series (What's this?)
Series title:
Volume:
Edition number (optional): (What's this?)
Kindle
Description: (What's this?)
There's more to good and evil than meets the eye...
When human remains are found in her pre-war fixer-upper in an east Vancouver neighbourhood, Claire Dawson's grand plans to fix the house—and her life—take a disturbing turn. Suspicious there might exist a relationship between the discovery and her own tragic past, Claire insinuates herself into the investigation, unknowingly placing herself in harm's way and Homicide's Detective Dylan Lewis in an impossible conflict of interest. And when Dylan's
Book contributors: (What's this?)
M. A. Demers (Author)
Add contributors
Language: (What's this?)
English
Publication date (optional):
03/20/2011
Publisher (optional): (What's this?)
Egghead Books
ISBN (optional): (What's this?)
9780986891403
2. Verify Your Publishing Rights
Publishing rights status: (What's this?)
This is a public domain work.
This is not a public domain work and I hold the necessary publishing rights.
3. Target Your Book to Customers
Categories (What's this?)
Add categories
Search keywords(Up to 7, optional): (What's this?)
Baby Jane, murder, mystery, paranormal, Vancouver, Native, Coast Salish
4. Upload Your Book Cover
Upload image (optional):
The product image is your book's cover. Customers see your book cover in search results, the book's detail page, and in their Kindle library. A good cover looks good as a full sized image, but also looks good as a thumbnail image. If you do not upload a cover image, a placeholder image will be used.
See placeholder image example. You can change or upload a new cover image for your book at any time
Product Image Guidelines
Browse for image...
5. Upload Your Book File
Select a digital rights management (DRM) option: (What's this?)
Enable digital rights management
Do not enable digital rights management
Book content file:
Browse for book...
Learn KDP content guidelines
Help with formatting
Upload and conversion successful!
Preview your book to make sure your converted file looks good in Kindle format by clicking Preview Book.
Preview book
<< Back to Your Bookshelf
Save and Continue
Save as draft
FAQs
Who are contributors?
Contributors are the people involved in creating your book. You can identify your book's author, editor, illustrator, translator and more. To publish your book, at least one contributor name is required, and all contributors of any public domain content are required. Enter contributor names in the order in which you want them to appear in the Kindle store.
Should I use my physical book's ISBN?
Do not use an ISBN from a print edition for your digital edition. If you want to include an ISBN for the digital version of your book, it must be a unique ISBN. Learn more
How do I target my book to customers?
You can target your book to customers using browse categories and search keywords. Browse categories are the sections of the Kindle store (History, Fiction, etc.). Search keywords help customers find your book when they search the Kindle store. Learn more about browse categories and search keywords.
Should I enable Digital Rights Management?
DRM (Digital Rights Management) is intended to inhibit unauthorized distribution of the Kindle file of your book. Once you publish your book, you cannot change its DRM setting. Learn more
How do I know if my book is in the public domain?
Once the relevant term of copyright for a work has expired, the work falls into the public domain. The duration of copyright varies between countries, so ensure that you set your territory rights to only include those territories where you have determined the book is in the public domain. The 70% royalty option is not available for works that consist entirely or primarily of public domain content. Learn more

Fig. 8

Language is self-explanatory. Publication date, publisher, and ISBN are optional but if you input these they must match the data you inputted when you assigned the book its ISBN.

Regardless of whether you add an ISBN, Amazon assigns its own internal cataloguing number (ASIN) to each title. Both will appear on the title's product page on the Kindle website.

2. Verify Your Publishing Rights

Here you will be asked if the work is public domain or not, and if not you must declare you have the rights to publish. If you check this box and you do not own the rights, then this is copyright infringement and if you are caught Amazon will punish you (eventually), as most likely will the rights holder.

3. Target Your Book to Customers

Here you will be asked to select your book's categories from the list of BISAC categories. Kindle allows a maximum of two categories. You can then add up to seven keywords to assist searching.

4. Upload Your Book Cover

This is actually the product image for the Kindle website. You upload the same cover JPEG that you embedded in your ebook.

5. Upload Your Book File

Here you will be asked to select between enabling digital rights management or not.

You then browse to your Word file and upload it. If you hired a formatter/converter, you upload your mobi file here instead of your Word file. After your file uploads it will be automatically converted. If the conversion is successful a message will appear telling you so. If the conversion is not successful an error message will occur and you will have to fix the file.

You then use the online Kindle Previewer to test how your book looks. Using the menu in the lower right-hand corner, you can check the Go to Table of Contents and Go to Beginning options, but if you uploaded a Word file the Go to Cover option will be greyed out. (Do not panic. The Go to Cover option will still work on the actual Kindle if you added the bookmark.) If the conversion is successful, click on "Save and Continue." You will then be taken to page two (Fig. 9).

6. Verify Your Publishing Territories

If you own worldwide rights (most self-publishers do), you can select Worldwide. If you only own the rights to selected territories, or if you want to restrict distribution because of concerns over your book's content, you can do so by selecting all territories you want the book sold in and by not selecting those territories you have concerns about. For a discussion of your book's content issues, see Chapter 4: Errors & Omissions.

7. Choose Your Royalty

After inputting your book's price in U.S. dollars, Amazon will then provide you with your royalty options and calculate your royalties for you. It will also show you how large your file is and the delivery charge.

8. Kindle Book Lending

Kindle book lending is now checked by default but you may opt out if you selected the 35% royalty; you may not opt out if you have allowed lending in any other sales channel. If lending is enabled, a consumer can loan their ebook to a friend for up to fourteen days, during which time the book is unavailable on the consumer's Kindle.

Terms and Conditions

Once you are done, check "By clicking Save and Publish below, I confirm that I have all rights necessary to make the content I am uploading available for marketing, distribution and sale in each territory I have indicated above, and that I am in compliance with the KDP Terms and Conditions." Of course you should actually have read the Terms and Conditions because by clicking this box you are entering into a contract, a contract that you should understand before you click to accept. If you do not understand the Terms and Conditions you can contact Amazon and ask for clarification or you can seek independent legal counsel.

Save and Publish

You can save your book in draft form first if you discover you are not ready to publish. If you are ready, click "Save and Publish."

Your book will then show up on your dashboard as "In Review." English titles are typically reviewed and published within 24 to 48 hours, while non-English titles take 3 to 5 days.

If you upload your book but do not yet "Save and Publish," the book's status will be "Draft."

Once the review process is finished the status will change to "Publishing." You will get an email confirming this. After your book goes live it can still take up to 24 hours for the product image, search keywords, and product description to display or become functional on the Amazon Kindle site.

Once the title is available for purchase on the Kindle website your status changes to "Live." If you later make changes to your manuscript and upload a new file, the status will revert to "In Review" but the file currently for sale will remain so. During this time you cannot upload any

Fig. 9

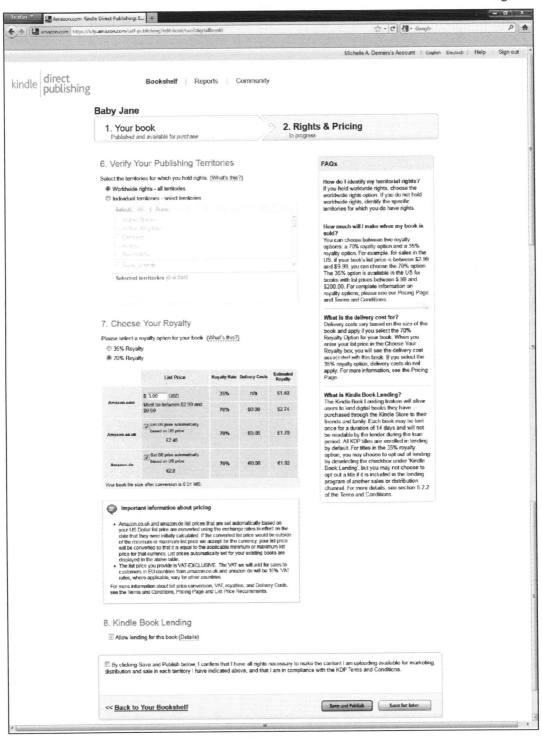

further revisions until the book's status returns to "Live." (Note that often your book will go live on Kindle before this is indicated on your publisher's dashboard. So do not wait to see the status change before you check to see if the book has gone on sale.)

Customers who bought earlier copies of your book will not get the revised version unless they delete the book from their device then download again. However, I have noticed with my Kindle for PC that revised copies are not automatically downloaded to my app.

If your status changes to "Blocked" it is because you requested it be so, someone has filed a copyright violation claim, the content has been flagged by a consumer as "adult" yet you failed to indicate this when uploading your book, or you have violated some other term or condition. Amazon will then view the complaint and notify you of the outcome. If the file meets the definition of adult content, Amazon will mark your book as such and restrict its sale to minors.

Market Your Book

Now that your book is on Kindle, if you have not already read Chapter 17: Marketing Your Book, and Chapter 18: Getting Paid, do so now. The first provides some practical suggestions for reaching your audience, while the second outlines the banking and tax issues you will now need to address in order to maximize your royalties.

Useful Links

To create an Amazon Kindle account.
https://kdp.amazon.com/self-publishing/signin?ie=UTF8&Id=AZEbooksMakeM

Amazon's own forum for all things Kindle, including formatting and conversion issues.
http://forums.kindledirectpublishing.com/kdpforums/forumindex.jspa

MobileRead is a popular forum for the discussion of all things ebooks including technical issues.
http://www.mobileread.com/

BISAC categories.
http://www.bisg.org/what-we-do-0-136-bisac-subject-headings-list-major-subjects.php

2/ Beyond Kindle: the ePub Format

While Kindle sells only its proprietary format, the rest of the ebook retailers sell the open source ePub format. Some ereaders will also read PDF and text files—and many classic books have been scanned and are sold as PDFs—but for current releases the main players sell ePubs. Thus you will need an ePub if you wish to expand your sales beyond Kindle.

For U.S. residents, the simplest and cheapest way is to publish directly to Barnes & Noble's PubIt! program, which is its version of Kindle Direct Publishing. You must, however, possess a U.S. tax number, credit card, and bank account. The first is because Barnes & Noble must report author earnings to the IRS; the second is so that if your account goes into arrears due to customer returns or fraud claims, the balance will be charged to your card; and the third is necessary because B&N pays only by electronic funds transfer. Authors who do not possess these qualifications, or who are outside the U.S., cannot deal directly with PubIt!; instead you must contract with an aggregator to distribute your ePub to B&N and other retailers.

More importantly, however, B&N only sells ebooks to American and Canadian consumers; authors wishing to sell globally need to look into selling through Apple, Sony, Kobo, and the myriad of smaller ebook retailers that exist around the world.

As with the previous chapter, this chapter offers only the easiest way to expand your ebook distribution. Where noted, authors are advised to read later chapters on specific issues such as ISBNs and ebook pricing models before going ahead, so as to avoid potential problems or later regrets.

Hiring a Professional Formatter/Convertor

As with Kindle, you can produce your manuscript in any word processor then save as a Word document and send it to a professional for conversion to ePub. Some of the companies listed on the B&N website overlap those found on Kindle. Many companies will convert your manuscript to both the Kindle and ePub formats for the same price, while others will offer a lower fee if converting only to the ePub. Ask around the forums for recommendations and prices then get a quote before you proceed.

Barnes & Noble's PubIt!

Formatting

If you have formatted your Word manuscript correctly for the Kindle, you can upload the same document to PubIt! with just a few minor changes.

The first is that ePubs do not include bookmarks for the cover, table of contents, or beginning. Remove the bookmarks from your Word document.

Barnes & Noble recommends that you do not use superscript or subscript as this can cause extra leading between lines of text. If you have used these text effects convert them to straight text. For example, type in "1/4" instead of using the symbol.

B&N asks that you restrict your font choices to Times New Roman, Arial, or Courier New.

B&N will not accept ebooks that do not have a title page. If you have followed the formatting for Kindle and added in your title page, all will be well.

EPubs do not include an embedded cover in the Word document. Instead, you add the cover when uploading.

Cover Image

If you created the cover as suggested for Kindle, you can use the same cover/product image for your ePub.

ISBN

An ISBN is not required to publish with Barnes & Noble. Like Kindle, B&N assigns an internal cataloguing number. If you elect to assign your own ISBN, you *must* assign a different one from that which you assigned to your Kindle book, and adjust your copyright page accordingly.

BISAC

Barnes & Noble's website suffers from the same issues as Kindle. So, again, you need to check which categories are available in the PubIt! catalogue, compare them to BISAC, and select the best ones for your title. B&N also has many, many subcategories that do not exist in BISAC; if you need to be in one of these categories you can contact PubIt! and request it.

Digital Rights Management

B&N offers DRM at the author's discretion. If you enable this it is not reversible so before you choose I recommend you read Chapter 6: Digital Rights Management to decide if DRM is right for you.

Royalty Structure

B&N pays a 65% royalty on ebooks priced between $2.99 and $9.99, and a 40% royalty for books published outside those figures (but they cannot be priced less than $0.99 or greater than $199.99). However, the list price cannot be greater than a competitor's list price in any sales channel. If your price on B&N is found to be higher, B&N may reduce your list price to match the competitor's price and will pay a royalty based on the sale price.

If you sell through PubIt!, the price match clause in your Kindle contract will also potentially come into effect. If you price your ebook lower on B&N than on Kindle, Amazon reserves the right to lower their price to match. If it does, Amazon will pay a royalty based on the actual sale price, not the original list price.

Opening an Account

If you have a consumer account with Barnes & Noble, you can use the same email and password to open your publishing account. If not, go to the PubIt! registration page to open your account (see this chapter's Useful Links).

Canadian authors take note: while you can open a consumer account with B&N, you cannot open a publisher's account.

When you open your account, you must do so under your personal name but you can add your publisher's imprint in a separate field.

On the next page you fill out your bank account, tax identification, and credit card information. Once everything is processed by B&N, you will receive confirmation and then you will be able to access your publisher's page.

Uploading to Barnes & Noble's PubIt!

Go to your publisher's page and click on the "My Titles" tab at the top of the page then select "Add a Title." You will find that the publisher's interface is essentially the same as Kindle's in terms of the information you need to input, with only a few differences.

Section 1: Product Data

The following information is required for all PubIt! titles: Title, List Price, Date of Publication, Publisher, Contributor(s), Language, Subject Categories, and Product Description. These follow the same rules as Kindle except:

Publication Date. This field defaults to the day you set up the title so if you want a different day you have to input it. Your publication date can be previous to the date of title set-up but not after.

Publisher: This field is automatically filled with the publisher name that you submitted during the PubIt! registration process.

Contributor's City and State of Residence: PubIt! is planning on adding location-based promotions so if you or other contributor(s) wish to participate you can provide each contributor's city of residence.

If you have your own ISBN you can input it in Section 1. Enter the 13-digit number without hyphens and select "Validate ISBN" on the Add a Title page. If you have a 10-digit ISBN you will have to convert it first to the 13-digit system. Regardless of whether you add an ISBN, B&N assigns its own internal cataloguing number (BN ID) to each title. Both will appear on the title's product page on the Nook Book/PubIt! website. If you also have a print version you can add its ISBN as well; the formats will then be linked on the B&N website.

In addition to required data, PubIt! also offers the option to add further data:

Target Group: From a drop-down list you can add an age range suitable for your book; customers can browse by target age group. If you choose "Juvenile" further options exist to narrow it into specific age ranges. If the book contains adult content you need to specify this; otherwise you will get complaints that might result in your book being pulled from the site.

About the Author(s): You can add biographical information about yourself and any co-authors, as long as it complies with PubIt!'s content policy, which is identical to their policy on book descriptions. See the section "Write a Great Book Description" in Chapter 17: Marketing Your Book for restrictions.

Editorial Reviews: If you have external reviews you can quote a portion of the review and state where it was published but you cannot add a hyperlink to any external reviews. You must also credit the person who wrote the review and you must have sought permission prior to posting. You can add up to five reviews for each ebook.

In Section 1 you will be asked to decide upon digital rights management. You must also specify your publishing territories. The same rules as those found at Kindle apply except that distribution in the U.S. is mandatory.

Section 2: Upload Your Book

Click on "Browse" to locate your Word document. If you have hired a formatter, you upload your ePub here instead. Click "Upload and Preview." A pop-up window will open with a NOOK emulator. Scroll through your ebook and make sure it looks correct. If it is not you can either fix your original file and then upload the amended file for conversion or you can download the ePub from PubIt!, amend the ePub using Tewak_epub, then upload the new file using the "Replace and Preview" option. If you hired a professional formatter, they will need to fix the file at no charge. If they will not fix the file, let other authors know not to hire that formatter.

Section 3: Add a Cover

Here, as with Kindle, this refers to the product image that will appear on the PubIt! website. Click on the "Browse" button to locate your product image on your computer, then click "Upload." The image will appear in the box on the left side of the screen. This cover will also be added to your ebook if you upload a Word document to PubIt!.

Put on Sale

If you are not ready to put the book on sale you can save it in draft form and the title's status will appear as "Not Yet Put On Sale."

Once you are ready to go live you will need to check the box that confirms you have the necessary rights to publish and you understand and abide by the Terms and Conditions, then you can choose "Put on Sale." Your title will show a status of "Processing." It usually takes between 24 and 72 hours for your books to go on sale.

Once the book is available on the site, its status will change to "On Sale." If you make changes to your title information or upload a revised manuscript, the status will change to "Processing." The title will remain available for sale but until it is "On Sale" again you cannot upload further changes.

As with Kindle, Nook customers who bought earlier copies of your book will not get the revised version unless they delete the book from their device then download again.

If your book status changes to "Off Sale" it means the sale of your book has been suspended either because you changed its status or because Barnes & Noble received customer complaints or noticed a violation of a term or condition.

Distributing Via an Aggregator

An aggregator is a company that specializes in converting manuscripts into the various ebook formats, sells your ebooks through their own online bookstore, and also distributes your ebook to a selection of retail partners like Amazon, Barnes & Noble, Apple, Sony, et cetera. The retailers pay your royalties to the aggregator who then takes a percentage as its distribution fee before passing the remainder on to you.

Most aggregators allow you to opt in or out of their various retail channels: you can still deal directly with Amazon and/or Barnes & Noble and hire an aggregator to distribute your ePub to the remaining retailers. Pay attention to who distributes to whom and for what percentage as aggregators vary considerably in the royalties paid and the amount deducted as their fee; and some charge a recurring annual fee. Also, while most distribute to the same set of major retailers, the number of minor retailers on their roster varies and therefore the breadth of distribution. Finally, some retail partners may pay based on the suggested list price while others, like Amazon and Apple, pay only according to the actual selling price. Choosing which distributor or aggregator is best will therefore depend on which retailers you want to distribute to. For a list of some of your options, see the section "eBook Aggregators" in Chapter 16: Distribution and Royalties.

Formatting, Conversion and Distribution

Some digital aggregators, for example eBookIt, include manuscript formatting and conversion in the fee you pay to sign up with them, and produce both mobi files and ePubs. EBookIt's fees start at $149.00 and depend on the length and complexity of your book. Other aggregators such as BookBaby include conversion to mobi and ePub but do not provide formatting services. Fees start at $99.00.

The popular aggregator Smashwords converts to multiple formats and does not charge a conversion or sign-up fee; however, Smashwords does not format your manuscript. Instead, authors must format their manuscript in accordance with Smashwords' style guide (available for download from their website). Upon submission, your manuscript is then put through Smashwords' "Meatgrinder" software and converted into the various ebook formats. Manuscripts that fail to follow the guidelines will be rejected and you will have to keep reformatting until your manuscript passes. Consequently, while Smashwords does not charge you for conversion, you may need to hire a professional to format your manuscript to Smashwords' specifications. Note, too, that Smashwords will not accept a pre-made ePub file; Smashwords will only accept a Word document, which it then converts. (Smashwords has indicated they may in future accept ePubs for distribution, but that has not yet been implemented.)

Hiring an aggregator can solve two problems at once—conversion and distribution—and can be an economical way to get your ebook to market. Turnaround times vary with each company and can sometimes be several weeks, but that is time you can use to investigate the various ways in which you can market your ebook, and perhaps work on some pre-release advertising.

A few words of warning: aggregators will *not* provide you with a copy of your converted files; they will only distribute them. This locks you into that aggregator, and you will have to pay for another conversion if you later change aggregators or if you decide you would rather contract directly with a retailer. I would advise that you instead hire an independent formatter/convertor to create your mobi and/or ePub files and submit those to the aggregator, who will usually charge a lesser fee if you have distribution-ready files (eBookIt reduces their fee to $49.00 if you have fully compliant files.) The exception to this is Smashwords; paying someone to convert your files is pointless as Smashwords will not accept them.

ISBNs

Apple, Sony, Kobo, as well as the myriad of smaller retailers worldwide require that ebooks submitted to them for distribution bear an ISBN. You can acquire an ISBN yourself by contacting your national ISBN registry or you can accept the free or inexpensive ISBN provided to you by the aggregator you sign up with. If you accept the aggregator's ISBN they will be listed as the publisher of record, and some, like Smashwords, will demand this be indicated on your copyright page prior to submission. Other aggregators may add their publisher information to your copyright page when you submit your manuscript for formatting and conversion. For the pros and cons of your ISBN options, read Chapter 7: ISBNs and Other Book Identifiers.

Agency Pricing Versus Distributor Discount

There are two pricing models for self-published ebooks, agency pricing and the distributor discount model. Agency pricing is where you set the retail price for your ebook and the retailer pays you a commission for every unit sold, but the retailer retains the right to set a lower price and pay accordingly. This is the pricing model used by Amazon, Apple, and the aggregator Smashwords. Agency pricing is also used by Barnes & Noble if you contract directly with them or distribute to B&N via Smashwords.

The distributor discount model is where you set a suggested retail price and sell your ebook to the retailer at that price less an agreed upon discount, anywhere from 25-55%. The retailer pays you this wholesale price regardless of the price they sell your ebook for. This is the pricing model used by the distributor Ingram Digital. The aggregators BookBaby and eBookIt use both pricing models depending on the retailer.

The two pricing models conflict with one another and can cause serious headaches for indie authors. For a history of ebook pricing and how indie authors are affected, see "Agency Versus Distributor Discount: The eBook Price War" in Chapter 16: Distribution and Royalties.

Useful Links

To create a PubIt! account.
http://pubit.barnesandnoble.com/pubit_app/bn?t=pi_reg_home

LuLu.
http://www.lulu.com/publish/

Smashwords.
http://www.smashwords.com/about/how_to_publish_on_smashwords

BookBaby.
http://www.bookbaby.com/

eBookIt.
http://www.ebookit.com/

PART II

Going the Distance

The remainder of this manual goes into much further detail regarding self-publishing, including print production for those ready to take that final step. Many chapters, in particular those on editing, errors and omissions, copyright, marketing, and getting paid, are essential reading for all authors, and those who ignore these important issues risk later problems. Other chapters provide the rationale for the instructions provided in Part I, while still others offer technical information on formatting for greater control and more complex ebooks, and how to test them before uploading to Kindle or other retailers. We then end with some marketing advice and an exposé of a typical author services company.

Those who have read the whole of the earlier chapters may encounter some duplication here, which is unavoidable. I have endeavoured not to repeat myself, but in the interest of not forcing my readers to recall information they may have read days or weeks earlier and will likely have forgotten, I have allowed some duplication where expedient to do so. For lengthier sections, such as those on the Kindle and PubIt! publishing interfaces, I will ask that you return to those earlier chapters.

Part II also includes anecdotes from my experiences self-publishing *Baby Jane*, problems I ran into and what I learned as a result. I have included as well the first four chapters of my novel so you can see how it all came together in the end.

3/ Manuscript Editing

Spelling and Grammar

Before you begin to format your manuscript for any given ebook or print format, you first need to create your final draft. And since nothing says "amateur" faster than poor grammar and spelling, the first step in this process is a thorough edit. *This cannot be emphasized enough.* The number one negative comment in indie book reviews is that a book was laden with errors. Typos are a way of life—no manuscript is perfect—but if your readers are slowed down and annoyed by all your errors, you will have lost your audience and any chance of success. And with print self-publishing, since the hardcover or paperback sells at a higher price point than ebooks, poor grammar, spelling, and formatting usually result in very unhappy readers, poor reviews, and returns.

Thus, the first order of business is to proofread your manuscript for spelling and grammatical mistakes. Put your manuscript aside for a few days before you begin proofing so you are tackling your work with fresh eyes. Run your manuscript through spell check but do not rely solely upon this as spell check will miss errors such as "form" where you intended to type "from" since "form" is also a word. Read each word as if it existed alone since the brain is adept at filling in gaps. A trick once suggested to me is to read your manuscript backwards.

Similarly, do not rely solely on a word processor's grammar checker. Most processors do not understand style, so sentence fragments and such that are often part of every writer's style are misinterpreted as errors. And many grammar checks are often simply wrong. Nevertheless, a pass through with grammar check might pick up a few strays so it is worth a look.

One useful editing tool is text-to-speech (TTS) software that reads your book back to you. Windows used to have a built-in program but it was discontinued with Win 7; Mac has a built-in program, Speech, found in Preferences. There are also free and proprietary TTS programs available on the market. Check online for what is available to you. Bear in mind, however, that TTS software will not catch homophones (words that sound the same but are spelled differently, like "there" and "their"). You can also read your own manuscript aloud.

Lastly, always proof a print-out of your manuscript. We learned to read on the printed page and so we tend to pick up more errors when reading a hard copy than when reading on a monitor.

Professional Editing Services

If you can afford to do so, hire a professional to read your manuscript as it is so easy to miss one's own mistakes. Editors may charge by the hour or the word; the latter is easiest for you to calculate an estimated cost.

Many self-publishing companies offer editing services. To give you an idea of cost, one self-publishing imprint offers a basic proofreading service for $0.0175 per word with a minimum charge of $175.00. So for example, my novel, *Baby Jane*, which has 99,876 words including title page and copyright information (yes, have these proofed as well!), would cost $1747.83 (plus any applicable taxes) to have proofed.

I am an advocate for hiring an editor directly, especially as you can likely negotiate a *much* better rate since third parties are using the same freelance editors and simply charging you a premium over what they pay the editor. Also, remember that if you use a foreign service, taxes charged in foreign jurisdictions are not deductible, but if you are registered for your local tax (e.g., GST or HST in Canada, VAT in Europe) then you can deduct any similar tax charged to you by a local editor (all sales taxes are input-output taxes). And if you are unhappy with the service, if you and your editor live in the same country or, better still, same city, more options to deal with any perceived breaches of contract are available. That said, sales taxes are often not charged to foreign clients (every jurisdiction has its own rules); if you are not registered for sales tax then sometimes using a foreign editor may be less expensive. Before making a choice you need to consider convenience, rates and exchange rates, possible taxes, and the reputation of the editor.

When hiring an editor, you also need to make sure your editor knows and understands which language and style you need to adhere to. Are you using U.S. or British spelling, for example, or a hybrid of the two? (Canadian spelling is a hybrid: we typically use British spelling but accept both American and British.) Do you need to adhere to the Chicago Manual of Style or the Oxford Manual of Style? A good editor will have multiple style guides and dictionaries (I have six and three, respectively).

If you wish to go further with an editor and receive advice on improving your writing, the structure of the book itself and/or specific elements, expect to pay another 10% on top of proofreading. Understand this is for advice only; the editor is not going to rewrite your book. Ghostwriting services are significantly more expensive than the review process.

Also, if your grammar and spelling acumen is very weak (for example, if the written language is not your native tongue), most editors will charge extra—as much as 80% more—because there will be considerably greater work involved.

And when all is said and done, expect and accept there may still be errors. The human brain is particularly skilled at filling in missing letters or words. And when proofing it yourself, since you know what you meant to say, your brain can fool you into thinking that what you wrote is what you meant. So perfection is next to impossible. Believe me, I know: a week after I ordered fifty copies of *Baby Jane* for local distribution, a rather embarrassing typo was discovered: I had typed in "site" instead of "sight" in three places. I wanted to crawl under a rock. Misspell "onomatopoeia" perhaps, but "sight"? That's just pathetic. (And a clear indication I spend way too much time online.) It was also a hassle: I had to upload an amended file to Kindle, suspend print production and fix the manuscript. And then I had to try (in vain) not to think about it as I sold those fifty copies.

That said, if after paying for an edit you notice mistakes, your editor should offer to do another pass at their own expense.

Focus Group

The second most common negative comment made about a self-published book is that it was badly written or that it appeared promising but was released prematurely. Before you publish your book it is essential to have your manuscript read by a focus group (often referred to as "beta readers") to determine beforehand where weaknesses exist in your story. Bear in mind that friends often do not want to hurt your feelings so you need to a) make it clear to them that this is your only opportunity to fail privately instead of publicly so honest but constructive feedback is essential; and 2) take every criticism they offer and double it.

When choosing your focus group, mimic your intended audience. If you are writing a romance aimed at women, for example, having men in your focus group is unlikely to provide you with anything useful. Similarly, if your target demographic is teens, asking your mother to read it probably will not help you much. It is the same if you are writing non-fiction: a travel guide, for example, needs to be more accessible than an academic text aimed at Ph.D.s; your focus group needs to reflect this. And if you can include fellow writers in your focus group, all the better.

For fiction, ask your focus group a list of targeted questions such as:

Did the first line/paragraph/chapter entice you to continue reading?

Did the chapter endings entice you to turn the page, or was it easy to put the book down?

How was the pacing? Too slow? Too fast? Inconsistent?

Did you connect/sympathize with the protagonist(s)?

What were your feelings toward the antagonist(s)?

Other main characters: like or dislike?

Were the main characters well-rounded and believable, or shallow and cliché?

Was the storyline interesting or boring and cliché?

Did the story lag anywhere or was your interest maintained?

Did you guess the outcome before you reached the end?

Was the language accessible? Did it make you feel uneducated, pleasantly challenged, or irritated by its simplicity?

Did you find the dialogue engaging? Realistic?

Did the book meet the expectations of the genre? For example, was your comedy funny? Was your horror novel scary?

And in all the above questions ask your readers Why? or Why not?

For non-fiction, ask questions such as:

Was the information presented in an engaging way?

Was it presented in a logical way?

Was the information lacking sufficient details? Did the writer assume the audience is more knowledgeable than they are? Conversely, was the information too detailed? Did the book assume that audience knowledge was insufficient and annoyed them with this assumption?

Did the book include illustrations? If not, would it benefit from them? If illustrated, were the illustrations sufficient? Were they of good quality or did they cheapen the book?

And, of course, no matter the genre, if your readers find any typos or grammatical issues they should bring them to your attention.

Never underestimate the value of a focus group or independent editor. Every great writer has sought out peer review, and every great book ever published has benefitted from editorial feedback. So you need to embrace this stage of your writing and listen to your readers and editors. It does not mean you have to accommodate every criticism, but if you cannot reply to a criticism with a valid rationale for the creative choice you made, then chances are your reader or editor is right and you should take heed.

You must remember that as the author of the book you know the story and its characters; your audience does not. So while you will fill in the gaps, your readers cannot. For example, feedback from my *Baby Jane* focus group indicated the scenes involving the minor character Becky Wilson were too far apart: by the time her next scene came along the reader had forgotten her storyline. This was not apparent to me because I, of course, knew who Becky Wilson was and her story. The feedback resulted in my adding further scenes with Becky and carefully placing them at regular intervals to keep her storyline active and in the mind of the reader.

Similarly, I was once asked in an author interview about character development. I responded that my characters tend to arrive in my imagination fully formed; my job is to make sure that I am describing them properly. Because I know what my characters are thinking and feeling, there is a tendency to assume that what I am writing is an accurate representation of those thoughts and feelings. But sometimes it is not. For example, in the early drafts of *Baby Jane*, the heroine, Claire Dawson, was quicker to anger: this is a woman who was hurt deeply and she has become very isolated; she is having to learn all over again how to be a social being. Her anger stems from her insecurities and her embarrassment for past transgressions. But reader feedback was that, until they got to know her, Claire appeared cold so it was hard for them to connect with her; they couldn't see the pain behind the anger. That was not my intention. I had to change how Claire responded to others and her situation. I removed some of her anger and expressed more of her vulnerability.

You may also find that some of the criticisms of your focus group mirror your own concerns. This provides the twin benefit of validating your concerns and reminding you to listen to your instincts and not to rationalize them away. This happened to me not only with *Baby Jane* but with this manual as well.

Your focus group, as a microcosm of your target demographic, may also expose you to possibilities you did not see yourself. For example, the final beta reader for *Baby Jane* felt that, although there was certainly the romance angle to my novel, the mystery was strong enough and the male protagonist so realistic that she felt the book would also appeal to men. This encouraged me to market *Baby Jane* as a murder mystery with a paranormal twist, leaving out any reference to romance, a decision that later proved effective: my very first sale was to a man who loved the book and gave it a 5-star review on Amazon.com.

Useful Links

Wikipedia list of various style guides.
http://en.wikipedia.org/wiki/Style_guide

University of Chicago grammar resources.
http://writing-program.uchicago.edu/resources/grammar.htm

Merriam-Webster online dictionary.
http://www.merriam-webster.com/

A list of the alleged top 100 creative writing blogs.
http://www.bestcollegesonline.com/blog/2009/02/05/top-100-creative-writing-blogs/

4/ Errors & Omissions

Please be aware the following does not constitute legal advice; it is information I have gleaned through experience and research only. For questions related to a specific project, please seek out independent legal counsel.

While you are waiting for your focus group to get back to you, you can use the time to perform some basic errors and omissions (E&O) research (see this chapter's Useful Links for some good places to start). E&O research helps to protect you from lawsuits pleading defamation, copyright infringement, or trademark infringement. When you write anything intended for public consumption you are responsible for ensuring you have not infringed upon the rights of named parties or organizations, trademarks, copyrighted material, et cetera. Your publisher, including third party publishers or distributors, will include in any contract an indemnity clause along the following:

> You represent and warrant that your Work nor any materials embodied in the content nor its sale or distribution as authorized in this Agreement will violate or infringe upon the intellectual property, proprietary or other rights of any person or entity, including, without limitation, contractual rights, copyrights, trademarks, common law rights, rights of publicity, or privacy, or moral rights, or contain defamatory material or violate any laws or regulations of any jurisdiction; ... To the fullest extent permitted by applicable law, you will indemnify, defend and hold [publisher], its officers, directors, employees, affiliates, subcontractors and assigns harmless from and against any loss, claim, liability, damage, action or cause of action (including reasonable attorneys' fees) that arises from any breach of your representations, warranties or obligations set forth in this Agreement ...[16]

As illustrated, these clauses are always far-reaching and make you legally and financially responsible for any lawsuits that arise from actions taken by an offended party. Moreover, even if the party is unsuccessful you will still incur legal fees, not to mention the stress of a lawsuit. So it is always time well-spent to ensure you have not libelled anyone or used protected works or trademarked items with reckless disregard.

All book retailers including ebook retailers such as Amazon's Kindle and Barnes & Noble's PubIt! naturally reserve the right not to sell your book; doing so is purely at their discretion even if you have set up a publisher's account. Moreover, they warn you upfront that they will not publish any material they deem offensive or pornographic, promotes illegal activity, infringes upon another's copyright or right to privacy or publicity, or is comprised solely of marketing lists.

Errors and omissions issues are not confined to the content of your book but also apply to the cover. See the section "Sourcing Imagery" in Chapter 9: Cover and Interior Images, for information on potential issues with cover imagery.

Libel

Libel is defamation in written form (slander is verbal defamation). Libel is both a civil and criminal offence in most countries, and can usually be pursued both at the state or provincial level as well as federally. In my home country of Canada, for example, libel is covered by both provincial civil law statutes and by the federal Criminal Code of Canada, Sections 297 to 317. Section 298 defines defamatory libel as:

> (1) A defamatory libel is matter published, without lawful justification or excuse, that is likely to injure the reputation of any person by exposing him to hatred, contempt or ridicule, or that is designed to insult the person of or concerning whom it is published.[17]

Libel statutes are similarly worded elsewhere; what differs between jurisdictions is what is considered "lawful justification or excuse." Due to First Amendment protection, U.S. libel laws tend to be less favourable for plaintiffs than laws found in Europe and in Commonwealth countries where statutes are often based on British law. Perhaps more than others, then, Americans need to be aware that if you publish worldwide you will be subject to other criminal and civil jurisdictions: the offence occurs not where the book is written but where it is sold. If this is a concern, then when you self-publish you should elect to exclude from distribution individual territories where you believe you may run into problems. Usually the distributor will present territorial exclusions under Rights Management, meaning that you must exclude territories for which you do not hold the rights to publish within, but you can also use this option to deselect territories for which you fear possible controversy. For example, many orthodox Islamic countries have draconian blasphemy laws, so if your book deals with sensitive issues around Islam you may wish to restrict sales to these jurisdictions.

Many Western countries also have blasphemy laws. Canada, for example, has an archaic criminal code violation of "blasphemous libel" (Section 296), which is defined in the negative: blasphemous libel is not specifically defined ("It is a question of fact whether or not any matter that is published is a blasphemous libel"[18]) but rather there is a "saving" clause that determines whether or not you can be convicted: "No person shall be convicted of an offence under this section for expressing in good faith and in decent language, or attempting to establish by argument used in good faith and conveyed in decent language, an opinion on a religious subject."[19] This saving clause is what distinguishes legitimate discourse on religion from hate propaganda, which is also a criminal offence in many Western countries.

Characters in fiction are assumed to be just that, fiction; thus cases of libel against fiction writers are rare and cases that are commenced rarely survive summary judgment. Nevertheless, they are a potential hazard that you should be aware of. When doing your due diligence, all characters that are identifiable must be checked: do not assume minor characters are exempt from libel.

While positive portrayals may not seem blameworthy—for libel to exist the characterization must be false or partly so, and it must portray the character as engaging in untoward acts—you cannot assume a person will be flattered to be in your book, that your definition of what is and is not shameful is shared by the person portrayed, or that their acts of personal courage or heroism are subject to public consumption. For example, you write a story based on your sister's heroic battle with breast cancer only to discover that she is horrified her private health issues were turned into a work of fiction that everyone knows is really about her. More importantly, though, an unflattering portrayal can land you a lawsuit.

Libel cases in fiction arise when an author bases a character on someone they know or has read about elsewhere and makes little effort to conceal the identity of the real person. The portrayal is almost always unflattering and the person's real characteristics are mixed in with fictional ones. Simply changing a person's name is insufficient if there are enough other details—such as age, ethnicity, physical characteristics and mannerisms, and personal history—that make it possible to identify the real person. Your best strategy is to change as many characteristics as possible and never use a name that is similar to that of the real person.

Truth is the only defence against libel, so where libel arises in fiction is where the fictional elements of your character are plausible, making it unlikely that the reader will be able to distinguish between the truth about the real person and the fiction of your character. The most famous current example of this is the case of "SuSu," a character in author Haywood Smith's novel *The Red Hat Club*. Smith modeled her character SuSu after long-time (and now ex-) friend Vickie Stewart, a member of the Red Hat Society. SuSu shared over thirty similarities with Stewart including where she grew up, her employment, and even the details of her first husband's death, but *The Red Hat Club* then went on to portray her as a promiscuous drunk. Stewart sued Smith and was awarded $100,000 in damages. So before you decide that a novel is your best revenge against your ex-spouse/boss/employer, ask yourself if it is worth the lawsuit.

Often writers are advised to avoid defamation lawsuits by imbuing their character with additional characteristics that are so far-fetched that no one would believe them to be true. One somewhat infamous strategy is to write that a male character has a small penis because, it is alleged, no man will stand up in court and declare, "That character with a very small penis, that's me!" Known as the "small penis rule," it was referenced in a dispute between journalist Michael Crowley and author Michael Crichton. Crowley alleged that after writing a negative review of a Crichton novel, Crichton retaliated by including in his novel *Next* a character named Mick Crowley, a child rapist described as a Washington-based journalist and Yale graduate with a small penis. Unfortunately for Crichton, Crowley, who is Washington-based and a Yale graduate, did stand up and declare he was libelled, though he elected to fight in print instead of in a courtroom.

With non-fiction, truth is not always an adequate defence. In some jurisdictions the courts will also look at the context of the revelations: whether they were made with "malice intent" or "ill will," and whether or not they serve the "public good." There is also the concept of right to privacy, whereby revealing private but true facts not intended for public consumption can lead to a cause for action. For example, instead of fiction you write a non-fiction book about breast cancer and reveal your sister was a sufferer and had a mastectomy; she would have a cause for action against you: that your sister personally was affected by breast cancer and had a mastectomy is of no concern to the general public in need of information about the disease. So proceed carefully and if in any doubt seek legal counsel.

Portrayals of Public Persons

Portrayals of public persons are handled differently in libel legislation. Public persons are generally exempt from right to privacy legislation but they are also more likely to benefit from right of publicity legislation, that is, the right to be the sole beneficiary of the sale or use of their name and likeness. You should definitely consult an attorney before you publish an unauthorized biography or exposé, dramatic recreations, or "faction."

Libelling the Dead

In general, you cannot libel the dead but you can indirectly libel living relatives of the dead if your dead character interacts in such a way with other characters that this impugns the reputations of living relatives. For example, you base a character on someone's dead father and portray him as a pedophile who indoctrinated his sons into a pedophile ring; even if the sons are not characters in your novel, you have implied by the actions of your character that the sons are pedophiles, and if untrue then this would be potential grounds for them to win a lawsuit.

Copyright Infringement

Plagiarism is the act of representing the work of another as your own, which is the most heinous of copyright infringement, but infringement also applies to using another's work, even if referenced, to an extent that exceeds fair use or fair dealing.

"Fair use" is a U.S. term, while in Canada, the UK, and Australia the term is "fair dealing." Both attempt to define the parameters under which you may use excerpts of another's work, or even the whole of the work, without the copyright holder's permission. (Note: the author of a work may not be the copyright holder. The author may have produced a work-for-hire, may have sold or assigned the copyright, or may have died and the copyright is controlled by his/her heirs.) While the popular belief is that as long as you only reproduce a few lines or paragraphs at most you are not violating copyright, this is not actually true: length is only one determination of infringement; other determinants include intent, context, and purpose of use. Thus even short excerpts of copyrighted works may land you in trouble and you should seek legal advice before using them, or request permission to reprint. For example, in one of my screenplays I wrote a scene where a segment from a medieval play is reproduced, and while the play is obviously public domain now, the dialogue made use of a modern translation that is copyrighted. Were the screenplay to be produced, that scene might require permission from the author. If so, and if the producers were unable to acquire a release or negotiate a reasonable royalty, then that scene would have to be rewritten or cut.

Titles, ideas, character names and personalities, and plots are not copyrightable, only the expression of them. In other words, an idea for a novel is not copyrightable but the manuscript is, as are any outlines and earlier drafts that may have been written. Facts are also not copyrightable but a non-fiction book that makes use of those facts is. And a work may be in the public domain but a modern interpretation of that work would be protected, for example a new translation of *The Iliad* or a new illustrated *Cinderella*.

But while fictional characters per se do not benefit from copyright protection, many, for example comic book characters, have been trademarked. Moreover, some characters have become iconic—for example, James Bond or Miss Marple—so using them without permission could run you into legal problems. Do not use a character from another work unless the work is now public domain or you acquire permission to use, or you first consult an attorney as to the risk.

Copyright of a work exists immediately upon creation even if no formal copyright declaration is made or the work is not publicly available. You must not assume that you can help yourself to stuff off the Internet or that you can use the unpublished work of another writer. To determine if a work is usable, ask yourself this simple question: Did I write it? If not, it is not yours.

Works in which the copyright has expired are considered public domain, but while you can reproduce excerpts without permission or even publish a public domain work in its entirety, you must always acknowledge original authorship. Also, what is public domain in one country may not be in another; if you intend to publish internationally you need to be doubly careful (see Chapter 5: Copyrighting Your Manuscript).

To acquire permission to use, contact the author directly or through their publisher.

Trademark Infringement

Similar to copyright is the issue of trademarks. For example, does your character drive a generic sports car or a BMW? Does your character take an Aspirin for her headache or some acetaminophen? "BMW" and "Aspirin" are trademarked; "sports car" and "acetaminophen" are generic terms. Whenever possible, use generic terms as these do not require permission to use.

Some trademarks have become so common that they have become generic in the eyes of the public. Two examples are Kleenex and Band-Aid. These trademarks are deemed "diluted" and are no longer protected by trademark. Nevertheless, unless the trademark is integral to your plot, use of the generic term is preferable.

In non-fiction, a writer may use trademarked items so long as the facts are correct. For example, if you wrote a biography of a famous drug addict hooked on OxyContin, the makers of the drug, Purdue Pharma, would have no claim for trademark infringement. But if your addict was taking the generic version, oxycodone, then Purdue Pharma might have a case against you for trademark infringement (and also likely defamation).

In fiction, it is common practice to use trademarked items because doing so can be a shortcut to defining or illustrating your character. It is highly unlikely that it makes a difference to your story whether your character uses a Band-Aid (trademarked) or a bandage (generic), but if your character drives a Lamborghini this provides an immediate image of his or her wealth and priorities, much more so than if your character simply drove a sports car.

A fiction writer may use a trademarked or copyrighted item without permission as long as the reference is incidental, not essential to the story line, and of infrequent use so as not to suggest association or endorsement. Your character can thus drive a Lamborghini, but if the Lamborghini is referenced repeatedly or is an essential component of the story line—if you are writing, for example, the next *Knight Rider*—then the reader might assume Lamborghini has endorsed the use of their product and if they have not then this would be deemed beyond fair use.

Some attorneys thus suggest that you include a disclaimer on your copyright page that lists the trademarks used and indicates they are being used without permission and that the use of a trademark is not authorized by, associated with or sponsored by the trademark owner. It is easy to find out who owns the trademark: most large corporations have set up Wikipedia pages, and you can check the various government trademark online databases.

Often corporations are more concerned with context than actual trademark use. Is the connection to your character positive or negative? If positive, you will find many companies will ignore a trademark infringement or be happy to give you permission to use as this amounts to free advertising; but if your character drinks a Coors and dies (and it is implied the beer killed him), or if the driver of the Lamborghini is a drug dealer, you may find yourself receiving a cease-and-desist letter, especially if your book becomes popular. And while it might transpire that the corporation you have offended has no case, they also have much deeper pockets than you do to finance a lawsuit through which to air their grievances.

Simply changing the trademarked name to a similar name is another strategy since such use is not considered infringement, even if the connotation is negative. So instead of "Coors" beer your character drinks "Cores" beer (and dies).

If it is necessary to reference a trademarked item beyond fair use, you will need to procure what is known as an "Authorization to Use" release signed by an authorized person, often in-house legal counsel, on behalf of the company who controls the trademark. If the company does not have in-house counsel, you will need to do a company search and see if a law firm is listed as the provincial or state contact. Or contact a local branch or affiliate and ask if they know who represents the company in legal matters.

You may find yourself playing detective here, and your creativity will serve you well. Years ago I was in charge of securing product releases for a TV show and needed to procure a release for a poster featuring a popular rock band. But a call to the record company revealed a closed system whereby I could not get through to a customer relations person or a receptionist; I had to know the name of the party I wished to speak with and dial their extension. I figured most large companies have at least one person named Smith working for them so I dialled "Smith" into the company directory and up came an extension. Once I got Smith on the line I was able to explain why I was calling and was given the number to the legal department, from whom I was able to acquire the signed release.

If asked about the context in which the trademark will appear, do not be tempted to lie because if you do any corporate release is unlikely to protect you in court.

When checking for trademark infringement, remember to check any imaginary businesses that you have created for your book, just in case. Also, do not assume something is generic or public domain. For example, if your characters are playing Scrabble, that is trademarked, but if they are playing Rumoli, that is not, but you will not know that for certain unless you check.

When using trademarks without permission, you will have to balance the value that a trademark can add to your work—by providing the reader with an immediate visual reference—versus any potential legal action.

And finally, you can sell a company the use of their trademark in your book; this is known as "product placement." However, it is unlikely that a company would be willing to pay for a negative connotation, and also if you are a new writer it is unlikely anyone will consider your book a valuable advertising venue. But if your book does well you can certainly entertain the idea for later projects.

Government Agencies, Public Buildings, and Academic Institutions

Government agencies (e.g., FBI, RCMP, Interpol, IRS, Revenue Canada, Scotland Yard), public academic institutions, and public buildings are not trademarked or trade-named. Thus these do not need to be avoided unless you are libelling the organization itself. If so, check with legal counsel.

Do not assume, however, that all buildings are "public." Many privately owned or built buildings have become trademarked, for example the Sears Building in Chicago or Trump Towers in New

York. Also, do not assume a building is governmental. A good example of this is the New York Stock Exchange: the exchange is a privately held entity, not a government body. Similarly, most airports are privately held entities and holders of trademarks and trade names. And check whether a private educational institution is trade-named.

You can do an online search for trademarks and, if the building or institution you are using is trademarked, treat it the same as you would any other trademark.

Use of Phone Numbers, Addresses, and Other Personal Identifiers

In a work of fiction never use a real phone number or address because the holder of that phone number or address could have a claim for violation of their right to privacy. Consider also the possibility that a psychologically unbalanced person, unable to distinguish between reality and fiction, could attend at an address and harm its inhabitants, for which you could be held liable if it is determined the attack was based on belief in the content of your book. Similarly, if someone were to receive threatening or harassing phone calls because you put their phone number in your novel, you would be liable. (This is why phone numbers used in U.S. television shows and movies always start with "555": there are no real phone numbers anywhere in the U.S. that start with "555.")

The same principle applies to driver's license numbers, social security numbers, and so on. Always use a fictional sequence, for example by adding in an extra digit or changing a number to a letter and vice versa.

In non-fiction, real phone numbers and addresses are statements of fact BUT if your book promotes hatred or violence against an individual or group not only can you be charged under hate crime legislation but you can also be found civilly liable if harm occurs as a result of the release of private information.

Onus on the Defence

While incidental use of a copyrighted work or trademark is allowed, the onus is on the defence (you) to prove fair use or fair dealing. To complicate matters, the definition of "fair" differs among jurisdictions, as does the uses for which fair use or fair dealing applies, and judges are free to apply their own subjective evaluation to the term. So if you are planning on making your work available worldwide, it is best not to rely on any concepts of "fair" in cases where you intuit that you have likely entered a grey area. It is safer to acquire the necessary permissions or rewrite the copyrighted or trademarked item out of your work. And writers may find it less expensive to pay a royalty than to fund a civil defence, even where no breach is likely to be proven.

Should You Hire Counsel? Buy Insurance?

You can hire a lawyer to read your work, do the research, and advise you. It is expensive but offers some protection; and if you are incorrectly advised you may have a case for negligence against your lawyer. There are also errors and omissions researchers that you can hire but they will not provide legal advice; their job is simply to identify potential infringements and procure releases (search online for "E & O Services").

You can purchase errors and omissions insurance but it is expensive and if you take the proper precautions you should not need it. But if you are publishing a risky book and decide to purchase insurance, check the fine print for exclusions that void the insurance if you act recklessly or with intent.

If working in fiction do not overly fret about this issue. Libel suits against fiction writers are rare, as noted earlier, and the plaintiff will have to show knowledge and malice. It is often enough to check the name of your character and geographical area; if a conflict exists, do more research on the real person if possible or simply change your character's name. And not all characters or persons referenced will need to be checked: a passing reference to a generically named person will not require any research. (The purpose of your exhaustive list is to ensure you do not make any mistakes that go unnoticed and which might come back to haunt you later.) Observe caution if your character is based upon a real person, and do not use a trademarked character from another work without permission.

Remember, too, that it is not just a character's name that identifies them but the details or context they appear in. So if your character is a cardiac surgeon named Dr. Mark Smith and he is based in Los Angeles, and your search brings up Dr. Mark Smith, family practitioner based in Boston, there is no need to change your character's name. If, on the other hand, your search brings up Dr. Mark Smith, cardiac surgeon in Los Angeles, ask yourself what other details about your character are mentioned. If it is a minor character and there are no further details, chances are you're good; but if he is a major character and there is the possibility those who know him will see him in your character, then I would suggest changing the name.

And while checking a long list is not only tedious but time-consuming, the process is useful for making sure your book is factually correct or plausible. For example, my character Detective Dylan Lewis jokes about Canada Immigration not doing their job properly at the airport by letting his partner, a UK citizen, back into Canada, but immigration control at Canadian airports is not performed by the Department of Citizenship and Immigration; border control is handled by the Canada Border Services Agency, a mistake my character would not have made. My research gave me the opportunity to fix my error.

Performing Errors & Omissions Research

To perform E&O research, your first task is to create an inventory of every character, major or minor, including any persons referenced even if they are not active characters in the novel, any uses of or references to copyrighted works and characters (including any which are likely public domain), any references to or use of trademarked items, and fake business or product names you created. Do a thorough analysis of your manuscript; do not assume you can remember every reference you made because chances are you cannot: I found that my list grew longer and longer and longer with each pass through my manuscript. Include in your list the geographical location your character is based and rudimentary details such as age and ethnicity, if specified or implied in your book.

Once you have made your list, research sources include Internet search engines, Facebook, LinkedIn, Wikipedia, phone books, libraries, professional associations, government organizations, and trademark databases. There are also fee-based services that do extensive checks including criminal, civil, and financial records.

The following are examples of the main characters in *Baby Jane*, their characteristics, and where I searched for potential conflicts:

Claire Cynthia Dawson, elementary school teacher, Vancouver. Brunette, green eyes, 5'8"; born 8 July 1981 in Calgary; thirty years old; never married. Had an affair with Dr. Eric Mellor, a cardiac surgeon; suffered a miscarriage. After miscarriage launched a medical negligence lawsuit against Dr. Harold O'Connor and St. Martin's Hospital, Vancouver. Both parents alive. One brother: studied at Carleton University in Ottawa and now works in finance and lives in Toronto. Not based on a known person.

I called the Ministry of Education of British Columbia. There were no teachers by that name in the BC school system so I stopped there.

Detective Dylan Lewis, Homicide, Vancouver Police Department. Half-Native, 5'11", approximately forty years old. Mother was addict on Downtown Eastside. Father unknown. Orphaned at age eight. Grew up on the Capilano Reserve in North Vancouver. B.A. in Criminology (with Honours). Martial arts training. Relatives include an aunt Sylvie (married to an archaeologist named Tim), cousin Kurtis (married to Denise), nephews Jeremiah and Jason, grandmother Sarah "Ta'ah" Lewis. Not based on a known person.

For Dylan, I called the Vancouver Police Department. There were no officers by that name in the department.

Sarah ("Ta'ah") Lewis, octogenarian medicine woman, mother to several named characters and grandmother to Dylan Lewis. Native (Coast Salish). Lives on the Capilano Indian Reserve, North Vancouver. Not based on a known person.

I found contact information for the band online at Indian and Northern Affairs Canada and called the band's membership coordinator. There was a real Sarah Lewis living on the reserve but she was born in 2007 so no worries there.

Benjamin Keller, criminal defence lawyer, Vancouver. Divorced (ex-wife Samantha); two children. Son of Randolf Keller; nephew to Armin and Therese Keller; cousin of Elisabeth Keller and the deceased Karl Keller. Named partner at Keller Jamieson Clark & Associates, situated in the Grosvenor Building, Vancouver. Drives a Mercedes. Assistant is Linda, an attractive blonde. Not based on a known person.

I went online to the BC Law Society lawyer lookup. There were no matches to the name so I stopped there.

Armin Keller, elderly German-Canadian man, former member of *Hitler-Jurgend* and member of resurrected Nazi group. Resides in elder care facility. Father to Karl Keller (deceased) and Elisabeth Keller (mid-50s); married to Therese Keller. Pedophile and child abuser. Not based on a known person.

A search of the phone book resulted in an A. Keller in east Vancouver; I called, with negative results. Some Internet finds that were easily eliminated:

> Armin Keller, artist, Berlin;
> Armin Keller, Facebook, graduated 1956 (makes him too young);
> Armin Keller, Volkswagen, Head of Sales, India.

Rafael Juarez, accountant, money launderer for the Morelia Cartel (lead by Cesar Morelia), Mexican, Canadian resident. Two sisters, both married with children. Son of Antonio Juarez, owner of a Mexican grocery store chain; grandson of Ernesto Juarez. Average height and build. Handsome. Not based on a known person.

Both Google and Facebook searches brought up several Rafael Juarezes, including a few accountants, but none resided in Vancouver, or Canada, and I felt confident the remaining details would eliminate any other potential conflicts. However, an Internet search of "Morelia Cartel" revealed that the town of Morelia is a major battle ground in the Mexican drug wars, and one of the cartels is called the "Juárez Cartel." I decided to change both names. Rafael Juarez became Rafael Morales (and relatives' names changed accordingly) and Morelia Cartel became Baja Cartel.

Remember that even minor or referenced characters can be a cause for concern. In the original draft of *Baby Jane*, a Karen Palmer, surgical nurse, Vancouver, though not a character per se, was referenced in the book in a negative way: the mistress of Dr. Eric Mellor, she has the "skills of a porn queen." A search brought up a Karen Palmer on the faculty of a nearby university, so I changed the character's name to Katie Palmer.

And, most importantly, one of my characters is based on a real person: Constable Charles Brown, Media Relations Officer, Vancouver Police Department, is portrayed as handsome, popular and ambitious, authoritative but with a baby face that inspires trust. He plays on the VPD's Centurions hockey team, and subtly blackmails Dylan into buying tickets to a charity game. Because Charles Brown is based on a known person—a good and supportive friend for whom the character was an homage to our friendship—I told him in advance of his "role" and received his blessing. I also sent him a draft of the manuscript, giving him the opportunity to express any concerns prior to publication.

Baby Jane used or referenced seventeen potentially copyrighted or trademarked places, works or characters; nineteen government agencies or academic institutions; fourteen real potential trademarks; and twenty fake business names that had to be checked in case a real counterpart existed. The only concerns that arose were:

> Agencia Federal de Investigación, Mexico. The agency is portrayed as plagued by corruption, but the agency *is* plagued by corruption, as government reports and news stories relay. I kept copies of these reports and news stories.

> Robert Jay Lifton's *The Nazi Doctors: Medical Killing and the Psychology of Genocide*. I had originally quoted from this book but decided it was not worth the hassle to track down permission so I rewrote the passage to remove the reference.

> The Lamplighter Pub, Cambie Street, Vancouver. Of all my imaginary businesses, I only had to change this one when a search revealed an identically named establishment in Gastown, Vancouver.

Useful Links

A Wikipedia article on defamation with information on specific international jurisdictions including countries within North and Latin America, Europe, Asia and Oceania.
en.wikipedia.org/wiki/Defamation

A Wikipedia article on fair dealing with information on specific international jurisdictions: the U.S., Canada, the UK, Australia, New Zealand, Singapore, and South Africa.
en.wikipedia.org/wiki/Fair_dealing

Citizen Media Law Project, hosted by the Berkman Center for Internet and Society. In addition to U.S. law, this site offers useful information about foreign libel laws. It also offers details of cases brought against authors and their publishers, and against film and TV producers.
www.citmedialaw.org

An excellent article on fair use of trademarks in fiction, by Lloyd L. Rich, an attorney based in Denver, CO.
www.publaw.com/article/fair-use-of-trademarks

United States Patent and Trademark Office, with searchable database.
www.uspto.gov

UK Intellectual Property Office.
http://www.ipo.gov.uk/tm.htm

Canadian Intellectual Property Office with trademarks database.
www.ic.gc.ca/app/opic-cipo/trdmrks/srch/bscSrch.do?lang=eng

Australian trademarks database.
http://www.ipaustralia.gov.au/trademarks/search_index.shtml

A blog on libel in fiction, by New York entertainment attorney Mark Fowler.
www.rightsofwriters.com/2010/12/could-i-be-liable-for-libel-in-fiction.html

A CBC article on the libel lawsuit commenced against crime writer John Grisham.
www.cbc.ca/news/arts/books/story/2007/09/29/grisham-lawsuit.html

A *Wall Street Journal* article about the libel suit against the producers of *Law & Order*. The suit was the first of its kind in 25 years to survive summary judgment in New York State.
blogs.wsj.com/law/2008/03/20/libel-in-fiction-claim-rarely-successful-survives-summary-judgment/

New York Times article on defamation feud between Michael Crowley and Michael Crichton.
www.nytimes.com/2006/12/14/books/14cric.html

Details of the successful suit against Haywood Smith, the writer of the bestselling *The Red Hat Club*. The plaintiff was awarded $100,000. The suit has become a benchmark case study of what NOT to do when basing your character on someone you know.
www.lexisone.com/lx1/caselaw/freecaselaw?action=OCLGetCaseDetail&format=FULL&sourceID=bdjgjj&searchTerm=eTfC.WQea.UYGT.Ddii&searchFlag=y&l1loc=FCLOW

5/ Copyrighting Your Manuscript

Legally speaking, any artistic work is automatically copyrighted by virtue of being created. In general, copyright lasts for the life of the author, the remainder of the calendar year in which the author dies, and then for a set period of time—usually fifty or seventy years—as determined by the legislation of the country in which the copyright is protected. After that, the work becomes part of the public domain and anyone can use it. There are exceptions to this general rule: books published in the U.S. prior to 1978, for example, are protected for a set term from the date of publication, not the death of the author, and many countries have similar exemptions. Some countries base copyright on the nationality of the author while others base it on the country of first publication.

Although your own country may have copyright legislation, there is actually no such thing as international copyright. Copyright is only protected by the laws of any given country, so your work is not protected in countries where copyright laws are lax or non-existent. This is why countries like China are a haven for bootlegged product. You cannot oppose the unauthorized reproduction of your work in a jurisdiction where it is not protected, only the importation of those unauthorized copies into a treaty nation.

Many countries are signatories to copyright treaties, which means the signatories agree to respect the copyright of one another's authors. These treaties may further define the nationality of the author/work and the date a work becomes public domain. For example, generally speaking Canada delivers a work to the public domain after fifty years but the United States waits seventy years. If Dan Brown died this year (2011), then in the absence of a treaty to the contrary *The Da Vinci Code* (and Brown's other books) would become public domain in Canada on 01 January 2062 but public domain in the U.S. on 01 January 2082. This would mean that in 2062 a Canadian publisher could publish *The Da Vinci Code* without permission and sell it in Canada but could not export it to the United States. However, if Canada has a treaty with the U.S. that states Canada will respect the seventy-year period for American authors, then Brown's work will not be in the public domain in Canada until 2082.

Copyright treaties may be bilateral, meaning between two countries, or multilateral, between several countries. Since one's country is often a signatory to several copyright treaties, the copyright notice you see in a typical book published in North America is therefore all encompassing: "All rights reserved under International and Pan-American Copyright Conventions."

Even where your copyright is protected, owning copyright and proving it are two different things. If you are concerned about copyright theft, especially if you intend to send your work out to be edited or analysed prior to publication, then there are steps you can take to create proof of authorship.

The most common method is to register the work with your national copyright agency. (If you search "copyright registration" and your country, your national registry will come up.) This is done by filling out the requisite form, paying the requisite fee and, in some cases, sending either an electronic or physical copy of your manuscript, or both. In support of this process, the U.S. Copyright Office states:

> Many choose to register their works because they wish to have the facts of their copyright on the public record and have a certificate of registration. Registered works may be eligible for statutory damages and attorney's fees in successful litigation. Finally, if registration occurs within 5 years of publication, it is considered *prima facie* evidence in a court of law.[20]

There are many writers' associations, unions and guilds that have a copyright service for their members. Most are pay-per-use, and the entity keeps a copy of your manuscript in their files for a set time period, usually one to three years. There are also commercial registries that provide the same service.

You can leave a copy of your manuscript with an attorney, who will date and seal the envelope with their notary seal and keep it in safe offsite storage.

There is a long-held belief that you can create your own registry of sorts by mailing yourself a copy of your manuscript, either printed out or saved to disk, and then leaving it sealed and stored in a safe place: the postmark serves as your proof of date, and the envelope can then be opened in court, witnessed by the judge, if conflict arises. Called "the poor man's copyright," this method will not prove that you wrote the work in question—it only indicates date of creation—and there are no provisions in copyright law that formally recognize this method. Its usefulness will thus be very limited, but depending on the facts of the dispute it might be better than nothing.

If you publish under a pen name, you can copyright the work in your pen name or in both your pen and real name; the latter is preferable because otherwise, if conflict arises, in addition to proving your copyright you would have to prove your identity as this fictitious author. And if the relationship between your fictitious self and your real self is not established, this can also complicate the later selling of subsidiary rights and reprint rights, and the transfer of your rights to your heirs upon your death.

When it comes time to publish your final manuscript, the copyright date used for the book should be the date of publication even if you registered earlier drafts or have been writing the book for years. Remember that every unique expression of an idea is individually protected, so each early draft of your manuscript is accorded protection from the moment of its existence whether formally registered or not; copyrighting your final manuscript using the date of publication does not negate your copyright of the earlier drafts, and there is no loss of protection by using the date of publication.

Who is Entitled to Copyright?

At the heart of copyright law is the issue of who is entitled to the proceeds of that copyright, that is, its royalties. So if copyright is shared then so too must be the royalties. If a book is jointly authored then copyright is shared and would be identified as such in the book—"Copyright 2011 by Writer X and Writer Y"—and in the absence of a contract to the contrary all contributors would be entitled to an equal share of royalties. Consequently, if one writer contributes more than the other(s) then the writer needs to enter into a contract with his/her partner(s) that outlines what each party's contribution is and what portion of the proceeds each is entitled to.

In the case of illustrated works it all depends on the contract between the parties as to how copyright is shared. If the writer and illustrator have collaborated without payment to the other, then copyright is shared as it would be between co-authors and must be identified as such. Again, a contract stipulating the division of royalties is recommended.

If an author hires an illustrator to produce drawings for a book, the copyright to the book remains solely with the author but the images would either be owned by the author or licensed from the illustrator, depending on the terms of the contract: if the contract states copyright of the illustrations remains with the artist, then the author licenses the images from the illustrator for a set period of time and over a defined geographical area; if the contract states the illustrations are a "work-for-hire," then copyright of the illustrations is owned by the commissioning author. In either case, the contract usually stipulates a credit must be given to the illustrator on all versions of the book and all marketing materials.

If you contract out for any services whether they are for research, editing, illustrations, cover art, translations, and so on, it is always recommended that you have a written agreement that specifies it is work-for-hire, that copyright is not conferred upon any other parties, and that any and all claims against the author are limited to payment of the invoice. It is also wise to keep all correspondence between yourself and anyone, including your focus group, who is privy to your manuscript prior to publication.

Legal Deposit

In most countries where copyright legislation exists, it is mandatory for the publisher of a work to provide one or more copies of the published work free of charge to the national literary agency within a specified time after publication; this includes copies of ebooks where the means for deposit exists. This is known as Legal Deposit and it ensures your book becomes part of your nation's literary archives.

In most countries, too, this legislation applies to any copyrightable work that is distributed for public consumption regardless of whether an ISBN is assigned to the work. Copies of ebooks must usually be submitted in a non-proprietary format; in other words, Legal Deposit can accept a mobi file but not a Kindle file. While this might seem like semantics, it is not because the Kindle file contains additional data that specifically turns the mobi into a Kindle device-specific file. At the moment, then, some national archives do not have the means to accept a Kindle file but you can send in ePubs or PDFs if you publish to those formats. You will need to check with your national registry for specifics.

In the U.S., copies of ebooks are exempt from Legal Deposit unless the Library of Congress specifically requests a copy. If a physical edition of the title exists, two copies are mandatory unless the publisher requests and is granted an exemption. Mandatory deposit with the Library extends to physical works published outside the U.S. and imported either as part of an American edition or distributed in the U.S.

Copyright registration is voluntary in the U.S. but you can kill two birds with one stone by applying to the Library of Congress for copyright registration of the published work, upon which you must submit two copies: this simultaneously satisfies Legal Deposit. Registration is possible online—the Library prefers it, in fact, and encourages online submissions by reducing the fee from $50.00 to $35.00. Online submissions are processed faster, can be tracked online, and the fees are payable by credit card. Your manuscript can be submitted as a Microsoft Word Document (2003 or earlier), Microsoft Word Open XML Document, HTML, PDF, Rich Text Format (.rtf), text file (.txt), WordPerfect Document, or Microsoft Works Word Processor Document (version 9 or later).

In Canada, Legal Deposit requires one copy for print-on-demand titles with an initial print run of less than one hundred books, including ebooks; two copies are otherwise required. New Zealand requires two copies; South Africa requires one copy for print runs of less than one hundred copies or POD. In the UK and Ireland you must provide six copies of your published book: three for the National Libraries of Scotland, Wales and Ireland, and three more for the Universities of Oxford, Cambridge, and Trinity College, Dublin. In Australia, Legal deposit requirements vary among provinces. For details on any exemptions, handling of ebooks, and other details check the website of your applicable national agency.

I have noticed a great deal of discrepancy among author services companies regarding Legal Deposit. Some ignore the issue while some, like iUniverse, only submit copies to the Library of Congress if an author buys a package that includes copyright registration with the Library; this is not sufficient to fulfil the company's Legal Deposit obligations as your publisher, and it *is* your publisher (see "The Hidden Cost of Free ISBNs" in Chapter 7: ISBNs and Other Book Identifiers). The same principle applies to any author services company or POD hybrid that supplies free ISBNs.

Legal Deposit, as the name suggests, is a legal requirement and failure to comply is punishable with fines. If the national agency decides to enforce the matter, the publisher is first sent a notice and given an opportunity to comply voluntarily before the matter is escalated. I have not yet heard of an indie publisher being fined or even sent a letter demanding compliance; nevertheless, you need to be aware that this legislation exists. More importantly, voluntary compliance means your work becomes part of your national archives—how cool is that?

Useful Links

Wikipedia article "List of parties to international copyright agreements."
http://en.wikipedia.org/wiki/List_of_parties_to_international_copyright_agreements

Wikipedia article "Copyright."
http://en.wikipedia.org/wiki/Copyright

Wikipedia article "List of Countries' Copyright Length."
http://en.wikipedia.org/wiki/List_of_countries%27_copyright_length

U.S. Copyright Office.
http://www.copyright.gov/

Circular 7D, "Mandatory Deposit of Copies or Phonorecords for the Library of Congress."
http://www.copyright.gov/circs/circ07d.pdf

Tutorial on electronic filing for U.S. copyright.
http://www.copyright.gov/eco/eco-tutorial.pdf

Canadian Copyright Office.
http://www.cipo.ic.gc.ca/eic/site/cipointernet-internetopic.nsf/eng/home

UK Copyright Office.
http://www.ipo.gov.uk/copy.htm

Australian Copyright Office.
http://www.ag.gov.au/cca

Wikipedia article on copyright laws of the European Union.
http://en.wikipedia.org/wiki/Copyright_law_of_the_European_Union

6/ Digital Rights Management

When you upload your ebook for sale you will be asked if you wish for digital rights management (DRM) to be applied to your title. This is a highly controversial issue and opponents tend to be quite polarized, with evangelicals at both ends. Before you upload your ebook, then, you need to familiarize yourself with what DRM technology is and what the arguments are, for and against.

Digital rights management technology attempts to prevent the unlawful copying of ebooks for sharing and/or selling. It can also allow but limit the user's ability to loan an ebook to a friend, print out pages, or copy pages to another electronic format. There are currently four main DRM technologies, one each from Adobe, Apple, Barnes & Noble, and Amazon; and two earlier players, Microsoft and Sony, whose technology has not achieved broad adoption. Of the four main players, only Adobe's is cross-platform: Apple's Fairplay is designed for Apple devices only, B&N's is a modification of Adobe DRM to make it device-specific (Nook), and Amazon's is a modification of an earlier Mobipocket encryption method.

Contrary to common belief, DRM-controlled ebooks can be read on multiple devices: if a single user has several devices the user can download the ebook to these devices without having to buy additional copies of the ebook, provided the user registers their devices with the relevant retailer. The exception to this is that Kindle books cannot be read on a competitor's ePub device and their ePubs cannot be read on the Kindle.

If the retailer sells an ePub encrypted with unmodified Adobe DRM, ePubs purchased from that retailer can be read by a competitor's device if the ePub is first registered with Adobe Digital Editions, a free utility that acts as conduit for legitimate copies of digital content. Users register with ADE and then instead of downloading an ePub or PDF directly to one's device, the user opens it first in ADE, the copy is validated and then made available for all devices registered to the user's Adobe ID. Adobe currently allows for up to six devices per ID. If a user does not register with ADE, then each time a book is downloaded to the user's device it is encrypted with their device's ID, which binds the book to that device and no other. There is no doubt that using ADE adds a step in the purchasing process and some consumers find this inconvenient or bothersome but, having tested it, I did not find it particularly onerous.

The confusion over which devices can read which competitor's ePubs arises from older versus newer versions of ADE and whether your device is newer and has the latest firmware. In general, Kobo ebooks can be read on any ePub device because Kobo leaves the Adobe code unmodified. Nook ebooks are only transferrable to newer competitors' ereaders because Barnes & Noble used to amend the DRM code to render their ebooks device-specific and is only now moving in the direction of portability. Sony ebooks were previously encrypted with device-specific DRM, which Sony has since abandoned in favour of unmodified Adobe DRM. Apple's ePubs are not transferrable to a competitor device.

If the author permits book lending, DRM allows a user to loan a book to a friend for fourteen days; during this time the book is rendered unavailable on the user's device. After fourteen days the book is automatically removed from the friend's device and resent to the lender's device. This lending option is also only allowed once per title. Critics have complained that the time limit is unreasonable as one could loan a print book for longer than fourteen days, and more often than once. These are valid issues that must be addressed if DRM is to achieve acceptance among consumers.

A similar technology but considered less restrictive is digital watermarking. Here, the file is not controlled and can be shared, but when purchased the ebook is embedded with the user's account information; if pirated copies are later found circulating around the Internet, the publisher can identify the original purchaser who can then be held civilly and criminally liable for copyright infringement. J.K. Rowling, who recently announced she would be selling e-versions of the *Harry Potter* series from her own website, is using the digital watermarking system.

There are various arguments made against DRM, mostly by those who believe in unfettered access to content, who believe anti-piracy measures serve to hinder legitimate sales and, paradoxically, encourage sales of legitimate copies. Let's look critically at some of these arguments.

Obsolescence

The first argument made is that all digital formats contain by their nature built-in obsolescence and therefore users are being denied the same longevity in their ebook library that they are with their print library, and many users have already lost their investment in proprietary formats that were later abandoned due to lack of consumer support. This is all true, but how many of us can still play records or cassette tapes or VHS (or Betamax, for that matter)? How many old cars can be driven without first being modified to meet modern environmental standards? Knob and tube wiring is a fire hazard. Your analogue TV signal just went the way of Johnny Carson. Obsolescence is the nature of the technological beast. If the consumer is concerned about longevity they have the option to remain analogue: to buy print books. As long as a market remains for print books they will continue to be produced.

DRM is a Corporate Conspiracy to Promote Their Brand

Anti-DRM advocates point to Apple and Barnes & Noble specifically to illustrate how DRM is used to bind the consumer to a specific device: the user risks losing their ebook library if they abandon one ereader for another. The use of DRM to force consumer fidelity is very real—and very obvious—but the market has been punishing manufacturers for such behaviour: Sony started out with a proprietary DRM, its sales were abysmal, and Sony has now abandoned its DRM for Adobe Digital Editions; Barnes & Noble appears to be following suit after losing content sales to Kobo. Apple's ebook sales are anaemic and will likely remain so because its competitors have built Apple reading apps. Apple has stubbornly refused to listen to consumer complaints and is now trying to compensate for poor sales by forcing competitors like Amazon to pay Apple a 30% fee for sales made through ereader apps, a battle no one expects Apple to win.

The other holdout is Amazon, whose Kindle is a different format from the open-source ePub, which is fast becoming the JPEG for ebooks. Whether Amazon will be forced to adopt the ePub, or make conversion of DRMed Kindle files to ePubs possible, will depend on market pressure.

Years ago a similar situation developed with the advent of professional digital cameras: Nikon cameras produce a proprietary image format, the NEF, while Canon cameras produce a CRW file, and so on; there are now over three dozen proprietary digital negative formats. The sole purpose of proprietary formats is to force fidelity to the brand and to force users to adopt the manufacturers' imaging software—as if professional photographers are suddenly going to abandon their much loved Photoshop. What has happened instead is that Adobe developed a free convertor that converts these proprietary camera formats to a single format, the DNG (digital negative). The DNG is now the only format recommended by the Library of Congress for the archiving of digital image content, and the photographic industry is pushing manufacturers to give up on proprietary formats and adopt the DNG. It does not surprise me that Adobe, having seen what happened in the digital imaging industry and recognizing a similar issue developing with digital books, jumped at the opportunity to be at the forefront of cross-platform DRM.

If consumers are offended by corporate behaviour like Apple's or Amazon's the consumer can vote with their wallet. To promote the idea that unfettered consumer access is the only way to stem corporate ambition is disingenuous.

Cheap and Easy is the Ticket

Opponents to DRM insist that the way forward is not to prevent illegal sharing but to make the product so cheap that theft is not worth the hassle and risk anymore. And yet you can buy a song off iTunes for a dollar and that has not stopped rampant music piracy. There are many for whom stealing is a philosophy, who simply feel entitled to whatever they want and do not see the harm they cause to artists. Awhile back I got into a debate with a twenty-something man about this very topic; his argument was that if the creators will not price their work at a level he can afford then this entitles him to steal it. "If Sony prices a video game at $50.00 and I can't afford that and I want the game, I have no choice but to steal it," he argued. "No," I replied, "you do have a choice. You have the choice to accept that you don't get everything you want in life, and to live with it." I'd like a Porsche, I remarked, but I can't afford it; should I be allowed to steal one? That's different, was the reply, because when someone steals a car they rob the original owner of their possession; when someone steals digital content they do not: the original owner still has their copy and the thief has his; everyone is happy, no harm done. No amount of explaining how this robs the *artist*, the *creator* of that content, of their livelihood could change this young man's mind. I pointed out that if artists cannot afford to create they will stop, then where will we be as a culture? His response? "No they won't. They'll keep creating; they'll just find another way to earn a living." Of course we will: would you like fries with your novel?

I think as a society we need to take an aggressive stance against this ideology. Artists have a right to earn money from their talents. Some will hit it big, most will not, but they are all entitled to be paid for their creations. Moreover, they are entitled to name their price. If the market will not bear it, the artist will not sell. If the market will bear it, the market has spoken. Not everyone gets to own a Warhol.

Restricted Use is Inherently Unfair

The argument here is that the consumer should never have to worry about obsolescence, never have to be tied to a brand or even a technology, and never be restricted in any way in their use of their ebooks. Putting aside the improbability of this technological Utopia, the foundation of this argument is the fallacy that if one buys a print book there is the unrestricted right to use it in multiple ways including the right to resell or repurpose in any way imaginable. This is simply not true. You can certainly sell your book to a used bookstore but you cannot photocopy or scan a book and sell or give away those copies. If you only have one physical copy of a book you cannot start the book at home then finish it on the bus after work unless you carry the book with you. If you loan a physical book you cannot read it while it is not in your possession, and you incur the risk that the borrower may fail to return it. So while one book may indeed change hands multiple times, anyone who wishes to retain possession of the book must buy their own copy.

What is the difference, this argument further asks, between loaning a physical book and sending a copy of an ebook? It is one book read by a multitude of friends and family, they say, so there is no loss of sales. Or, it is no different than buying a DVD and watching it with the whole family. What is wrong with this argument is that a book, unless you are reading it aloud to someone, is not a shared experience. A book read among family or friends is not read simultaneously; people have to wait their turn. Arguing that they should be allowed to replicate the book to satisfy their demand for instant gratification only feeds into a sense of entitlement, and then we are back to Cheap and Easy is the Ticket.

One thing that is not mentioned in this argument is that the owner of a digital book, DRMed or not, is actually getting a *better* deal than the buyer of a print copy. Why? Because a buyer with more than one device does not have to carry one specific device with them as they do with a print copy: the buyer can start a book on their Kobo, continue it on their iPad, and finish it on their mobile phone. Moreover, if the buyer has more than one device registered to their account they can loan a device with the same book on it that the buyer can also read on another device. Which means the buyer and their friend get to read the same book simultaneously, something they cannot do with a print book. How much more do people need? How much more can we artists be expected to give away to an ever-insatiable consumer base?

I agree that the consumer should have the right to sell forward their ebooks as they currently can with print books, and I believe this will happen as the industry develops—but it will only be through DRM that such sales can be legally made: there will need to be a way to ensure the removal of the digital content from the seller's e-library when the ebook is resold. DRM will thus actually facilitate the possibility of a future legitimate used ebookstore.

The Real Money is in the Ancillaries

Another argument against DRM is to point out that musicians make most of their revenue through performing concerts and via merchandising, so giving away their music encourages revenues where they really matter. This same argument is then applied to publishing, and we are told to learn from the mistakes of the music industry. But this is nonsensical: unless you are J.K. Rowling, authors do not get paid to perform in public. Readings are free events meant to encourage book sales. And except for comic book characters, how much merchandising do you see happening in our industry, or celebrity endorsement contracts? How many Stephen King whiskeys are there? How many J.K. Rowling fashion lines? When was the last time you saw Dan Brown selling razor blades on the sports channel?

Musicians also make money every time their music is played on the radio, in the local shopping mall, and while people are stuck on hold, to name only a few secondary uses. Beyond the aforementioned merchandising of comic book characters, authors have really only one secondary use for their books: film and TV adaptations. Having a film made out of your book is a long shot. And you are never going to hear excerpts from *The Da Vinci Code* read to you while you are on hold with the cable company.

Piracy Encourages Broad Adoption

This strategy compares ebook piracy with software piracy: software companies have been known to encourage piracy, or to give away early versions, in order to achieve broad adoption. Once the user is hooked, it has been proven, eventually they will pay voluntarily for newer versions rather than suffer the possible consequences of piracy such as viruses or corrupted programs. Yet once again we are comparing radically different beasts: software is continually updated, year after year after year. A popular program can mean a lifetime of purchases from the same user. But a book? An author does not update the same book year after year after year—unless, of course, it is a software manual. Or some other similar non-fiction title. But not fiction. A publisher can release a book with a new cover, or perhaps add a guest forward, or release an anniversary edition, or a new format such as an ebook, but there is only so much you can do to milk the cow. Once a user owns a book they are not required by necessity to upgrade. Moreover, there is a thriving used book trade that discourages purchases of new copies. Software does not have a similar aftermarket, at least not one that counts.

eBook Sales Are Forever

Another argument against DRM is that, while the legacy published author has to make their money within a short timeframe before the book is taken out of print, the ebook author does not have to worry about piracy killing the goose: what the ebook author loses to piracy in the short term they make up for with a longer earning term. As one notable proponent put it, ebooks are forever. My response to this would be that if your title is widely pirated among users, forever quickly shortens. What promise do we have that our ebooks will be offered by a retailer in future? There is no current obligation to offer a title; what makes anyone believe this will change? There is also a cost to keeping massive catalogues: storage and computing power. Somebody has to pay the electricity bill; somebody has to pay for the servers. I do not see how ebooks will be *guaranteed* a longer shelf life than a print book.

There is also the matter of copyright legislation. It runs out a few generations after our death, ebook or not. So just because a book exists digitally does not translate into income for our heirs in perpetuity.

The Pirated Copy is Not a Lost Sale

This argument proposes that the type of person who will steal a $3.00 book is not going to pay for it no matter what, so if the book were not pirated this same person would not pay for a legitimate copy; hence, no lost sale. Moreover, this same person might steal your book, love it, and spread the word—it's a win-win! While this might all be true, open acceptance of piracy encourages the broad adoption of an attitude of entitlement, which brings us back again to Cheap and Easy is the Ticket.

Non-DRM Books Sell Better

This argument I find particularly interesting because while I have heard it parroted repeatedly I have yet to see it supported with statistical evidence. For example, on its website the indie aggregator Smashwords states:

> There is a growing body of evidence indicating that DRMed works do not sell as well as non-DRMed work because customers resent limitations and don't appreciate being mistrusted. Non-DRMed works often outsell DRMed works by leveraging the viral nature of uninhibited sampling and sharing which can dramatically increase your total audience and sales opportunities. By pricing your works for less than printed equivalents, and by maximizing the distribution of your books, you make it easier for readers to acquire legal, paid copies of your book...There are many who argue that illegal piracy of your work actually benefits your overall sales.[21]

Where is this "growing body of evidence"? The assertions are not footnoted. And what evidence does Smashwords founder, Mark Coker, have to support the rest of that statement?

Similarly, vocal anti-DRM proponent Joe Konrath has stated that non-DRM books sell way better than DRMed books and that he has "a lot of evidence," but I have never seen this evidence posted on his blog: Konrath expects us to accept his anecdotal experience as is. Yet he has the ability to offer some empirical evidence because his books are not sold DRM-free everywhere: Apple, Sony, and Kobo all apply DRM to his titles. Konrath sells DRM-free on Amazon and Smashwords and elsewhere, so what I would like to see from Konrath is a market analysis: are his DRM-free books really selling better in proportion to the retailer's market share? In other words, it is of no empirical use that Konrath's DRM-free books on Amazon sell better than his DRMed books on Apple because Amazon has the lion share of the market; but if it were to be revealed that his books on Apple are only 1% of his sales but they have 4% of the market, or that 95% of his sales are on Amazon but they only have 70% of the market, that would be interesting and worthy of a closer look.

Also, DRM is only one part of the buyer's decision, so how can Konrath assume his books are selling so well because he elects not to apply DRM where the option exists? How does he know his sales are not instead linked to the popularity of his blog?

I think it more evidentiary to look at the only two indie authors who have reached the million unit mark on Amazon, Amanda Hocking and John Locke, and compare. Hocking sells mass market young adult fantasy fiction; Locke sells short mass market thrillers. Both have been at it for a little over a year and both release a book every few months. Both sell their books at $2.99 or less. Hocking does not apply DRM; Locke does. Yet if we were to accept as fact that DRM-free books sell better, why do Locke's sales not reflect this? And why does Locke sell better than Konrath? Should we assume that Locke would have sold *two* million books had he not applied DRM? Truth be told, unless consumers weigh in to say they would have bought his book if it were not for that annoying DRM, we can never know for certain. And if a legitimate consumer poll has ever been taken on the issue, I have not seen the results.

It's Not That Big of a Problem

On its website, Authors OnLine offers this nugget of wisdom: "Firstly in our experience we ... don't have any evidence [book piracy] happens to any great extent, and if it does then it is only amongst small groups."[22] Question: If you do not have any evidence that piracy happens to any great extent then how do you know it only happens amongst small groups? I would direct Authors OnLine to do a simple test, as I did: Google "Stephen King PDF." The top result was not a legitimate site at which to buy a PDF of a Stephen King novel but a blog that directs you to a torrent site. Second runner-up was another torrent site and then another.[23] The list of torrent sites went on for pages. A search for other formats such as the ePub was also populated by page after page of torrent sites.

In comparison, a search for *A Different Kind of Girlfriend* by Chris Pope, currently #1 on Authors Online, brings up only three hits on Google, all of which are from the Authors OnLine website. Thus, when Authors OnLine claims the problem does not happen to any great extent, perhaps what Authors OnLine really means is that it does not happen to any great extent to their clients, unknown indie authors.

What is also of anecdotal interest is that a search for "John Locke ePub" returns significantly fewer torrent sites than does "Amanda Hocking ePub." As noted, John Locke uses DRM.

And never mind just file sharing: also of anecdotal interest are the complaints that indie authors have made about pirated copies of their work being *sold*, and often *on the same platform!* How cheeky is that? Pirated books, sometimes with the same cover and author, sometimes under the guise of a new name, are being sold on Amazon who, in turn, has been accused of not responding to the infringements aggressively enough. Authors have had to resort to social networking contacts to post reviews on the offending book's page stating it is a stolen manuscript. And as one poster on Goodreads noted, ebooks are turning up in DVD collections being sold on eBay with the sellers claiming the ebooks are in the public domain or that the sellers have taken out a GNU General Public License on the anthology.

Not that big a problem? That's a matter of perspective.

The Actions of the Crooked Few Unfairly Affect the Honest Majority

This is another declaration that I hear parroted often: that DRM is an inconvenience the masses of honest people must suffer because of the actions of the dishonest few, and this is inherently unfair. While I agree with the first half of that assertion, I do not agree with the conclusion.

This argument brings to mind the annoyance I often incur while clothes shopping, trying to determine the fit of an item burdened with those security tags that the sales staff always put in the most inconvenient places, like around the waist. I have often had to ask that a tag be removed so I can determine a proper fit. Is this annoying? Definitely. Is it unfair? No. While I expect the store to accommodate me by removing a tag, I also have to acknowledge that shoplifting is a billion dollar retail problem. Just because security tags annoy me as a consumer does not mean retailers should forgo the use of tags and accept the large losses associated with theft. Moreover, those losses are ultimately passed on to the consumer in the form of higher prices. This is where the honest majority are really affected. If anything, the honest majority should be opposing piracy and reporting abuses.

The bigger question is, Why do most of us tend to support file sharing instead of reporting abuses? Why does the man mentioned earlier feel he is entitled to steal anything he wants so long as it is digital? Dishonesty is subjective. The man in question believes himself to be "a very moral person." And as his female friend remarked, "There's a lot worse things people can do than steal a book." Digital piracy is perceived as a victimless crime, like stealing cable, or office supplies from work. If that fails to nullify our complicity, we then depersonalize the victim so as to mitigate our guilt, or we erase them altogether: it is declared that publishers are greedy, they overcharge for ebooks, and they deserve what they get; there is no mention of the author. It is as if people think the author gets paid no matter how much money the publisher does or does not make, as if authors were employees. For the indie author this disregard is doubly troubling because we suffer from the disdain directed toward these perceived greedy corporate monoliths without receiving any of the perks of such an association.

More unfortunate still, even truly honest people will steal books if they are led to believe what they are doing is not stealing: you cannot feel guilty if you don't know you've been bad. How many of us download movies or television shows from free websites and do not consider that to be wrong? If we keep perpetuating the idea that stealing digital content is not the same as stealing a car because we are only stealing a *copy* of the content, not the content itself, then there is no moral compass to guide us.

If you want an idea of where we are headed without DRM, one only has to look at the photographic industry, particularly stock photography, which has been decimated in part by theft. In the 1990s, the stock photography industry enjoyed healthy growth and expansion, and many professional stock photographers were able to make a good if modest living. The reasonable return on investment encouraged these professionals to take more and ever better pictures, to invest in new equipment or incur travel expenses and other expenditures. But when digital became ubiquitous so did theft of imagery. It has become so commonplace that the image tracking service Picscout claims that 90% of the images they find online are used without authorization.[24] A 2006 white paper by the Stock Artists Alliance adds to this, saying:

> In addition to outright piracy, digital media has also increased the potential for legitimately licensed images to be used outside the scope of the original licence. Once downloaded, image files can be easily repurposed and redistributed to other users. File names are commonly changed and identifying metadata is stripped or altered, making these images vulnerable to misuse.[25]

So many professionals have since left stock photography that the Stock Artists Alliance will close its doors this year, no longer able to support a dying industry. While DRM may be an inconvenience to some users, until we can find another way to enforce—or at least try to protect—the author's copyright, I do not see any other option.

DRM Forces Honest People to Become Dishonest

Some have proposed that DRM forces honest people to steal books when a consumer with multiple but incompatible devices wants to read your book on all devices: they have no option, they claim, but to seek out a way to strip the DRM and convert the file to a format that can be read on their incompatible device. This is not actually illegal anymore than it was illegal to tape your records so you could play the music in your car: as long as the principle user is one and the same the law allows you to make one copy for personal use. That said, if the user is concerned about cross-platform portability they should consider that when choosing their ereader rather than assuming the author has to accommodate the user's poor consumer choices.

A variant of this argument proposes that if a book is not available in the consumer's preferred format then they are "forced" to steal a copy that has already been converted to the user's required format. Once again, if digital limitations are a concern, the consumer still has the option to buy analogue—to buy the print version—or to choose their technology more carefully. If an ebook is not available to you, then *c'est la vie*. Sometimes the shoes simply do not fit or that dress doesn't come in blue. Life goes on.

DRM Violates Privacy

Of all the arguments against DRM, this is the one that I believe is the truly valid one. DRM has been used by certain retailers as a means of collecting consumer information, to track consumer habits, and to deliver advertising. A 2007 white paper by the Canadian Internet Policy and Public Interest Clinic reported privacy abuses by DVD, computer software and video game manufacturers, and ebook retailers. The writers only looked at one ebook device/retailer, Sony's eReader, though they did look at Apple's iTunes music and video store. Abuses by both Sony and Apple were reported, some associated with the ebook device itself and others with the retailer's websites. It is not clear what violations, if any, are associated with newer ebook DRM like Adobe's and Amazon's: the report, as noted, is from 2007. This concerns me the most: all the studies I found regarding DRM and privacy are from 2007 or earlier. Privacy issues are just not attracting the same attention as accessibility issues. The potential violation of one's privacy, and abuses of one's personal information, is a much more serious issue than consumer inconvenience, yet convenience has eclipsed all other arguments. This is a worry because, as the report indicates, the use of DRM to protect copyright does not for the most part require the sharing of consumer information with third parties, or certainly not to the extent the report found among some offenders.

Ideology Versus Economics

How much of the anti-DRM crusade is actually hidden economics? DRM is expensive: the licence for Adobe Content Server 4, which administers DRM to Adobe clients, costs U.S. $6500.00 plus a pay-per-use subscription to their digital signing service. Is it a coincidence that the most vocal opponents to DRM among the retailers are the smaller players like Authors OnLine and Smashwords for whom DRM would be a significant cost? The large retailers all apply it, either mandatorily or by author's choice, and they all had the means to develop their own DRM software or to licence and modify Adobe's. As noted, for sales from her own website J.K. Rowling is using a watermarking system, which is also not cheap. But then she is a billionaire. Authors OnLine's Richard Fitt and Smashword's Mark Coker are not. If their objections to DRM are really about philosophy and not money, then why not offer their authors the option and let them choose for themselves?

As you wade through the treacle that is the DRM argument, remember that it is the individual authors, not the aggregators, that piracy hurts the most. Aggregators and vanity publishers do not care whether your book is pirated because they have tens of thousands of books and authors to build their fortune upon; it is *you* who has only your own books from which to earn a living. When these people tell you piracy is not such a big deal, maybe it is really just not such a big deal for them.

Useful Links

Wikipedia page on digital rights management.
http://en.wikipedia.org/wiki/Digital_rights_management

Collection of *Guardian* articles on DRM-related issues.
http://www.guardian.co.uk/technology/drm

"Digital Rights Management Technologies and Consumer Privacy: An assessment of DRM applications under Canadian Privacy Law." Study paper by Canadian Internet Policy and Public Interest Clinic, 2007.
http://www.cippic.ca/sites/default/files/CIPPIC_Report_DRM_and_Privacy.pdf

Berkeley Technology Law Journal essay, "DRM and Privacy," by Julie E. Cohen, Professor of Law, Georgetown University Law Center.
http://www.law.georgetown.edu/faculty/jec/drmandprivacy.pdf

Website of the research and dialogue project INDICARE: Informed Dialogue about Consumer Acceptability of DRM Solutions in Europe.
http://www.indicare.org/tiki-view_articles.php

7/ ISBNs and Other Book Identifiers

The ISBN System

ISBN stands for International Standard Book Number. The rules and regulations governing the use and distribution of ISBNs are determined by the International ISBN Agency, based in Berlin. The international agency allots ISBNs to national agencies, who in turn allot them to their publishers; thus, a publisher cannot acquire an ISBN from a foreign national agency: a British publisher, for example, cannot buy an ISBN from the American ISBN agency and vice versa. Publishers then assign their ISBNs to their books. ISBNs are thus owned by the publisher, not the author. An author can, of course, also be the publisher, but they own the ISBN in their capacity as publisher.

Not Mandatory, Just Practical

ISBNs are not legally required to publish; however, they are the primary means by which retailers, wholesalers, distributors, libraries, and national cataloguing agencies identify a work and its format. The ISBN is the primary metadata that retailers use to catalogue their books and provide search data. If you do not assign an ISBN to your print book it cannot be distributed through traditional means, and it cannot be registered in the various databases from which book buyers make their purchasing selections; your potential audience must find you solely through your advertising efforts. And most retailers as well as libraries will simply not purchase a book, including an ebook, that does not contain an ISBN.

To understand why this is, you need first to understand a bit about publisher imprints and formats. If you were to look, for example, at the website for the publisher Alfred A. Knopf, you would see that it is actually an imprint—a subsidiary—of Knopf Doubleday Publishing Group, which is a subsidiary of Random House Inc. Random House Inc. owns eight similar publishing groups, all but one of which own multiple subsidiary imprints. Each imprint is deemed a separate publisher, and large houses will often publish a novel in its initial hardcover form under the publishing group's most prestigious imprint, then publish the paperback under a less prestigious imprint. A title may also be published by different publishers in the various jurisdictions the rights were sold in; for example, British author P.D James' *The Private Patient* was published in the UK by Faber and Faber Limited and in Canada by Alfred A. Knopf. Sometimes, too, a writer may elect to change publishers upon termination or expiration of a contract. So one publisher may have the first hardcover and another publisher the second hardcover or the paperback. Since the ISBN is unique to the publisher, the market can keep track of who publishes what and where.

The ISBN system also keeps track of a book's various editions: the hardcover edition, the trade paperback edition, the mass market paperback edition, and so forth; thus one title may have several ISBNs. The system ensures that when a customer requests the hardcover of a title they do not get the paperback instead. The system also ensures that when a title changes publishers, or a public domain work is published by multiple publishers, the customer is able to differentiate between the editions.

(When we speak of editions, there are two understandings of the word that mean different things. The first use arises out of a marketing technique: when a book is printed the publisher orders a specific number to be printed and, if and when sold, will then order another print run. Sometimes the title page of the first print run will be inscribed with "first edition" to differentiate those copies from subsequent print runs, which encourages buyers to rush out to acquire said first edition because of its perceived greater value, especially over time. Thus one often hears of someone acquiring the coveted first edition of a book, even though later editions might actually be more valuable for different reasons.

The second meaning of edition is what we use here when speaking of ISBNs, and refers to the publisher/format combination: one can order the paperback Penguin Classics edition of *Little Women* instead of the paperback Bantam Classics edition of *Little Women*, and so on.)

ISBNs also help to defend a publisher's territorial rights. Publishers often pay dearly for the sole right to publish a title within a given jurisdiction, and it is illegal to import another publisher's version into a jurisdiction for which it does not have the right to publish, at least for a prescribed time. Imagine if you will the UK publisher of *Harry Potter* paying a fortune for the rights only to have cheaper U.S. copies imported, replacing the UK publisher's sales. When an ISBN is assigned to a title, the publisher's rights are inputted into the system and travel with the ISBN within a title's ONIX code (discussed later in this chapter), serving as a guide to importers and retailers.

ISBNs for eBooks

With ebooks, the same principle applies: different ISBNs must be applied to a title's different digital formats—Kindle, ePub, PDF, and so on—to ensure that the consumer does not order the ePub when they need the PDF. It should also be applied to multiple versions of the same file format if different digital rights management (DRM) software is applied, and it should also be applied to the same file using the same DRM if different versions apply different levels of security: one PDF might allow printing, for example, while the other PDF of the same title may not. And if you were to publish a static PDF and later create an interactive PDF version of your book, that interactive PDF would also need a new ISBN.

However, most ePubs are distributed via aggregators, and the indie author is not given the option to upload different ePubs with different ISBNs for distribution. The indie author really has no choice here but to distribute a single ePub with a single ISBN.

The Kindle format is proprietary to Amazon and is not distributed outside of Amazon, so you can publish to Kindle without an ISBN; Amazon applies an internal cataloguing number, an ASIN, to Kindle books. This does not prevent you from applying an ISBN to a Kindle title, however, and if in time Amazon makes the Kindle format available outside its walls your ISBN may prove useful (Amazon has recently announced it will soon implement library lending).

Barnes & Noble's PubIt!—the indie wing of Nook—also applies an internal cataloguing number so an ISBN is optional for B&N.

Apple, Sony, Kobo, and other online retailers will not carry ebooks without an ISBN, so you cannot distribute to these retailers without one.

When Does a Book Need a New ISBN?

Minor changes to a manuscript do not require that a new ISBN be assigned. Typos and such can be fixed at any time without concern. You can also add new marketing pages without issue, or modify the cover to advertise an award, for example, or to add a new endorsement. It is only when the manuscript itself undergoes material changes—for example, if a foreword is added or new illustrations are created—or a whole new cover is put on the book, that you need to assign a new ISBN (and the new edition must be indicated on the copyright page).

ISBNs and Copyright

ISBN designation does not confer or register copyright; ISBN and copyright have no bearing on each other whatsoever.

What's in a Number?

There are five parts to an ISBN, separated by either a hyphen or a space. Only the first three digits and the final check digit are of a fixed length; the remainder vary according to language, publisher identifier, and the number of ISBNs assigned to the block. The five parts of an ISBN are:

- the current ISBN-13 prefix of "978";
- the group or country identifier;
- the publisher identifier;
- the title identifier; and
- the check digit which validates the ISBN.

For example, the ISBN for the Kindle version of *Baby Jane* is:

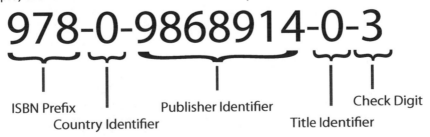

75

ISBN Prefix

The ISBN prefix of "978" arose out of product barcode regulations that use the first three digits to identify the country of origin. When the ISBN and barcode systems were integrated for the purposes of publishing, books became a "country" in themselves, assigned the 978 prefix.

Publisher and Title Identifier

The next section, which is between one and five digits long, indicates the country identifier, with countries divided into language groups. The ones you will most commonly come across are single digits: "0" and "1" indicate English-language countries, "2" is for French, "3" is for German, "4" is for Japanese, and so on. Countries like Canada where we have two official languages, French and English, will see French-language books assigned "2" for the country code. Books published in an English-language country in a language other than English will still see "0" or "1" applied as the country code. For example, I noticed that Spanish-language books published in the U.S.—where Spanish is broadly adopted but not an official language—have "0" as their country code.

The publisher identifier and title identifiers are adjusted according to the number of ISBNs allotted in the block. If you are allotted a block of 10 numbers, the title identifier section will only be one digit (0 through 9); if you are allotted a block of 100 numbers, the title identifier section will be two digits (00 through 99); if you are allotted 1000 numbers your title identifier is three digits (000 through 999).

The publisher identifier is then lengthened or shortened to maintain the thirteen-digit format. Thus an English-language publisher allotted a block of 10 ISBNs will have a seven-digit publisher identifier while the same publisher allotted a block of 1000 ISBNs will have a five-digit publisher identifier number. Large publishers may be allotted even larger blocks, of 10,000 or even 100,000 numbers. The ISBN below is owned by Pocket Books; in this case their identifier number is only four digits and the four-digit title identifier indicates the block allotted was 10,000 numbers (oooo through 9999).

978-0-4391-0281-7

ISBN Prefix
Country Identifier
Publisher Identifier
Title Identifier
Check Digit

What Your Number Says About You

I have read on the Internet that a seven-digit publisher number tells all and sundry that you are a first time publisher with less than ten titles to your name. This is not true. In jurisdictions where numbers are given out free of charge, common sense dictates that all new publishers be granted only a block of ten ISBNs to begin with and are then simply allotted a new block of ten with a new publisher identifier number when that initial block of ten numbers is used up. Thus a single publisher may have multiple publisher identifier numbers. So whether you are on book one or book eleven is not indicated by your number. Your publisher identifier number merely indicates how many ISBNs were allocated to you in one go.

If you publish in a jurisdiction like the U.S. where ISBNs must be paid for, your publisher number only indicates how many you could afford to buy in a single purchase. Obviously a larger, wealthier publisher can buy a 1000-block of ISBNs to save money, while a smaller publisher with a stricter cash flow may only be able to afford a block of 100 ISBNs and simply have to pay the higher price.

It has also been rumoured that a publisher identifier number ending in "14" indicates a self-publisher. Since my number ends in "14" I queried Library and Archives Canada about this and was assured this was a fallacy: prefix "9868914" was simply the next one to be assigned.

How to Purchase an ISBN

If you elect to use the ISBN system, and to purchase your own numbers, you do this *before* you put your book on the market as you must include the number on your copyright page.

In some countries the ISBN agency and national registry are one and the same—in Canada, they are combined into Library and Archives Canada—while in others they are distinct agencies: in the U.S., Bowker is the ISBN agency while the Library of Congress is the national literary registry. You thus need to determine who administers and/or sells the ISBNs for your country.

United States and its Territories

In the U.S. and its territories, Bowker sells a single ISBN for $125.00; a 10-block of ISBNs costs $250.00; a 100-block of ISBNs costs $575.00; and a 1000-block of ISBNs costs $1,000.00.

Canada, New Zealand, and South Africa

In Canada, ISBNs are free to publishers including self-publishers. You must register first with Library and Archives Canada and be vetted, after which you will be given an account; the process takes about ten to fourteen days. ISBNs are also free in New Zealand through the National Library of New Zealand, and in South Africa through the National Library of South Africa. These latter registries may also have a vetting process because of the free service, though I have been told anecdotally that New Zealand does not.

UK and Ireland

In the UK and Ireland, purchases are made through the Nielsen UK ISBN Agency. ISBNs are sold in a minimum block of 10 numbers at a cost of £118.68 inclusive of 20% VAT. A publisher can elect to buy larger blocks at a progressively diminishing rate: 100 numbers costs £222.00, and 1000 numbers costs £576.48.

Australia

In Australia, the ISBN agency is Thorpe-Bowker, affiliated with Bowker in the U.S. In Australia, new publishers pay a one-time registration fee of $55.00. ISBNs are then purchased individually at $40.00 or in a block of 10 ISBNs for $80.00, a block of 100 for $435.00, and a block of 1000 ISBNs for $2,750.00.

How Big a Block Do You Need?

When considering how big a block to buy, remember that each format of your book will require its own ISBN, so if you release a single title as a hardcover, paperback, Kindle, ePub, and PDF, that is five already. ISBNs do not expire, so if you plan on eventually releasing a second title this will take up the rest of a block of ten numbers. So while you may have to pay in advance for the whole block of ten they sit in your account until you need them. Similarly, when applying to an agency for free ISBNs, you will be asked how many publications you are likely to publish in the next year or how many ISBNs you will likely need; this determines how big a block they give you. Sometimes the question is worded as "publications," in which case each format you publish is a publication; sometimes it will be worded as "titles," in which case you need to specify how many formats each title is likely to be published in; and sometimes it will be worded as "ISBNs," in which case you need to add up how many formats you will need an ISBN for and request that many.

Bowker Books in Print

Bowker in the U.S. maintains the global Books in Print database, which is the main book database of record used by independent retailers, libraries, and search engines. Originally, Bowker separated its domestic Books in Print database from its Global Books in Print database, but has since combined them into Books in Print2. Purchase of a U.S. ISBN automatically enters your title in the Books in Print database but the publisher needs to input the information (Fig. 10). Titles by foreign authors who purchased/received their own ISBNs can also be added to the database by registering at MyIdentifiers.com. There is no fee to register.

Note that the publisher information you supply to Books in Print is accessible by those with a Books in Print account (or other Bowker database account), meaning libraries and retailers, et cetera. It is not accessible by the general public, and it is not accessible by other publishers through their MyIdentifiers account.

Similarly, in the UK and Ireland the purchase of an ISBN registers your title in the Nielsen book publishers database, Nielsen BookData. Foreign publishers may apply to be added to the registry.

Fig. 10

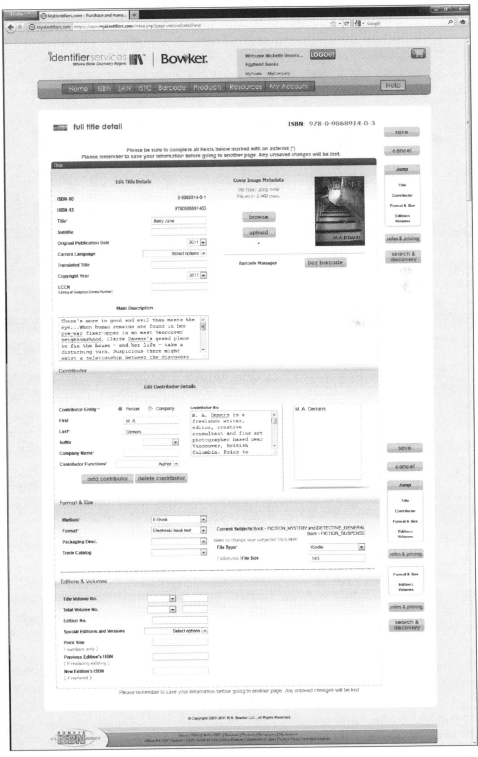

Registering for an ISBN Account

When you register as a publisher in order to acquire ISBNs, you may do so under your name, under the name of a company you control if the rights to publish your book have been assigned to it, or under an imprint regardless of whether the imprint is formally registered or not. You cannot open an account under a pen name or any other pseudonym.

In all the registries I checked, registration and purchases can be made online. It is generally a straightforward process: you fill out your personal information and pay by credit card if applicable. A few things to note, though: if you decide to create your own imprint or register under the name of a company you own or control, pay attention to whether the registry wants your personal name as the account holder and your imprint listed as the publisher, or whether they want your imprint/publisher name as the account holder and your personal name as the account contact and administrator. Each registry is a little bit different.

At the time you buy your block of ISBNs you do not need to set up your titles immediately. And when you assign an ISBN to a title you do not need to input all information at once, or even ever. In fact, if you are publishing a print version you have to assign the ISBN before you can produce the book and fill in the information on, for example, the book's dimensions: how can you know what the size will be until it is made? It can be a bit confusing at first but mandatory fields are usually clearly marked so you will know what must be inputted upfront and what can be added later. So make a note of what is mandatory for your registry when you set up your account so you will have this information ready when you set up your title. At minimum you will need your title and names of all contributors, the book format, publisher or imprint, price, and geographical territories in which the title can be distributed. Later on you can add a product description (your book's marketing synopsis), your primary Book Industry Standards and Communications (BISAC) categories, a cover image, contributor's bio, product dimensions, et cetera. Obviously, the more info you provide to your potential buyers the better.

The Hidden Cost of Free ISBNs

The high cost for individual ISBNs in some jurisdictions versus the inexpensiveness of a block of 1000 ISBNs—costing as little as $1.00 per unit—has created an opportunity for vanity press ("author services") companies and ebook aggregators to offer free ISBNs to their clients. Most vanity publishers, in fact, make use of their ISBN mandatory. But there is a hidden cost to accepting this ISBN: by doing so the indie author is technically no longer self-publishing: the vanity press or aggregator becomes the publisher of record. This has legal as well as practical implications.

Legally, as the publisher of record the vanity press or aggregator is entitled to reproduce and distribute your book as it sees fit, within the parameters of your contract with it. Some contracts give the publisher full control over pricing and distribution while others allow the author to set the price and to opt in or out of specific retail channels. Whichever it may be, most contracts give greater powers to the vanity press or aggregator who becomes your publisher as opposed to acting merely as your manufacturer and/or distributor, so you need to read the contract carefully to understand exactly what you are handing over when you accept a "free" ISBN. This is not to say you should not accept the ISBN, only that you should be aware of what it means to do so, so that your decision is an informed one and not one that has been manipulated by the vanity publisher or aggregator.

The Not-So-Non-Exclusive Contract

Most of these publishing contracts will state they are "non-exclusive" and, while it is true that you are not prohibited from entering into a similar contract with another publisher to publish your title, or to publish directly to another retailer, you cannot publish the same book with a different ISBN attached. This is because most vanity publishers contract the services of wholesale distributors such as Ingram or Baker & Taylor, but wholesale distributors only allow one publisher/distributor per ISBN. The same goes for the Bowker Books in Print database: duplicate publishers for an identical book are not allowed. So if you use more than one vanity publisher or digital aggregator and each assigns its own ISBN to your book, they are barred from offering the exact same book as this would create confusion in the marketplace. Instead, you must change the book in some fundamental way for each publisher: usually this means a different cover but it can also be the size of the print book, for example the mass market paperback instead of the 6" x 9" trade paperback, or it can be the digital format, the PDF instead of the ePub for example. So instead of paying for your own ISBN you pay for multiple covers or book designs. Not very sensible.

As you can see, then, the "non-exclusive" contract is really exclusive *as it pertains to your title/ format combination*. You can offer the same *title* across multiple publishers, but not the same *book*. Which is something none of the vanity publishers or aggregators want you to know and none will tell you until you run into problems.

ISBNs are Not Transferrable

If you accept a publisher's ISBN, you cannot use their ISBN to distribute your book directly to other sales channels. For example, say you decide to accept an aggregator's ISBN for your ePub format, for distribution to Apple, Sony, Barnes & Noble, and Kobo. You then contract directly with Amazon and upload your book in the Kindle format. You cannot attach the aggregator's ISBN to your Kindle book because you do not own the ISBN, doing so is a breach of your contract with the aggregator, and the Kindle format is different from the ePub. You must either purchase your own ISBN for the Kindle format or publish to Kindle without an ISBN.

Or say you sign up with an aggregator but opt out of B&N because you want to contract with them directly too, uploading your own ePub. You cannot use the aggregator's ePub ISBN for your B&N ePub because you do not own the ISBN. No problem, you say, since PubIt! does not require an ISBN you can publish to it without one. This is true, but what is hidden in there is that a retailer or library who searches for your book via the Bowker Books in Print database will only be directed to the aggregator, that is, to the publisher of record. If an interested party Googles the ISBN, they will be directed only to those sites where that ISBN is indicated, in this case the aggregator's website and retail partners but not B&N's PubIt! because your ePub there does not bear the ISBN.

None of the above precludes Internet searches by your name and book title, which means your readers can still find your book. What it does do is bind you to the owner of the ISBN, thereby limiting your distribution options. Most aggregators and vanity publishers have a limited number of retail partners—sometimes only one—so you have to weigh the value of the free ISBN against the limitations of their retail channels.

Books in Print Database

Moreover, if you publish your title to multiple formats, but only one format has an ISBN attached, only that format will show up in the Books in Print database. This means you cannot tie all the formats together so that, at a glance, a library for example can tell what formats the book is available in. They will only know about the registered format and will thus not be presented with the option to buy other formats.

Also, some aggregators only provide Books in Print with the minimum information required by the registry. You will find the title and author, and of course the aggregator listed as the publisher, but optional information like a synopsis or contributor bio will be absent from the record.

Brand Promotion

The primary reason vanity publishers and ebook aggregators want you to use their ISBN is because doing so promotes their brand. If you look on any retail site you will see the publisher listed in the book's information; and if the publisher is also listed in the format, its name may be displayed as prominently as the author's. Whether this is bothersome for you or not is a personal matter, but I feel strongly that since I am the one incurring the costs to bring my book to market, it is *my* brand I want to promote, not that of a vanity publisher or aggregator.

I also take issue with any aggregator or vanity publisher who understates the significance of accepting its ISBN. Vanity publisher iUniverse writes on its website, "By utilizing iUniverse's services, you are simply granting us a non-exclusive license to publish and distribute the work for you";[26] but as you have learned in this chapter, it is not so simple or non-exclusive as iUniverse suggests. The aggregator Smashwords goes even further, claiming that accepting its ISBN does not make it your publisher:

> The free ISBN … although it registers Smashwords as the "publisher" in the Bowker record, we are not your publisher. This designation is due only to the legacy limitations of Bowker's categorization options for ISBNs. If Smashwords is listed as your publisher in the ISBN record, it in no way limits your ownership of your book, and in no way makes us your publisher.[27]

It is true that accepting an ISBN in no way limits ownership of your work—it does not with a legacy publisher, either, since you grant a publisher only a licence to publish your work, not the copyright—but it does make Smashwords your publisher. Hence Smashwords makes it mandatory that authors put "Smashwords Edition" on the book's copyright page: as you now know, an "edition" denotes the publisher/format combination. Smashwords even requires author/publishers who supply their own ISBNs to put "Published by [your name] at Smashwords" or "Published by [your name] via Smashwords" on the book's copyright page; if you do not your book is rejected for distribution. This I find particularly audacious: it is the equivalent of a wholesale distributor like Ingram forcing legacy publishers to put "Published via Ingram" on a book's copyright page. Considering how many distribution channels a single title may utilize, it is outrageous to suggest that a wholesaler or distributor be included on the copyright page, yet this is precisely what Smashwords mandates.

This distinction is also reflected contractually. With Smashwords, "The Author hereby grants and assigns to Smashwords the nonexclusive worldwide right to digitally publish, distribute, market and sell ('Publish')" your book.[28] Compare this to the ebook distributor Ingram Digital, which does not assign ISBNs: "[Ingram Digital] is granted a limited, non-exclusive, non-transferable right and license to ... display, distribute, reproduce and store the Digital Media Files on LSI's on-premises systems and off-site systems operated by third party service providers."[29]

ONIX Code

What the vanity press or aggregator is also not telling you is that the information about the publisher travels with the ISBN in the form of ONIX code (discussed in more detail later in this chapter). This code identifies you as the author but the vanity press or aggregator as the publisher, and contains the publisher's contact information. Thus all inquiries by interested parties are directed to the publisher and not to you, the author. So if, for example, an agent, legacy publisher, reviewer, film producer, or another author wishes to contact you, they will be directed to the publisher, who is not obligated to pass the inquiry on to you, and it cannot legally give out your contact information to the inquirer because this would be a violation of your privacy. You have to rely on the discretion of the publisher to pass the inquiry on to you or for the inquirer to search for you through other means such as your website or blog, assuming you have one.

Pricing and Distribution

While most digital aggregators and print-on-demand manufacturer/vanity publisher hybrids like CreateSpace or LuLu allow the author to decide upon price and distribution, a vanity publisher like iUniverse usually does not: it sets the price and distributes as it sees fit. Now, without going into specifics here, CreateSpace pays a considerably higher royalty for sales off Amazon.com than vanity publishers do; but if the publisher were to notice that a duplicate title is available via its competitor CreateSpace, what is to stop the vanity publisher from lowering the price of your book to undercut the price you set on CreateSpace and thereby divert sales to the vanity publisher? You will have no say in this yet your list price will not only be lowered, it will be lowered by the publisher who is paying you the lesser royalty, doubling the negative effect on your income.

One other interesting complaint I discovered about free ISBNs was the length of time it took to acquire said ISBN because the vanity publisher or aggregator "ran out" of ISBNs: some clients were expressing frustration with delays of up to three or more weeks.

The high cost of ISBNs in the U.S. and elsewhere has created resentment among many indie authors and so there is rampant misuse of ISBNs. This misuse hinders distribution of your book because misuse creates confusion in the marketplace and more work for retailers. And it is creating conflict between the agency and indie authors. Thus it is of benefit to use it correctly or simply avoid it since it is not mandatory.

The Advantages of Owning Your ISBN

(Note: It is not permissible for a publisher to sell or transfer their ISBNs to another publisher or individual. The practice of some aggregators or vanity publishers to sell to their clients an ISBN that specifies the author as the publisher and the aggregator or vanity publisher as the distributor, thus strikes me as suspect.)

The upside of accepting a publisher or aggregator's ISBN is obvious: less cost if you live in a jurisdiction where you have to pay, less work on your part, you are not responsible for Legal Deposit, and you will have access to your publisher's full complement of sales channels. With CreateSpace, for example, if you assign your own ISBN to your title you will be barred from some of the distribution channels offered through its Expanded Distribution, specifically the libraries and academic markets. You will be told this is "because of rules set by [the wholesaler] Ingram," but no one will tell you what the specifics of those rules are. Thus you will feel you have no choice but to accept CreateSpace's ISBN if you want access to these markets.

Increased Distribution Options

What CreateSpace does not want you to know is that, if you own your ISBN, you can contract with a print-on-demand company such as Lightning Source, which is owned by Ingram, to manufacture and distribute your book, and you will have access not only to the additional libraries and academic markets but also to the longer list of wholesalers with whom Lightning Source does business. Many vanity publishers only use the services of one or two wholesalers— usually Ingram and Baker & Taylor—but a POD manufacturer like Lightning Source distributes via Ingram, Baker & Taylor, NACSCORP, Espresso Book Machine, Bertrams, Blackwell, Coutts, Gardners, Mallory International, Eden Interactive Ltd., I.B.S - STL U.K., and directly to retailers Amazon.com, Amazon.co.uk, Barnes & Noble, Adlibris.com, Paperback Shop, Aphrohead, and The Book Depository. Lightning Source also has manufacturing centres in three countries—the

U.S., UK, and Australia—meaning orders outside North America are generally fulfilled faster. And with both ebooks and print books you control pricing, not just in the U.S. but globally.

One other advantage to owning your ISBN is that you can contract with CreateSpace to fulfil your Amazon.com orders, which not only pays you a higher royalty and results in faster fulfilment times than if you use another POD company, but it does not prevent you from using another POD manufacturer/distributor to fulfil all other sales channels. How is this possible? It is possible because Amazon.com does not look beyond its subsidiary CreateSpace for a title's distributor if CreateSpace offers it. So the fact that Lightning Source might be offering the same book to Amazon.com is simply ignored. Note, however, that this only works if you do not choose CreateSpace's Expanded Distribution for your title (see Chapter 16: Distribution and Royalties).

Optics

Then there is the optics of owning your ISBNs. If your book is published by any of the known vanity publishers or aggregators, everyone will know your book is self-published. If, on the other hand, you create your own imprint, it is not necessarily apparent that your book is self-published. While at first this might be nothing more than semantics—and with only a modicum of digging the gig will be up—over time you can build your brand and even expand to publishing other authors. For example, my imprint, Egghead Books, is intended to be an authors' collective.

Books in Print

Having your own ISBN means you control the information available through Bowker's Books in Print. This is done through the MyIdentifiers website (which is replacing BowkerLink). It is free to sign up and is available to all authors who own their ISBNs. Use of MyIdentifiers also entitles you to free use of the basic SEO Title Card service from Bookwire (owned by Bowker); you can also elect to use their premium service at a fee of $60.00 per title/year.

You can then tie all your title's formats together in the Bowker Books in Print database so that, at a glance, the user can tell what formats the book is available in. Thus they may decide to buy the print, the ePub and the Kindle version, a decision they will not make if they are only aware of one format. Fig. 11 is the SEO card for *Baby Jane*.

Free National Agency Advertising

Finally, owning your own ISBN means you can take advantage of free pre-release advertising (if available) via your ISBN registry. Library and Archives Canada, for example, has a program called Cataloguing in Publication whereby in advance of publication publishers can voluntarily make available to LAC information such as the intended date of publication, the title page, list of contributors, genre and primary audience, your book description, and its table of contents

Fig. 11

and preface (if applicable). This information is then disseminated to libraries and retailers via the New Books Service, an on-line service showcasing new Canadian publications; via the national bibliography *Canadiana*; LAC's bibliographic database, AMICUS; and in Canadian Books in Print. The intention of the program is to provide advance promotion for publishers and to assist booksellers and libraries to plan their purchases. It is not currently available for ebooks and is limited to print books with an intended initial print run of 100 or more copies. The Library of Congress has a similar program.

And the Disadvantages

The first and most obvious disadvantage to owning your ISBNs is the expense if you live in a jurisdiction where you have to pay. This can be reason alone for many indie publishers to accept an ISBN from their digital aggregator or POD/vanity press company.

The second disadvantage is that you, as the publisher, are legally responsible for fulfilling the requirements of Legal Deposit both in your own country and additionally to the Library of Congress if you are a foreign publisher distributing in the U.S. This is an additional task and expense.

The third disadvantage is that you have to do the work. You have to sign up for the account, keep track of your ISBNs, and input and maintain the information in the Books in Print or similar database(s).

If you and the publisher are one and the same, meaning your publisher address and phone number are also your personal address and phone number, your personal contact information will be available to anyone with a subscription to the Books in Print or similar databases (mostly libraries and retailers). So if you are concerned about this—if you intend to publish a book you believe may be controversial, for example—then it might be better to use a vanity publisher or aggregator's ISBN. Historically, the publisher stood between authors and their critics and/or rabid fans, providing a modicum of privacy or security, but how much of a firewall they can provide in the Internet age is debatable. Even before the advance of the Internet, the firewall provided by a publisher certainly did not protect Salman Rushdie. It does not keep weirdoes from sorting through J.K. Rowling's trash. The thing about being a writer or any other public figure is that success comes at the expense of anonymity. So if this is an issue for you, write under a pen name and then either legacy publish, vanity publish, engage the services of an aggregator, or e-publish only without an ISBN.

Ease Versus Control

Only you can decide if the advantages of owning your ISBN outweigh the disadvantages. Again, it all comes down to ease versus control. Just as the legacy-published author acquiesces control to their publisher in exchange for less work and expense, by accepting an ISBN from a vanity publisher or digital aggregator the indie author acquiesces some control in exchange for less work and expense.

That said, sometimes the ease of accepting a publisher or aggregator's ISBN proves fleeting: the author discovers after the fact the problems and limitations we have discussed in this chapter. Vanity publishers also have an agenda to sell additional services to you, services that will be expensive and usually overpriced. The best course of action will thus depend on your long-term goals as an independent author/publisher.

Which path did I choose? I elected to own my ISBNs: I have been a self-employed writer for over fifteen years so signing up for an ISBN account seemed a logical and natural extension of my business. Moreover, as I began my self-publishing experiment it dawned on me that we indie publishers are all on our own, trying to make a go of it, and wouldn't it be beneficial to have a writers' collective, similar to the early writers' collectives that published each other's books? With that intention in mind I created an imprint, Egghead Books, registered it with Library and Archives Canada, created a logo, bought the domain name, and created a Facebook page. It will still be awhile before I can pursue my goal of creating a true writers' collective, mainly for lack of time, but the foundation is now in place and can be built upon.

Owning the ISBN also meant I could contract with CreateSpace for fulfillment of Amazon.com print orders, and then Lightning Source for all other print orders in the U.S. without having to create a new cover or change my book in any other way. I could also contract with Lightning Source UK and Australia for quicker distribution in Europe and Oceania. Similarly, with ebooks I was able to distribute my ePub directly to Kobo and to all other e-retailers via both Ingram Digital and eBookIt, again without having to change the file in any way, something I could not do if I did not own the ISBN.

It was also through my control over the information in the Books in Print database that I learned that many retailers get their information from the Bowker database and not from the distributor: due to slight variations in the book description (the use of em dashes versus hyphens due to limitations in the Books in Print database that did not exist in my distributor's database), I could tell where each of my retailers was getting their information from. This should serve as a warning to those using an aggregator/vanity publisher who inputs title information into the Books in Print database on your behalf: if there are problems you may have no idea why your information is wrong, you will have no access to fix it, and you will have to rely upon your publisher to make the corrections, if it could be bothered to.

International Standard Text Code

A new identifier is being developed called the International Standard Text Code (ISTC). This number is attached to the work itself and not to the publisher/format. The advantage of this number is that it allows for identical textual works published by different publishers or in different formats to be identified as a group. So if a library, for example, wanted to know who published a specific author's work and in what formats, they only have to know one example of the work to find all the rest.

The ISTC also helps to differentiate between different works with the same title by the same author. For example, a playwright might first publish a play then expand that into a novel or a screenplay, and oftentimes the same title is used so as to benefit from the reputation of the original.

ISTC numbers are currently dispensed by many of the same agencies who currently dispense ISBNs: Bowker and its affiliate sites, Nielsen Book in the UK and New Zealand, Cercle de la Librairie-Electre in Paris, and MVB Marketing-und Verlagsservice des Buchhandels GmbH in Frankfurt. Which agency you apply for an ISTC is irrelevant as there are no territorial restrictions on ISTCs.

The ISTC is still in its infancy but the self-published author may benefit from its use if you create derivative works or you publish under multiple entities. The ISTC is also a solution to the problem of publishing without an ISBN to sites such as Amazon and Barnes & Noble but then publishing to Apple and Sony with a vanity publisher or aggregator's ISBN: an interested party who searches for your work using the ISTC will find all formats as opposed to only those where the ISBN is in use.

ONIX for Books

ONIX for Books is a metadata language that publishers use when distributing electronic information about a book to anyone involved in the production, review or sale of books. It was jointly developed by the UK-based EDItEUR corporation, the Book Industry Communication (UK), and the Book Industry Study Group (U.S.) and is now maintained under the guidance of an international steering committee.

ONIX code is basic HTML with specific tags to identify such things as the author and other contributors, the publisher, book format, publication date, availability, price, rights information, BISAC categories, and so on. It can also include such things as biographical data on the contributors, website and email contacts for the publisher and contributors, the book's synopsis, review quotes and links to their sources. And of course the book's ISBN. Below is a portion of the ONIX code for *Baby Jane*:

```
<Title>                        .
<TitleType>01</TitleType>
<TitleText>Baby Jane</TitleText>
</Title>
<Contributor>
<SequenceNumber>1</SequenceNumber>
<ContributorRole>A01</ContributorRole>
<NamesBeforeKey>M. A.</NamesBeforeKey>
<KeyNames>Demers</KeyNames>
</Contributor>
<Language>
<LanguageRole>01</LanguageRole>
<LanguageCode>eng</LanguageCode>
</Language>
<NumberOfPages>270</NumberOfPages>
<BASICMainSubject>FIC022020</BASICMainSubject>
<Imprint>
<ImprintName>Publisher Name</ImprintName>
</Imprint>
<Publisher>
<PublisherName>Egghead Books</PublisherName>
</Publisher>
```

The ONIX code "travels" with the ISBN to the various distributors and retail channels around the world. Each retailer then decides which fields of the ONIX code they wish to display to their customers. They will all make use of the basic data such as the title, publisher, and author, then pick and choose from among the optional data. For example, an online retailer might display the author's bio but is unlikely to display reviews found on a competitor's website as this would encourage the user to leave the retailer's site; or a site that sells your book for higher than the list price you set will not display that data.

This code can also be added to your website's source code to optimize search engine relevancy rankings, crawling and indexing. It can also be incorporated as part of fan pages on social networking sites and book sites such as Goodreads.

When you upload your book to a direct-to-retail site such as Amazon or PubIt!, or to a distributor or aggregator, you are asked to fill out web forms that request information about you and your book. This information is translated into ONIX code and forms the backbone of the various retailer and distributor search engines.

Similarly, when you input your book data into the Books in Print web form, the information is translated into ONIX code that is used by the database's subscribers. Some ISBN agencies have the option for you to export your book data to ONIX code, which can be useful if you know how to use it. I have to confess that, while I can wrap my head around the basics of ONIX code, I do not know enough yet about HTML to incorporate ONIX into my website or blog or Facebook page without the use of a widget (which MyIdentifiers sells for $60.00/year). And it does not help that most ISBN agencies are still catching up to technology—most do not even have the digital formats listed yet—so the code may be incomplete and therefore in need of amendment.

You will likely never have to learn ONIX code; it is only useful to know what it is and how it functions to disseminate information about your book to retailers around the world.

BISAC Categories

When you upload a file to your POD printer/distributor, or your ebook to a retail site, you will be asked to select your book's categories, and will be allowed anywhere from one to three selections. These categories are known as BISAC (Book Industry Standards and Communications) categories, and are used by booksellers and consumers to determine the primary subject or genre of a book. Each category is represented by a code and a title; the codes are used by the booksellers while the category titles are used on the back of print books and on retail sites to inform the reader. If you stroll around the sections of your local bookstore you will see some of the classifications such as science fiction, literature, romance, self-help, cookbooks and history. These in turn have subcategories. There are numerous main, or "parent," categories and even more subcategories. The parent category Fiction, for example, has over ninety subcategories, of which are included the following, chosen at random:

FIC002000 FICTION / Action & Adventure

FIC049000 FICTION / African American / General

FIC044000 FICTION / Contemporary Women

FIC009000 FICTION / Fantasy / General

FIC022000 FICTION / Mystery & Detective / General

Many of these subcategories in turn have secondary subcategories to further differentiate. For example, FIC009000 Fiction / Fantasy includes the following subcategories:

FIC009010 FICTION / Fantasy / Contemporary

FIC009020 FICTION / Fantasy / Epic

FIC009030 FICTION / Fantasy / Historical

FIC009050 FICTION / Fantasy / Paranormal

FIC009040 FICTION / Fantasy / Short Stories

FIC009060 FICTION / Fantasy / Urban Life

Unfortunately, the use of the BISAC system is not consistent across the industry. For example, Amazon asks you to choose from among the full complement of BISAC categories when you upload your Kindle book but then inexplicably does not use all of the categories in its catalogue. If you assign your book to a category Kindle does not use, it assigns the nearest category to the one you selected. For example, you can choose for your vampire novel the category Fiction / Occult & Supernatural but Kindle does not include this category on its website; instead, such books will be found in fantasy or in science fiction, or can end up unclassified.

To make matters even more problematic, the categories for print books are not based on BISAC but use Amazon's own system. Yet when your print book is assigned its categories upon upload to your distributor, you will be using BISAC. As you can imagine, the results can be even more unpredictable than with Kindle. Fantasy writers, for example, share their category with science fiction; there is not a print book category for Fantasy / Paranormal despite the popularity of *Twilight* and all its cousins. Why is this? Only Amazon knows. And since Kindle and print books use slightly different cataloguing systems, if you have both a print and ebook version of your title they may not end up in the same categories.

This problem is not limited to Amazon. I have noticed on sites such as Barnes & Noble many, many subcategories that do not exist in BISAC; while these additional subcategories help to further differentiate books, how does one get into these categories if they do not exist in BISAC? My novel, *Baby Jane*, would benefit greatly from B&N's subcategory Fiction / Mystery & Crime / Multicultural Detectives but I have no way to indicate this anywhere outside of my synopsis.

Conversely, the Bowker Books in Print database greatly reduces the number of BISAC categories available. So *Baby Jane* could not be categorized as either Fiction / Mystery & Detective / Police Procedural, or Fiction / Occult & Supernatural, because neither category is on offer. Instead I had to settle for Fiction / Mystery & Detective / General and my third category, Fiction / Suspense.

When using a distributor, and inputting to Bowker, you must select from BISAC categories and hope you do not end up with weird results because every retailer is going to use a slightly different system. There is nothing you can do about it: you cannot personalise your selection(s) for each retailer. For advice on selecting BISAC categories, see the section "Choose Your BISAC Categories Carefully" in Chapter 17: Marketing.

Useful Links

A Wikipedia article explaining the ISBN system.
http://en.wikipedia.org/wiki/International_Standard_Book_Number

Home page of the International ISBN Agency.
http://www.isbn-international.org/

U.S. ISBN agency.
http://www.bowker.com

UK and Republic of Ireland ISBN agency.
http://www.isbn.nielsenbook.co.uk

Library and Archives Canada ISBN page.
http://www.collectionscanada.gc.ca/ciss-ssci/041002-2000-e.html

National Library of New Zealand ISBN page.
http://www.natlib.govt.nz/services/get-advice/publishing/isbn

Australian ISBN Agency.
http://www.thorpe.com.au/isbn/

The National Library of South Africa.
http://www.nlsa.ac.za/NLSA/

Nielsen BookData.
http://www.nielsenbookdata.co.uk

MyIdentifiers website.
https://www.myidentifiers.com

Books in Print database.
http://www.booksinprint2.com

Bookwire by Bowker.
http://www.bookwire.com/

U.S. Library of Congress.
http://www.loc.gov/index.html

An interview with Bowker's Andy Weissberg about the uses of ISBNs and the conflict between ebook distributors and the ISBN Agency.
http://www.thebookdesigner.com/2010/05/bowkers-andy-weissberg-on-isbns-and-the-future-of-the-book/

EDItEUR website.
http://www.editeur.org

Website of the International Standard Text Code (ISTC).
http://www.istc-international.org/html/

BISAC categories.
http://www.bisg.org/what-we-do-0-136-bisac-subject-headings-list-major-subjects.php

8/ Interior Book Structure

Every book is divided into three sections: front matter, body, and end matter. Front matter refers to items such as the title page, copyright page, acknowledgments, and table of contents; body refers to the manuscript; and end matter refers to items such as endnotes, bibliographies and indices, and author biographies. A book may also contain marketing materials for other works by the author or publisher but those materials must then bookend the text: they must not appear after the title page or before end matter.

In print books, the title page is always on a right-hand page followed immediately (no blank pages in between) by your copyright page. This is then followed by your acknowledgements (if applicable) and your table of contents (if you have one), and then the first page of your manuscript. The acknowledgments, table of contents, and first page of your manuscript should all start on a right-hand page; if necessary, blank pages can be inserted between front matter sections.

In ebooks, the structure is the same except there are no blank pages inserted; and oftentimes the copyright page and acknowledgements are placed at the end of the document. This is because some e-retailers offer free sample pages from the manuscript—usually no more than the first 10% of the file—so by pushing some of the front matter to the back the consumer receives more of the story in their sample pages. This is considered advantageous to the writer as the greater the taste the more likely the consumer will want to read the rest of the book. If you elect to do this you should include links to these pages in the table of contents for easy reference. Do not place your table of contents in the back: Kindle will reject your book.

Front Matter

The most common items found in front matter include, in this order, your:

- title page;
- copyright page;
- dedication or acknowledgements;
- table of contents;
- foreword;
- preface; and
- introduction.

Title Page

The title page of your book *must* contain the title, including any subtitle, as it appears when you assigned the title's ISBN. The title page must also contain the names of anyone else accredited, for example the illustrator if it is a picture book, the editor if it is a compilation, or the translator if the original is in another language. It must contain any edition number, and it must contain the name of the publisher.

Copyright Page

The copyright page always follows the title page, with no blank page(s) in between. The order of information contained on your copyright page is not written in stone; however, each element should be separately contained within its own section. In other words, your copyright declaration should not be in the same paragraph as your trademarks declaration, which in turn should be visually separated from your cataloguing information, and so on.

Your copyright declaration should read "Copyright © [year] [name of copyright owner]" on a single line (no quotation marks). The copyright owner is usually the author, and usually written using their full name though some, such as J.K. Rowling, still use only their initials. The copyright holder can be different from the author—for example, you might be publishing your late mother's secret novel because you inherited it from her estate, or you might have written a new translation of a public domain work. If you publish under a *nom de plume*, the copyright notice can be in either your pen name or your real name, though using the latter would defeat the purpose of a pen name.

This is followed on the next line by publisher information. If you have created your own imprint you can use this as your publisher information whether the imprint exists as a formal entity (a corporation, limited partnership, or sole proprietorship) or not; however, the imprint listed must match the imprint registered with the agency from which you acquired your ISBN. If you have not created an imprint you can write "Published by the author."

If you signed on with an author services company or digital aggregator and elected to assign its ISBN to your book, then technically speaking the owner of the ISBN is the publisher of a work and you must put the author services company or aggregator down on your copyright page as the publisher. Some aggregators will do this for you when they format and convert your manuscript prior to distribution.

This is then followed by a paragraph containing the copyright notice. You can create your own or you can use the following standard text:

> All rights reserved under International and Pan-American Copyright Conventions. No part of this book may be reproduced in any form or by any electronic or mechanical means, including information storage and retrieval systems, without permission in writing from the author, except by reviewer, who may quote brief passages in a review.

If your book is a work of fiction, it should contain the following declaration:

> This is a work of fiction. Names, characters, places and incidents either are the product of the author's imagination or used fictitiously. Any resemblance to actual persons, living or dead, events or locales is entirely coincidental.

If you use trademarks in your work you can add an optional paragraph for this as well. Each trademark should be listed along with its registered owner, followed by a declaration that you are using these trademarks with or without permission, as the case may be. For example:

> BMW is a registered trademark of Bayerische Motoren Werke AG. Mercedes is a registered trademark of Mercedes-Benz, a division of Daimler AG. Trademarks are used without permission. Use of the trademark is not authorized by, associated with or sponsored by the trademark owner.

If you use any copyrighted passages in your book with permission of the author(s) or their publisher(s), you should add a paragraph for them as well. For example:

> Excerpt from "Flights of Fancy" from *Flights of Fancy and other poems* by Fake Poet. ©1995 Fake Poet. Reprinted by permission of Fake Poet's Publisher.

If you received any government or private foundation grants to write your book, acknowledge them next:

> This book was written with the kind support of X&Y Foundation.

If the book had been published earlier in other formats, or with other publishers, it is industry practice to specify this along with the ISBN, if applicable. For example:

> First published in paperback by Egghead Books, May 2011, ISBN 978-0-9868914-1-0

or

> Published to Kindle, March 2011, ISBN 978-0-9868914-0-3.

This is then followed by the book's ISBN information, and your national literary registry cataloguing information if applicable. Each agency has its own rules for the information that should be included, so you need to check with them for the appropriate information and presentation format.

Included in this section will be the author's name and year of birth and, if applicable, year of death. Since copyright expiration is dependent upon the death of the author, this information indicates when a work will become public domain. This information is followed by the book title and author's name as it appears on the cover, followed by the title format and edition number if so desired. Then the title's ISBN.

The title's format may also include the publisher information, as in "Egghead Books trade paperback edition." However, you will never see distributor or manufacturer information on the copyright page.

Amazon owns a proprietary format known as "Kindle"; its digital extension is .azw. Thus the Kindle is not just the device but the format, and so a book published to the Kindle would say on the copyright page "Kindle Edition." Note that it is not the "Amazon Edition" because Amazon is a retailer, not a publisher or format.

Publishers have the option to register their titles with their national literary cataloguing agency in advance of publication and this information is then disseminated to libraries and booksellers. This cataloguing information—called Cataloguing in Publication (CIP)—must then be added to your copyright page so librarians and book buyers can confirm their purchases. The information contains the title's subject headings, its Library of Congress classification number, the book's Dewey decimal classification number, and its national control number, in that order. (The Library of Congress classification number is not to be confused with a Library of Congress Control number. The classification number is from the Library's cataloguing system, which is used mostly by research and academic institutions, and is an alternative to the Dewey decimal system, which is used by most public libraries.) For example, the Vintage Canada paperback of *The Private Patient* by British author P.D. James contains the following registry information:

I. Title.

PR6060.A56P75 2009   823'.914   2008-905509-8

whereby "PR6060.A56P75 2009" is the Library of Congress number, "823'.914" is the Dewey decimal number, and "2008-905509-8" is the Canadiana (the national bibliography) control number.

And finally, you should credit the cover image creator or stock agency (as dictated by the sales contract) and the cover designer. For example:

Cover image by Jane Photographer/Getty Images.

Cover design by Joe Designer.

Put this all together, then, and for example the copyright page for Carol Shields' *Unless* looks like this (Fig. 12):

Fig. 12

Copyright © 2002 Carol Shields

All rights reserved under International and Pan-American Copyright Conventions. No part of this book may be reproduced in any form or by any electronic or mechanical means, including information storage and retrieval systems, without permission in writing from the publisher, except by reviewer, who may quote brief passages in review. Published in 2002 by Random House Canada, a division of Random House Canada Limited, and simultaneously in the United States and the United Kingdom by The 4th Estate. Distributed in Canada by Random House of Canada Limited.

Random House Canada and colophon are trademarks.

National Library of Canada Cataloguing in Publication Data

Carol Shields, 1935—
    Unless

ISBN [978-]0-679-31179-3

    I. Title

PS8587.H46U55 2002   C813'.54   C2001-903484-9
PR9199.3.S514U55 2002

www.randomhouse.ca

Text design: CS Richardson

Printed and bound in the United States of America

"Steam Heat" by Richard Adler and Jerry Ross. Copyright 1954, renewed. All rights controlled by Lakshmi Puja Music and J&J Ross Music. Used by permission. All rights reserved.

Acknowledgements or Dedication

If you wish to acknowledge anyone who assisted in the creation of your book, or you wish to dedicate it to someone special, you do so on a separate page after the copyright page. Most people will be flattered to be included here but you should always check beforehand in case anyone wishes to be excluded.

Table of Contents

A table of contents is optional, particularly in a novel, although with ebooks the trend is to include one. In ebooks the table of contents includes all front matter like the title page, acknowledgements, and copyright information so that the user does not have to scroll through the book to access this information.

In print books the table of contents follows the acknowledgements or dedication, always starts on a right-hand page, and does not include any material that precedes it like the title page or copyright information.

Foreword, Preface and Introduction

A foreword is an introduction written by a guest of the author. The name of the guest writer is always given at the end of the foreword, flushed right and separated by the text by a line or two. Forewords are often written by a more famous or established writer, or by an industry expert, and is essentially a marketing tool, a stamp of approval by a distinguished peer.

A preface is written by the author and explains why the author wrote the book, and their research methodology if applicable. A preface may also integrate acknowledgements if these have not already been made on a separate page.

An introduction introduces the subject matter, and often places the book in its historical, sociological, intellectual, or academic context.

Body

In ebooks the first page starts right after the front matter. Since ebooks do not contain any header or footer information (more on that in Chapter 11: Manuscript Formatting for eBooks), the first page is formatted no differently from subsequent pages.

In print books the first page of the body text always starts on a right-hand page and usually does not contain any header or footer information. Subsequent chapters may or may not start on a right-hand page and may or may not contain header and footer information; this is personal preference.

End Matter

End matter usually consists of the appendix, notes or endnotes, glossary, bibliography, and the index.

Endnotes, Bibliography and Index

With ebooks, footnotes are amalgamated into endnotes though the Kindle plug-in for InDesign does allow for chapter endnotes. A bibliography comes after any endnotes. Indices are not recommended due to the complexity of creating one and the volume of unsightly hyperlinks that would result.

In print books, whether you use footnotes or endnotes is personal preference, though heavily referenced texts often opt for endnotes for aesthetic reasons. Those that opt for endnotes either use chapter endnotes or combine all endnotes into one section after the close of the body; these are sometimes subdivided into chapters for ease of reference.

The bibliography usually follows the endnotes and follows the style appropriate to the subject matter and geographical area (consult a style guide for details). This is then followed by the index.

Contributor Biographies

If you like you can add information about the author and any other contributors. In ebooks you can add hyperlinks to websites or blogs or social media sites, et cetera.

9/ Cover and Interior Images

Every book needs a cover, and many more will contain interior images such as a publisher's logo, or graphs and illustrations. Whichever the case, you need to learn a few basics so you can properly prepare your images for print or ebook use. How these images are then placed in your documents will differ between book formats; see each format's dedicated section.

A new breed of picture books are emerging, particularly on the Apple platform, including interactive PDFs that behave almost like a webpage, and talking children's books that highlight each word as it is being read. These are complex documents that require professional technical support and as such are not covered in this manual.

Image Formats

Before I get into the technical details of formats, color space, and resolution, if learning about pixels and compression and stuff like that makes your eyes glaze over, skip straight to the section "Book Cover and Product Image" and read to the end of the chapter so you know what you require from the professional you will hire to create your cover. If, on the other hand, you have already been playing about with imaging programs like Photoshop or GIMP and wish to try your hand at designing your book cover, soldier on.

Vector Versus Raster Graphics

There are two main types of digital images, vector and raster graphics. Raster graphics, most commonly recognized by their use in digital photography, are created using pixels, which can be thought of as square building blocks of color stitched together like an elaborate quilt. Raster graphics are constrained by the amount of data present (the number of pixels in the image) and thus suffer a degradation of image quality when the limits of the pixel information are exceeded. Vector graphics, on the other hand, are built mathematically by plotting points on a two-dimensional grid and filling the space between those points with blocks of color, and are used most often in digital illustration. Because vector graphics are mathematical constructs they can be resized without any change to image quality. But even if you start with a vector graphic for your images (you might have your cover digitally illustrated instead of using a photograph), vector graphics must be rasterized before they can be used in an ebook; for example, an Adobe Illustrator file must be converted into a JPEG or a TIFF.

Raster graphics are split into essentially three categories: uncompressed, lossless compressed, or lossy compressed. Compression is the means by which a large image is reduced in file size by software that uses a formula for erasing multiples of the same pixel that are then redrawn when the image is opened by a viewer. The advantage of this is that large image files can be made significantly smaller, resulting in more space for images on a hard drive or camera card, and smaller file sizes for documents that contain images, such as an ebook with embedded images. Lossy compression produces the smallest and therefore most portable of the file options but will result in degradation of image quality, a problem which can be compounded every time changes are made to the image and it is resaved. Thus, whenever possible you should work in and save your source file in a lossless format, only converting to a lossy compressed file upon completion.

Acceptable Formats for eBooks

Most ebook distributors will ask for images to be uploaded to their website or embedded in your book as either a Graphics Interchange Format (GIF), Portable Network Graphics (PNG), Bitmap (BMP), JPEG, or Tagged Image File Format (TIFF).

JPEG is the most common image format since it is the format created by compact digital cameras and is an option for higher-end digital cameras as well. JPEG is a lossy format, however, and so image quality can become an issue: each time the image is compressed then redrawn, small errors are made that create flaws in the image called artifacts (the newer, lossless JPEG format, the JPEG 2000, is not yet fully supported and thus is not accepted by most ereaders). The more often you change and resave a JPEG, the more artifacts are created. When using JPEGs they must be saved at maximum quality (no less than an image quality of "40"; "12" in Photoshop) and formatted to "baseline standard," not "baseline optimized" or "progressive."

TIFF is the most versatile of the accepted file formats as it can be saved as uncompressed, lossless compressed, or lossy compressed. TIFFs can also retain editable image layers, such as the title text layer laid overtop your cover image, which means you can make later changes to individual layers without having to redesign your whole image from scratch. However, they create a large file and are not widely supported by web browsers and digital devices, and thus are best used as an uncompressed source file before converting a copy to a more popular file format like JPEG, which "flattens" the editable layers into a single, compressed image layer. More importantly, if you embed a TIFF image in your manuscript, when converted to an ebook the TIFF is converted to a JPEG, and not always very well. It is much better to do the conversion to JPEG yourself so you can control or fix any undesirable results.

GIF is used for logos and line art and simple animations. It is a lossless format but severely restricted in its color spectrum, which is what keeps these files small in size. Kindle recommends GIFs for images that are primarily text, such as tables, but I disagree. My tests indicated that JPEGs are preferable because, despite their original larger file size, text-heavy JPEGs compressed slightly smaller than their GIF equivalents; and, when tested on the Kindle Previewer, GIFs displayed poorly on the iPad simulator. Nevertheless, if you do decide to use GIFs, do not use them with transparency enabled.

Bitmap is a Windows-only image similar to GIF. Since Bitmap is PC-based, web and ebook software will convert bitmaps to GIFs to create cross-platform compatibility.

PNG is a lossless format that, like GIFs, works best with simple graphics, but has a significantly larger color spectrum than GIFs. PNGs are particularly useful for logos and other images that contain areas of transparency, areas that would be filled in with white if it were a JPEG. However, most ereaders do not support PNGs so ebook conversion software will change them to JPEGs. It is best to do the conversion to JPEG yourself as I have experienced conversion that changed transparent areas in a PNG to black (yikes!). JPEGs are also smaller files than PNGs.

Acceptable Formats for Print Books

Which formats can be imported into a print book is wholly determined by the program used to design the book. In general, JPEGs, TIFFs, Bitmaps and GIFs are the most popular. Uncompressed TIFFs are usually preferred for their quality. Some printers will reject book files over a certain size—Lightning Source, for example, has a 250MB limit—so if you have a lot of images you will need to find a balance between image quality and file size.

Image Properties

When we speak about raster images, four key terms need to be understood: image size, resolution, document size, and file size. Image size refers to the number of pixels that make up an image; resolution is the arrangement of those pixels within a finite space; document size refers to the result of that arrangement when displayed or printed; and file size is the volume of pixels measured in bytes, and may be compressed or not.

Image Size and Resolution

A raster digital image is made up of a finite number of pixels, for example 1000 x 500 pixels. This is your "image size." But it is important to understand that a pixel is a unit of color information, not a unit of size like centimetre or inch. Rather, pixels are arranged into one-inch squares; thus, resolution is measured in pixels per inch, or ppi. The more pixels squished into one square inch the smaller and less visible they become and the higher the image resolution is said to be. Conversely, the fewer pixels fitted into one square inch the larger they become until they become visible to the naked eye, and the image is then said to have become "pixellated."

Image size can be increased or decreased by what is called image interpolation. To increase the size of an image, image editors like Photoshop add pixels based on surrounding pixel information ("upsampling" or "uprezzing"); to decrease the image size, image editors erase pixels ("downsampling"). However, while downsampling rarely results in a loss of image quality, upsampling often does: since the image editor replicates the existing pixel information, if an image is of poor quality to begin with, this is merely amplified. If the image has been retouched poorly or heavily processed, these actions can also create artifacts, which are also then amplified. Also, if you begin with a JPEG, which is a compressed format, the compression itself will have created artifacts and these will be replicated. Consequently, it is rarely advised to upsample an image more than 10%; if you must, try upsampling it in stages of 10%.

Fig. 13

Imaging standards dictate that you always write out image and document sizes as width by height. The easiest way to remember this is that you write on 8.5" x 11" paper, not 11" x 8.5" paper.

Document Size

Say you have an image that is 1000 x 500 pixels saved at a resolution of 100 ppi. Your pixels are arranged 100 pixels for every inch in either direction, so your 1000 x 500 pixel image will print at 10" x 5" (1000/100 = 10; 500/100 = 5); 10" x 5" is your "document size." Change the resolution and you change the document size.

Fig. 13 shows the same 225 x 150 pixel image at three different resolutions. The first is 100 ppi, and you can see the document size is 2.25" x 1.5". The second is at 50 ppi, doubling the document size, and you can see the degradation of the image quality. The third is a section of the image at 10 ppi. Here the document size is 22.5" x 15" and is completely pixellated. (And if you count the number of squares in the inch you will see there are ten.)

File Size

File size refers to the amount of data when a file is compressed or opened in an image editor like Photoshop, which decompresses the file. A 1000 x 500 pixel image is about 1.43MB when uncompressed; when compressed into a high quality JPEG, file size will vary depending on the complexity of the image content. This has to do with repetition of pixel information: the more the same pixel is repeated, the smaller the compressed file size will be. Blocks of the same color will compress more than a continuous tone image, so a 1.43MB image of a black box will compress all the way down to 41KB but a complex image might only compress down to 500KB.

Images in ebooks require higher rates of compression because ereaders are not designed to display large image files. This is why images in ebooks are not usually of great quality, and why producing the ebook equivalent of a beautiful coffee table book is currently impossible.

Color Space

Although most ereaders display everything in greyscale, other devices such as the iPad, mobile phones and computers will display your images in color, and of course your product image on a retailer's website will be displayed in color; thus all ebook formats accept color images. (And Nook has just released the NookColor, so color screens are the forward trend.) And if you intend to produce a physical edition of your book, you will of course be dealing with color printing, at least for the cover.

Color space refers to the range of colors (the "gamut") capable of being rendered by any given display device or reproduced in print. Print uses the CMYK—cyan, magenta, yellow, and black—color space while display devices express colors as RGB, which refers to the mix of the three primary colors, red, green, and blue. Each color in the spectrum is defined by the amount of each primary color in it; RGB is expressed in numbers between 0 and 255, with black expressed as R0-G0-B0 and white expressed as R255-G255-B255. Everything else is something in between: a shade of sky blue, for example, might be R25-G188-B241. The number of possible permutations is extraordinary. However, few devices are capable of reproducing the full spectrum that exists mathematically, and even if they could the human brain cannot differentiate between more than about ten million colors at most (the range is typically between seven and ten million).

Color Profiles

Over time, a number of standard color spaces, or "profiles," emerged that define specific gamuts. The only three you are likely to encounter are sRGB, Adobe RGB, and CMYK. Also known as sRGB IEC61966-2.1, sRGB most closely represents the color gamut of home computer monitors and compact digital cameras. The color space used by professional image makers is usually Adobe RGB (1998), which has a much wider gamut than sRGB, and which is rendered by professional grade digital cameras, pricier LCD monitors, and expensive hexachrome printers. Most commercial printing presses use the CMYK color space, which is smaller than sRGB in most ways but is actually capable of producing certain colors (mostly in the green/blue spectrum) that do not "live" in the sRGB color space. (For an excellent video explanation of color space, see this chapter's Useful Links.)

When a digital image that exists within one color space (the source profile) is converted to another (the destination profile), the imaging software must translate one set of numerical values to another. For example, that sky blue R25-G188-B241 in the RGB color space becomes C66%-M4%-Y0%-B0% in the CMYK space. When converting from one profile to another, colors that exist in the source profile that do not exist in the destination profile are "mapped" to the nearest producible color in the destination color space. This is where you will see shifts in color. Some color shifts are so subtle that you will not notice them but many can be quite pronounced and produce undesired results. This is particularly true of intense, highly saturated colors that exist only in the wider RGB gamut: when converted to sRGB or CMYK, intense RGB reds can go muddy, purples can turn magenta, teals will go blue, and so on. Skin tones are also finicky, with pink tones often mapping either toward magenta or yellow.

The point of telling you all this is that ebook software companies and online distributors such as Amazon's Kindle say they accept RGB images but that is misleading: you really need to submit your images as sRGB because sRGB is the color space of web browsers and most digital devices. Furthermore, when images are converted into an ebook they are stripped of their color profiles, and when an "untagged" image is read by a digital device in most cases the device will assume the color profile is sRGB. Thus, if you use an image that was saved in a color space other than sRGB you might discover unwanted color shifts when you view your image on the retail website or on a color-capable ebook device or app.

Bear in mind as well that few computer monitors and digital devices are calibrated, meaning they are not set to an international standard for color display. Devices that are calibrated will display an image identically (or nearly so) from screen to screen, and thus professional image creators and high-end print houses use calibration devices and software so creator and printer can work together to produce an image that maintains its color integrity. But a typical desktop monitor, laptop display, mobile phone and so on is not calibrated, and consequently images will appear differently from screen to screen. So no matter how good your image looks when you created it on your computer, understand it is highly unlikely the image will be replicated exactly on other color devices.

So, you may think, then what's the point? There isn't one if you are not the type to sweat over whether your red letters turn magenta or your cover model looks sickly. But if you are, if you have spent a lot of time and/or money creating a great book cover, then by using the sRGB color space you increase the chances that your image will look reasonably close to or even identical to what you laboured over.

Greyscale Images

If your image is greyscale ("black and white"), you can save it as sRGB or as Gray Gamma 2.2 (Gray Gamma 1.8 on the Mac). Saving a greyscale image as sRGB will give it a slight color cast (often magenta) but it will still look greyscale to the untrained eye. However, saving a greyscale image in the greyscale color space results in a significantly smaller file size, which is of benefit where the retailer charges a delivery cost to the author for each ebook sale.

Greyscale eReaders

Unfortunately, no matter how beautiful your color or greyscale images look on your computer, most ereaders are only capable of sixteen shades of grey, which means your images will appear flat and lifeless on those devices no matter what. Your color images will, however, display in all their glory on color devices like the iPad.

Color Space for Print

For print, you need to convert your images to the CMYK color space. As noted, color shifts from an RGB profile to CMYK are often quite pronounced, and if you submit a file in RGB or sRGB to the print house, their printer software will map out-of-gamut colors and you might not like the results. By working in CMYK to begin with, you can decide for yourself what colors to use if your initial preferences are out of gamut, and your final results will likely be closer to what you expect.

Where a print company says they accept RGB images, it is still safest to work within the CMYK gamut then convert the profile back to RGB. This is because by doing so you ensure that all your colors are printable in CMYK and will not be mapped with unexpected results.

For greyscale images, files are usually saved in one of several "dot gain" presets, or as a CMYK SWOP file. Check with your printer as to what profile they want greyscale images saved to since dot gain is printer-specific.

Regardless of what color space you are working in, unless you know what printer is being used and how it maps colors, there can still be unexpected results. Most printers will provide color profiles so their clients can proof to that profile, but my experience with print-on-demand is that they do not provide this information, partly because they often subcontract to third parties. Thus you will find in the fine print of your contract a note about not guaranteeing print quality, which is not just referring to the paper stock and binding but to the fidelity to your color files.

Image Resolution for Print

Generally speaking, most commercial print companies will ask for an image to be submitted to them at a resolution of 300 "dpi," which is a misnomer that arose from print resolution, measured in dots per inch or lines per inch (the terms are interchangeable): 300 dpi/lpi means there are 300 lines of dots for every inch of the printing plate.

All printing presses, whether digital or traditional, deposit color onto the paper using droplets of ink or toner. With CMYK printing, each pixel of color is translated into print by using a combination of three primary colors—cyan, magenta, yellow—and key black. To replicate an orange pixel, for example, the printer will overlap a drop of yellow and a drop of magenta to create the illusion of orange (yellow + magenta = orange). Different shades of orange are achieved by varying the relative size of the yellow and magenta dots, and adding black if necessary to darken the tone. Traditional printing presses control the amount of ink deposited onto the paper by adjusting the size of the dots on the printing plates, defined as a percentage: the higher the percentage the larger the dot and the more ink is deposited. This process is called halftone printing. Digital printing, though no longer using plates, mimics this process by adjusting the size of the ink droplets.

All printing devices have a "total print density" or "total ink limit" (TIL), which your print-on-demand manufacturer will relay to you. TIL refers to the sum of the percentages of the four CMYK values for any given color; for example, C60%-M40%-Y40%-K100% equals a TIL of 240. Most printers will not accept TIL limits that exceed 300, and prefer no more than 285. The reason for this is that print densities of a value greater than the printing device can handle will result in ink pooling on the surface of the paper, which will cause smearing and other problems.

As with pixels, the finer the droplets of ink or toner the more of them can be squished into a square inch and the greater the illusion of continuous tone. Conversely, the fewer the dots per inch the larger the droplets need to be to fill the space or the wider apart the droplets will be spaced, and the less refined the printed matter will look. As the traditional printing press developed over time, the most common resolution used for mass market matter became between 133 and 150 dpi/lpi: the more lines per inch on the printing plate the higher the volume of ink is used, and so 133 to 150 dpi/lpi was the balance arrived at between print quality and economy. Newspapers, which sell for much less than a magazine, commonly print at only 85 dpi/lpi, while an expensive coffee table book might print at 175 or 200 dpi/lpi.

So if the printer is printing between 133 and 150 dpi/lpi, why are you asked to submit a 300 ppi image or text document? It is because the software that translates pixels into halftone dots needs, depending on the printing device, between 1.3 and 2 times the print resolution to carry out its calculations. The outside number of 300 ppi is thus considered the safe resolution to request for submission.

The exception to this is for true black and white images that do not contain any shades of grey; these images, called "line art," should be submitted at 600 ppi.

Many photo-realistic printers will boast a high dpi, usually around 1440 dpi and some as high as 5000 or 6000 dpi, but this is using a very different and much more expensive system called stochastic, in which ink is sprayed ("dithered") in different directions. For production of a book for mass distribution, suffice it to say you will not be using this method so you needn't worry about it. Similarly, there are now printers that use up to eight different ink colors (the hexachrome system), but again these are more expensive devices to run and it is unlikely you will come across them for mass book production.

Due to the high resolution required to ensure quality print reproduction, if you intend to offer your book as a physical edition you need to plan in advance for this and ensure that you start with a cover image that will meet or exceed the print dimensions of your book. For example, my novel, *Baby Jane*, was released as a 6" x 9" paperback with a cover image that spanned the whole of the front cover; that 6" x 9" image therefore needed to be 1800 x 2700 pixels (300 ppi x 6" = 1800; x 9" = 2700). My cover image was thus shot using a camera that produces a 2848 x 4288 pixel uncompressed (lossless) image, well in excess of what I would need. Never try to take a smaller or lower resolution image created for digital and upsample it to fit a print book: the results will be horrid.

Image Resolution for eBooks

With digital display things become less predictable because, unlike printing which deals in finite measurements, different digital devices display at different resolutions: the default, or "native," resolution of Windows is 96 ppi while for the Mac it used to be 72 ppi but now varies with different models: the native display on the new MacBook Pro is approximately 113 ppi, for example, while the iPad displays at 132 ppi. Moreover, the display resolution on a personal computer is adjustable to suit user preference: my PC laptop can display anywhere between 57 and 98 ppi.

The significance of this is that with digital display it is not the resolution of the image that is relevant but the resolution of the device the image is viewed on. All that matters is the pixel dimensions of the image, which will then appear larger or smaller depending on the resolution of the device: if your image is 1000 pixels tall it will appear to be approximately 8.85" tall on a MacBook Pro (1000/113), 10.42" on a Windows monitor (1000/96), and 7.58" on the iPad (1000/132).

Specialized devices like ereaders have relatively high resolutions—for example, the Kindle's resolution is 167 ppi, the Kindle DX's is 150 ppi, Sony's Touch Edition 650 is 170 ppi, and Barnes & Noble's NookColor is 169 ppi. Screen sizes vary from 600 x 800 pixels (Kindle, Sony Touch) to 600 x 1024 (NookColor), to 824 x 1200 (Kindle DX). The entirety of the program menus are displayed on the screen, however, meaning a portion of a device's real estate is devoted to toolbars and to white space around the text to mimic the margins of a physical book. Thus, even if you were to embed a 1000 ppi cover image in an ebook, the cover would not display at its full size even on a Kindle DX despite its 824 x 1200 pixel screen. Moreover, each ereader scales images to fit the screen according to the device's software; predicting how an image will appear in any given ebook is therefore impossible without doing individual tests.

The Significance of 72 ppi

When preparing your images for use in an ebook, you will often be told that images intended for digital display should be saved at 72 ppi, or what is known as "web ready." This is because 72 ppi used to be the standard for digital display: when Apple first developed the personal computer, they chose 72 ppi as the native resolution because it correlated with the typographer's 72 points per inch, the measurement for fonts used in a printing press: 1 point equals 1/72 of an inch (thus your typical 12 pt font is 12/72 of an inch high). The rationale was that the user wouldn't need to imagine what their electronic document would look like when printed because what you saw on the screen was essentially identical to what was printed out. This choice of 72 ppi, however, resulted in a jagged appearance of fonts onscreen, and so when Windows arrived on the scene they elected to use a screen resolution of 96 ppi, which smoothed out the appearance of fonts.

When graphic design went digital, Mac was the platform of choice for many designers, and thus the same principle applied to images: coming from the print world, graphic designers were used to thinking of images in terms of their document size and were essentially unable to visualise an image in terms of its pixel dimensions, so working with an image saved at 72 ppi resulted in an image printing at the same size as it appeared on the designer's monitor. Thus, 72 ppi became the standard. But, as shown, Mac left 72 ppi behind ages ago and Windows never had it. So there really is no standard anymore—in fact, the trend is upward, with devices capable of ever-increasing resolution.

So is 72 ppi still relevant? The answer is both yes and no. No, because as noted there is no standard digital display; but yes because a great deal of web software still assumes this "standard" and will process and save all images at 72 ppi. If your original image has been saved at a higher resolution, downsampling can occur when converting to an ebook or uploading to a retailer's website, leaving you with unwanted results. So until old habits die and new ones keep up with technology, 72 ppi will continue to be requested for many web-based applications.

That all said, due to a quirk in Word that is discussed in more detail in Chapter 11: Manuscript Formatting for eBooks, it can be advantageous to save at 96 ppi any images intended for import into Word.

Limitations on Embedded Images

Kindle will not accept embedded images larger than 127KB, so embedding a large image inside your ebook may result in rejection. Large images also increase your file size and therefore your delivery costs. With ePubs, though the format itself technically does not have any restrictions on image size, some older ePub ereaders cannot display images larger than 300KB. And all device manufacturers have file limits that need to be considered if creating an image-heavy ebook: for example Nook Books must be no larger than 20MB and Kindle books have a 50MB limit.

Kindle recommends images be no larger than 600 x 800 pixels because if an image is larger than the display device, "the image will be shrunk to fit on the screen, which may lead to a loss of legibility." However, what they mean is that, if you can only read the image text and make out details if the image is larger than 600 x 800 pixels, then you have created an unsuitable image for display on a Kindle screen; it does not mean you are confined to 600 x 800 pixels.

Previously, Kindle stated that internal images for books had to be no smaller than 300 x 400 pixels. That recommendation has now disappeared off its website but images smaller than 300 pixels high or wide will generally be too small to be viewed appropriately. It really depends upon the content of the image: this manual contains an image 293 x 333 pixels and it looks fine and is perfectly legible.

Images that have an aspect ratio of 9:11 will fill the Kindle screen.

Ideal Image Size

Is there, then, an ideal image size to use in your ebook? Large images are pointless if they exceed the display capabilities of the reading device, but do you need an image of sufficient size that will meet the requirements of the current largest screen likely to view the document, the Kindle DX, that is, an image of 824 x 1200 pixels? And what about small images?

Currently, Kindle suggests that images not exceed 800 pixels wide, which is why in Chapter 1: To Kindle in Ten Steps I suggested you have a cover/product image made that is no wider than 800 pixels and between 1040 and 1200 pixels tall. Whether or not you can then use that same 800 x 1200 pixel product image for your embedded ebook cover image will depend on which technique you use to create your ebook. If you are using the Word-to-HTML technique outlined in Chapter 1, then my tests suggests an 800 x 1200 image will usually compress within the 127KB limit when converting the Word document to HTML: Word will downsample the image to 960 pixels tall and uses a medium compression level. A smaller image is problematic for Word because if the image fits on the page it will be exported at 100% and left uncompressed—Word exports the original instead—in which case if you start with an image larger than 127KB you will end up with an image larger than 127KB. Thus, using the Kindle-recommended 600 x 800 pixel image will likely result in this problem. Such an image would have to be compressed first in an image editor, something most authors building an ebook in Word likely wish to avoid.

If you are using Calibre, it does not compress images; you must compress them first in an image editor to fit within the 127KB limit. Larger images require greater compression to then reduce to 127KB; in this case limiting yourself to the recommended 600 x 800 is a better idea: a 600 x 800 pixel image is about half the size of an 800 x 1200 pixel image so it will require less compression.

If you are using a program such as InDesign, images are not compressed at source but are optimized by Kindle when the file is delivered to the client's device; the larger the image the more it will need to be compressed. That said, larger ereaders scale images to fit, in which case a 600 x 800 pixel image will be upsampled by the device. My conclusion is that using a slightly larger image—say around 960 pixels tall—does not increase the file size significantly, still compresses within 127KB, and requires less upsampling by a higher resolution device.

Regarding horizontal images, at one point Kindle recommended nothing wider than 600 pixels; this recommendation has also disappeared off its website but my own tests suggest between 600 and 720 pixels wide is fine.

And what about images narrower than 600 pixels wide? If they are smaller than 127KB, and if you use the Word-to-HTML system, or if you build a mobi file using Mobipocket Creator or Calibre, the images are not affected. This is ideal if you are starting with an image that is already small or low resolution to begin with (like the screen shots in this manual) and further compression will only make matters worse. If the image is greater than 127KB, however, then you have the same problem of needing to compress it first in an image editor.

If using the Kindle plug-in for InDesign, images smaller than 600 pixels, though exported at their native size, are coded by the plug-in to expand to fit the Kindle screen—at least they did during my tests—sometimes with undesirable results.

With ePubs, which do not compress images, you have to find a balance between the image size and quality if you elect to compress them within the recommended 300KB limit. The largest screen likely to view an ePub is the iPad, at 768 x 1024 pixels. You can start at that image size, compress as necessary, and see how your images look.

Note that these dimensions are for interior images and covers that are embedded into a document. For the product image that you upload separately to the retail sites when you upload your book, the dimensions required by each retailer are outlined next.

Book Cover and Product Image

Retailers such as Amazon use the terms "Cover Page" and "Product Image" interchangeably but they are not the same thing. When you upload your book to Kindle, for example, you will be asked to "Upload Your Book Cover," but this cover is not the book cover you see when you open a book on your Kindle; it is the product image on Amazon's website and the thumbnails on the Kindle device's home page. It is the same thing with all retailers and ereaders.

Each retailer or distributor will ask for different image dimensions so you need to check their documentation. Product images must be in JPEG format (not JPEG 2000; and baseline, not progressive) or TIFF (flattened, no layers or transparency). Most retailers will ask for the images at 72 ppi. Files must be in the RGB color space, and ideally in sRGB. The requirements of the more popular retailers and distributors are:

Kindle

Cover images (product images) for Kindle must be portrait style, cannot be smaller than 500 x 800 pixels or larger than 800 x 1280 pixels. You can upload a full 1280 pixel image here if you like, though at the moment Amazon does not appear to display the product image any larger than 500 pixels high at its largest, at least on its own website. Kindle will accept JPEGs or TIFFs but will convert TIFFs to JPEGs.

Barnes & Noble

Barnes & Noble's PubIt! requires cover/product images be a JPEG file between 5KB and 2MB in size. The longest side must be between 750 and 2000 pixels in length.

Smashwords

Smashwords requires cover images be rectangular, portrait style, a minimum of 600 pixels tall, and recommends 500 x 700 pixels. Images must be JPEGs or PNGs.

Ingram Digital

For ebooks distributed by Ingram Digital, product images must be in JPEG format, a minimum of 680 pixels tall, and saved at 96 ppi.

POD Manufacturers

Some print-on-demand manufacturers do not need you to submit a product image; they will create one from the book cover you submit with your manuscript. Others will ask for a product image; you can use the same one as for your ebook.

Cover Elements for eBooks

With ebooks you only require a front cover, which must include the book title and the author's name. Optionally you may add the subtitle, if applicable, and the names of anyone else accredited (for example, the illustrator if it is a picture book, the editor if it is a compilation, or the translator if the original is in another language). The cover does not have to contain all the information contained in the title page, and often whether a contributor such as an illustrator is added to the cover is based on contractual obligations between the publisher and the contributor. On the book cover you do not credit the book designer or the copyright holder of the cover image; you do that on the copyright page.

Cover Elements for Print

With print books you need a cover that includes in a single image the front cover, book spine, and back cover. When using a POD manufacturer, designing your cover is made simpler as these companies offer templates based on page number and paper choice: you input your options and the system creates the relevant template for your needs.

For example, *Baby Jane* was published as a 6" x 9" trade paperback. The finished cover image therefore needed to be 9" tall by 12" wide plus the width of the spine. The width of the spine is determined by the number of pages in the book and the weight of the paper used: the more pages and the thicker the paper stock the wider the spine needs to be. In the case of *Baby Jane*, the spine required was .69" wide.

The cover design must also include what is called a bleed. A bleed is a portion of the cover—usually .125" on all three sides—that is cut off when the book is manufactured: when a book is made it is printed on paper larger than the final size (the "trim size") then the book is cut down; this ensures that there are no embarrassing lines of white paper at the edges of your cover image. So *Baby Jane*'s cover needed to be 9" tall by 12.69" wide plus .125" for the bleed on each side, for a total of 12.94" x 9.25". Since the image must extend to the edge of the template and is cut off, you have to take into account the loss of the bleed when designing your cover to ensure your image will not be inappropriately cropped.

Cover templates also have what is called a "safe zone," which is usually .25" inside the final trim size. Important elements such as text and logos must be clear of the safe zone or you risk them being cut into during manufacture due to slight movement of the book as it goes through the cutter. The template you download from your POD manufacturer will have the bleed and safe zones clearly marked.

Fig. 14

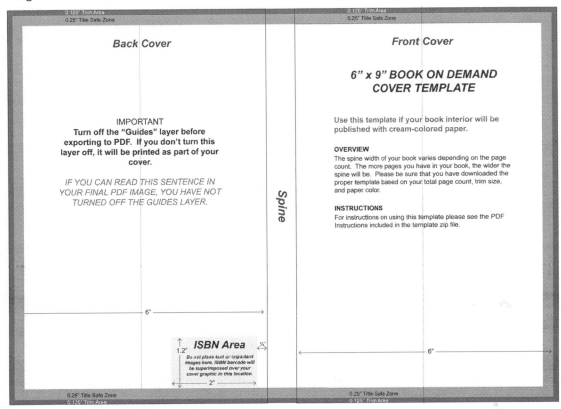

Spines are also designed with a safe zone, usually .0625" from the edge, to ensure spine text and images are not pushed into the crease due to slight variations in binding. For books with less than around eighty pages, the spine is often too narrow for any text and so is left blank. Fig. 14 is the CreateSpace template for *Baby Jane*.

The front cover must, as with ebooks, contain at minimum the book title and author. The spine usually contains the book title and author's name, and the publisher's logo (if applicable). The back cover usually contains a story synopsis or reviewer quotes, the publisher's logo (again if applicable), the BISAC categories, and a credit for the cover image and design. If intended for commercial distribution, your book must also contain on the back cover a barcode comprised of the book's ISBN, and may contain an optional price barcode.

For design ideas and examples of how different book covers incorporate the various elements, have a browse through your local library or bookstore.

Barcodes

Barcodes come in a variety of formats known as "Barcode Symbology." There are two symbologies used to generate barcodes for books, the older "Bookland" or "Bookland EAN," and the newer "EAN/JAN-13" or just "EAN-13." The difference is that the older Bookland symbology generated a 13-digit barcode from what was then a 10-digit ISBN; newer books, which have 13-digit ISBNs, can thus use the Bookland symbology or the newer EAN-13.

The five-digit retail price barcode is made up of the country code currency digit and the four-digit price. The British pound, for example, is "0," the U.S. dollar is "5," and the Canadian dollar is "6." Thus, a book retailing for CAN $17.95 would read "61795"; if it were U.S. $17.95 it would be "51795." A code of "90000" indicates the book does not have a suggested retail price, and is commonly used when a single cover file is used across multiple jurisdictions.

The price barcode is optional in some countries, which is why you usually do not see it on the back of most Canadian and British books, but is mandatory in the U.S. A specific price is, however, still optional, so it is common to see U.S. books with a 90000 barcode.

POD manufacturers provide you with a barcode, either on the template itself or at time of manufacture, so you do not need to source out software or pay-per-use websites to procure a barcode for your book.

Sourcing Imagery

If you cannot create your own images for use in your books you will need to source images that you can legally use. Do not for a moment believe you can simply swipe something off the Internet and use the image with impunity. That is copyright infringement and such behaviour will expose you to litigation and can get you banned from sites such as Amazon if they are served with the writ as well. (And don't forget that indemnity clause in your publishing contract.)

I have heard it argued that by putting images on the Internet, image creators are forfeiting their copyright, and thus the onus is on the copyright holder to protect their work rather than on the thief not to steal. This is a legally indefensible and morally bankrupt position. The only question you need to ask yourself to determine if an image is available for you to use without permission is this: Did I create the image? If not, it is not yours, and if you are unable to find the copyright holder or ascertain the image is in the public domain, then it is best to find another image.

Royalty-Free or Rights-Managed?

To use a copyrighted image legally, you need to procure from the copyright holder written permission to use the image for your purposes, commonly referred to as a "licence to use." Licences can be unrestricted (royalty-free, or "RF") or restricted (rights-managed, or "RM") by such things as time, territory, and print run. For example, a photographer might licence his or her photograph for your book cover for one year, in North America only, and for a print run of 5000 books. If you wish to expand the terms of the licence—if you print more books, expand globally, or decide to keep the book with that same cover in print longer than one year—

you must pay an additional fee to the rights holder. Generally speaking, with rights-managed images the longer you use an image or the greater the distribution, or if you restrict the sale of the image to other customers by demanding exclusive use of the image, the more you pay.

With ebooks and print-on-demand there is no initial print run, so calculating a rights-managed fee becomes problematic: you must pay the same fee whether you sell one book or one million. Stock photography agencies have tried, with varying degrees of success, to price images for the ebook/POD market by offering a one- to three-year term with worldwide usage and no limit on the number of units sold. An RM image for an ebook or ebook/print book combination can run you anywhere from $300.00 to over $3000.00 for a three-year term.

Royalty-free images are more flexible and affordable because you pay a one-time fee based on the image size and then you are free to use the image for as many uses as you like, in perpetuity, but for your own use only: the image cannot be shared or sold onward. For example, a royalty-free image might sell for $30.00 for a 580 x 830 pixel image, $50.00 for the same image at 1160 x 1650 pixels, and $70.00 for 2770 x 3945 pixels. Royalty-free images are usually older images or of lower creative quality (often created by amateurs), which is why they are considerably less expensive than rights-managed images, but as with anything else you get what you pay for. Expect to pay anywhere from a few dollars upwards to $300.00 for a royalty-free image.

If you intend to publish only to the ebook format, you may be tempted to buy only the size required to meet the requirements of e-publishing. While this might seem logical and cost-effective, keep in mind that you may wish to have bookmarks and postcards made to promote your book, or if it does well you may decide to take the plunge into print. By buying the largest image you can afford you increase the chances your image will meet your needs later on and you will not have to start all over again, which will save you money in the long run.

There are a multitude of stock image agencies to choose from, from the professional, well-known and generally more expensive Getty Images to the plethora of cheap microstock (also known as "penny stock") agencies that have been cropping up in recent years. Where you go for your images will depend on your budget.

Microstock agencies generally do not provide for refunds if you change your mind about an image, but the professional stock agencies do, anywhere from seven to thirty days. So you can buy a few images and test them in a design before choosing the final one, then return the rejected images to the agency for a refund.

When buying an image from a stock agency, it should be you that makes the purchase. This is because the licence to use is granted to the person or company named on the invoice and is non-transferrable. Thus, if your designer buys the image it is your designer, not you, who owns the licence, and with rights-managed images the licence granted to a designer only transfers to their client the right to use the image for that *one* purpose only. With royalty-free, the licence is for multiple uses but not *your* multiples uses. You are thus wedded to your designer for any further use of that image. But if you buy the image yourself, you are free to use whichever designer you please, and to use that image for whatever other purposes you please so long as they fall within the parameters of the licence.

Borrowed Images

You can use an image from a friend or flattered stranger who gives you permission, but if you do you still need to set out the terms in a written contract and you need to pay a fee of at least one dollar (or pound, or euro, et cetera) for the image. The contract need not be complex—it can be an email between two people outlining the uses and granting permission—but you need to pay the fee because all exchanges of rights are based on "due consideration," that is, a fee paid. If you do not pay the money there is no due consideration, and if at a later date good relations between you and the copyright holder break down the contract may be deemed invalid if no consideration had been paid. And you must pay the money upfront because the rights do not transfer until the fee is paid, and you do not want to go through the expense of creating your book cover only to have the image owner change their mind just before you release your book or, worse yet, after you release it.

Public Domain Images

Just as with any artistic media, artwork and photographs become public domain after a set number of years. In most countries the length is the same for all media—meaning if books are covered for seventy years, pictures are too—while some treaties, the Berne Convention for example, only provides 25 years for photographs unless the signatory provides for a longer term. If you are interested in an image you believe is likely public domain, if you know the date of creation or the date of the artist's death, it is easy enough to check online: there is an excellent list on Wikipedia (see this chapter's Useful Links).

Free Creative Common Images

There are free images on the web that image creators have made available for use in exchange for a proper credit, licensed under the Creative Commons Licence. You can search for such images using Google's advanced search options. However, the usual method of credit includes a link to the licence, which of course will not work in print. In that case, you should contact the rights holder and enter into a separate agreement for your print book.

Image Content: Potential Issues

Regardless of where you source your imagery, issues with copyright and trademark can arise. By this I do not mean the copyright of the image itself but of what the image contains. Does it contain a protected logo or trademarked building? Does it contain an identifiable person?

Is it of a private dwelling? If so, then along with a licence to use the image you may need permission from the trademark owner or person. If it is a person, you need what is called a model release; if a logo, you need a trademark release; and if a private dwelling or building, you need a location release. This is usually the responsibility of the photographer or illustrator who will acquire the necessary permission to sell the image for commercial use. If such permission had not been not sought or was denied, then the image will be marketed as not having a release or will say "not available for commercial use."

For the purpose of copyright and trademark law, books are considered "editorial" as opposed to "commercial," and so in most cases there is no need for a release because editorial use is not subject to the restrictions of commercial use (it is the same as with your book content: fair use laws apply since you are using the image to illustrate the text, as opposed to selling a product). However, as with your book content you need to be aware that grey areas can arise. For example, an image of a McDonald's restaurant on the cover of your novel about a serial killer who disposes of the bodies using his fast food chain is likely to get the kind of attention you really do not want. Or the image of an identifiable minor on a book about a child killer may make her parents uneasy and they could exercise what are known as "moral rights," which in this case are the rights of individuals not to have their likeness used in ways that impugn their integrity. So you need to exercise proper judgment and sensitivity.

If you are worried about the cover image, some of the major stock agencies will sell you indemnity insurance but it will not be cheap. If in doubt, it is often best just to move on to a different image.

Lastly, keep the cover content PG-13. Many publishers and retailers will reject a book if the cover contains nudity or graphic violence, or will label the book "adult content" and thereby limit its exposure to the marketplace.

Hiring a Professional

Author Services Companies

Many author services companies offer book cover design, ranging from inexpensive covers created using templates to more expensive custom covers. But understand that if you use one of these services they are almost always tied to your account with the company, and it will not give you the source files: the contract will state copyright remains with the company. At most it will give you a low-res PDF, which might be useful for email but likely not much else. Instead, if you want additional promotional items such as bookmarks and postcards you will be forced to purchase these items from the company, often at inflated prices. And since the company will be the one purchasing the cover image from the stock agency, as noted earlier it will be the company, not you, who will own the licence to use the image, so even if you negotiated the source files as part of services rendered you would not have the legal right to do anything further with the image. If you then change author services companies your cover stays behind, and you will have to pay again to have a new cover made elsewhere if you wish to keep your book on the market.

Low-Cost eBook Design

There are a number of companies out there who offer cheap cover design, sometimes as cheap as $35.00. You can find these companies or independent graphic designers by searching for "ebook cover design," or by posting queries on the various indie writer forums. Most digital aggregators offer cover creation services or provide lists of recommended designers.

A cover design under $100.00 is considered ridiculously cheap, and as with most things in life you get what you pay for: I have yet to see a $35.00 cover that didn't look like a $35.00 cover. And that low price will be for the ebook version only: most are designed using low-resolution penny stock images. If you request a print version of your cover the price will go up considerably; request a print version later on and you will discover the file is not of sufficient resolution. The file will also likely be of insufficient resolution even to print a postcard or bookmark, so if you are already pondering having these promotional tools made you need to ask upfront if your design package includes any print-quality files. It likely does not, and when you ask for this the price will go up. If you see a pattern here, you are right: often the low price is to lure you in, and when you later need additional services the prices are often inflated because the designer has you in a corner: accept the price or start all over again with a new cover and designer.

Low-cost design also does not include control over the cover image. Even if the designer gives you copyright of the cover itself, control of the image is retained by the designer (who will buy it from the penny stock agency) unless they used a public domain or Creative Commons image.

For the indie author just testing the waters, the low-cost option is obviously most affordable. As long as you understand the restrictions upfront, you will not get a surprise later on that makes you feel angry and cheated. If your book starts to do well, you can invest in a new, better quality cover then.

Copyright and Work-for-Hire

A book is judged by its cover, at least initially, so a great cover will translate into sales while a bad cover will likely result in a loss of revenue. If you decide to spend a bit more and go with a higher quality design, a full print and digital cover package will run anywhere from $300.00 to $1000.00 (more if you commission original artwork).

In addition to better quality design and resolution, there are a few other things you should demand in exchange for the higher fee, the first being copyright. As noted in the section on copyright, when you commission a designer to create a cover for you, strictly speaking this is a "work-for-hire" and copyright lies with the commissioning party. However, this is a common cause for conflict, and some designers will later claim you agreed they retain copyright, or they will send you a "standard" agreement that states they own the copyright and only licence the file to you for the purpose you commissioned. So if you want maximum flexibility and control over your cover, you need to be clear—in writing—that you own copyright.

This of course means you also need to control the main image. Instruct your designer to provide you with options for cover images, and after you decide upon an image buy the licence to use from the stock agency yourself or directly from the artist.

Source Files

When your designer creates your cover, s/he will do so in a program that uses individual layers: your image is one layer, then your title text will be another, your back cover synopsis is yet another, and so on. The advantage of this is that if later on you need to change any element— you might later replace your synopsis with review quotes, for example—then your designer only has to edit those layers; s/he does not have to start from scratch, saving your designer time and you money. Also, if you later decide to create additional marketing materials like bookmarks or a poster, the designer can reuse elements from your cover without having to do the same work over again. Consequently, you will want each cover provided to you as a layered file in whatever program your cover was designed in, which will usually be Photoshop or Illustrator, perhaps even InDesign or Quark. Even if you do not have the software capable of reading the files provided to you, you need to keep them anyway because they may be required again at a later date by a different designer.

Like their low-cost colleagues, many higher-end designers will not readily offer you these source files because they want you to come back to them for additional work—if you later want those postcards or bookmarks, or perhaps a poster made for a public reading. Most of the time this works out well anyway, but sometimes relations can sour and you do not want your cover files held hostage. It is imperative, then, that the contract specify that all source files must be included in the design package you commission. If your designer will not agree to this you will have to decide how badly you want to hire that particular designer. If you decide to go ahead anyway, at the least you should ask how long the designer keeps the source files; a good one will keep them for at least three years; many keep them indefinitely. The contract should specify how long the files must be kept at minimum.

How Large Do You Need?

If you are only publishing electronically, it is still advisable to have your front cover created large enough for print; your designer can then provide you with the source file as well as a 72 ppi, sRGB JPEG in the appropriate ebook size. It does not take your designer any more time to create a larger image than a smaller one, so there is not a difference in design costs (except for the royalty-free image if you are using one). The larger cover means you will have maximum future flexibility, and if you later publish to print you will only need to have the spine and back cover design added. The larger file also means the ability to print marketing materials.

You will also then need the front cover in the appropriate size for use as your product image as previously specified in "Book Cover and Product Image." Your designer should also provide you with JPEGs in relevant sizes for use in marketing emails, to add to a blog, or to submit to a reviewer. For example:

- 1800 x 2700 pixels, 300 ppi: front cover portion of a 6" x 9" trade paperback;

- 1200 x 1800 pixels, 300 ppi: print version for press releases or if you get print press coverage;

- 640 x 960 pixels, 72 ppi: ebook cover and product image;

- 300 x 450 pixels, 72 ppi: medium-sized image for marketing email and blogs; and

- 100 x 150 pixels, 72 ppi: thumbnail for use in a digital signature or blog.

Designing for Print

If you are publishing a print version, you should inform your designer of the templates available from the print-on-demand manufacturer. This will not only provide your designer with ready-made specifications but the barcode will also be provided along with instructions for its placement on the back cover.

For the print version you will need your full cover and your book interior files provided to you in their original program-specific formats, and as separate PDF files for submission to the print house (some printers will accept InDesign or QuarkXPress files, though the preference is for PDFs). For details on the specifications of the PDF, provide your designer with the POD manufacturer's documentation, which it will provide to you when you create your account or which it will direct you to download from its website. If your designer communicates directly with the print house and submits the files on your behalf, your designer must still provide you with full resolution copies of all relevant files.

Hire Locally

If you hire locally and retain the necessary files, it will be easier for you if you later decide to print copies of your book locally. This is of particular importance to authors outside the U.S., UK, or Australia as these are the three key countries where the POD manufacturer/wholesalers are based. Printing and shipping from these countries can be more expensive than printing locally, though certainly not always.

Useful Links

Wikipedia article on different file formats.
http://en.wikipedia.org/wiki/Image_file_formats

Wikipedia article on CMYK printing.
http://en.wikipedia.org/wiki/CMYK_color_model

Wikipedia article on the relationship between printing and screen resolution.
http://en.wikipedia.org/wiki/Dots_per_inch

A great webpage by dpbestflow.org that explains the different color spaces and has a video that illustrates in 3D the relationship between the different color spaces.
http://www.dpbestflow.org/color/color-space-and-color-profiles

Wikipedia article "List of Countries' Copyright Length."
http://en.wikipedia.org/wiki/List_of_countries%27_copyright_length

10/ Software

Unless you intend to hire the services of others to properly format and upload your book to the various ebook retailers and/or to design your print version, you will need a combination of software programs to achieve your self-publishing goals. Which software combination you need will depend on how complex your document is and which formats you wish to publish to; how you format your book will depend somewhat on which ebook conversion software you elect to use. It is best to learn what some of the different issues are with the various formats and then decide upon a plan of action before you invest in software or go through the process of formatting your book one way only to discover you needed to do it another way to satisfy the requirements of a specific conversion program or distributor's requirements. To learn about some of these issues read Chapter 11: Manuscript Formatting for eBooks; the section "eBook Aggregators" in Chapter 16: Distribution and Royalties; and, if you are planning a print version, Chapter 15: Print Production.

There are two main ebook formats on the market today: Amazon's Kindle (.azw), which is a proprietary version of a mobi file, and the open-source format ePub (.epub). Some ereaders will also read PDF and text files—and many classic books have been scanned and are sold as PDFs—but for current releases the main players sell either the Kindle or the ePub format: Amazon of course sells only the Kindle, while Barnes & Noble's Nook Books and the likes of Apple's iBookstore and Sony's eReader store sell the ePub and sometimes PDFs. In the UK, Waterstones and WH Smith sell ePubs. In Canada, Kobo sells ePubs; ditto for Kobo and Borders in Australia and Whitcoulls in New Zealand. Thus you will need to learn how to format for both the Kindle and ePub, and optionally the PDF, if you wish to sell across multiple sales channels.

Mobi and ePub files appear on your computer as a single file but they are actually what is known as an archive, a zipped folder containing separate subfolders and files. These subfolders and files contain the book's text, images, and metadata, and to which ebook retailers add code for such things as digital rights management (DRM), text-to-speech functionality, and so on.

Regardless of what the final format of your book is, it is built on HTML code in the same way that a website or a software program is built. This is why you will see and hear references to HTML wherever ebooks are discussed. Some HTML basics and how to amend the code are discussed in this manual.

If your book is a simple format like a novel, a word processor will often be sufficient as Word documents are accepted by Kindle, Barnes & Noble's PubIt!, and most aggregators. However, some aggregators will charge you a conversion fee, and others will charge less if you are able to upload your fully compliant ePub, so while it can mean an investment of time and sometimes money to acquire and learn a new program or two, it might save you money later on.

Many indie authors elect to publish only to the ebook format but you should consider offering a print version, not only because there is still a large market for print books but because print publishing carries cache. You can always start off with the e-version and, if it does well, add the print version then. If you plan ahead on the technical side (as outlined in the previous chapter) you can keep your options open.

Offering a print version is significantly more complicated, but the first book is really the hardest because there is a steep learning curve; once you get over that curve the road straightens for your second book. If you offer a print or a static PDF version, you will need to learn about desktop publishing programs and PDFs.

The following is an overview of the most likely software programs you will encounter in your pursuit of indie publishing, and some of their strengths and weaknesses. You will not use all of them as some of them are competitors while others perform multiple duties. Further details of their use follows in the sections on formatting and conversion, at least as they apply to our efforts: this manual is meant to provide the basics required to accomplish a typical book made up mostly of text and perhaps a few images. It is not intended for complex formatting or interactive books. For that you will need a manual on the specific software you are using or to hire a professional who has access to more robust (and expensive!) programs designed specifically for creating ebooks.

Before I continue, let me reiterate that you do not have to learn any of this: you can hire professionals instead. You can hire a graphic designer for both your print and ebook, or send your Word document out to be formatted and/or converted. Kindle Direct Publishing and Barnes & Noble's PubIt! websites provide a list of professional conversion service providers; you can find more by searching for "ebook conversion services" or by asking for recommendations from others on the indie publishing forums. Rates for a typical novel of 90,000 words will range anywhere from $150.00 to $300.00 for both the Kindle and ePub format; shorter works such as novellas or short stories will cost less while more complex documents like a manual will cost more. Some companies will convert to one format only for half the rate.

If that sounds too expensive, let me assure you that if your book is a simple format like a novel, learning how to format it yourself and even amend the code is nowhere near as daunting as it first appears. You can also start more slowly by creating the much simpler Kindle format yourself and leave the more complex ePub to a professional. To create and test a Kindle file you only need Word, your computer's built-in zip program (yes, it has one), Notepad, and the free Mobipocket Creator, Kindle Previewer and Kindle for PC (or Mac). If you fear becoming overwhelmed by information, read only about that software and leave the rest for when you are feeling more confident about your technical skills.

Word Processors

Obviously, if you are writing a book you will need a word processor. Most writers nowadays use Microsoft Word, whether on PC or Mac, while others use Oracle's free, open-source OpenOffice or the relatively obscure Atlantis. Many Mac users have adopted Scrivener. Whichever one you use, make sure the final format of your document is compatible with whichever ebook format you intend to convert to.

Microsoft Word

You can actually create an entire Kindle book (except for the cover) using only Word but you must use the .doc extension, not the more recent .docx extension. If your document is simple, the only real disadvantage to creating your entire Kindle book in Word is that your cover will be smaller on the Kindle screen. This is because the cover is embedded into the Word document and is then treated as a page in the Kindle: margins will then be visible so your cover will not fill the screen.

Kindle will accept book submissions as a Word document but I highly recommend you use Word's "Save as Web Page, Filtered" option instead and upload the resultant HTML document to Kindle. This allows you to test the book and even amend the code if necessary before upload. This is much easier than it sounds, and when you read the next chapter on manuscript formatting for ebooks you will see how amending the code solves numerous problems, saves you time, and results in fewer unwanted surprises.

If you sell your ebook through PubIt!, Barnes & Noble's Nook bookstore for indie writers, PubIt! will accept Word documents including the newer .docx files. However, I would suggest you not follow PubIt!'s formatting guidelines as some of what it says may result in problems with your ePub. It is better to follow the general formatting guide, below, since if you follow these formatting principles the conversion to any digital format will be smoother and more consistent.

If you elect to use an aggregator, some will *only* accept your manuscript as a Microsoft Word document, which the aggregator then puts through its own conversion software. Consequently, these aggregators often have their own style guides to comply with their technology, and some of what they suggest contradicts the formatting requirements of other options. Most author services companies also want Word documents, though some encourage authors to use the company's proprietary online book writing software. And if you intend to hand your work off to a book designer, giving them a Word document is usually best since all professional desktop publishing programs have Word import filters.

You can also use Word to create a PDF for a print version of your book, though there are better programs for this if the layout is complex. You cannot, however, use Word's built-in PDF exporter to create PDFs that are commercial printer compliant; you must use Adobe Acrobat Professional, using the Print function in Word instead of the Save As or Export function.

A note to Word for Mac users: when converting to HTML, I have noticed that the Mac adds a phenomenal amount of header code that I believe is completely unnecessary, merely increases your file size, and may interfere with conversion to ebook formats. I would advise Mac users to learn which of this code can be erased without harm and to do so.

OpenOffice

Oracle's OpenOffice is a free, open-standard office suite similar to Microsoft Office. It will let you save as a Word document, so you can use it for uploading directly to Kindle and others. However, its Save to HTML function is not particularly good; it returned errors that amending the code failed to fix, at least in my tests. As with Word, you cannot use the Export to PDF function in OpenOffice to create PDFs for commercial printing. OpenOffice has an export to ePub extension but when I tested the ePub it failed validation. Not recommended at this time.

Atlantis

Atlantis is an inexpensive word processor with the added convenience of an export to ePub option. It is only available for PC and is currently only 32-bit compliant. It costs around U.S. $35.00. I have not tested Atlantis so I cannot comment further.

Scrivener

Scrivener, by Literature & Latte, is a document creator which functions as a cross between a word processor and a digital wall board: you can have multiple windows open containing your document, images, virtual index cards, outlines and so on, which is quite handy when working on complex documents or non-fiction books. Scrivener is currently fully functional on the Mac and in its beta stage for Windows, but only the Mac version has an export to Kindle and ePub plug-in. The export to Kindle requires you to use Kindlegen, Amazon's command prompt utility that is not only confusing to the uninitiated but, if forum reports are to be believed, buggy. Users report that they instead export to ePub then use Calibre to convert to mobi. Scrivener currently costs around U.S. $45.00.

Apple Pages

Pages is part of Apple's iWorks suite, the Mac equivalent of Microsoft Office. Pages functions like Scrivener does, building a file from a set of documents. Pages has an export to ePub utility. Apple's iWorks cost around $70.00 or you can downloaded just Pages from the app store for $9.99.

Zip Program

If you elect to upload an HTML document to Kindle you will need to compress, or "zip," the HTML file and any image folders together into a single folder called an archive. You will also use this same zipped folder to convert HTML to mobi through Calibre, and you can use a zip program to open up, or "unpack," some mobi and ePub files to see the files hidden within; however, you cannot use these zip programs to re-zip a mobi or ePub file.

There are a number of zip programs available such as WinRAR, Winzip, or the free, open-source 7-Zip. Windows began including a built-in zip utility with XP; if you are using a Mac with a current OS, it too has built-in file compression software.

Kindle

If you own a Kindle, Amazon has a handy service whereby you upload a compatible file and it is converted into the Kindle format and then either downloaded directly to your device for a fee or emailed to you for free for you to transfer to your Kindle reader. To learn more about this service, you need to create a Kindle account and then visit the "Manage Your Kindle" page.

Mobipocket Creator

Mobipocket Creator is owned by Amazon, and the PRC files it creates can be read by your Kindle or Kindle application. PRC files are mobi files under a different name, and as noted the Kindle (AZW) format is also a mobi format under a proprietary name; hence the Kindle will read all three formats: PRC, mobi, and AZW.

Mobipocket Creator has not been updated in ages and the forums are full of people having problems with it, and its disadvantages are many: it does not compress the text portion of your file very well, resulting in larger files (compared to Calibre) and therefore a higher delivery fee on Kindle; it is more difficult to make a table of contents; it does not run well on 64-bit systems; it is not available for Mac; and its Help section is a misnomer. Moreover, you can upload an HTML file directly to Kindle so why would you bother with Mobipocket Creator? Its only advantage over Word-to-HTML is that you achieve a larger cover because it is not embedded in the text document. Hardly worth the bother of dealing with this frustrating program.

To be truthful, Mobipocket Creator is really only useful for testing your HTML file before you upload it to Kindle because Mobipocket Creator most closely resembles the convertor (Kindlegen) Amazon uses when you upload an HTML document to Kindle. You can then check your book out in Kindle Previewer or Kindle for PC and if all looks good you will feel more confident about uploading your HTML file to Kindle. And you do not have to learn the Mobipocket Creator software beyond a few clicks because you will not be using it to create your book; you only use its most basic functions for testing.

If you wish to go further with technology and create your own mobi files, the free program Calibre does a better job and is easier to use than Mobipocket Creator. And there was only one advantage over Calibre that I could detect: Mobipocket Creator compresses your cover when you add it during conversion; Calibre does not. So when using Calibre you have to first modify your cover to fit within the 127KB limit imposed by Kindle.

Kindle Previewer

Kindle Previewer is another free application provided by Amazon. Kindle Previewer is designed to read PRC, AZW, and mobi files, and it replicates a few different devices in size and layout: the Kindle, the Kindle DX, the iPad and iPhone. You can see how your book will look on these devices and you can test most of your book's functionality (text-to-speech is not a function of Kindle Previewer). Note, however, that the latest version of Kindle Previewer will display your book as it would be on the latest Kindle device and not how it might display on an older Kindle device.

Kindle for PC or Mac

The free computer apps for Kindle are also useful for testing your book. The Kindle for PC/Mac app does have one noticeable quirk, though: because you can resize the screen to a size that is larger than an actual Kindle, and your cover image is resized to fit the screen, the app is not useful for determining how the cover image size will display on an actual ereader. Kindle for PC/Mac will also not give a true indication of how interior images will display on the Kindle: the Kindle for PC/Mac app resizes images to fill the remainder of the screen after whatever text may be on the "page"; as the user increases or decrease the font size the images shrink or expand to fill the space. It's completely unpredictable.

Nook for PC or Mac

Just as Amazon has free apps for computer and mobile devices that allow consumers to read Kindle products without owning a Kindle, Barnes & Noble has free apps for reading Nook products without a Nook. You can use this free app to test your ePubs on the Nook platform.

Sony for PC or Mac

Another free app for computer and mobile devices. You can use this free app to test your ePubs on the Sony eReader platform.

Kobo for PC or Mac

Although Kobo has a free app for computer and mobile devices, if there is a way to add and test your own book I have not figured it out yet. So not useful at all for testing.

Calibre

Calibre is an open-source library program that converts non-digital rights managed books to other formats compatible with other ereaders; for example, a Kindle book can be converted to an ePub to be read on a Sony eReader or a Nook. Over time Calibre has become used for file creation as well. When using it to convert your HTML file to the mobi format, Calibre does a much better job of retaining your paragraph formatting than Mobipocket Creator.

Since Calibre is open-source, programmers are constantly tinkering with it, correcting bugs and quirks at a much faster rate than proprietary software. In one week alone Calibre released five updates. This is both good and bad, since it can mean sudden and unexpected incompatibility issues with other software.

Calibre compresses the text portion of your document better than Mobipocket Creator. *Baby Jane*, for example, was 398KB after conversion through Calibre and 827KB after conversion through Mobipocket Creator. This would result in a $0.06 per unit difference in Amazon's delivery fee. It is also much easier to make your table of contents in Calibre.

Calibre can also convert to the ePub format. However, while Calibre ePubs can be read in most ereaders, for technical reasons Calibre ePubs cannot be distributed. You will need to look elsewhere to create ePubs for distribution.

Sigil

Sigil is a free, open-source WYSIWYG (What You See Is What You Get) HTML editor for creating ePubs. In Sigil, the user can view the text document, the HTML document, or both simultaneously. It has a few functions that I really like such as an automatic table of contents creator based on heading styles, and an "Insert Chapter Break" function that allows the user to import a single long document and break it into the individual sections that ePubs require. However, it is not a convertor per se and it will return errors for many common Word functions such as footnotes; and if your file returns such errors you must be conversant with HTML to fix them. That said, I was contacted by the new lead developer for Sigil and he has adopted my suggestion that a Word-to-HTML import module be a development priority. So keep an eye on Sigil as it soon might be the best option Word users have to create their own ePubs.

Adobe Digital Editions

Adobe Digital Editions (ADE) is a free online tool that allows you to read ePubs on your computer and also to read Digital Rights Managed ePubs from one retailer on a different ereader. ADE is added here because it is useful for testing your ePubs before you upload them to a retailer since ADE has a built-in ereader.

ePubCheck

EPubCheck is a free tool for validating ePubs files. Some companies such as Apple insist ePubs are validated through ePubCheck prior to upload to the site, and wholesale distributors such as Ingram Digital require ePubs be validated and fully functional when uploaded.

EPubCheck is a command-line tool, so unless you are comfortable with this you may wish to have someone else do it for you. The ePubCheck site has detailed instructions if you want to give it a go or, better still, visit Threepress Consulting Inc.'s website where you can upload your ePub for instant validation. If your file fails, a list of errors and warnings are generated that you can use as a guide to fixing the errors. (If you Google the error, you will find various postings where someone has had an identical problem.)

FlightCrew

FlightCrew is a free tool for validating ePub files. It is beyond simple to use and unlike ePubCheck's online validation tool you do not have to be online to use FlightCrew. It is available for both PC and Mac, including 64-bit PC. Anecdotal reports are that it does a better job of validating ePubs than ePubCheck, the assumption being that if your ePub passes FlightCrew it will also pass ePubCheck. FlightCrew might also find problems that ePubCheck misses.

Tweak_epub

Tweak_epub, by Atlantis, is one of my favourite utilities as it allows you to edit the ePub's individual XML, CSS, and HTML files without the need to unpack the ePub. EPub files must be zipped in a specific order, and you cannot use programs like WinRar or 7-Zip to package ePubs without risking errors. By using tweak_epub you avoid this problem. Tweak_epub is a stand-alone utility, run off the executable, meaning there is no need to install it into your programs folder.

HTML Editors

If you are game to learn HTML code, you will have a significant advantage because a lot of the issues that arise with ebook conversion can be fixed by editing the code yourself. You can even create your own ePubs from scratch. Some common editors are Sigil, Adobe Dreamweaver, and the free KompoZer. Windows contains the text editor Notepad, which is all you will really need to fix the code in your Word-to-HTML document; Mac users have TextEdit.

Some authors elect to compose their books in an HTML editor since this affords them the ability to directly edit the HTML that the rest of us rely on our word-processing software to create automatically when we Save as Web Page, Filtered (more on that later). But I think such authors are a rare breed and so this manual assumes most authors are using a word processor.

Learning some basic HTML is not as scary as it first seems, and my initial reluctance to do so was quickly overcome once I got into the habit of cleanly formatting my documents: it is the bloated code of a messy document that overwhelms the uninitiated. As you will discover in this manual, in particular the sections on formatting, learning a wee bit of HTML will save you considerable time and grief. Also, if you later notice a typo in your text you can go into the code and fix it there without having to go through the bother of converting and testing your ebook all over again.

Adobe InDesign and QuarkXPress

InDesign is a desktop publishing (DTP) program used for creating multiple-page documents. Kindle has created a plug-in for InDesign CS4 and CS5, and InDesign has a built-in ePub builder, so in theory you can use one program to create your Kindle mobi file, your ePub file, and the PDF for print. As at time of writing, the Kindle plug-in is only at the beta stage and there are problems, which are discussed in more detail under the relevant formatting sections, and a few issues with its ePub convertor. And InDesign is not free: the full version will run you about U.S. $700.00 unless you are a student, in which case you may qualify for the educational price of U.S. $199.00. Adobe recently introduced a subscription option whereby you pay by the month, currently set at U.S. $35.00 per month; this is useful for the indie author who only needs to use InDesign once or twice a year.

Another popular DTP program is QuarkXPress, which at one point was considered superior to InDesign (when it was formerly known as PageMaker). You can use QuarkXPress for creating print versions of your book, and it has an ePub plug-in. It does not have a Kindle plug-in but Kindle accepts ePubs for submission, which Kindle will then convert. I have not tested QuarkXPress in almost a decade so I cannot comment any further.

Adobe Acrobat Professional

If you intend to publish a print version of your book, most commercial printers today prefer your file be supplied as a PDF. Adobe InDesign has a fully functional PDF export plug-in and creates excellent PDF files.

As noted above, you cannot use the Export to PDF plug-in that comes with many word processors to create commercially compliant print PDFs. This is because software developers like Microsoft only licence a portion of Adobe Acrobat, so when Word creates a PDF it does so with default settings that are not acceptable for commercial printing. Instead you need Adobe Acrobat Professional, which allows you to control all aspects of the PDF file creation—such as image compression, font embedding, print resolution, and color management—and thus to do so according to the requirements of the printer you have contracted with.

The patent on Adobe's PDF technology has expired and thus there are now a plethora of PDF file creation programs on the market and usually at a significantly lower price point than Acrobat Pro. But again, many of the lower priced programs do not contain the full range of options found in Acrobat Pro, and thus many printers will not accept PDFs made using aftermarket software.

Note also that the free Adobe Acrobat Reader does not create PDFs, it only reads them.

Image Editing Software

I personally use Adobe Photoshop to create my book covers but it is undeniably expensive (unless, again, you are a student and qualify for the educational version). Other less expensive but reasonably comprehensive options include Adobe Photo Elements, Corel Paint Shop Photo Pro, and Xara Photo and Graphic Designer. All are under $100.00. If you search for "Image Editing Software" in your browser, any number of compare-and-review sites will come up that can help you choose the right program for your needs and budget.

A free option is the open source GIMP, which is an acronym for GNU Image Manipulation Program. GIMP will do pretty much everything the less expensive image editors will do and is all you will need for a simple cover. GIMP will read the most common image formats as well as Photoshop's PSDs: if you have your cover professionally designed and delivered to you in the layered PSD file, you can open it in GIMP. They have a good website with screenshots, tutorials, user manuals, and FAQs.

GIMP is available for both PC, Mac, Linux, Sun OpenSolaris, and FreeBSD. It is not yet available for 64-bit systems but will load into the 32-bit section of Win 7.

Useful Links

Oracle's OpenOffice site.
http://www.openoffice.org/

Literature and Latte's Scrivener site.
http://www.literatureandlatte.com/scrivener.php

Official Atlantis site.
http://www.atlantiswordprocessor.com/en/

Official download page for 7-Zip.
http://www.7-zip.org/

Tweak_epub by Atlantis. The download is in their Tools sidebar.
http://www.atlantiswordprocessor.com/en/downloads.htm

To download FlightCrew.
http://code.google.com/p/flightcrew/

To download ePubCheck.
http://blog.threepress.org/2010/12/16/running-epubcheck-on-your-computer/

To download Mobipocket Creator.
http://www.mobipocket.com/en/downloadsoft/productdetailscreator.asp

To download Kindle Previewer, Adobe InDesign Kindle plug-in, and (if you must) Kindlegen.
http://www.amazon.com/gp/feature.html?ie=UTF8&docId=1000234621

To download Kindle for PC or Mac.
http://www.amazon.com/gp/help/customer/display.html/ref=sv_kinc_9?ie=UTF8&node Id=200127470/

To download Nook for PC or Mac.
http://www.barnesandnoble.com/u/free-nook-apps/379002321/

To download Sony eReader for PC or Mac.
http://ebookstore.sony.com/download/

To download Calibre.
http://calibre-ebook.com/

To download Adobe Digital Editions.
http://www.adobe.com/products/digitaleditions/

To download GIMP.
http://www.gimp.org/

11/ Manuscript Formatting for eBooks

Ebooks require different formatting than print production because ebooks do not have a fixed right margin, page length, or font size. Instead, the font is scalable—meaning the user can adjust the font size on their device to suit their reading preference (Fig. 15)—and thus there is no fixed placement of text on the screen: the text simply flows through. Due to the fluidity of ebooks, they are not ideal for complex book designs such as those with tables, text boxes, and sidebars.

Also, each device has a different screen size so you cannot design to a specific digital "page," and some devices even allow users to adjust the white margins around the text. Consequently, in ebooks there are no page numbers, though some formats such as the ePub have place markers added to the file so that the book can be quoted and properly referenced as a print book can be. These place markers are added by the conversion software, however, so the author need not worry about adding these to their document.

The ereader market is changing so rapidly that by the time you read this changes may have occurred that either fixed current issues or created new ones. In just the first three months after I published *Baby Jane*, Amazon came out with a new Kindle, Barnes & Noble came out with a color Nook, Kindle Previewer and Kindle for PC were both updated, and Calibre went through at least a dozen upgrades. So it is inevitable that even with this manual you may have to do some experimentation on your own to see what works best for your document.

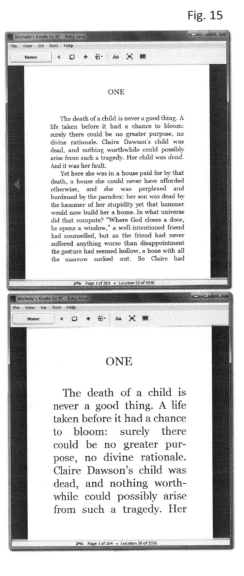

Fig. 15

Where specific instructions are offered here, they refer to Word 2003; and where later versions of Word differ I have mentioned those. If there are further differences in Word for Mac 2011 I have included these as well. Other word processors or book creators like Scrivener have equivalent functions.

As noted in the previous chapter on software, all ebooks are built on HTML; you will find numerous references and explanations to this code in this manual.

I advise that you read this section with your word processor open and try out the formatting instructions as you go along. It is also a good idea to save your manuscript to HTML by using the Save as Web Page, Filtered option in Word, open the document in Notepad, and refer to this Notepad document as you go through this chapter. This way you are not having to learn in the abstract.

Imperial Measurements

In most word processors and desktop publishers you have the option to use metric or imperial measurements. It is best practice to use imperial measurements because digital typography is based on print typography, which uses the point system, which is based on the imperial inch: 72 points = 1 inch. Depending on which software you use to create your book, when you convert to HTML you will find your margins, text indents and paragraph spacing coded either in inches or converted to points. So do not be alarmed if you see your .5" text indent expressed as 36 pt instead.

You also have the option to use either points or inches as your imperial measurement. Either one is acceptable.

Cascading Style Sheets

When a document is converted to HTML, code in the form of what is called "cascading style sheets" (CSS) is created from the styles and formatting options present in your document. For example, if your Normal paragraph is defined as 11 point Georgia regular, no left or right margin indent and no first line indent, and no Before or After spacing, the HTML code for your Normal style will look something like this:

```
/* Style Definitions */
p.MsoNormal, li.MsoNormal, div.MsoNormal
    {margin-top:0in;
    margin-right:0in;
    margin-bottom:0in;
    margin-left:0in;
    font-size:11.0pt;
    font-family:Georgia;}
```

If you use header styles, they too get their own style definitions. Thus if your Heading 1 is comprised of 16 point Georgia bold, centered on the page, with a Before spacing of 12 points and an After spacing of 24 points, the CSS looks like this:

```
h1
    {margin-top:12.0pt;
    margin-right:0in;
    margin-bottom:24.0pt;
    margin-left:0in;
    text-align:center;
    page-break-after:avoid;
    font-size:16.0pt;
    font-family:Georgia;}
```

Each unique paragraph and header style contained within a document gets its own CSS style definition, which is used to control the display of the text on the screen. When you modify text or a paragraph—for example, you highlight a heading and center it, or you italicize a word—the paragraph is still coded with its primary style and then additional code is generated that indicates the changes made. In your word processor (or desktop publisher) you would then see a "+" sign added to the style in use, followed by the modification(s) made. So if, for example, you modified a Normal paragraph to change the After space to 6 points, the paragraph's style would be "Normal + After: 6 pt." If you were then to check the list of formats in use in your document, "Normal" would be listed as a style (in Word this is indicated by the "¶" symbol) and the modification would appear below it as "Normal + After: 6 pt" (and no "¶" symbol). Too see the list of styles in your Word document, click on Format > Styles and Formatting (Mac: Styles submenu), and then hover over a style so that the information box appears. (In Word 2007+: Format > Styles > Description.)

The Normal Paragraph

Kindle will warn you first and foremost not to mess with the Normal paragraph style:

> The "normal" text in a Kindle book must be "all defaults". We encourage content creators to use creative styles for headings, special paragraphs, footnotes, tables of contents and so on but not "normal" text. The reason is that any styling on "normal" text in the HTML would override the user's preferred default reading settings. Users tend to report such behavior as a poor experience. Here are the most important points:

> "Normal" text must not have a forced alignment (left aligned or justified). [Note: in some programs the default alignment is "left." So unless you are going to amend the code, the alignment will be included.] "Normal" text must use the default font family ... "Normal" text must use the default font size ... "Normal" text should not be bold or italicized. Selected parts can of course use such styling. [These] guidelines only [prohibit books] that would be entirely bold for example.

> "Normal" text should not have an imposed font color or background color.[30]

In Word, the default Normal style is defined using the default font and font size, set to "regular"; paragraph alignment set to "left," all indents and Before/After spacing set to "0" and line spacing at "single"; your default dictionary; and widow/orphan control. Of these attributes, it is recommended that you only modify the font and default dictionary of the Normal paragraph.

To modify the Normal paragraph, select Format > Styles and Formatting (Word 2007+ select the Styles submenu; in Mac select Format > Styles). Your list of styles will appear on the right-hand side of your Word screen. Beside "Normal" you will see the ¶ symbol. Click on the symbol and it will turn into an arrow. Click on the arrow.

Fig. 16

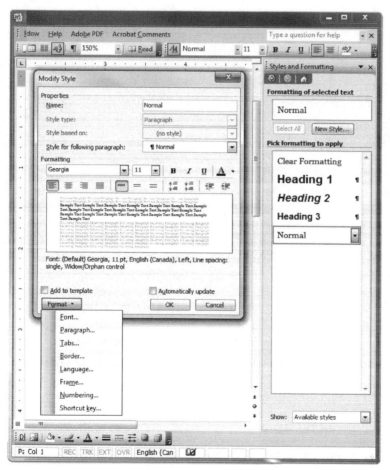

From the drop-down menu that appears select "Modify." (Mac: "Modify" is in the same dialogue box.) In the dialogue box that opens choose your default font and size. Then select Format > Language. In the submenu box that opens choose your language and click "OK." Click "OK" in the main box. You will get a warning message about affecting all future documents made using the Normal template; click "Yes."

Fig. 16 shows the list of styles and the Modify Style dialogue box in Word (the image has been cropped to fit).

In most word processors there are default header styles such as Heading 1, Heading 2, and so on. But if you check out how these styles were created you will see that most start with "Normal +." If you create a new heading style you cannot base it on another heading style; you must base it on Normal.

Styles

The cleanest code is that which has the fewest amendments to the styles in use, so it is best to plan your document around styles as opposed to reformatting the default Normal paragraph text as you go along. For example, this manual uses a style I call "Basic Paragraph." Basic Paragraph is based on Normal but has a justified margin and paragraph spacing of 12 points After. I also have styles for the different headers, the indented quotes, the useful links, and so on. All are based on Normal.

The beauty of styles is that if you later decide to modify your document you merely have to modify the relevant styles rather than having to go through your 300-page novel. For example, if you have a paragraph style that has a first line indent of .5" (a typical novel) and you later think that is too wide, you can change the first line indent in the style to, say, .3" and every paragraph based on that style will be adjusted without affecting other text not based on that style, such as your headers.

To create a new style, open your Styles and Formatting box. Click on "New Style." In the dialogue box that opens, set your basic attributes (and remember it must be based on Normal), then click on the "Format" button at bottom to access further dialogue boxes to modify the style's paragraph attributes and so on. Give the style a name and click "OK." Fig. 17 is the style box and paragraph attributes for my style Basic Paragraph.

Problems arise in many conversions because most authors will build their books using a word processor but word processors make for very messy HTML code. The reason for this is that they keep a memory of every font and formatting option you used even if you later erase all instances of their use from your manuscript. For example, while writing this book I copied off the web a number of links and article titles for my Useful Links sections; and even though I used the "clear formatting" function in Word it did not erase the code, so when converted to HTML the code had numerous font definitions and various paragraph formats that were not in the final manuscript. This hidden font and paragraph formatting code can cause unwanted changes when your text is viewed across a variety of platforms.

Consequently, if you use a word processor and bring in bits and pieces from multiple sources, it is recommended that you delete any styles that were imported when you imported text from other sources, including your other document files. After you clear the format of the imported text, open your Styles and Formatting box. At the bottom you will see "Show" beside a drop-down menu. Select "Formatting in use" and delete the imported style. You also need to select "Available styles" and "Available Formatting" and delete the unwanted style there too if it still appears. Note that when you import text you might end up with seemingly duplicate styles—the imported text might have a different Heading 2 for example—so you need to be careful that you delete the right one. Deleting these extraneous styles and formats increases the chances wayward code will not be created when you convert your document to HTML.

Fig. 17

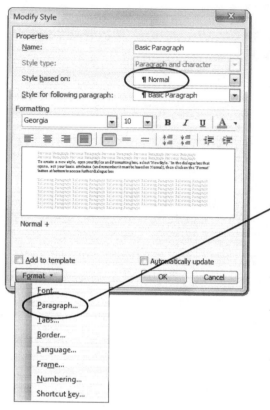

One way to avoid importing unwanted paragraph styles is to import any text first into Notepad and then copy and paste from Notepad into Word. The font style will still be imported (hidden) but the paragraph style will not.

Even if you do not use multiple sources, many word processors have several default styles and these styles may be exported to your HTML document even if do not make use of them.

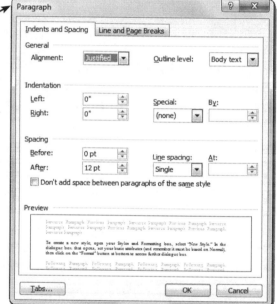

If possible delete from your document any unused styles.

If you later find that you are still experiencing odd formatting issues upon conversion, then you might have to resort to the "nuclear" method, which is to save your entire manuscript as a plain text file, close it down, reopen it again in your word processor, create your styles and paragraph formats, then reformat your entire manuscript.

Before you do anything so drastic, however, first consider trying to amend the HTML code. Now, before you panic let me tell you this is much easier than it sounds. When it was first suggested to me that I learn how to amend HTML code, my instinct was to arm myself with a silver dagger and a garland of garlic. Once I started tinkering, however, I discovered how easy it is to make minor modifications, which is all most authors will need to do. Note that you amend the code only *after* you have finished your manuscript and have saved as Web Page, Filtered.

First save a copy of your file (in case you make a mistake), then save that copy as Web Page, Filtered. Open the resulting HTML document in Notepad (Mac users: TextEdit is your equivalent). Scroll down until you find:

```
/* Style Definitions */
```

Beneath Style Definitions you will see all your various paragraph, header, and table of contents styles, and so on. Each style is easy to identify because its name is flushed left and its attributes are always indented. If you find any wayward styles you merely have to delete them from the HTML. For example, for some inexplicable reason Word puts Heading 6 into my HTML code even though Heading 6 is not used in this document and has been removed from the document's list of styles. In my HTML code, Heading 6 is found bookended by Heading 3 and my level one table of contents:

```
h3
     {margin-top:.25in;
     margin-right:0in;
     margin-bottom:6.0pt;
     margin-left:0in;
     page-break-after:avoid;
     font-size:12.0pt;
     font-family:Georgia;}
h6
     {margin-top:12.0pt;
     margin-right:0in;
     margin-bottom:3.0pt;
     margin-left:0in;
     font-size:11.0pt;
     font-family:Georgia;}
p.MsoToc1, li.MsoToc1, div.MsoToc1
     {margin:0in;
     margin-bottom:.0001pt;
     font-size:10.0pt;
     font-family:Georgia;}
```

Since my document does not use this Heading 6 style, I can delete it then save and close the file:

```
h3
     {margin-top:.25in;
     margin-right:0in;
     margin-bottom:6.0pt;
     margin-left:0in;
     page-break-after:avoid;
     font-size:12.0pt;
     font-family:Georgia;}
```

```
p.MsoToc1, li.MsoToc1, div.MsoToc1
    {margin:0in;
    margin-bottom:.0001pt;
    font-size:10.0pt;
    font-family:Georgia;}
```

You can then convert and test your new document and see if erasing the unwanted styles solved your problem. (Conversion and testing are covered later in this chapter and the next.) If it did not, scroll through your entire Word document first and see if you accidentally applied the wrong style to a heading or paragraph. (Here's a shortcut: use CTRL+ the down arrow to jump from paragraph to paragraph.) If there are no errors, go back into your HTML code and check each paragraph there. At the start of each paragraph, the code indicates what style is applied to the text, using the code "<p class="; Normal, for example, is "<p class=MsoNormal." Check for any unwanted or erroneous styles and if you find an error amend the code to apply the correct style. For example, if I find the Normal style has been applied to a paragraph and it really should be my own style Basic Paragraph, I can simply change the code from

```
<p class=MsoNormal
```

to

```
<p class=BasicParagraph
```

then save and close the file.

Header Styles

As noted, you should use heading styles for your chapter and section titles; however, doing so can cause page breaks before Heading 1 and Heading 2. The reason for this is that some conversion and/or ereader software assumes all uses of Heading 1 and 2, known as "h1" and "h2" in HTML code, are chapter titles and will add a page break before the heading if a page break is not already present.

If you want a page break before your headers then this is fine; but if you do not, you have two options: do not use Heading 1 or 2 for your headers—change to Heading 3 or higher—or perform a simple amendment to the code. If you use this latter option you cannot upload your Word document directly to Kindle; you have to upload the HTML file (which is preferable anyway).

To illustrate how this works, select Format > Paragraph and click on the Lines and Page Breaks tab. There you will see the box "Keep with next." In all of Word's main default heading styles this is checked by default. This prevents an unwanted page break occurring after a header. If you then look at the heading style in HTML, you will notice it contains the value "page-break-after:avoid"; this is how "Keep with next" is translated into code:

```
h1
     {margin-top:.25in;
     margin-right:0in;
     margin-bottom:6.0pt;
     margin-left:0in;
     page-break-after:avoid;
     font-size:15.0pt;
     font-family:Georgia;}
```

In the same Lines and Page Breaks tab, you will see Word offers the option to add a page break before a header. If you check this box, a page break will always occur before the header and you will not have to add a page break manually. If you then look at the code, you will see the value "page-break-before:always;":

```
h1
     {margin-top:.25in;
     margin-right:0in;
     margin-bottom:6.0pt;
     margin-left:0in;
     page-break-before:always;
     page-break-after:avoid;
     font-size:15.0pt;
     font-family:Georgia;}
```

Unfortunately, while Word provides the option to force a page break before a header, Word does not provide the option to avoid one. If you want to avoid a page break before a header, you must add "page-break-before:avoid;" to the header's style in the HTML code:

```
h1
     {margin-top:.25in;
     margin-right:0in;
     margin-bottom:6.0pt;
     margin-left:0in;
     page-break-before:avoid;
     page-break-after:avoid;
     font-size:15.0pt;
     font-family:Georgia;}
```

If you add this code, any ereader's software that by default adds a page break before Heading 1 will not do so; the "page-break-before:avoid" HTML code will override this. You can repeat this for any heading style.

Paragraph Formatting

While paragraph formatting and styles are translated in CSS, carriage returns and tabs are generally not: Kindle will recognize most blank lines (but not all; it's a bit hit and miss) but other devices may not and your desired effect will be lost; and if you convert the same file to an ePub, blank lines created by carriage returns are erased. Thus, do not separate lines of text or paragraphs by inserting blank lines created by carriage returns; instead, use paragraph formatting and input your desired space in the After option. For example, if you want the equivalent of a blank line between paragraphs when using a 12 point font, set the After option to 12 pt. If you want two lines, set it to 24 pt, and so on.

If you want your chapter headings to start part way down your page (to mimic a printed book), use the Before spacing option to add the equivalent of blank carriage returns and the After option to add space between your chapter heading and first line of text.

Line Spacing

Ereaders do not recognize line spacing greater than single even though HTML does. Double line spacing, et cetera, is changed to single when converted to an ebook format.

Paragraph Alignment

Regardless of whether or not you specify justification, Kindle and other ebook readers automatically justify the text unless the user has changed this in their device's preferences. So justifying your paragraphs is not necessary. That said, since the user can alter their preferences to avoid auto-justification, if it is essential to you that your paragraphs be justified I do not feel there is any harm in formatting your paragraphs this way.

Conversely, there may be instances where the auto-justification will look horrible and you will want to override this. This is particularly true of poetry, headers, and lengthy website addresses. My experience is that headers, particularly those that are flushed left (as in this manual), look very unsightly if they are forced justified by the ereader. Lengthy website addresses look even worse. Poetry is destroyed. To avoid this, you have to amend the code because if you leave the style with the default left indentation, Word does not add a text-align value to the code and auto-justification will occur.

For example, in this document I apply a style to my website addresses called "Links 2." Since Links 2 uses the default left indentation, a text-align value is missing from the code:

```
p.Links2, li.Links2, div.Links2
    {margin-top:0in;
    margin-right:0in;
    margin-bottom:12.0pt;
    margin-left:0in;
    font-size:10.0pt;
    font-family:Georgia;}
```

To avoid auto-justification of my website addresses, I need to add a "text-align:left" value to the code after the margin values:

```
p.Links2, li.Links2, div.Links2
    {margin-top:0in;
    margin-right:0in;
    margin-bottom:12.0pt;
    margin-left:0in;
    text-align:left;
    font-size:10.0pt;
    font-family:Georgia;}
```

I can do the same with my heading styles:

```
h1
    {margin-top:0in;
    margin-right:0in;
    margin-bottom:24.0pt;
    margin-left:0in;
    text-align:left;
    page-break-after:avoid;
    font-size:18.0pt;
    font-family:Georgia;}
```

Centered Paragraphs

Fig. 18

If you need to center a lengthy sentence or paragraph, do not use carriage returns to break your text on the line after certain words so that it looks good on the page in your word processor or desktop publisher. If you do this, the text will reflow on the Kindle but the carriage returns will be honoured, and you will end up with a mess (another reason why ebooks are not very good for poetry). For example, in the print version of *Baby Jane*, the copyright information is centered and forced line breaks are used to control how the text looks on the page; the breaks are after "Conventions," "means," and "author." Yet when converted to an ebook and viewed on the Kindle at a larger

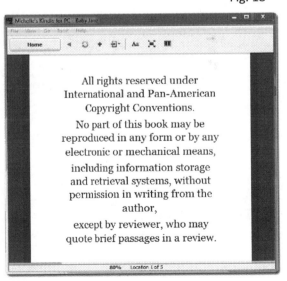

font (Fig. 18), you can see how the lines break wherever necessary to fit the text on the screen but then also break wherever I had put in a forced line break, which you want to avoid.

Hanging Paragraphs

Ebooks cannot read hanging paragraphs. This is because hanging paragraphs make use of hidden negative indents, which HTML will register but which are lost upon conversion. For example, if you format a paragraph to have a hanging indent of .25", behind the scenes your word processor has actually created a left margin indent of .25" and a text indent of minus .25". So the code looks like this:

```
<p class=MsoNormal style='margin-left:.25in;text-indent:-.25in'>
```

When the HTML is converted to the ebook format the negative text indents are removed and you end up with a paragraph the whole of which will be indented at .25".

(By using Calibre I have actually managed to create a true hanging paragraph in a mobi file that displays properly on the Kindle and other devices, but this true hanging indent is only possible if there is not a left margin indent.)

Tabs and Right Margins

Do not use tabs anywhere in your document. Tabs do not translate into HTML. Use Paragraph Formatting to indent your lines or paragraphs. Do not indent your right margin as right margins are not recognized due to the resizable text option in ebooks.

Kindle's Auto-Indent

If you send your Word document or unadjusted HTML file to Kindle, Kindlegen has an irritating default whereby it will automatically indent the first line of every new paragraph if no first line indent is defined by the author (Fig. 19). This is a pain if you wish to have paragraphs flushed left with no first line indent (like this document), especially for section headers. The reason for the automatic first line indent is simple: if your paragraph style does not contain a first line text indent then no code exists in your HTML to indicate this; the Kindle converter then adds one, and it adds a value that, as far as I can tell, is approximately .39" (38 pixels/28 points/1 cm).

For those who wish to work solely with a word processor, your options are either a tedious workaround or a simple fix. Obviously the latter is preferable yet for the longest time the tedious workaround has been touted as a solution, mainly because Kindle accepts Word documents for upload and the workaround means one does not have to mess about with HTML. However, once the two options are explained you will see the benefit of amending the code.

Before I explain the solution, let me first explain what Kindlegen (the Kindle converter) does. In a nutshell, when converting your Word document or your Word-to-HTML file, Kindlegen respects a first line indent set by the author *only* if the indent is greater than zero; this is because, as noted, a text-indent value of zero results in the absence of a text-indent element

Fig. 19

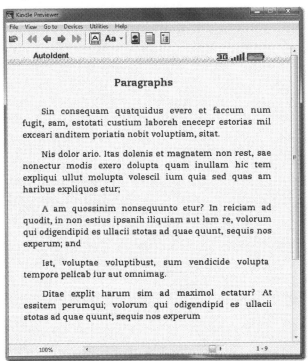

in the HTML. However, if you set your paragraph first line indent at, say, .5", it will appear so in your Kindle book because now there is a text-indent element in your HTML that says either "text-indent:.5" or "text-indent:36pt." The remainder of the paragraph then flushes left as one would expect.

The workaround for those wishing to have block paragraphs is thus to cheat the Kindle by inputting .01" as your *first line* indent: Format > Paragraph > Special > First line (Word 2007+: Paragraph submenu). You thus end up with code that says "Text-indent:.7pt" (.7pt is the equivalent to .01". You can elect to work in points instead, as noted earlier in the manual). The .01" indent on your first line is so miniscule it isn't noticeable and the paragraph appears flushed left.

On its website, Kindle offers a way to amend the HTML code so that the above workaround is not required. Amazon states: "The first line of each paragraph indents by default. You can change the indentation of the first line of a paragraph using the text-indent style on the 'p' tag. For example: o p style='text-indent:0' - no indentation of the first line."[31] However, this is tedious because it means you have to amend each paragraph in your file, and it assumes you did not use styles when formatting. A much simpler way is to add the missing HTML code to your paragraph style.

After you save your file as HTML, open the HTML in Notepad (or an HTML editor). Since you will have followed this manual and used styles, you merely have to amend the Normal paragraph style definition (or whichever main paragraph style you are using in your document) to include "text-indent: 0in;" so that

```
/* Style Definitions */
p.MsoNormal, li.MsoNormal, div.MsoNormal
    {margin-top:0in;
    margin-right:0in;
    margin-bottom:0in;
    margin-left:0in;
    font-size:11.0pt;
    font-family:Georgia;}
```

now reads

```
/* Style Definitions */
 p.MsoNormal, li.MsoNormal, div.MsoNormal
    {margin-top:0in;
    margin-right:0in;
    margin-bottom:0in;
    margin-left:0in;
    text-indent:0in;
    font-size:11.0pt;
    font-family:Georgia;}
```

and then save and close the file. (Note: the font size and family will reflect the font you have used, not necessarily 11 point Georgia.) Fig. 20 illustrates the results of adding this bit of code.

Fig. 20

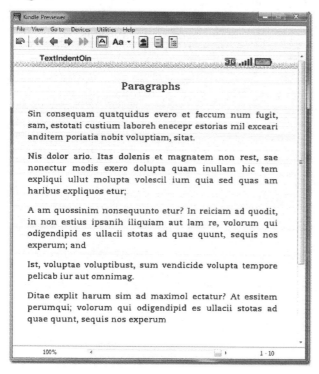

Paragraph Indents

Paragraph indents are problematic on the Kindle because the mobi format, as one kind techie put it to me, "doesn't have very robust margin support." Which is another way of saying the Kindle reader fakes paragraph margins, and how it fakes them is dependent on the way the different convertors code the indent.

To put it simply, indented paragraphs are cheated by one of two ways: the first codes in a hard space (a margin of sorts) that is not collapsible, meaning it has a set value and that is it, you cannot make it smaller or larger; this is the method used by Kindlegen and utilities such as the Kindle plug-in for InDesign. The second method uses a code called a blockquote, which also has a set value that is not adjustable; this is how Calibre does it. There is no real difference between the two systems from the perspective of the user; what is important is that Calibre has multiple blockquotes, meaning you can have more than one level of indent, but Kindlegen has only one hard space. Fig. 21 illustrates how Kindlegen indents all paragraphs exactly the same regardless of whether you set them at .2" or .35" or .5" and so on because there is only the one hard space; Fig. 22 illustrates the multiple blockquotes offered by Calibre.

My experiments suggest that Calibre creates multiple-level indents at values of multiples of 12 points: 12 pt (.2"), 24 pt (.35"), 36 pt (.5"), and so on. When I set a value in between these, for example at 30 pt, Calibre set the margin indent at 24 pt. My tests also show that Calibre does not have a limit on the number of indents or the degree of indentation: I tested a document with eight levels at 12, 24, 36, 48, 60, 72, 84, and 96 point intervals and all displayed correctly on the Kindle for PC. On the Kindle Previewer, however, at 96 points the paragraph indents began displaying incorrectly. I would therefore limit your indents to 84 points.

What this means for you, the author, is that you cannot use only Word to create your ebook if you need multiple level indents. Instead, after saving as Web Page, Filtered, you will need to convert the HTML to a Kindle (mobi) file using a program like Calibre or InDesign, or hire someone to do it for you.

Page Layout

When converted to HTML, a document's page margins are ignored, headers and footers are erased, and any text divided into columns is recombined into one column. Text frames, regardless of where they are placed on the page, are moved to the left margin and the text is flowed around it.

While tables are supported by HTML, they are not supported by many ereaders. If you need to insert a table

Fig. 21

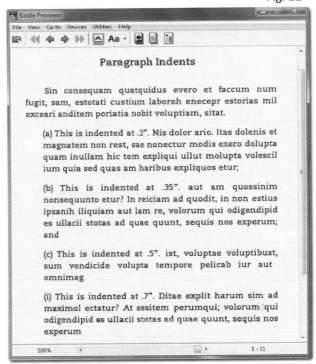

Fig. 22

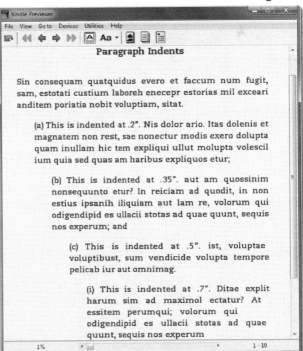

you should first convert it to an image file at a size that renders the lowercase "a" no smaller than 6 pixels in height (see "Adding Images to Your Document" later in this chapter).

Use page breaks, not carriage returns, to force text to start on a new page. If you do not use page breaks your pages will run one into the other. To insert a page break, click Insert > Break > Page break (Word 2007+: Insert tab > Pages > Page Break). The exception to this is if you added an automatic "Page break before" to your heading style. In fact, you can format any individual paragraph to add a page break before it, which works better and is more stable than a page break marker. (Format > Paragraph > Lines and Page Breaks > check "Page break before.")

When viewed in HTML there are no obvious page breaks; however, if you left space above and below your chapter headings using paragraph formatting you will see some white space. But when viewed on an ereader the page breaks will be there.

Miscellaneous Text Formatting

Clean out spaces before carriage returns. Since a space is required between a period and the start of the next sentence, many of us, myself included, have a habit of adding in that space when we come to the end of a paragraph and before we hit "Enter." These spaces are read as characters of text and so they can cause odd text alignment. You can check for unnecessary spaces by clicking on the Show/Hide icon (¶) on your toolbar to view hidden characters, then delete these redundant spaces.

Do not use character spacing, for example to increase the distance between points of an ellipsis ("..."). As noted earlier, horizontal spacing is erased when converted to HTML. Word's Autocorrect automatically increases the spaces between the dots of an ellipsis but this will not translate into HTML. If you use an ellipsis, do not put spaces between the points (". . .") as one would in a print manuscript because each point will be read as an independent character and so your ellipsis might end up divided between lines of text. To use ellipses, I elect to format the text using a space between the text and the ellipsis, then no spaces between the points of the ellipsis, then if text resumes another space between the ellipsis and the text ("text ... text").

If using an en dash ("–") or em dash ("—"), do not leave a space between the preceding text and the dash, or after it. Doing so can create odd text alignment. (So "text—text" not "text — text.")

Bullets and Lists

If using bullets or lists, do not use tabs and do not use symbols that are not recognizable. If using Word it is not recommended that you use Word's bullet tool because some options make use of tabs and Wingdings. It is better to format your own bulleted lists using paragraph formatting and something simple like an asterisk for the bullet.

Internal Hyperlinks

You can create internal hyperlinks in an ebook that allow the user to jump to a graphic or to a place in the text and then return to their previous place using their device's back button.

If you are linking to a header in your document, first select the text you wish to turn into a hyperlink. Select Insert > Hyperlink. In the box that appears, on the left-hand side, choose "Place in This Document." In the window you will see "Top of the Document" followed by "Headings." Select the relevant header. Click "OK" (Fig. 23).

If you are linking to a graphic or to text that is not a header, you must first create a bookmark to be hyperlinked to. To insert a bookmark, place your cursor at the *beginning* of the text you wish to link to, or click on the image you wish to link to, then select Insert > Bookmark.

Fig. 23

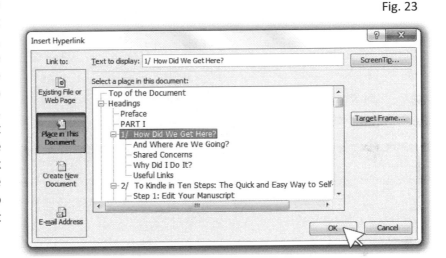

In the box that appears, type in a name for the bookmark. (There are three default bookmarks to choose from, OLE_LINK1 through 3; delete these.) Note that spaces and punctuation marks of any kind cannot be used and each bookmark must have a unique name.

To link to the bookmark, select Insert > Hyperlink. In the box that appears, on the left-hand side, choose "Place in This Document." Scroll down to the bottom where you will find your list of bookmarks. Select the relevant bookmark. Click "OK" (Fig. 24).

An Annoying Quirk in Word

If you insert a page break before a header and then later create a hyperlink to that header, when you test the link you will discover an annoying quirk in Word: it applies the heading style to the page break and then links to the page break line instead of to the header. This means that when you click on the link you are taken to the end of the page that precedes your header.

Luckily, there is a way around this. Rather than manually inserting a page break before each chapter heading, you can modify the style to automatically insert a page break as illustrated earlier in the section "Header Styles." Your hyperlink will then go to the header text as required.

Fig. 24

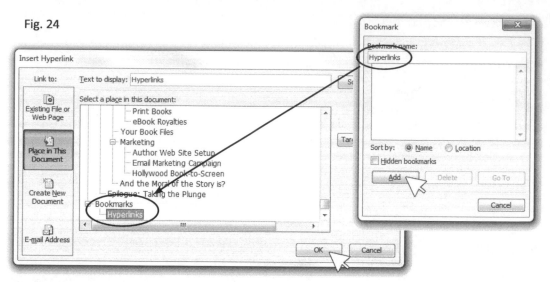

Footnotes

When converted to HTML, footnotes' hyperlinks are maintained but the target bookmarks (the footnotes) are moved to the end of the document into one page of endnotes. When the user wishes to read a footnote they click on the hyperlink and are taken to the endnote in the document; to return to their place in the text they merely have to click the back button on their device or click on the footnote number.

Most word processors have a function whereby you can start each section's footnotes at "1," so you can have footnote 1 in chapter 1 and footnote 1 in chapter 2. But when you convert to HTML, this sectioning will be ignored and footnotes will be renumbered into one sequential list based on order of appearance in the manuscript. So if, for example, you have eight footnotes in chapter 1, footnote 1 in chapter 2 will be renumbered "9."

If you have a plethora of footnotes—for example, in a heavily referenced academic text— where the volume can result in footnotes numbered in the four or five digits (which can look odd), you can elect to manually create chapter endnotes. To do so you must *not* use Word's automatic Insert > Footnote function. Instead, you must manually mark each footnote by typing in its number and formatting the number to superscript: Format > Font > check "Superscript." Then at the end of your chapter type in your footnotes. Once this is done you bookmark each footnote for hyperlinking as outlined in the previous section: place your cursor at the start of the footnote, then Insert > Bookmark. In the box that appears, type in a name for the bookmark. So for footnote 1 of Chapter One, your bookmark might be C1F1; for footnote 1 of Chapter Two, C2F1.

Once you have bookmarked all your footnotes, you then manually create the hyperlinks. Go to your place in the text, highlight the superscripted number, then Insert > Hyperlink. In the box that appears, on the left-hand side, choose "Place in This Document." Select the bookmark name that corresponds to the footnote; click "OK." Repeat until all notes are done.

This manual method is, as you can see, tedious, and in a voluminous work it can be very difficult to keep proper track of your footnotes while you edit. I, personally, do not see the benefit of having chapter-specific endnotes in an ebook since the reader merely has to click on a hyperlink to read the footnote and then click to return to their place in the text: there is no tedious scrolling required. So you will have to weigh the benefits of convenience over the aesthetics of large-numbered footnotes.

Fonts

Digital devices (and websites) have a limited number of fonts they can properly display, so if your book contains a font that the device cannot display, the font will be displayed as the next closest font the device has or as its default font; and in some cases the text will simply disappear off the digital page. To be safe, then, you need to use only the few fonts that have the four basic font styles in their family, are known as "websafe," and do not make use of unrecognized text effects.

Font Styles

A font is actually made up of a number of separate font styles that make up a font family. Font styles include the four basics—Regular, Bold, Italic, Bold Italic—and can also include styles such as Black, Light, Semibold, Slanted, Condensed, Medium, Narrow, and Demibold. Thus, if you are using Georgia as your font and you italicize selected text, the Georgia Regular font is actually replaced by its sibling Georgia Italic; if you bold the text, it is replaced by Georgia Bold; and if you bold and italicize the text, it is replaced by Georgia Bold Italic. When you then export your text to HTML the font family is exported; when you export to a PDF for print, your font is not exported as a single font family but as its separate font styles.

Digital devices can read Regular, Bold, Italic, and Bold Italic font styles, but they cannot read Black, Light, Semibold, Slanted, Condensed, Medium, Narrow, and Demibold. Thus if you use Arial Black as your header, it will be converted to Arial Regular and the bolded look of your header will be lost. You must instead use Arial and bold it (the Arial family contains Arial Bold).

Many fonts do not contain all four basic styles, and if they do not your word processor fakes the missing style. So if, for example, your font does not have italic, the word processor uses an algorithm to slant the text. In this case the text is not a true italic font but is an italic "text effect."

Text Effects

Digital devices in general will recognize italics, bold, underline, superscript, subscript, and strike-through text effects. All other text effects cannot be read and will be converted to regular text. This includes double strike-through, shadow, outline, emboss, engrave, small caps, all caps, and hidden, and also horizontal scaling, raised and lowered text, text in different colors, and kerning. Moreover, even recognizable text effects can be easily misread by a device, and in some cases they will not display properly at all, and thus it is recommended that you use a font family that contains all four basic styles. To find out if a font family contains the four styles, open up the font folder in your operating system and see what font styles are listed. In Windows this is C:\Windows\Fonts. (On a Mac it is Macintosh HD > System > Library > Fonts, but unfortunately it does not list the individual font styles, only the font family.)

Open Type and Websafe Fonts

Digital devices are also limited in the types of fonts they can read. Most will read True Type Fonts but some devices will only read Open Type fonts. Open Type fonts are the next generation in font development, and are paving the way for better digital rendition of non-Latin alphabets such as Chinese, Hebrew, and Arabic. Since Open Type is the way forward it is of benefit to use these fonts. You can tell if a font is True Type or Open Type by going into your font folder in your operating system as specified earlier.

A small number of fonts have become adopted across the industry for web and other digital display, and have thus become known as "websafe." These websafe fonts are Arial, Courier New, Georgia, Tahoma, Times New Roman, Trebuchet MS, and Verdana. There are four more fonts considered websafe—Arial Black, Comic Sans MS, Impact, and Webdings—but ereaders have not yet developed capability for Webdings; Arial Black is, as noted earlier, not usable; Comic Sans only has Regular and Bold font styles in its family; and Impact only has Regular. Thus none of these four are recommended for use in an ebook.

Symbols and Subsets

You can use symbols as long as they belong to the same websafe font families and are a recognized subset. It is not always possible to know which font subsets will be recognized, so if a symbol is uncommon it is best avoided. Do not use Wingdings as they cannot be read.

What is a font subset? In Word, if you click Insert > Symbol, in the box that appears you will see on the left a field naming the font and on the right a field titled "Subset." Most of the common fonts—such as Times New Roman, for example—have the subsets Basic Latin, Latin-1, Latin Extended-A, Latin Extended-B, IPA Extensions, and so on. Basic Latin, Latin-1, and General Punctuation will generally be recognized by ereaders but not the other subsets; test first before using. If you are writing in a language that does not use the Latin alphabet, you will definitely need to do tests first.

eReader Default Fonts

That all said, even if you select the Open Type version of one of the seven recommended websafe fonts, or a recognized font subset, this does not mean every ereader will display them.

This is because some ereaders are programmed to ignore font definitions and instead apply their own default font; the Kindle does this and displays all text as a Monotype font (and a rather hideous one, in my opinion) called Caecilia. Other devices allow the user to choose from among a limited selection of fonts, and their selection overrides the embedded font definition. So while the text effects will be respected—your italics will still display, for example—the font family will not be. Consequently, many authors elect not to include font definitions in their books at all. Either way, when you test your book do not be alarmed when the ereader does not display your font style, but do change any symbols that cease to display properly to ones that will.

Fig. 25

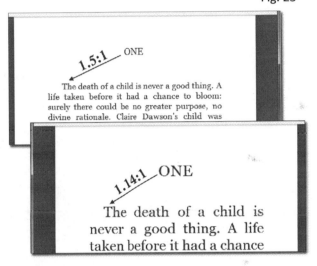

Digital devices in general do not display fonts larger than 18 points or smaller than 10 points; if you use a font size outside that range it will be mapped to the nearest size available. Since ereaders have scalable fonts, the device does not really conform to the font size you set; rather, your fonts are scaled in relation to each other. For example, if you use 12 pt for your body text and 16 pt for your chapter heading, the ereader merely maintains the 12:16 ratio as best it can within the limitations of the device. As the user increases the font size on their ereader, once the largest font available is reached, the ratio begins to break down. Fig. 25 illustrates how the relation between the header and body text size changes as the font size is increased on the ereader: the ratio of header to body text on the left screen is 1.5:1; on the right screen it has dropped down to 1.14:1. At the largest size available the ratio will drop to 1:1.

Font Definitions

If you bring in text from a multiple of sources, the font definition of the imported text will remain in your document's code even if you remove the font from your document, import via Notepad, or use the Clear Formatting function. These font definitions should be deleted from your HTML code prior to uploading to Kindle. This document, for example, due to all the links and titles imported off the Internet, contained over 150 hidden font definitions that needed to be deleted from the HTML.

To erase unwanted font definitions, open your HTML file in Notepad. Near the top of the code you will find the font definition header:

```
/* Font Definitions */
```

159

This will be followed by each font family that was used at some point in your document. For example, these are the font definitions for Helvetica, Courier, and Times New Roman:

```
@font-face
    {font-family:Helvetica;
    panose-1:2 11 6 4 2 2 2 2 2 4;}
@font-face
    {font-family:Courier;
    panose-1:2 7 4 9 2 2 5 2 4 4;}
@font-face
    {font-family:»Tms Rmn»;
    panose-1:2 2 6 3 4 5 5 2 3 4;}
```

Simply delete all font definitions no longer used in your document, and the font definitions will be gone with no harm done. If you use only Times New Roman, for example, delete everything except:

```
/* Font Definitions */
    @font-face
        {font-family:»Tms Rmn»;
        panose-1:2 2 6 3 4 5 5 2 3 4;}
```

Adding Images to Your Document

You can place images—including your cover—directly into your Word document if they are in any of the following formats: Graphics Interchange Format (GIF), Portable Network Graphics (PNG), Bitmap (BMP), and JPEG. As noted previously, PNGs and Bitmaps are converted by Kindle into JPEGS and GIFs, respectively, since the device can only recognize internally these two formats. If you have PNGs or Bitmaps I would suggest converting them yourself rather than risk Kindle's conversion: there are fewer surprises that way.

Before inserting an image into your document, however, you need to ensure the image is of sufficient size and the appropriate resolution. See Chapter 9: Cover and Interior Images.

Also set your page view to Print Layout. If you have your view set to Normal, when importing images sometimes they will import at full size instead of conforming to your margins, which you will likely need them to as will be illustrated shortly.

To insert an image into the body of your text, place your cursor at the point in the page where you want your image to sit, and, if you want the image centered, set your paragraph formatting to centered. In Word you then select Insert > Picture > From File. Navigate to the folder where your image is stored and select it. Click "Insert."

Once it is imported, click on the picture and select Format > Picture. Click on the Layout tab and select "In Line With Text." (In Word 2007+, when you click on an image the Format toolbar comes up automatically. In the Arrange menu, click on Text Wrapping > In line with text. Mac users: When you click on an image the Format toolbar comes up automatically. In the Arrange menu, click on Wrap Text > In line with text.)

That said, you can use text wrap, but remember that while text is resizable images are not so you will get strange text flow not only from device to device but also depending on the font size the user selects. If your images are small, you might wish to risk text wrap in order to obtain a certain page look when viewed at a small font size, but understand the results will be unpredictable and are ill-advised.

Thus, if your image is connected intrinsically to your text—for example, if it is a graph or image that explains the preceding text—the best way to insert it is to center it using paragraph formatting and use the aforementioned "in line with text," then begin your next paragraph after the image.

If you are creating a children's picture book, the best way to do so, in my opinion, is to create images that include the text as part of the image. Make the text large enough to read when the page is viewed on a Kindle. Images with an aspect ratio of 9:11 display at maximum screen coverage on the Kindle.

This concept also applies to comic books. One of the stumbling blocks with comic ebooks thus far has been that, when the page is shrunk down to fit a Kindle, the dialogue becomes illegible. Comic ebooks are thus best viewed on larger devices like the Kindle DX or the iPad. One other option is to divide the traditional comic book page into its frames and set those in your document as individual images.

Bear in mind, too, that such image heavy ebooks may exceed the file size limit of the retailer, or will increase your delivery costs where applicable, so you need to take that into consideration when contemplating the feasibility of comic or picture ebooks.

Importing Your Cover Into Word

To insert a cover image, place your cursor at the top of your document and set your paragraph formatting to centered. Import your image as per the previous instructions on importing images. You then need to add a page break after the image so that it remains at all times a separate page.

If you intend to build a mobi file instead of uploading your Word document or HTML file to Kindle, then do not embed your cover image. This will be added at the build stage (see Chapter 13: Building a Mobi File).

How Images Are Exported From Word

When you place an image in Word, if your image is larger than will fit on your document page Word will automatically shrink the picture to fit the page. For example, if your page is set to letter size (8.5" x 11") and your margins are set to .5" all around, your document working area is 7.5" x 10". You may recall that Word displays at 96 ppi, so if the imported image is larger than 960 pixels high (10" x 96 ppi) or 720 pixels wide (7.5" x 96 ppi), Word proportionally resizes it to fit the 7.5" x 10" working space. Thus if you click on the picture and select Format > Picture > Size (Word 2007+: Size submenu on the Format toolbar) you will see that the image is not scaled at 100% but some fraction thereof. The importance of this is that when you export to HTML the size of the picture is exported at the pixel equivalent of the displayed size in Word at 96 ppi, not the original image size. For example, if you import an image that is 1000 pixels high, Word will shrink it to fit within the 10" working space then export it at 960 pixels high (10" x 96 ppi).

So what can you do if you want, for example, to maximize your image for the iPad, which has a display size of 768 x 1024? You do so by formatting the picture so it displays at 1" for every 96 pixels you want. To do so, click on the image, then select Format > Picture > Size and adjust your height and/or width. For a final image of 1024 pixels high, set the image height to approximately 10.66" (1024/96). If you have a horizontal image and want it to export at the maximum 768 pixels, set your width to 8" (768/96). Do not worry if the image disappears off the edge of the document page: when exported to HTML the image will appear in its entirety.

A word of warning: as indicated in Chapter 9: Cover and Interior Images, images must be compressed to within 127KB to fit the Kindle. Images that are shrunk to fit the page in Word are compressed when exported to HTML, but images exported at 100% are not. You have to take this into consideration when using images that fit on your document page.

Word for Mac

For Mac users, the same principles apply but the math is based on 72 ppi instead of 96. So a 10" high image in Word will export at 720 pixels. You have the option to change picture display to 96 ppi but this does not affect export when saving to HTML.

Mac users will discover, however, two irritating quirks. The first is that the Mac exports all images in Word as both the original image as well as the resized image as a PNG; you thus get two images but only the PNG is linked to the HTML. This creates two problems: the first is that Kindle will convert the PNG to a JPEG upon converting your HTML, which may be fine but, as noted in the chapter on imaging, may also result in some unwanted image degradation. And you cannot merely change the code to link to the original images because they will not be compressed as you need them to be to meet the 127KB limit of the Kindle. You must either hope the conversion back to JPEG goes well or you must create JPEGs that fit within the 127KB limit, replace the images in the HTML image folder with the new JPEGs, and amend the HTML code to point to the JPEGs instead of the PNGs. This is not as difficult as it sounds, but if you have a lot of images it will be tedious.

The second problem is that you should remove these original images from the adjunct image folder (more on that in a minute) before sending your HTML files off to Kindle.

By the way, if you uncheck "Enable PNG as an output format" under Web Options > Pictures in the hope of avoiding this issue, alas it only gets worse: Mac then turns your JPEGs into GIFs!

Other Word Processors

Users of alternative word processors will have to do their own experiments to see how individual programs export images upon conversion to HTML. But if you are using Scrivener or Atlantis you can use the export to mobi and/or ePub options instead, since Kindle will also accept ePubs for conversion, and the ePub is required for Barnes & Noble, Kobo, and Apple, et cetera.

The Advantage of Using 96 ppi

As noted, Word for PC exports all images at 96 ppi regardless of their native resolution. This means that an image saved at 72 ppi is reconfigured at 96 ppi when exported. If your image is larger than 960 pixels high and you display it to fit on your 10" page, then you will not notice any change. But if your image is set to display at a size that when multiplied by 96 ppi yields a greater pixel volume than your image currently contains, Word upsamples your image. This means you will end up with a *larger* image file than what you started with, and likely a degraded one.

For example, if I embed an image that is 768 x 1024 pixels, 72 ppi and set the image to display at 100%, the image's document size is approximately 10.6"x 14.15". When that image is exported into HTML, Word upsamples the image to 96 ppi and exports the image at 1018 x 1359 pixels (14.15" x 96 ppi = 1359), an increase of about 33%. Thus the HTML-compressed image file size (of the image I tested) went from 105KB to 175KB, in excess of Kindle's 127KB limit.

Conversely, if you embed into your Word document an image of a resolution higher than 96 ppi, Word maintains the higher pixel resolution when displaying the image BUT when converting to HTML the conversion engine in Word downsamples your image to 96 ppi. So it will look alright when viewed in Word but the exported image will be considerably *smaller* than you anticipated. For example, if you import the 768 x 1024 pixel image saved at 150 ppi into a Word document, the image will display at approximately 5.12" x 6.83" (1024/150 = 6.83"); but when you export it to HTML, Word will downsample the 150 ppi to 96 ppi and the result will be an image 492 x 656 pixels, or about 1/3 your original image size! (150/96 = 1.56; 1024/1.56 = 656.)

(Mac users: because your Word exports at 72 ppi, it is more advantageous for you to use images saved at 72 ppi since this will yield the most consistent results, and you can ignore this subsection.)

You may thus find it easier to maintain control and consistency of results if you use images saved at 96 ppi when embedding them directly into Word. Fig. 26 below summarizes the results of exporting the 768 x 1024 pixel image.

Fig. 26

Image Size	Resolution	Document size fit into Word page (7.5"x 10")	Exported Image Size	Document Size in Word at 100%	Exported Image Size
768 x 1024	72	7.5" x 10" (70%)	720 x 960	10.6" x 14.15"	1018 x 1359
768 x 1024	96	7.5" x 10" (94%)	720 x 960	7.97" x 10.63"	768 x 1024
768 x 1024	150	5.12" x 6.83" (100%)	492 x 656	5.12" x 6.83"	492 x 656

Creating a Table of Contents

You can create a table of contents in one of two ways: by manually inserting TOC markers or by using Word's built-in TOC creator using styles. Regardless of whether you use styles or manual insertion to determine your TOC entries, you do not use page numbers; you use hyperlinks.

Styles Method

If you have followed the advice of this manual and used heading styles, to create your table of contents you first type in its title at the top of your TOC page ("Table of Contents" or "Contents"—whatever is appropriate). Then on the next line select Insert > Reference > Index and Tables (Word 2007+: References > Table of Contents > Insert Table of Contents).

In the Index and Tables dialogue box, click on the "Table of Contents" tab. Uncheck boxes "Show page numbers" and "Right align page numbers." Check "Use hyperlinks instead of page numbers" if it is not already checked.

If you want your TOC to have multiple levels, meaning subsections are indented from the parent chapter heading (as in this manual's TOC), use the "Show levels" option to decrease or increase the levels you want included. Word will automatically assign a level to match the heading number—Heading 1 will be assigned Level 1, Heading 2 will be assigned Level 2, and so on—and Word will automatically apply an indent to each level, indenting further as the levels descend: Level 1 will be flushed left, Level 2 will be indented .17", Level 3 will be indented .3", and so on. If you are not using Heading 1 or 2 so as to avoid inadvertent page breaks, or you want certain levels to be indented the same amount, you can modify these defaults by clicking on the "Options" and "Modify" buttons in the TOC dialogue box.

Under "Options" you need to check the "Styles" box and uncheck "Outline levels" and "Table entry fields." Click "OK." The table of contents will now be automatically created. Fig. 27 illustrates the settings for an indented table of contents created using styles.

Fig. 27

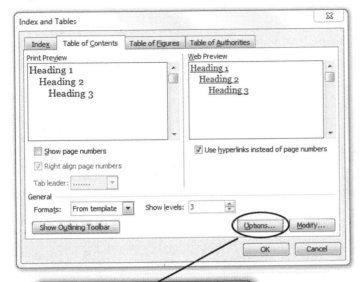

Note, however, that the same problem with indents in your paragraphs reappears in your TOC: Kindle does not go any further than an indent of about 28 points, so your Level 3 entries appear flush with Level 2 entries. Once again, if you have more complex formatting, you will need to consider an alternative to using Word-to-HTML.

Manual Method

If you did not use styles you can use a manual method to create a table of contents. There is one small advantage to doing so: it affords you the option to use different formatting or even different words altogether in your TOC than in the body of your document. For example, the chapter headings in *Baby Jane* were spelled out in all caps but when listed in a table of contents it appeared as if the TOC were being yelled at the reader (ONE, TWO, THREE, ...) and yet at the same time the TOC did not specify "chapter." So I elected to insert my table of contents manually, which allowed me to have a TOC entry that read "Chapter 1" even though the actual chapter heading is "ONE."

This method is also useful for creating a TOC entry for pages where you do not want an actual header, for example your copyright page, because the manual method uses hidden markers. For *Baby Jane* I simply placed a TOC entry called "Copyright Information" flushed left at the top of the copyright page. I also had entries for "Acknowledgements" and "About the Author."

To add these hidden markers, place your cursor at the *beginning* of your heading, then press Alt+Shift+O. (Note: if you have space before your chapter heading so that it starts below your top page margin, then if you wish to preserve this look in your Kindle book you need to place the marker at the top of your page and flushed left, not before the chapter heading. This is because when you use the Go to function, it hyperlinks to the hidden marker and places it at the top of the screen. Similarly, you must not place the marker within or after your heading text as any text placed before the marker will then "disappear" off the page.)

In the Mark Table of Contents Entry dialogue box that pops up, type into the "Entry" table the name of your chapter. This is the name that will appear when you auto-create your TOC, and as noted it does not have to match exactly your actual chapter heading.

The default "Table identifier" is "C"; leave all entries at the same letter identifier. However, if you have a subchapter heading you can use the Level to indent subchapter headings: Level 1 is flushed left, Level 2 is indented below Level 1; and Level 3 is indented below Level 2, and so on. Click on "Mark" (Fig. 28).

Fig. 28

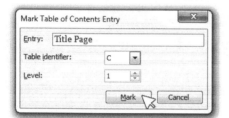

Once you have everything marked you can now create a table of contents. You do this as you would for the styles method except that under Options you uncheck the "Styles" box and check "Outline levels" and "Table entry fields." Click "OK." The table of contents will now be automatically created.

Note that the manual method does not work with Mobipocket Creator.

Styles Method + HTML

You can have the best of both worlds by using the styles method then modifying the HTML after you have finished your document and saved it to HTML (which is discussed in detail later in the next chapter). This way you do not have to put a header called "Title Page" at the top of your title page, or "Copyright Information" on your copyright page, and so on. Instead you format your first line using a header style then modify the text in HTML.

For example, using heading styles, the first entries in my table of contents are "BABY JANE" (the first line of my title page), "Copyright © 2011 Michelle A. Demers" (copyright page), "With thanks to" (acknowledgements page), and "ONE" (chapter one). This is not what I want, so I can amend the text in HTML. I can also remove or modify any level indents in my TOC.

First I open my HTML document in Notepad. I scroll down until I find my TOC style definitions:

```
p.MsoToc1, li.MsoToc1, div.MsoToc1
    {margin:0in;
    margin-bottom:.0001pt;
    font-size:12.0pt;
    font-family:"Times New Roman";}
```

```
p.MsoToc2, li.MsoToc2, div.MsoToc2
    {margin-top:0in;
    margin-right:0in;
    margin-bottom:0in;
    margin-left:12.0pt;
    margin-bottom:.0001pt;
    font-size:12.0pt;
    font-family:"Times New Roman";}

p.MsoToc3, li.MsoToc3, div.MsoToc3
    {margin-top:0in;
    margin-right:0in;
    margin-bottom:0in;
    margin-left:24.0pt;
    margin-bottom:.0001pt;
    font-size:12.0pt;
    font-family:"Times New Roman";}
```

If I do not want a cascading table of contents, I can simply delete the "margin-left" entries and all entries will be flushed left. Or I can amend the left margin of any of them to increase or decrease the margin.

Next, I go to my TOC entries:

```
<p class=MsoToc1>>a href="#_Toc297103599">BABY JANE/a></p>
<p class=MsoToc1>>a href="#_Toc297103600">Copyright © 2011
Michelle A. Demers/a></p>
<p class=MsoToc1>>a href="#_Toc297103601">With thanks to/a></p>
<p class=MsoToc1>>a href="#_Toc297103602">ONE/a></p>
```

As I do not want this text for my TOC entries I can amend the code to read:

```
<p class=MsoToc1>>a href="#_Toc297103599">Title Page/a></p>
<p class=MsoToc1>>a href="#_Toc297103600">Copyright Information/
a></p>
<p class=MsoToc1>>a href="#_Toc297103601">Acknowledgements/a></p>
<p class=MsoToc1>>a href="#_Toc297103602">Chapter 1/a></p>
```

Save and close.

Amending the HTML TOC text does not affect the heading text at all; it only changes the text in the table of contents.

If you upload your HTML file to Kindle this method will work. It will also work in Calibre because Calibre will base its table of contents on the HTML entries (as long as you do not use the "Force use of auto-generated Table of Contents" option). But if you use Mobipocket Creator, this method will not work because Mobipocket Creator will ignore the HTML TOC.

For Mac Users

In order to create a table of contents in Word for Mac you must use heading styles from the style sheet. You then create an automatic table of contents based on your heading styles but you must manually create the TOC entries.

First, create a manual table of contents by typing out your TOC entries. As with the manual method in Word, the advantage of this is that your text does not have to match your actual headings. For example, your TOC entry might say "Chapter 1" but your actual chapter heading might be "1" or "One."

Next, in your table of contents, highlight the entry then hit Cmd+K. In the hyperlink dialogue box that appears, click on "Display." You will see your highlighted text there as the title. Click on "Document." For the anchor, click "locate." A submenu will appear. Click on the arrow beside "Headings." Click on the corresponding heading (e.g., "1") and click "OK." Then "OK" again. Repeat until the table of contents is finished.

"Go to" Menu Markers

To take advantage of the Kindle's "Go to" menu items (Cover, Table of Contents, and Beginning) you need to add bookmarks.

If you have elected to embed your cover in your text document, click on the image then select Insert > Bookmark. Under "Bookmark name," change the default name to "cover" (no quotation marks or uppercase; in Word 2007 there is no default title, just a blank box). Click on "Add." You will not see the bookmark but you will be able to check that it is there when you convert to HTML.

Also, as noted in the instructions, you need to click *on* the image and then place the bookmark; if you click above the image and the image later fills the screen of the device the book is being viewed on, the bookmark will get pushed back and create a blank page. If you place the bookmark below or beside the image, you will get a blank page after your image and the reading device will assume the blank page is your cover (because the bookmark says it is).

For your TOC marker, click at the start of your Table of Contents, then Insert > Bookmark. In the dialogue box name it "TOC" (no quotation marks but all uppercase). Click on "Add."

To add a Go to Beginning function, choose where you want your book to open when the consumer first opens it on their Kindle. This is usually your title page though some prefer the first chapter. Wherever you choose, place your cursor at the top of the page and, like before, click Insert > Bookmark. Type in "Start" (no quotation marks). Click "Add."

If you do not include a "Start" bookmark, an ereader will assume the first page after the cover is the beginning and will link to that page.

Upload to Kindle

If your book formatting does not require you to amend the HTML, you can upload your Word document directly to Kindle and/or Barnes & Noble's PubIt! However, doing so is a leap of faith and, while you have the opportunity to view your book in Kindle Previewer on the Kindle upload page, I believe it smarter to test your book first for errors. This gives you the opportunity to fix any problems without feeling pressured by time or worried that your book will accidentally be put on sale with errors in it. Nevertheless, if you feel confident in your file, return to Chapter 1, Step 10 for instructions on uploading to Kindle.

If you want to test your book before uploading, or if you needed to amend the HTML for greater control of your formatting, the next chapter will teach you how to test your efforts.

Useful Links

To create an Amazon Kindle account.
https://kdp.amazon.com/self-publishing/signin?ie=UTF8&ld=AZEbooksMakeM

Kindle Direct Publishing website help pages.
https://kdp.amazon.com/self-publishing/help

Kindle Community forum.
http://forums.kindledirectpublishing.com/kdpforums/forumindex.jspa

Mobile Reads forum, a popular site for ebook authors and formatters.
http://www.mobileread.com/forums/

Kindle Boards, another popular community site.
http://www.kindleboards.com/

12/ Build and Test Your HTML File

If you own a Kindle you can take advantage of Amazon's @free.kindle.com service whereby you can upload your Word document to the service and it will convert it to the AZW format and download it to your Kindle for a fee or email it to you for free. You can also send an HTML file (see next section).

If you do not own a Kindle, Windows users can save their Word document to HTML and use Mobipocket Creator to create a test book that can then be viewed on the free Kindle Previewer and Kindle for PC app. You can check the validity of the book's formatting and most menu functions, its images, as well as any footnotes or hyperlinks in your document.

Mobipocket Creator is not available for Mac. Mac users can build a test book in Calibre, but if you intend to upload your HTML file to Kindle, know that Calibre produces multilevel paragraph indents and a three-tier table of contents that will not display as such when you upload HTML to Kindle: Kindlegen has limitations on both, as discussed in the chapter on formatting. Mac users can instead use Calibre and upload the mobi file it produces. Alternatively, if you have the iWorks suite installed, you can use the Apple Pages ePub plug-in to produce an ePub that Amazon will convert to the Kindle format.

Amazon and HTML

My experience of interacting with authors on the Kindle forums is that uploading a Word-to-HTML file is one of the more popular methods of publishing a book to Kindle, yet despite this, and despite the fact that Kindlegen converts these HTML files, Amazon makes no mention of this on its site. Instead it instructs the user who wishes to upload HTML to make their own NCX files and to input code, and "to create separate Cascading Style Sheets (CSS) in a dedicated CSS file, which is separate from your HTML content, and to use a tag to link the CSS file to the HTML file"[32]—all of which is confusing, daunting, and unnecessary if you built your HTML from Word.

Moreover, Amazon instructs the user that:

> All the files in the ZIP archive must be in a single folder, without any files in subfolders (such as image files). Save your details in the web browser using the "Save As Web Page (Complete)" option or similar, which will include any images on the page. Then the resulting files can be put inside a ZIP file.[33]

Not only does Word not have a Save as Web Page (Complete)—you find that in an HTML editor—but if you remove the images from the adjunct image folder the link from the HTML code to the image will be broken. So what do you do? In my case I simply copied the images from the adjunct folder and pasted them into the same folder as the HTML document and then zipped everything together. It meant Kindle received two copies of each image, but no one seemed to know what the alternative was. When later the issue came up again in the forums I queried Amazon and was told the duplication was unnecessary; that you only need to zip the HTML file and the image folder together and send that—even though on the surface of things that contradicts their online instructions for HTML.

The reason for the confusion is that the instructions found on the Amazon site regarding HTML assume you are building your ebook from scratch using code. Since you are not building the code from scratch, you will need instead to follow the instructions here.

Save to HTML

Before you Save as Web Page, Filtered (Save as Web page (.htm) on the Mac), save your document. This is because Word will automatically close your document after converting to HTML and it will do so *without saving any changes*!

Also before you save to HTML, you should input file information into your document as this metadata is exported along with the text. To do this, select File > Properties. Under the Summary tab input the book title and the author's name as it appears on the title page.

When you save to HTML, you will always get a warning that saving this way will remove Office-specific tags; click "Yes." After conversion, Word will open up the HTML. Close it down.

Open Explorer (Finder on the Mac). When you check the folder you saved the file in, you will notice there both your HTML file and an adjunct folder called "[title]_files." In this adjunct folder are compressed copies of all the images contained in your document and renamed in order of appearance: your cover becomes "Image001" and so on. For example, my "Baby_Jane.doc" became "Baby_Jane.htm" and a folder called "Baby_Jane_files" that contained "Image001.jpg" (my cover) and "Image002.jpg" (my publisher logo). This folder and the HTML file are inextricably linked: delete one and you delete the other; move one and the other moves with it.

Image File Sizes

Before you make any changes to your HTML, check that your images fall within the 127KB limit. Open Explorer (Finder on the Mac) and navigate to your HTML file's adjunct image folder. Check the file sizes of the images contained within. If any are above 127KB, you will need to resize the image(s) in your Word document to make them smaller and then resave as Web Page, Filtered again until all files are within the limit.

Check for Menu Markers

If your image files are okay, open your HTML document in Notepad, TextEdit, or an HTML editor like Dreamweaver to check if your "Go to" menu bookmarks are there. You do not have to understand the code; you just have to make sure the bookmarks are there.

The HTML will start with your font and style definitions and such; scroll past these until you find the line of code that contains the text "<a name=cover>." The example below is from *Baby Jane*:

```
<p class=MsoNormal align=center style='text-align:center'>
<a name=cover><b><img width=658 height=960 src="Baby_Jane_files/
image001.jpg">
```

The element "<a name=cover>" tells me the cover bookmark is there; "658" and "960" are the pixel dimensions of my cover; "Baby_Jane_Files" is my adjunct folder name; and "image001. jpg" is my cover image.

If the pixel dimensions are incorrect (conversions from Word are often off by a pixel or two, so do not worry about a small anomaly), or your bookmark is missing, you will need to redo your Word document then Save as Web Page, Filtered again until you get it right.

(Some formatters will tell you that if your pixel dimensions are incorrect you can simply amend the code to input the proper dimensions. This is true, provided the image in the adjunct folder is the correct pixel dimensions and you have not accidentally exported the image from Word at the wrong size. To check this, open the folder in Explorer [Finder on Mac]. If the pixel dimensions are not already displayed, right-click on any column and check "Dimensions." If the pixel dimensions are correct here you can simply amend the HTML code to fix the width or height dimensions. If not, return to Word, figure out what you did wrong, and Save to Web Page, Filtered again.)

Next you need to check for your TOC marker. Scroll down until you see code similar to this:

```
<p class=MsoNormal><a name=TOC></a><span style='font-
size:8.0pt'> </span></p>
```

The element "<a name=TOC>" tells you the bookmark for your TOC is there. This will be followed by all your table of contents entries.

Next, scroll up or down to find the place where you added your "Start" bookmark (if applicable). You should find something like this:

```
</b><a name=Start></a></p>
```

This is your Go to Beginning bookmark.

If you find all the above code, your cover, TOC, and Start bookmarks are there and should work in the Kindle file. If you are missing any, you need to return to your Word document and input the missing markers.

Amend Your Code (Optional)

Once your images are correct and your markers have been confirmed, you can make any deletions or changes to your HTML as illustrated in the previous chapter. You can edit the code in Notepad, TextEdit, or an HTML editor like Dreamweaver. Once you are done, it is this final HTML file that you will test.

Build a Test Book With Mobipocket Creator

Windows users can test their HTML files by creating a partial mobi file using Mobipocket Creator. I say partial because you will just put your file through the basic steps to mimic Kindlegen, Amazon's convertor. Note that the resulting PRC file is only good for testing; *you must not upload it to Kindle*.

(Mac users: you can upload your Word document to Kindle without first testing, you can build a mobi file using Calibre and upload that file instead—see next chapter for instructions—or you can use Pages or Scrivener to build an ePub and upload that to Kindle for conversion.)

To build your test book, open Mobipocket Creator. On the right-hand side of the program window, under "Import From Existing File," click on "HTML document." This will change the window to Welcome to the Import File Wizard. The "Choose a File" field will be empty; browse to find your HTML (.htm) file. Click on "Import." This will change the window to Publication Files.

In the Publication Files window you will see your HTML document. Highlight it using a *single click only*. From the top toolbar, click on "Build."

The window will change to Build Publication. Leave Compression Options and Encryption Options checked at the default "No Compression" and "No Encryption." Click on the "Build" button at the bottom of the window.

The book will now be built. In the next window, leave "Open folder containing eBook" checked and click "OK." Do not worry about any warnings at the bottom of the box. You can now test it in Kindle Previewer.

Test in Kindle Previewer

From the open folder, drag the PRC file created in Mobipocket Creator to the Kindle Previewer icon on your desktop; this will open your book in Kindle Previewer.

In Kindle Previewer you can test your Go to Cover and Go to Beginning menu functions, but the Go to Table of Contents menu item with be disabled. This is because Mobipocket Creator builds a TOC differently. You need not worry about this: if you put the TOC marker in and if your hyperlinks are working when you click on them in the Previewer, the table of contents will work when your book is converted by Amazon into the Kindle format.

The Kindle Previewer will illustrate how your book will look in the Kindle DX, the iPad, and iPhone: the Previewer simulates these devices. Click on "Devices" in the Kindle Previewer menu to see the variations.

Kindle for PC

You can also test your book on the Kindle for PC app to see how it will look there. I always check my book here as well as in Previewer because I hate the Kindle font and the Kindle for PC app displays the book much more nicely.

If you view your book in Kindle for PC, it will import the book into its library. Once you are done previewing your book you can leave it in your Kindle for PC library or you can delete it: click on the book's thumbnail on the app's Home page and then select File > Remove From Device, or delete the file from the My Kindle Content folder in your My Documents folder.

Zip Your Files

If all is well, you can upload your HTML file to Kindle for publication. First, however, you need to zip your HTML file and the adjunct image folder into what is called an "archive." An archive is simply several files bundled together into one compressed folder for ease of delivery.

Using a zip utility, zip your files into the archive; if you are given compression options, choose the least amount of compression available to you. Use the "zip" extension. Do not create a self-extracting archive and do not apply encryption or password protection.

If using Windows' built-in compression utility, open Explorer and select both the HTML and adjunct image folder, then right-click and choose Send to > Compressed (zipped) folder. On the Mac, select the files then select File > Compress. These will create a zipped archive.

Once you have your zipped folder you can upload the archive to Kindle. Return to Chapter 1, Step 10 for instructions on uploading to Kindle.

You can also use the zip file to build your book in Calibre. This option is discussed in the next chapter.

Useful Links

See Useful Links in Chapter 10: Software for all software download links.

Kindle's @free.Kindle com service.
http://www.amazon.com/gp/help/customer/display.html/ref=hp_navbox_email_200375630
?nodeId=200375630&#email

To create an Amazon Kindle account.
https://kdp.amazon.com/self-publishing/signin?ie=UTF8&ld=AZEbooksMakeM

13/ Building a Mobi File

As mentioned in the chapter on formatting, if you have a document that makes use of multilevel indented paragraphs, or you need a cascading table of contents with three levels, Kindlegen will not support these options. If you need these you cannot upload a Word or HTML file to Kindle.

Mobipocket Creator will also not support more than one paragraph indent, but it will create a three-level table of contents. This is a small consolation for putting up with a program that is out-of-date and finicky. Worse still, Mobipocket Creator will also ignore any modifications you made to the table of contents in your HTML and will use your headers instead, which will defeat the purpose of the modifications. If you made such changes to your TOC code, do not use Mobipocket Creator; use Calibre instead.

The free, open-source Calibre will support both multilevel indents and a three-level table of contents. Calibre is also more flexible and less finicky than Mobipocket Creator. Nevertheless, in the interests of comprehensiveness I have included a section on building a mobi file with Mobipocket Creator.

If you use either of these programs, you should not have embedded your cover image in your Word document; if you did, remove it and save your text document as Web Page, Filtered again before proceeding. If you have already made modifications to the HTML and would prefer not to have to redo them, you can simply delete the line of code that points to your cover image, and delete the image from the adjunct image folder. If your cover is your only image, you can delete the adjunct image folder altogether and use the HTML file only.

Mobipocket Creator

Open Mobipocket Creator. Under "Import From Existing File" select "HTML document." In the next window, use Browse to find your HTML (.htm) file. Note that here you do not send the zipped folder since Mobipocket Creator will automatically detect the adjunct image folder if there is one. Click on "Import." This changes the window to Publication Files.

Add Your Cover

In the Publication Files window, along the left blue sidebar, you will see a list of menu options. Click on "Cover Image." Click "Add Cover." Navigate to your cover image; click on the file and click "Open." Then click "Update."

Create a Table of Contents

In mobi files, the table of contents is created and stored in its own NCX file. When the user selects "Go to Table of Contents" they are taken "outside" of the text to the external NCX file. The internal TOC that you created in Word remains but is ignored by the "Go to" menu. The internal TOC's hyperlinks will still function but they are redundant and accessible only by navigating in the text to the table of contents page.

If you wish to proceed with Mobipocket Creator, select Table of Contents from the left-hand (blue) menu. The window will change to Table of Contents Wizard. Click on "Add a Table of Contents." This opens the wizard.

The default title is "Table of Contents"; you can leave as is or change to suit. Below this is the Table of Contents Generation Rules. Here you must input the tags and, if applicable, the values that tell Mobipocket Creator which of your heading styles to build your TOC from. For example, if you used Heading 1 for your chapters, input "h1" (no quotation marks) in the First Level under Tag Name.

One of the limitations of Mobipocket Creator's TOC builder is that if you used multiple heading styles they are automatically cascaded; you cannot tell Mobipocket Creator to put h1, h2, and h3 headers all on the same level, nicely flushed left. Mobipocket Creator also cannot distinguish between heading styles used out of order. For example, if you tell it you want h2 in the first level and h1 in the second level, Mobipocket Creator will not do it: you have to cascade your headers in numerical order.

You can preview your table of contents by clicking on the "Preview in Browser" in the Table of Contents Wizard panel. Note that it will automatically open in Internet Explorer and is not compatible with IE9.

Once you are finished, click on "Update." This will add the table of contents to your list of publication files and return you to the Publication Files window.

Input Your Metadata (Optional)

You can input metadata such as title, author, publisher, ISBN, et cetera, into your book file. However, this data will be inputted into the Kindle website when you upload your book, so it is not necessary to do so here.

Guides

In this window you can add guides for the "Go to" menu in Kindle. If you built a table of contents in Mobipocket Creator, a guide will have been automatically added. When you add your cover, a guide is added for that as well, though you will not see it automatically added to the list. This leaves only your Start marker. If there is a way to get Mobipocket Creator to recognize the marker already in the code, I have not figured it out and, judging by the forum users, few there have figured it out too. If the Start marker is not recognized, the default in the Kindle device is to land on the first page after the cover, which will be your title page. I would not worry, then, about figuring out how to link to your Start marker and simply leave the Guides alone.

Build Your Publication

Select the HTML file under your Publication Files. Then click on "Build" from the top toolbar. In the next box, leave Compression Options and Encryption Options checked at the default "No Compression" and "No Encryption." Click on "Build."

In the next dialogue box, leave "Open folder containing eBook" checked and click "OK." If there are warnings, check what these are, fix your file as necessary, then redo.

Mobipocket Creator stores the publications it creates in a folder called My Publications, which is the folder that will open by default when you finish building your publication. You can later retrieve these files at any time or delete them.

You will notice, too, that in addition to the PRC file there will be other files and possibly folders with extensions such as .html, .opf, and .opfcache. These are copies of the internal PRC files. When uploading a Mobipocket Creator file to Kindle you only upload the individual PRC file and not the many adjunct files.

Calibre

When I first discovered Calibre I tested one of its mobi files by using Kindle's @free.Kindle service to convert the Calibre mobi to AZW and tested it in both Kindle Previewer and Kindle for PC. The file worked. Excited, I posted to the Kindle forum that one could use Calibre instead of Mobipocket Creator for creating a mobi file for upload to Kindle. However, it was then revealed that Calibre's mobi files were not compatible with Kindle because the file did not contain sufficient room in its header for the metadata that Kindle adds when you upload a book (things like Kindle's catalogue number, digital rights management metadata, text to speech function, et cetera). A post to another forum resulted in a discussion among Calibre programmers and an update. I have thus been assured that Calibre's mobi files will be accepted when uploaded to Kindle, but as I have not used this software to create my final files I cannot attest to this.

Add Your Book

Open Calibre. On the toolbar you will see "Add books"; click on this. Browse to your HTML file or the archive that contains your HTML file and adjunct image folder, whichever is applicable, and click "open." The file will be downloaded into the Calibre software and will appear as a title in the main window.

Click on the title and then click on the toolbar icon "Convert books." This opens the conversion program. In the program window, in the upper right-hand corner, you will see "Output format." Select "MOBI" from the drop-down list.

Along the left-hand side is a panel bar. "Metadata" is highlighted as this is the window that by default first opens.

Metadata Panel

In the Metadata panel you must input your book's title, author as it appears on the cover, and publisher.

In the Metadata panel you have the option to add your cover during the conversion process or check the "Use cover from source file" box to ask Calibre to detect the cover image embedded inside the HTML (from Word) file. I have found it best to add the cover at the time of conversion rather than detect an embedded file. Downsample your cover to 127KB and add it using the "Add Cover" option.

Do not use TIFFs for your cover or interior images. These are by necessity converted to JPEGs and in the process are often degraded.

Look & Feel, Heuristic Processing, and Page Setup

Unless you know what you are doing, leave the Look & Feel panel alone, as well as Heuristic Processing. (Heuristic processing is the process of scanning a manuscript for common mistakes, or what the program thinks are mistakes. If you have edited properly, this is both completely unnecessary and potentially destructive.)

Under Page Setup, choose "Kindle" for your Output profile; leave the Input profile at "Default."

Structure Detection

If you modified your headers to add or avoid page breaks, as explained in the section "Header Styles," you do not have to deal with Structure Detection. Structure Detection asks you to define where your page breaks are and amends the code to suit; since you will have already added this code, there is no need for Calibre to do so.

Instead, delete the default values for "Detect Chapter at (XPath expression)" and "Insert chapter breaks before (XPath expression)" and leave them blank.

If you did not modify your headers to add page break information, you need to fill in the appropriate values in the Calibre fields. If your heading structure is simple, meaning you did not use the same heading style with different page break attributes applied, Structure Detection is simple.

The field "Detect chapter at (XPath expression)" tells Calibre which header(s) you used for your chapter titles. For example, if only Heading 1 has been applied to your chapter titles you simply amend the "Detect Chapter at (XPath expression)" to read:

```
//*[name()='h1']
```

You then have a choice to separate your chapters with a page break, a black line ("rule"), both, or neither. The default "Chapter mark" is set to "pagebreak."

The next field, "Insert page breaks before (XPath expression)," tells Calibre where to place a page break. If you want a break only before your chapter headings, you replicate the code from above:

```
//*[name()='h1']
```

If you have more than one header that should be preceded by a page break, you can add to the "Insert page breaks before (XPath expression)" field the appropriate header value(s). For example, to add page breaks before both Headings 1 and 2 the code would need to read:

```
//*[name()='h1' or name()='h2']
```

Fig. 29 illustrates the above configuration.

Fig. 29

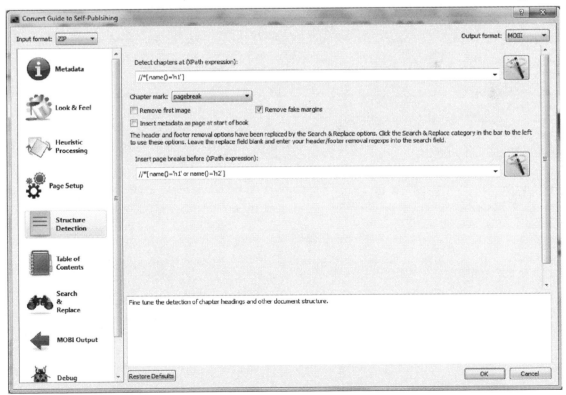

If you used the same heading style for different headers, but only some of them require a page break before, things become more complicated because now you will need to tell Calibre which heading text requires a page break and which does not. The default "Detect Chapter at (XPath expression)" is:

```
//*[((name()='h1' or name()='h2') and re:test(., 'chapter|book|
section|part|prologue|epilogue\s+', 'i')) or @class = 'chapter']
```

The default "Insert chapter breaks before (XPath expression)" is:

```
//*[name()='h1' or name()='h2']
```

These values tell Calibre that all h1 and h2 headers with any of the words "chapter(s)," "book(s)," "section(s)," "part(s)," "prologue(s)," or "epilogue(s)" appearing in the heading text, or if there is a class expression that equals "chapter," are chapters and to insert a break before them. If this is not appropriate, then you have to set the value(s) for Calibre to use as the filter. For example, if your chapters make use of Heading 1 and always start with the word "Chapter," and your subsections also use Heading 1 but do not start with the word "Chapter," you would amend the "Detect Chapter at (XPath expression)" instruction to read:

```
//h:h1[re:test(., "chapter", "i")]
```

In the "Insert page breaks before (XPath expression)," if you only want page breaks before your chapters, you replicate the code you inputted into "Detect Chapter at (XPath expression)." If you want additional page breaks, you amend it to suit. For help on more complex Structure Detection, see the Calibre help files (see this chapter's Useful Links).

Table of Contents

If your book has an embedded table of contents, Calibre will replicate it, which is especially useful if you did not use a heading system and manually created your TOC instead.

When the TOC is replicated, Calibre stores a copy in its own external NCX file and leaves the internal TOC intact. This internal TOC will work but will not be linked to the Go to Table of Contents menu option.

However, Calibre's TOC builder may not necessarily replicate exactly the table of contents in your document, due to a few quirks. The first is that Calibre will interpret any footnotes or hyperlinks in your document as TOC entries if the number of TOC entries permitted is greater than the actual number of TOC entries in your document. Thus you need to go to the Table of Contents Tab and adjust the defaults. Calibre's default "Number of links to add to Table of Contents" is "50"; you need to change this value to the actual number of entries in your TOC to avoid footnotes or hyperlinks from being added (if you have these in your document; if not, do not worry about it). So if, for example, you have ten chapters in your book plus entries for your title page, copyright page, and acknowledgements, you would set the value to "13." (Editor's note: this issue seems to have been resolved in the latest version of Calibre that I tested, version 0.8.20. However, the default number of links and chapter threshold values remain, so perform your own tests.)

Secondly, if you amended Structure Detection to limit chapter breaks to Heading 1, Calibre will only include in its TOC the Heading 1 entries; if you want your other headers to be included in the TOC you have to tell Calibre to include them. So if, for example, you want any uses of Heading 1, Heading 2, and Heading 3 to be in the TOC, and you wish for the TOC to cascade, you input into the Level 1 TOC (XPath expression):

```
//h:h1
```

In the Level 2 TOC (XPath expression) input:

```
//h:h2
```

And in the Level 3 TOC (XPath expression) input:

```
//h:h3
```

Fig. 30 illustrates this configuration.

Fig. 30

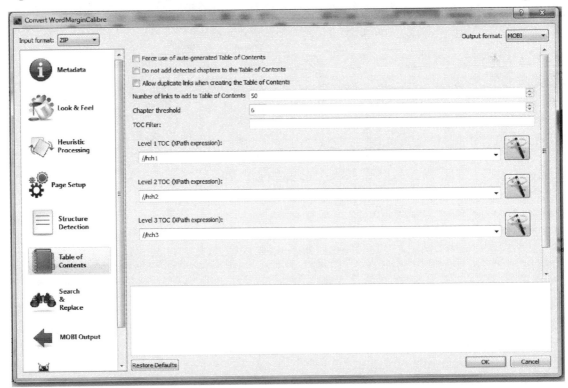

Alternatively, if you want for example both Heading 1 and Heading 2 at the same Level 1, you would input into the Level 1 TOC (XPath expression):

```
//*[name()='h1' or name()='h2']
```

You can add as many heading styles as you wish but you are limited to three levels.

If you did not first create a TOC inside your text document for Calibre to copy, Calibre can create one. You do this by inputting the values as you see above, but in addition you need to check "Force use of auto-generated Table of Contents" option and "Do not add detected chapters to the Table of Contents."

One unfortunate feature of Calibre's table of contents is that it uses nested blockquotes to create the cascading TOC and these blockquotes are indented too much, in my opinion, especially between Level 2 and Level 3 (Fig. 31).

Search & Replace, MOBI Output, and Debug

Leave the Search & Replace and Debug panels alone. In MOBI Output, the only thing you need to do is input a title for your table of contents if you do not like the default "Table of Contents" (why this is not in the Table of Contents panel is anyone's guess).

Fig. 31

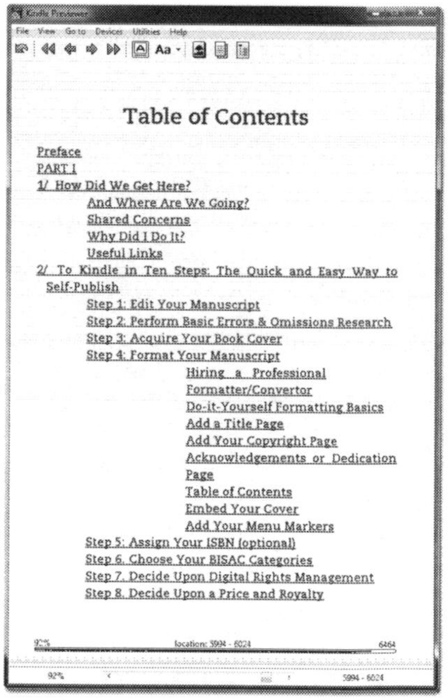

Build Your Book

Once you are finished entering your data, click the "OK" button at the bottom of the window. You will see a "Jobs" icon in the lower right-hand corner. When the icon stops spinning your book is done.

Calibre stores the files it creates in a folder called Calibre Library in your My Documents folder. Publications are further subdivided by author. In the publication's folder you will find the mobi file, a zipped archive, and an OPF file. If you elect to upload a Calibre file to Kindle you only upload the single mobi file.

Testing Your Calibre Mobi File

On the right-hand side of the Calibre window will be the cover image of your book and below that the list of formats it is now available in. Below that will be "Path: Click to open." This opens the publication's subfolder.

If you double-click the mobi file it will open in your Kindle for PC (or Mac) and will automatically store a copy of the file in your My Kindle Content folder. You can also drag and drop the book file onto the Kindle Previewer icon to open and view your book there. If you encounter any problems, return to your file or to Calibre to determine and fix the problems.

InDesign

As at time of writing, the Kindle plug-in for InDesign was in the beta stage, and I did report some unfortunate bugs, one of which is detailed below. InDesign's Kindle plug-in, which uses Kindlegen as its foundation, is being developed by Amazon itself, which is good in that you know your file will be accepted by its system when you upload. The other advantage to using InDesign is that with only minor adjustments you can use the same document to produce a Kindle, an ePub, and a PDF for print. That said, I recommend building your ebook first and then amending it as necessary for print because otherwise you will end up with bloated code.

Because InDesign is a specialized program that is not widely used by anyone outside the design industry, I will assume a degree of knowledge on the part of the reader and only mention those issues that are specific to the Kindle plug-in.

If you are a graphic designer who has been contracted to build a mobi file from an InDesign document, there are things you can advise your client to do to reduce the volume of formatting changes that may be required for a successful conversion:

- text and paragraphs should be formatted as outlined in the chapter on formatting;

- if importing a Word document into InDesign, do not use endnotes. InDesign will recognize footnotes and maintain the hyperlinks but it will not recognize endnotes: endnotes are formatted as text when imported from Word documents. InDesign will not allow for duplicate numbering: when imported, chapter-specific numbering is ignored and footnotes are renumbered in order of appearance in the manuscript;

- if there are hyperlinks in the Word document, when importing into InDesign external hyperlinks are maintained but internal bookmarks are erased and must be redone; and

- if you intend to make an ePub using InDesign's book function, you can optionally split the document into individual files, one for each chapter and one for each section of front and end matter.

Only Text Frames

When creating ebooks in InDesign, there can be only one text frame per page and all contents of the page must reside in the frame, including any images, which need to be anchored to the text. If you place an image outside of a text box, the image will automatically be flushed left and may or may not be preceded by a page break. More complex anchoring is possible; see Adobe's White Paper on this issue (see Useful Links below).

Paragraph Formatting

InDesign's default paragraph format is "Basic Paragraph"; you can use this as it is the equivalent of Normal. If you import a Word document that uses Normal then this paragraph format will be imported with the file and will appear as a paragraph format option in your InDesign document. In the interest of streamlined code, use the imported Normal style. If you delete the imported Normal style and apply Basic Paragraph to the document, any amendments to the text such as italics will be eradicated and you will have to go through the entire document and reformat any necessary text. All other Paragraph Styles must be based on Normal.

Blank lines must be created using paragraph formatting. Blank lines created by carriage returns are erased when exported to Kindle.

Narrow indents (for example, .125") and paragraphs flushed left are respected: there is no automatic Kindle first line indent because a text-indent value is added to the code.

In order to create a hanging paragraph in InDesign you have to indent the paragraph then use a negative first line indent. But as with Word-to-HTML, negative first line indents are not recognized, so hanging paragraphs are not possible using the Kindle plug-in for InDesign.

If you need to create multilevel indented paragraphs, you can do so by inserting multiple consecutive space characters via the Non-breaking Space character. Using the alternative paragraph formatting option will result in a single indent value only, as it does with HTML-to-Word; this is due to Kindlegen having only a single hard space.

Importing Styles and Font Definitions

When importing Word files, heading styles in use in the Word document are imported but appear as modifications to the style: you will see "[style]+". These styles need to be redefined to remove the "+" sign. If you do not, this will have an effect on exporting the table of contents: if a header appears with a "+" sign beside it, even though InDesign will add the heading to its text document TOC, when converting to mobi any modified headers will be ignored and removed from the TOC.

Font definitions, even if no longer used, are also imported; you need to use the font replace utility to remove unwanted hidden fonts.

If you use a font that is not websafe, it will not be converted to a websafe font; it will disappear off the page when converted.

Page Breaks

Page breaks must be identified by inserting the page break marker. If you do not insert the break character, pages will run into each other regardless of the layout in InDesign. The exception to this is if a paragraph or style is modified to include a page break before it. This method is, in fact, preferable because it results in more stable code.

Hidden Layers

When exported to Kindle, hidden layers are printed.

Table of Contents

When exporting to Kindle, if you want a table of contents you must create it first in your InDesign document. Then when exporting to Kindle you check "Include InDesign TOC entries" and a TOC will be added to the mobi file. The text TOC will then be automatically deleted from the mobi file to avoid duplication.

Footnotes

When InDesign exports to mobi, footnotes are converted to endnotes; however, while HTML moves all footnotes to the end of the document, InDesign offers the option to place endnotes "In place," "Before break/new chapter," or at "End of book."

Alas, this is where the bug appeared: if you choose "Before break/new chapter" the file exports properly, but if you choose "End of book" the footnotes export properly but suddenly the page breaks are ignored and chapters simply flow into each other. I reported this and Kindle requested my files so they could try to determine the source of the problem; their reply is as follows:

> We had a look at your InDesign file and we were able to reproduce the issue[. We] regret to say that this is a bug in the plugin.

> There is a workaround for this issue and that should help you in fixing your book. Remove all your existing page breaks at the end of each chapter. Instead of inserting a page break please use Paragraph Styles for each of your chapter headings. In the paragraph style options, navigate to the Keep Options page and select the Start Paragraph On Next Page option from the drop down list. Applying this paragraph style to the chapter title will ensure that each chapter starts on new page.

> We tried this on your book and the page breaks were exported fine even when the footnotes were placed at the end of the book.

Do not choose "In place" for your footnotes option: not only do the page breaks cease to function but each footnote is inserted into the text not after the footnote but after the paragraph that appears at the bottom of the page in InDesign; that is, whatever was right above the footnote on the page in the source document. Completely useless.

Images

With the Kindle plug-in you add the cover image during the export process; do not embed it into the document.

Kindle's documentation recommends that you place images in your document at 300 ppi to "future-proof" your images. It also recommends that you do not use InDesign's image optimization, especially for images that contain text; instead, you set the export option to use the original images, which Kindlegen then optimizes. Since you are sending the original, uncompressed images, your mobi file will be quite large. I contacted Amazon about my concern that this would result in images in excess of the 127KB limit, which would cause the book to be rejected. I was also concerned this huge file would translate into an increase in the per-MB delivery charge. Amazon's response was that neither issue is a concern:

> When you create a Mobi using Kindlegen or Kindle Plugin for Adobe InDesign, we create and store multiple versions of the content in the Mobi file in order to provide the best customer experience. For example, the image needs for the Kindle device are different from the image needs on an iPad. So we store multiple versions of the same image in the Mobi file. This is the cause of the file size increase. When we fulfill your book to customers, we only send the content version that is most appropriate for that device. Amazon sends the trimmed content to the reading device and hence this increased file size during book compilation does not affect the download charges.
>
> So, in the case where you export original images, due to larger input images, the mobi file size will increase proportionally.
>
> When you upload your file for publishing, we make sure that only the smallest and optimal size of the mobi file is considered while bracketing the book into a price range. So you need not worry about the increased file size. Any extra files and data will be removed from the mobi file and only the smallest file size will be considered. You could upload the mobi to KDP (without publishing it) to see what the actual charges will be for your Mobi book.

The importance of this information is that it tells you where Amazon is heading regarding device development. The forward trend will be for higher resolutions, and if your book contains the higher resolution images they will likely continue to look good on future devices.

Remember, however, that it is the pixel dimensions, not the resolution, of the image that ultimately matters most. If your images are small, the higher resolution will not future proof your book. A 300 x 400 pixel image at 300 ppi is still only a 300 x 400 pixel image.

Another consequence of sending original images is that changing the display size of the image in InDesign is irrelevant: you are not using InDesign's image optimization engine.

Amazon's documentation states that images embedded in InDesign are exported at 100% if they are within the 127KB threshold; anything larger than this is optimized by the convertor to bring them within the limit. However, as the email indicates, this optimization does not take place at the mobi creation stage; it takes place upon delivery. This information really should be included in the Kindle plug-in documentation as otherwise you are likely to assume, as I did when I checked my image file sizes, that the plug-in is not working properly.

In the tests I performed, using images saved at 300 ppi did result in improved image quality when compared to the same images saved at 96 ppi. I did not interpolate the images: the image size remained constant; I only changed the resolution. There was one unfortunate exception to this: where an image was less than the width of the Kindle screen (about 600 pixels wide), the smaller image was upsampled to fill the width of the screen, with terrible results. (The actual image was exported at its native pixel dimensions but was inexplicably upsampled by Kindle Previewer, something that did not occur with mobi files created in Calibre or Mobipocket Creator.) And where my images contained text, the recommendation that you do not use InDesign's built-in optimizer was dead on: the resultant images would render any book unsellable.

On the surface of things, the ability to use 300 ppi images is quite convenient because it means you can use the same images in your Kindle file that you use for your print file: no need to downsample and save additional images. However, images meant for print require sharpening to compensate for the printing process as this softens the image; the sharpened image will print properly but it looks terrible on the screen. Moreover, uncompressed TIFFs are preferable for printing, and these are converted into JPEGs—and not particularly well—during ebook conversion. Thus you really need to use different image files for your print and digital versions.

Useful Links

See "Useful Links" in Chapter 10: Software for all software download links.

Calibre help files.
http://calibre-ebook.com/help

Adobe's White Paper on Kindle Plug-in.
http://www.adobe.com/devnet/digitalpublishing/articles/indesigntokindle.html

14/ ePubs

The ePub (short for "e-publication"), developed by the International Digital Publishing Forum, is intended to be for ebooks what the JPEG is for digital imaging: a non-proprietary, cross-compatible digital format. This, of course, has not stopped the device manufacturers from trying to capture market share by encoding the ePubs they sell to be device-specific, a practice that has raised the ire of users.

EPubs are similar to mobi files except that ePubs are designed to load faster in an ereader because the book is segmented into files that cannot exceed 300KB each. These files consist of the metadata, the content OPF, the text HTML file(s), the CSS template, and the table of contents NCX file (image files are contained within a subfolder which is not subject to the same limitation). A default has developed among software developers to segment ePubs into sections of approximately 260KB to ensure they remain within the 300KB limit.

The 300KB limit is not a limitation of the ePub format itself but is a limitation of reading devices. This means that ePubs with larger sections may pass validation but might fail to open on the consumer's ereader or will cause the device to crash. Newer devices are overcoming this limitation but because there are sufficient numbers of older devices still in the hands of consumers, larger files are not recommended and may be rejected by retailers.

Creating ePubs is thus a bit more tedious because this 300KB limitation means for lengthier documents like novels or a manual like this one, one has either to design the ebook in sections or use a program that will allow you to control the separation of the document, and which will do so in a way that produces a file acceptable for distribution. Windows users will run into a wall here because there are currently no free or commercially available programs that will create a compliant ePub from your text document or HTML files. Mac users have an advantage in that two programs, Pages and Scrivener, have a convert to ePub plug-in that produces viable ePubs.

One visual difference in the ePub format is that the table of contents is nested, meaning its format is a collapsible tree structure like that which you see in your computer's Explorer or Finder, a "+" appearing beside those chapters containing subsections. These TOCs are useful for lengthy documents where numerous subsections exist.

To create a properly formatted ePub, you need to follow the same manuscript formatting principles you followed for Kindle files.

Images in ePubs

Unlike with Kindle's mobi files where images are restricted to 127KB and are often heavily compressed to make them fit, ePubs do not compress images. This makes ePubs particularly attractive for picture and comic books. However, each digital book device displays pictures differently, making the creation of a picture or comic book that will look good across all devices difficult. Such books require a greater degree of technical knowledge than the average author possesses, and thus if you are intending to produce such a book expect that you will need to hire a professional.

The 300KB limit does not apply to images; only oversized XHTML and CSS files will cause a device to crash. However, on some older devices, images that exceed 300KB will fail to display even though the book itself will otherwise function properly.

The downside to this is that if the program you use to build your ePubs does not compress your original images sufficiently (or not at all), and if you are concerned about images failing to display on older devices, then you must optimize your images first before building your ePub. In some cases you may even have to swap out the images exported by your ePub software for images you optimize in an image editor such as Photoshop.

Barnes & Noble's PubIt!

U.S. residents who elect to contract directly with Barnes & Noble's PubIt! can upload their text document to the B&N website and it will convert your book to an ePub. Acceptable formats are HTML, Rich Text Format (.rtf), text (.txt), or Word (.doc or .docx).

Aggregators and Vanity Publishers

Most aggregators will convert your document to the ePub format. Most charge a fee, some do not. See the section "eBook Aggregators" in Chapter 16: Distribution and Royalties to view your options.

Most author services companies (vanity publishers) that offer ebook distribution want your Word document already converted to an ePub or they will charge you a hefty conversion fee (one company charges between $175.00 and $495.00 depending on your page count). This is something to keep in mind if contemplating contracting with a vanity publisher.

Software Options

There are only two ways to produce a viable ePub: with one of the limited conversion programs available on the market, or by building an ePub from scratch using HTML. If you are familiar with code you can build your ePub with Notepad or TextEdit. This manual is not, however, a manual on writing code, so I will only look at the conversion options.

Calibre and Open Office

Calibre will build an ePub from a single HTML file—like that built from Word— but it does so by separating your book into "split" HTML files to conform to the ePub structure. Unfortunately these ePubs, while they will work when you test them in Adobe Digital Editions, will not pass ePubCheck and thus will not be acceptable for distribution.

Some users have suggested converting to mobi first in Calibre then converting the mobi to ePub, but my tests were unsuccessful in passing ePubCheck.

There is an OpenOffice extension called ODFToEPub that lets you save a document as an ePub. Unfortunately, it does so using the same method as Calibre; my tests failed validation.

There are also some online pay-per-use conversion sites that will convert a Word document to an ePub. Perform due diligence first before you use one of these sites since their software may simply split the document the same way that Calibre or OpenOffice does. Unless a pay-per-use site offers a refund if the file fails ePubCheck, I would look elsewhere.

Pages and Scrivener

Apple's Pages, and Literature and Latte's Scrivener, are useful for building ePubs because their native files are built in a similar fashion, meaning they are actually file archives: images, chapters, the table of contents, style sheets, and so on are segmented into separate files contained within the archive. The conversion to ePub is therefore quite simple.

However, you cannot use a Pages' template to create an ePub; you must design your document from scratch. In both programs you also embed your cover on the first page of the document; when converting you tell the program to use that image as your cover. See this chapter's Useful Links for tutorials on exporting to ePub from Pages or Scrivener.

Neither of these programs, however, give you control over image compression. If your images are too large or small as a result, you can swap out the images later using a zip program, which is discussed below in the section "Check for Image Size."

InDesign

InDesign has the advantage of a book function, meaning that you can take multiple files and combine them into a single book file comprised of the sub-files. This makes for easy conversion to ePub since the document is already segmented.

In the alternative, InDesign can properly segment a longer document, delineated through the use of headers. This is convenient for a document where there are many hyperlinks that would be a pain to create using the book function.

InDesign's Export to ePub utility is not without its quirks, however, and users will have to tinker a bit with the code; but with a few simple fixes the files pass ePubCheck.

Unlike Pages or Scrivener, InDesign gives you options for formatting your images, though here too there are quirks.

ePubs From InDesign CS5

If you choose to use the book function to create an ePub from InDesign CS5, you must first create your book's various chapter, front, and back matter as separate files. The book cover must be embedded in the document as a separate file.

The table of contents is created by the individual file names. This eliminates the need for page titles such as "Copyright Information" or "Title Page": you simply name those files as desired and include them in your table of contents.

Before you export your book to ePub, in your first document (your cover), you can create a custom table of contents style that you can then later choose instead of the default option when you build your ePub. If you do not create a custom TOC style then InDesign will use its default style, which does not designate any sub-headers or a multilevel, tree-style TOC.

Before you build your book you should also input basic document metadata such as document title, author's name and title (author, co-author, et cetera), and copyright information; you only need to do this for the first file of the book. You also have the option to add the product description (the book's synopsis) but as this is usually inputted when a book is uploaded to a distributor or retailer it is not necessary to include it here.

Images

InDesign exports all images at 72 ppi, so if you use images of a higher resolution, downsampling will occur. It is thus best practice to use 72 ppi images. (CS5.5 allows you to choose from among three resolutions, 72, 150, and 300 ppi.)

If you select "Formatted" when you export your images, image special effects such as drop shadows are exported with the image. If you crop an image, only the cropped portion will export. And if you resize the image, the scale is also exported. For example, if your image is 500 pixels wide and you scale it 80% in InDesign, it will export an image 400 pixels wide. If you resize it larger than 100%, upsampling will occur, usually with undesirable results.

If you leave "Formatted" unchecked, InDesign exports the original image at its original size, but will still downsample if the original is a higher resolution than 72 ppi.

All images are compressed using your choice of Maximum, High, Medium, or Low. And this is where the quirk reveals itself. For example, say you have a JPEG that is 600 x 800 pixels and 750KB when saved at maximum quality. You are worried about this image failing to display so you decide to compress it further in Photoshop, which reduces the image quality but also the file size. So now you have an image that is 200KB, well within the 300KB limit. Problem is, when you export from InDesign, if you select "Maximum" as your output option, InDesign returns to the original pixel information and compresses it at Maximum quality, and your image balloons back up.

If you only have one image, you can simply reduce the output quality to bring the image back to size. But what if you have many images in your document (like this manual) and choosing a lower output quality will degrade the rest of your images? The workaround is to choose "Maximum" for your output then later swap out any renegade images, the process for which we discuss shortly.

Build Your ePub

Once you have your book designed and compiled, right-click on the book submenu and select "Export Book to EPUB." If working from a single file, select File > Export for > EPUB.

In the dialogue box that opens, under the General tab, "Include Document Metadata," "Base on Page Layout," and "Map to Unordered Lists" are checked by default; leave as is and input the publisher and the unique identifier, which is usually the ISBN (if a default unique identifier appears, delete it and replace with your ISBN). Note that since many retail systems prefer the ISBN without hyphens, leave them out when inputting the ISBN into InDesign's metadata panel.

In the Images tab, "Formatted" will be checked by default. If you have already optimized your images, uncheck this box and images will be left as is. If you need them to be formatted, change the "Image Conversion" to "JPEG" and "Image Quality" to "Maximum." "Format Method" will be at the default of "Baseline"; leave it there.

In the Contents tab, "XHTML" and "Generate CSS" will be checked by default. Under "Table of Contents" check "Include InDesign TOC Entries." Then select from the drop-down menu the TOC style you created, if applicable. Check "Suppress Automatic Entries for Documents."

If you are using InDesign's book function, leave "Use First Level Entries as Chapter Breaks" unchecked. If you need InDesign to split a longer document, check "Use First Level Entries as Chapter Breaks." You then need to ensure that any header where you need the document to split into is set to the first level in your table of contents. Note: this is not the same as inputting page breaks. This is only about where InDesign will split the document into invisible sections.

Under "Generate CSS," uncheck "Include Embeddable Fonts."

If you include embeddable fonts, when you validate your ePub through ePubCheck you will incur the following warning for every font you included, in this example Times New Roman:

WARNING: [book title].epub: item (OEBPS/Fonts/times.ttf) exists in the zip file, but is not declared in the OPF file.

I was never able to find out how to correct this and was instead instructed by others not to embed the fonts. Thus disabling "Include Embeddable Fonts" solved that problem.

Fix the Bug

Another, even more bizarre bug, is that InDesign includes in the content file an invalid date end tag (and no start tag) that will result in this error message:

ERROR: [book title].epub/OEBPS/content.opf(4): date value '' is not valid. The date must be in the form YYYY, YYYY-MM or YYYY-MM-DD (e.g., "1993", "1993-05", or "1993-05-01"). See http://www.w3.org/TR/NOTE-datetime.

To correct this problem you need to amend the Content.opf. This is easiest to do with Tweak_epub.

Open your ePub with Tweak_epub. Select the Content.opf file and select "Edit File" (Fig. 32). The default editor in Windows is Notepad. Scroll through the code until you find:

```
<dc:date/>
```

Change that to:

```
<dc:date>[your date of publication]</dc:date>
```

For example, the ePub version of *Baby Jane* was published in July 2011, so the code was amended to read:

```
<dc:date>2011-07</dc:date>
```

Fig. 32

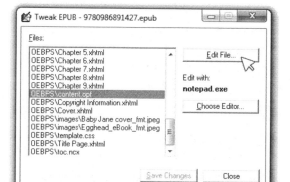

Note that the end tag needs to be fixed so that that "/" sign is placed at the front of the end tag, not the end as it appears in the original CSS generated by InDesign. Also, the date must be entered in the format noted in the error warning: YYYY, YYYY-MM, or YYYY-MM-DD (e.g., 2011, 2011-05, or 2011-05-01).

Once you have edited the code, click "Save" in Notepad. Then "Save Changes" in Tweak_epub.

Check for Image Size

Before you proceed to validate your ePub, you can check the size of your image files and swap them out if necessary. The way to do this is to copy your ePub file and put it into a separate folder on your computer. Then rename the file to change the extension from .epub to .zip. You will get a warning that changing the extension can render the file unusable; select "Yes."

Double-click the new zip file. A window will open that contains all the files within the archive. Click on the OEBPS folder. Click on the Images folder. (Windows users: you must have your Explorer window set to "Details" to see file size. If it is not revealed by default, right-click on any column title and check "Size." Mac users: you must be in "List View." If the size is not displayed, select CMD+J to open View Options and check "Size.")

If any of the images did not export at the right pixel dimensions, or at an unsuitable compression level, you can swap the images for ones you optimized inside an image editor like Photoshop or GIMP. First, create copies of your images and rename them exactly as they appear in the ePub folder. Inside the archive folder window, delete any unwanted image files. Then drag your optimized images from their folder into the archive folder. Close the folder.

Rename the archive to restore the file extension back to .epub. Then open the ebook in Adobe Digital Editions to ensure the swap went smoothly and the images display. If all is well, this is your new file and you can delete the original.

Note that large images in Adobe Digital Editions will often display as cropped inside the ADE window. ADE used to scale images to fit the reader window, but now ADE displays all images at their full pixel dimensions. Do not panic: ereaders will scale the images to fit the screen.

Validate Your ePub

While your ePub will technically work when you test it in Adobe Digital Editions, it may still not be suitable for upload to a distributor or retailer. This is because there are often hidden errors in the file that, while they might not affect the file's display in an ereader, they will affect the ability of the distributor or retailer to add digital rights management code or device-specific code, or even just cataloguing code. So before you upload you need to validate the file through a validation program such as ePubCheck or FlightCrew. If your ePub passes validation you can then view it and test functionality.

ePubCheck

EPubCheck is easiest to use by visiting the Threepress Consulting website (see this chapter's Useful Links). You then simply use the browse button to source your ePub file and click on "validate." In a few minutes or less your file will receive either a large checkmark indicating a pass, or a list of the file's errors. You can then use this list to source and hopefully fix the problems.

FlightCrew

After installing FlightCrew on your computer, open it up. All you will see is a simple white window with a browse button and an empty frame below it. Navigate to your ePub file then click "Go!" You will get a result of either "No errors found" or a list of errors. As with ePubCheck, you can then use this list to source and hopefully fix any problems.

Adobe Digital Editions

When you install Adobe Digital Editions you can set it as the default program for all ePubs, which is convenient because then double-clicking on an ePub file will automatically open it in Adobe Digital Editions. ADE does not store your ePub in its library folder, My Digital Editions, unless you specifically add it, which is also convenient because you do not then have to delete your test files.

Nook for PC or Mac and Sony for PC orMac

Both Nook and Sony have computer apps so you can view your ePubs on either. However, you must first add the file to your library, and then you have to delete it if you do not want to keep it in there.

Useful Links

A webpage that lists some popular ePub conversion programs.
http://www.lexcycle.com/faq/how_to_create_epub

How to build an ePub using HTML.
http://www.ibm.com/developerworks/xml/tutorials/x-epubtut/index.html or
http://www.jedisaber.com/eBooks/tutorial.asp

PubIt! website help pages.
http://pubit.barnesandnoble.com/pubit_app/bn?t=support

Adobe webpage for ePub creation.
http://help.adobe.com/en_US/indesign/cs/using/
WS8c5bc4f64c7a4a3d44f3b18d12dbcdf377a-8000.html

Apple webpage for ePub creation from Pages.
http://support.apple.com/kb/HT4168

Scrivener tutorial page; scroll down to the one on ebooks.
http://www.literatureandlatte.com/video.php

Threepress Consulting page for validating ePubs.
http://threepress.org/document/epub-validate

15/ Print Production

Before you set out to design your print book, or to hire a designer, you need to decide what size you want your book to be and whether it will be released as a hardcover or softcover (paperback), and whether perfect bound, coil bound, et cetera. If you are publishing a novel the most common formats will be perfect bound hardcover, paperback, and mass market paperback. Hardcover books are made with thick cardboard covers and the pages are either stitched into the spine or, more commonly now, glued in ("perfect bound"); a paperback has a cardstock cover and its pages are attached to the spine using a heavy glue; while a mass market paperback is smaller and usually made with cheaper paper and glue.

Most printers offer the option of crème paper or white paper for your interior. Crème paper tends to be thicker and more textured than white paper. Which you use is purely personal preference, though if printing in color then white paper is more appropriate since crème paper will affect color perception. White paper, being smoother, is also preferable for imagery because textured paper will soften the appearance of images.

Color printing is more expensive than black and white, for obvious reasons. Among color books, higher end "coffee table" books are often printed on smoother, more expensive paper stock to enable higher resolution printing; both the paper stock and ink usage will increase costs. If you are creating such a book you will need to enlist professional help as the file preparation and printing process can be quite complex.

A book's size is called its "trim size"; this is what it will be called in the literature from your manufacturer. Look at the books on your shelf for inspiration and use the size you like most as your starting point. You can then check the websites of popular POD manufacturers like Amazon's CreateSpace to see which trim sizes are considered "industry standard" and which are custom sizes; industry standard sizes are cheaper to manufacture and some custom sizes cannot be distributed through certain channels. You will also see what the minimum and maximum page counts are for each available size.

Formatting

If you use the same formatting techniques in your print version as with your ebook version, you can save yourself a lot of time because then the same file can be used for both with only minor tweaking:

- in your print version you can choose any font you wish as long as the font is embeddable when you export to PDF;

- you can use carriage returns to control the line breaks of centered text;

- you can use bullets and lists, tables, sidebars, columns, and any other more complex graphic element;

- you need to amend your Normal paragraph to turn off Widows and Orphans as this can cause unwanted spaces at the bottom of a paragraph or page; you want to control the layout of the text manually. Widows and Orphans refer to fragments of a sentence carried over to the next page, or to a single word that ends a paragraph on its own line. You want to control these using character spacing: individual words or even whole passages can be expanded or contracted so that the lines break aesthetically (in Word it is Format > Font > Character Spacing). This is particularly helpful because it also looks better if you do not use hyphenation;

- with a print book you have page numbers so you need to add a footer to your manuscript; you can also add an optional header;

- if you want all your chapters to start on the right-hand page you need to insert blank pages where necessary to ensure this;

- if you want a table of contents you use page numbers instead of hyperlinks. Same goes for an index; and

- hyperlinked text is not possible so any hyperlinks need to be removed so they will print in black and not be underlined.

Book Covers

Book covers are always designed as a separate file from the book content; when you upload your book to the manufacturer you will always be uploading two files. Most manufacturers want your file name to be your book's ISBN, followed by "cover" or "content." For example, *Baby Jane* consists of two files, "9780986891410_cover.PDF" and "9780986891410_content.PDF." Exactly how your manufacturer needs the files to be named will be included in the documentation it provides to you.

Cover Lamination

Covers are usually printed directly to the cover stock then sealed and protected by a clear laminate. Most laminates will yellow over time and some cheaper laminates will peel off, leaving the cover image unprotected but still visible. A newer process digitally prints to a laminate that is then heat sealed onto the cover stock. This process, though heralded as newer and more advanced, is actually inferior: when the cover is cut, if any air bubbles occur at the edges between the laminate and the cover stock, the laminate will lift off the paper. This problem is more pronounced in areas of high humidity where the moist air expands inside the air bubbles. The problem is also more likely to occur with dark covers because the density of the toner does not allow the glue of the laminate to adhere properly to the page. Unfortunately, because the cover image is printed directly to the laminate, when the laminate peels away it takes the cover image with it.

Amazon's CreateSpace uses the print-to-laminate process, a process I had no idea even existed until a few covers from an order of fifty copies of *Baby Jane* began to peel in the humidity of a rainy Vancouver spring. A check of the forums revealed other authors having the same problem. CreateSpace has indicated it is not happy with the laminate process and is looking into alternate technologies, but when it will abandon this process is not known.

Cover Templates

As noted earlier in this manual, POD manufacturers such as CreateSpace and Lightning Source provide cover templates to make your cover design easier. However, my experience reveals there can be technical glitches in their systems: when I inputted my information into CreateSpace's system, it returned a template for a 280-page book instead of a 276-page book, which resulted in a spine for *Baby Jane* that measured .72" instead of .69". Later measurements also showed the template's bleed was shy of the .125". Both issues caused my cover to be rejected, and it was weeks before the problem was sourced and corrected. So if your cover is rejected by the manufacturer's system and you used their template, demand a thorough investigation before you accept that the error is on your part.

Also, if using more than one POD manufacturer, pay attention to the finer points of their technical requirements and do not assume you can always use the same cover and interior files for everyone. For example, I use both CreateSpace and Lightning Source to produce *Baby Jane*, and while both companies allegedly use 55lb crème paper, the cover template generated by Lightning Source's system had a spine three millimetres narrower. It also requires files supplied in the CMYK color space while CreateSpace uses RGB; both the spine and color space differences forced me to modify my file. In the end, even though both companies produce a 270-page, 6" x 9" trade paperback on 55lb crème paper, the Lightning Source book is slightly narrower and 26 grams lighter than the one printed by CreateSpace.

For details on book cover design see Chapter 9: Cover and Interior Images.

Designing Your Book Using a Word Processor

If your book is simple, like a novel for example, you can create your own PDF using your word processor if you know how to use its basic layout functions. By "simple" I mean that your book does not use anything like a bleed or graphics in the header or footer.

To create your print book PDF, you set your page size to your book's trim size: File > Page Setup > Paper > Paper size > Custom size. Apply to "Whole document." Also in the Page Setup, click on the Margins tab and under "Pages: Multiple pages," change it from the default "Normal" to "Mirror margins." Then adjust your top and outside margins to no less than .5" and your inside margin to no less than .75". (Note: your POD manufacturer will further specify minimum margins based on your page count.)

To export to a PDF, you must not use the Export to PDF utility in Word; you must use Adobe Acrobat Professional and follow the guidelines provided by your POD manufacturer.

Using a Desktop Publisher

If you intend to send your book out to a designer, do not do any of the above to your manuscript as this will all be done by your designer in the desktop publishing program they use. If you wrote your manuscript using double spacing (for easier editing), change it to single spaced before you send it to your designer. And if you otherwise follow the same principles as preparing your manuscript for an ebook convertor, all will go more smoothly.

If you hire out your book design, the same principles apply as those regarding cover design: this is work-for-hire and all files must be supplied to you upon payment for services rendered.

Fonts

As noted, print books can use whatever font you like so long as it is embeddable in your PDF file. However, not all printers will print the same font exactly the same way. Printers "interpret" font information and so variations will occur. I noticed, for example, that the Adobe Garamond Pro font I used for *Baby Jane* printed much closer to the monitor display when printed at CreateSpace than it did at Lightning Source: the latter was heavier in appearance.

Book Signatures

Books are manufactured with two, four, six or eight pages printed onto both sides of a single sheet of paper then folded, cut and bound. These individual sheets that contain the multiple pages are called signatures. Depending on which signature is used, if your book has a page count that is not divisible by two, four, six or eight, as applicable, then blank pages will appear at the end of your book.

Manufacturers require at least one blank page at the back of the book to print their manufacturing information on, so if your book does not result in any blank pages the manufacturer will add a half sheet—that is, two pages—to the end of your book. This is done by the manufacturer so you or your designer should not add any blank pages at the end of the book unless required to do so to meet a minimum page count. For example, if your book has 257 pages and is printed on four-page signatures, 257/4 equals 64.25 signatures. The manufacturer will use 65 signatures and print their manufacturing information on the last of the three blank pages that result (65 x 4 = 260 pages).

Manufacturing costs are based on page counts and are charged by a divisible of two. So using the above example, if your book has 257 pages you will only be charged for 258 pages even though you will actually end up with 260 pages. On the other hand, if your book has 260 pages and is printed on a four-page signature, this will result in no blank pages. The manufacturer will then add a half sheet to create an available blank page for their information, and charge the author for 262 pages.

If your book has blank pages within itself so that chapters or front matter start on right-hand pages, these internal blank pages count toward your book page total and are included in the manufacturing charge. Also, when determining your page count, you do not count only the story pages; you include all front and end matter as well.

Proofing Your Book

Before you upload your PDF to your printer, print out your entire book and check for any errors such as missing pages or changes to formatting.

Once you have uploaded your book to the manufacturer, they will not put your book into production without first producing a proof. This proof is then sent to you for approval. If everything is as it should be, you approve the proof and your book will be put up for sale. If there are changes that need to be made, you will have to redo your book and go through the proofing process again. Some manufacturers will allow typos to be fixed without requiring you to pay for another proof; others will not. Inquire with your manufacturer.

Cross-Climate Transport

Paper is a porous material, so when books travel from one climate to another the paper expands or contracts with the changing humidity levels, which can cause the pages to go wavy and the book not to lie flat. If that happens you need to let the books sit for a week or two to acclimatize and flatten. If you are ordering books for a specific event like a book signing or reading, I would advise you to order them sufficiently ahead of the event to allow the books to acclimatize to your geographical area.

16/ Distribution and Royalties

Before you begin the process of publishing content, you first need to create accounts with Amazon's Kindle Direct Publishing (KDP), and/or Barnes & Noble's PubIt!, and/or a distributor, and/or an aggregator, and/or a print manufacturer/distributor.

When opening your accounts, you will sometimes be offered the option to sign up under your personal name or your publisher name, if they differ. If your company is a partnership or incorporated, you may need to assign to the company the proceeds from your copyright in order for the payer (e.g., Amazon) to pay royalties arising from copyright held by an individual. You should seek legal advice before proceeding. If you are a sole proprietor, unless you have a bank account in the name of your proprietorship, my advice is to sign up either under your personal name or as your name "doing business as" your sole proprietorship (e.g., Michelle A. Demers dba Egghead Books). This ensures both your personal name and sole proprietorship are linked to your account.

Most importantly, you must possess the rights to the material you are publishing. That means either you wrote the book, you inherited the rights to the book, or you bought or were granted a licence to publish. Amazon's Kindle will allow you to publish public domain works but you may be asked to prove the title is public domain, and if a free version of the same title is offered by Amazon then your version will only be accepted if it is differentiated from the free version, meaning it is significantly changed. Acceptable changes include a unique translation, unique annotations such as study guides, literary critiques, detailed biographies, or detailed historical context, or if the book contains ten or more unique illustrations. These ebooks must include "translated," "annotated," or "illustrated" in the title.

Barnes & Noble's PubIt! program does not accept public domain works. Kobo has partnered with the Gutenberg Project to provide public domain titles. Smashwords does not publish or distribute anything in the public domain. LuLu, eBookIt, and BookBaby accept public domain works but most warn these works may be rejected by the retailers.

The Distribution Chain

As a self-publisher you will encounter terms such as distributor, wholesaler, and aggregator. But what is the difference between a distributor and a wholesaler, and between a wholesaler and an aggregator? It is easy to become confused because the terms are used interchangeably, many of the players fulfil different functions depending upon with whom they are dealing, the word "distribute" is used indiscriminately to refer to all stops along the distribution chain, and— just in case we were not confused enough—wholesalers like to call themselves "wholesale distributors" or just "distributors" for short. Regardless of what they call themselves, however, those that control the book information highway have stricter rules: Ingram and Baker & Taylor, often called the "largest book distributors in the U.S." are, technically speaking, wholesalers, meaning they buy a book from the distributor and sell it on to the retailers; consequently, in the Bowker Books in Print database, wholesalers such as Ingram or Baker & Taylor cannot be listed as a title's "distributor."

Every publisher is by default a title's primary distributor: the publisher has the book printed (or digitally created) and then is responsible for ensuring the title makes its way into retail. A publisher may have their own marketing and distribution division that supplies large retailers directly and supplies smaller bookstores via wholesalers such as Ingram; or the publisher may contract with a distribution firm to distribute on behalf of the publisher. In this latter case, the contract to distribute is always *exclusive*. The publisher has the books printed and delivered to the distributor who warehouses the books, fulfills orders, and issues invoices. The distributor may sell directly to retailers or via a wholesaler. A wholesaler has a *non-exclusive* contract to buy books from the distributor and sell them to retailers.

With indie publishing the lines become blurred. When you contract with a print-on-demand company like Lightning Source or CreateSpace to manufacture and sell directly to a retailer like Amazon, the POD manufacturer is your manufacturer, wholesaler, and distributor. When you sell to wholesalers like Ingram, the POD company is your manufacturer and distributor. The self-publisher who pays in advance for printing then sells directly to a retailer is acting as their own distributor.

The fluidity of the publisher/POD manufacturer relationship, and its (alleged) non-exclusivity, means Bowker does not officially recognize POD manufacturers as distributors so you cannot input Lightning Source or CreateSpace as your distributor; the self-publisher is limited to calling themselves the distributor unless you print in advance and contract exclusively with a recognized distribution company. Regardless of this, for all practical purposes your POD manufacturer is also your distributor because they are fulfilling orders and issuing invoices on your behalf.

When the self-published author contracts with an ebook aggregator, the aggregator is acting as your wholesaler and distributor; but, like Ingram or Baker & Taylor, an aggregator is not technically regarded as your distributor because the contract is non-exclusive; the aggregator is regarded solely as a wholesaler, an intermediary between the author/publisher/distributor and the retailer. Once again, though, this is semantics because the aggregator is collecting revenues on your behalf and, in the case of Ingram Digital, is also fulfilling orders. Fig. 33 illustrates the various ways in which the indie author's work is disseminated.

There are very few wholesalers available to the indie publisher. Ingram, for example, will only do business with a publisher who has 200 titles; instead, the indie author must work with a publisher or POD manufacturer who contracts with Ingram; Baker & Taylor has similar terms. On the ebook side, wholesalers such as Overdrive are only available to publishers with a

Fig. 33

Author with own ISBN

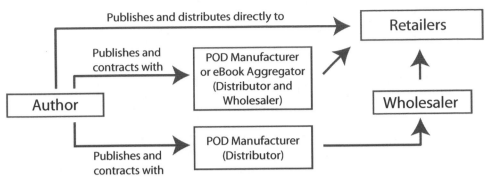

Author with vanity publisher or aggregator's ISBN

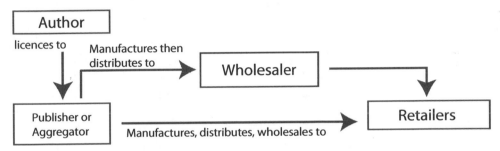

minimum of twenty titles and five authors; similarly, INscribe requires that publishers have a minimum of five titles, though the company promises additional services for smaller publishers are in the works. Ingram's CoreSource and MyiLibrary are only available to large publishers—CoreSource costs $5000.00 if you have less than 2500 titles—but Lightning Source has a digital wing open to indie authors. LibreDigital has a publisher set-up fee of between $5000.00 and $10,000.00, monthly charges on top of that, and the publisher must have direct agreements in place with the marketplaces to which they wish to distribute; LibreDigital will, however, place your indie title on Apple's iBookstore at no cost upfront and 15% of net sales.

You do not have to be an American to contract with an American company, nor are American authors barred from doing business with foreign firms. The only difference is how one gets paid: American companies cannot send funds electronically to an individual outside the U.S. so foreign authors are paid by paper cheque unless they set up a U.S. bank account; note this must be an account in a U.S. bank, not a U.S. dollar account in your own country. Some publishers and aggregators use PayPal instead of electronic funds transfer (EFT). Where a U.S. company has foreign subsidiaries, payments can be converted and paid by EFT into accounts in the subsidiary's country of location. Before signing on with a company always inquire first as to how you will be paid since the full details are rarely available on a company's website.

What's in a Price?

Anyone who has shopped online for print books will notice that the retailers all offer a discount off the "list price." But what, exactly, is the list price? And which is your royalty based on, the list price or the discounted selling price, what retailers like Amazon call their "customer price"? And what about ebooks? The answer, as with all things in publishing, is "It depends."

Traditionally, the publisher of a print book decided upon a suggested retail price for their title; this was the "list price." The publisher then sold their book to their distributor at a discount, usually around 45% off list. The distributor took a cut of that and sold the book to a wholesaler or directly to the retailer for around 38% off list. Smaller retailers who had to buy from the wholesaler paid between 25 and 32% off list. The retailer then sold the book for the list price, higher than list, or lower than list price as a special promotion to lure in customers or to discount unwanted stock. This is called the distributor discount pricing model.

For example, Publisher X lists a hardcover book at $35.00. The book is printed at the publisher's expense and sold to the distributor for $19.25 ($35.00 less 45%). The distributor sells it on for $21.70 ($35.00 less 38%), pocketing the $2.45 as its fee. The wholesaler, if applicable, then takes its cut. The retailer sells the book for $35.00, making a net profit of between $8.75 and $13.30 (depending on their wholesale discount level). If it sells below the list price the retailer earns less; if it sells above the list price the retailer earns more.

The publisher thus earns $19.25 less printing costs. Say, for example, the cost to manufacture and deliver is $8.75; the net profit is $10.50. The publisher keeps 50% of net and pays the author 50%, or $5.25. That amounts to a royalty payment of approximately 15% of the list price. Out of the publisher's $5.25 comes all overhead including the development of future titles.

In this model, the publisher earns the same amount regardless of what the retailer sells the book for. So if Amazon for example discounts a book from $35.00 to $26.00, the $9.00 comes off Amazon's share, not the publisher and author's.

Now, Amazon could afford to discount books because it had no bricks and mortar stores to finance. Bookstores could not compete and many went out of business. Of those that survived, most consolidated and began squeezing out the wholesalers, insisting publishers supply directly but at the same discount once offered the distributor, that is, 45% off list. Over time more pressure was exerted until the standard discount became 55% off list. Smaller bookstores, however, did not have the purchasing power to order directly from the publisher and had to continue to order via the distributor or wholesaler and pay a higher price. This tiered system continues today with wholesalers managing about 50% of books sold in the U.S. and the other 50% are sold by publishers directly to retailers.

The tiered system also affects smaller publishers who do not have the resources to manage their own distribution and must therefore supply solely through a wholesaler: this makes their books more expensive to retailers. Consequently, titles from smaller publishers have a hard time securing a spot on the shelf.

Agency Versus Distributor Discount: The eBook Price War

With ebooks, the print model was initially adopted as the basis for the new format: Amazon bought ebooks at 50% off the list price then sold them for whatever Amazon wished. However, to encourage the proliferation of ebooks and with them the Kindle device, Amazon began selling newly released ebooks for $9.99, often at a loss. What was frightening for the publishers was the potential to create in the mind of the consumer an expected price point of $9.99 which, if ebooks were to begin outselling print books, Amazon would then be able to force the wholesale price of ebooks down to a level where publishers and authors would simply not make enough money to continue to produce content. What Amazon refused to acknowledge, and what the consumer did not understand, is that while printing costs are indeed high, they are not the most significant cost to bringing a book to market. Acquisition, editorial development, design and marketing are much bigger expenses; printing accounts for only about 8-10% of a book's actual costs. To then suggest that an ebook should be half the price of a paperback is to ignore the true economics of publishing.

Needless to say, war broke out. Five of the largest U.S. publishers—Hachette, HarperCollins, Macmillan, Penguin, and Simon & Schuster—tried to pressure Amazon into raising its prices and to stop taking a loss. When Amazon refused, the publishers began delaying the release of a title's ebook until well after the release of the hardcover and paperback. Apple then saw an opportunity to take control of the ebook market away from Amazon by wooing publishers with an offer to sell ebooks at a higher price than Amazon *and* accept an agent's commission of only 30%, meaning the publisher set the list price and paid a 30% commission to Apple. A showdown finally ensued with Macmillan delivering Amazon an ultimatum: that the publisher would now set the list price and pay a 30% seller's commission to Amazon too; if Amazon did not comply, Macmillan would take their business solely to those who were prepared to accept this new "agency pricing." Amazon retaliated by removing *all* Macmillan books off its virtual shelves, not just ebooks.

Amazon spun their decision as that of a concerned parent looking out for the interests of the consumer, but this was really a battle between Apple and Amazon, with each trying to shore up support for their hardware: content drives device adoption. Yet the price on the Kindle was too high for a dedicated device and if consumers decided that the iPad, though more expensive, was the more economical option because of its multi-functionality, they would defect to the ePub format—and with it possibly also to rivals Kobo, Sony eReader and Nook whose devices are also ePub-based.

What was not making the news was that Apple was not, and does not, give publishers *carte blanche* control; rather, Apple sets a maximum price based on the physical book price. For example, a new release in hardcover priced at $30.00 cannot have an ebook edition priced higher than $14.99. Similar restrictions are placed on books featured on the *New York Times* Bestseller List. Only ebooks without a physical edition counterpart can be priced at the publisher's true discretion but—and it is a big but—Apple is not obligated to carry the title if Apple determines the list price is "unrealistic."[34]

The other fine print that was not advertised was the "price match" condition that Apple imposed: that a title could not be made available on a competitor's site at a lower price and, if it were, Apple had the right to lower their price. Moreover, since payment was by commission based on the actual selling price, a price reduction also meant a reduction in the amount paid to the publisher.

Nevertheless, and to make a long story short, Macmillan—and by proxy Apple—won that early battle but the war was not over. In March 2010, Amazon accepted agency pricing and the same commission level paid by Apple, but only for the Big 5 publishers who were demanding it, and only for books priced between $2.99 and $9.99; books priced outside this were paid at a rate of 35%—meaning the publisher was now paid 35% instead of 50% of list on those titles it insisted be priced higher than $9.99. Amazon also adopted the price match caveat that Apple had imposed.

Amazon then took another shot at Apple by allowing ebooks subject to the 35% royalty to be priced as high as the lowest list price for any physical edition of the book—that $30.00 hardcover could have an ebook version priced as high as $30.00 instead of Apple's $14.99, at least until the lower priced paperback was released—but Amazon added the caveat that the ebook had to be made available for sale in all jurisdictions for which the author or publisher had rights. Ebooks subject to the 70% royalty option could be priced as high as 80% of their physical counterparts; however, Amazon also added a per megabyte delivery charge for ebooks paid at the 70% rate.

This, however, did not end the agency pricing model as the five publishers decided to accept Amazon's penalty if it meant ensuring the price of ebooks remained at a sustainable level. However, the real loser was the author: to compensate for the financial penalties imposed by Amazon, publishers demanded from their authors a higher share of ebook earnings, 75% instead of the 50-50 split they pay on print books.

Barnes & Noble also eventually adopted agency pricing where requested by the publisher, as has Kobo. Terms vary slightly from Amazon's and Apple's but the principles are the same.

In May 2010 the war went global when Borders in Australia matched Amazon's prices and offered to refund consumers 10% of the difference. This led to a price war between Borders and Amazon. A few months later the insanity infected the UK when WH Smith, in an attempt to undercut rival Waterstones, dropped the price of its entire ebook catalogue by 50%. This led to some UK publishers imposing agency pricing on UK retailers as had happened in the U.S. Currently about one-third of ebooks sold in the UK are done so using agency pricing; the remaining two-thirds are not. (The ratio in the U.S. is not known.)

How Agency Pricing Affects Indie Authors

When Apple opened its doors to indie ebook publishers, Apple imposed agency pricing on us too. Amazon's Kindle and Barnes & Noble's PubIt! do so as well despite their continued insistence that agency pricing is abhorrent. So why impose it on indie writers? Simply put, because they can. To the indie author, then, it appears that agency pricing has become standard across the industry when, in fact, it has not: not all publishers agreed with the fear-mongering or the tactics of the Big 5 and consequently did not adopt their position: the majority of legacy publishers continue to sell ebooks to retailers, including Amazon and B&N, using the wholesale pricing model; only Apple imposes agency pricing across the board. So while legacy publishers have the option to choose their pricing model, for the most part indie authors do not.

For indie writers who contract with an aggregator whose retail contracts are mixed, this two-tiered system is creating havoc. Contracts that still use the distributor discount model lead to price discrepancies and inevitable reductions on rival retail sites. This inevitability became painfully real to indie authors in the summer of 2010 when Kobo began discounting ebooks, triggering price reductions on other sites. Some indie authors were hit twice when the reduction dropped their Kindle price below $2.99 and took them out of the 70% royalty bracket and into the 35% bracket: not only had their book price dropped but their royalty rate was halved. Among the more vocal victims were Smashwords authors, and many elected to remove their books from Kobo and some removed their books from Smashwords altogether. Smashwords eventually convinced Kobo in December 2010 to adopt the agency model but in April 2011 an alleged technical glitch resulted in Smashwords books sold on Kobo changing in price, mostly lower. This again caused significant grief and financial losses for authors whose books were then reduced on Amazon as well; and some authors were unconvinced by Kobo's assurances the problem had been accidental, or that it had been fixed. The issue is not whether the glitch was indeed accidental or deliberate, but rather that it illustrates the danger indie authors face with agency pricing. Without agency pricing the technical glitch would have been Kobo's problem and no one else's.

Hidden here, too, is the problem of lag times: the agency model allows the retailer to lower their price if a competitor does so as well, but there can be a significant lag time between a publisher changing their price and the price making it onto a retailer's site: retailers do not all update their metadata simultaneously or with the same frequency. This is particularly problematic for the self-publisher who sells through a distributor or aggregator: the lag time can be as long as two months. So the author who tries to put his or her book on sale for a limited time discovers to their dismay that when they raise the price back to full retail on their direct-to-retail sites like Amazon and input the change into their aggregator or distributor account, the new price does not make it as quickly onto their retail sites and the updates are staggered, triggering a possible price match on Amazon. Then once the higher price is restored on the aggregator or distributor's retailers, the lower price on Amazon can trigger an automatic price match on, say, Apple and Barnes & Noble. So what was intended to be a one-day or one-week promotion turns into an indefinite sale the author has little control over.

Where Will This All Lead?

Personally, I do not believe the agency model is sustainable both for legal and practical reasons. The agency model is price fixing and this is illegal in the U.S. and most Western jurisdictions—a manufacturer cannot dictate the retail price of a product, only the wholesale price. Sooner or later there will be a consumer or legislative challenge in the U.S.; agency pricing is already under investigation in the UK, where the February 2011 decision by the Office of Fair Trade to investigate complaints has put a halt to expansion of the agency model. If the UK rules against agency pricing, what effect will this have on agency pricing elsewhere? Agency price contracts speak to *all* retail channels: the contractual clauses do not have any geographical limitations placed upon them, and Apple's contract goes so far as to force parity across international jurisdictions. The only counter to this is where a publisher does not own worldwide rights: the publisher of a title in one jurisdiction cannot be bound to the terms a publisher in another jurisdiction has agreed to regarding distribution of the same title. Again, though, most indie writers own worldwide rights, so we more than any other publishers are adversely affected by this mess.

On the practical side, agency pricing only works if all retailers comply but retailers do not like the agency model: it removes their ability to compete on price alone or to offer promotions or discounts. Without competitive pricing with which to lure consumers, the retailer has to offer something else: exceptional customer service, loyalty programs, or brand recognition. To afford that you need resources, but if you are a small retailer what are the chances you will get the same commission structure as the larger ones? Or that you can offer your indie publishers the same deal as Amazon and Apple?

Even if everyone were onboard with agency pricing, compliance takes time. Contracts between publishers and retailers, between publishers and distributors, and between distributors and retailers all have to be renegotiated. In the interim there is pricing chaos and unintentional non-compliance. This creates too much uncertainty for the publisher because you never know if one of your distributor discount retailers will lower their price below the suggested list price and cause a backlash among your agency price retailers: agency pricing without the "lowest price" clause would have been workable (if still illegal) but agency pricing with the automatic right to price match is a nightmare. Agency pricing also creates more work for publishers because you have to adjust your pricing depending upon whom you are selling to, and you constantly have to monitor your pricing across sales channels. And the ideology behind Apple's decision to offer agency pricing was to create a monopoly. Once you have that, the monopolist dictates terms: will we see in ebooks precisely what we have already seen with print books: major retailers dictating more and more price cuts while incurring none of the risks that a publisher does? Apple and Amazon offer 70% now but will it be 60% later and then 50% after that and then ... who knows?

The decision by the Big 5 to accept Apple's agency pricing was, in my opinion, based on fear and short-sightedness. It made competition among retailers the publishers' problem. The distributor discount model is superior because it means certainty for the publisher: you get paid the same amount for your book regardless of whether Amazon wants to sell it for $9.99 or Apple wants to sell it for $12.99. What the Big 5 publishers should have done was accept Apple's 30% commission (70% royalty) but reject the automatic price match clause, and then offer product to Amazon at the same 30% discount instead of the 50% discount it had theretofore been enjoying. What this would have meant is that the loss Amazon incurred by selling ebooks at $9.99 would have increased, and even a company like Amazon cannot sustain losses over a long period of time. More importantly, it is illegal to price products at less than the retailer's cost: this is called predatory pricing and has been banned by the U.S. Supreme Court (and similar legislation exists elsewhere). Granted, a legal challenge would have taken time; would Amazon have held out long enough to create the idea in the mind of the consumer that ebooks should not be priced higher than $9.99, which is what the publishers feared and which would have rendered any legal win moot? Maybe, maybe not. It was a game of chicken and Amazon blinked, but I think they blinked because they realised they had not actually lost.

What publishers also lost in this battle was the ability to target specific audiences or geographical areas for promotion at the exclusion of others. For example, a publisher of romance novels might have a special offer on its own website for members, but with agency pricing the other retailers can simply follow suit and the membership is devalued. Or a publisher might want to offer a special price through a specific retailer who agrees to author readings and book signings; again, no can do without risking that special price across the board.

Do as I Say, Not as I Do

One has to wonder how real is this publisher control over pricing: read the Amazon and Barnes & Noble contracts and you will discover the retailers "have sole and complete discretion to set the price at which your eBooks are sold to the customer"[35]—which means they can, if they choose, discount your so-called agency price even if another retailer has not lowered the list price of your ebook. While this may merely be a clause to get around anti-trust legislation, the fact remains that the clause exists and can be invoked if market forces suggest to retailers that the clause would be advantageous to exercise.

Take a look, too, at actual practice and there is already nonconformity, even among publishers who demanded agency pricing. For example, when I checked the ebook version of Stephen King's *Full Dark, No Stars*, published by Scribner, an imprint of Simon & Schuster, it was selling for $9.99 on Apple, Sony, Barnes & Noble, BooksOnBoard, Diesel, and Google, but $11.99 on

Kobo and $14.48 on Amazon. The $14.48 ebook price meant it was subject to the 35% royalty and therefore the ebook could be priced as high as the lowest priced physical edition, in this case the paperback at $16.00. However, the $9.99 competitor price meant the Kindle book should have been priced to match. The Amazon website stated the Kindle book was sold not by Amazon Digital Services but by Simon and Schuster Digital Sales Inc. and "This price was set by the publisher" but really, what difference does that make? Simon & Schuster's website is still defined as a retail channel. Similarly, B&N was selling the paperback for $8.90 and the ebook for $9.99 yet B&N's contract states the ebook cannot be priced higher than any physical edition.

And what of Apple, who started this mess? Their iBookstore is doing poorly, mostly because Apple's reading apps are only available for Apple products, which despite having a sizeable market share are not the only game in town, and the iPad is next to impossible to read in a bright sun. Amazon has brought the price of the Kindle down, as has the likes of Kobo and Sony, making the economics of a dedicated device more affordable and the iPad considerably more expensive in comparison; consequently, Apple's ebook market penetration has not lived up to expectations. The drop in the price of the Kindle and competitor devices also reveals what the manufacturer/retailers have learned: that the money lays in delivering content, not hardware. This is why we have also seen over the past year the proliferation of free reading apps for computer and mobile devices from all the major players.

Legacy publishers shot themselves in the foot over this one, and now they are trying to save face by promoting agency pricing as a victory. Some aggregators also promote agency pricing as beneficial to their clients, but it only works so long as your aggregator's retailers all comply. But as Smashwords authors learned when their books were discounted on Kobo, all it takes is a single retailer who does not comply to create havoc for your titles and your bank account. And agency pricing is a form of bondage: Smashwords is now thus tied to the agency model, which limits their retail expansion to those willing to adopt the model unless Smashwords authors are prepared to risk a similar situation to the Kobo fiasco.

Whether this all proves in the end to be a short-term transitional phase, a short-lived experiment, or a permanent two-tiered system one thing seems certain: agency pricing is not a victory, at least not as far as I can see.

eBook Distribution and Royalties

Ebook distribution is achieved in three ways: the first is direct-to-retail sites like Amazon's Kindle, the second is through an aggregator, and the third is through ebook wholesalers who do not have retail sites of their own but often have a much larger network of retail partners than an aggregator does, and may also supply the library market as well, something aggregators do not do.

For the global indie author there is only one real ebook direct-to-retail option: Amazon's Kindle. It is the most flexible of the main players, allowing anyone who is of majority age, including non-U.S. residents, to open an account. Apple is also a possibility if you own a Mac and have a U.S. tax ID. PubIt! is not open to the foreign author: authors must be resident in the U.S. and possess a U.S. bank account, credit card, and tax number. Kobo, which is majority owned by Indigo Books & Music, announced in the late spring of 2011 that it will add an indie publishing division that will allow self-publishers to upload directly to Kobo instead of having to distribute through an aggregator; however, the site has not been launched yet so I cannot comment on its interface. I expect it to be similar to Kindle's and PubIt!'s.

Of course you can also sell your ebooks directly off the various publisher sites like LuLu or Smashwords, but these sites are small players in ebook retail and make more money distributing your work than selling it. You can also sell from your own website.

Amazon's Kindle

Amazon currently sells its Kindle books through four sites, the U.S., the UK, Germany, and France. Each site serves specific geographical areas, meaning a consumer in North America usually cannot purchase from the UK site and vice versa. The Kindle device ships to over 100 countries but from the U.S. only, and the Kindle apps are available for download in most countries. Kindle books currently support English, French, German, Spanish, Portuguese, and Italian languages only.

Ebooks are delivered via 3G and Wi-Fi networks through Amazon's Whispernet network, which is built on partnerships with companies like AT&T. Users must thus have access to a Whispernet partner network and in some areas users are subject to a hefty 3G network download fee, which increases the cost of ebooks. Once the ebook is downloaded, however, wireless access is not necessary except to sync across Kindle devices using its WhisperSync utility.

If you possess worldwide rights then Amazon places your books on all its Kindle sites. If you do not possess worldwide rights, or if you choose not to distribute to certain countries, books not available in a geographical area are either not listed when the user accesses the Kindle site or are indicated as "Not Available in Your Area." Books uploaded to Kindle can be DRM-controlled or not (author's choice).

When Amazon places your book on its UK or Continental Europe sites, in pounds sterling and euros, respectively, it does so at a price converted from the U.S. price the author sets or you can opt to set individual prices for each jurisdiction. Authors in the UK, Germany, and France who set up accounts there will have their books converted to other currencies in the same way. If the ebook is subject to sales tax it will be included in the list price or added at point of sale, depending on the rules of the sales jurisdiction.

As of January 2011, Amazon has two royalty levels for its ebooks, 35% and 70%. The lower royalty is mandatory for ebooks with a list price of less than $2.99 or more than $9.99, and optional for those books priced in between (all prices are in U.S. dollars). The 70% royalty is optional only for books priced over $2.99 and no more than $9.99. Your list price cannot exceed the list price offered in any other sales channel, including if you sell directly an electronic or print version of your book. If you select the 70% option you may also not offer your ebook at more than 20% below the list price for any physical edition offered in any sales channel, including direct sales. If you offer your book for free anywhere as a promotion, Amazon will do the same. Note that since the list price in the UK includes its Value Added Tax (VAT), the royalty is paid on the list price less VAT (otherwise Amazon would be paying you a royalty on the sales tax).

The 70% royalty only applies to sales in the U.S., Canada, the UK, Austria, Guernsey, Isle of Man, Jersey, Germany, Lichtenstein, Luxembourg, Switzerland, France, Monaco, and Belgium. Sales to other jurisdictions are paid at 35%. For sales paid at 70% Amazon charges the publisher a delivery fee of $0.15 per megabyte, which is deducted before the royalty is calculated.

Moreover, if Amazon sells at a lower price to match a competitor's price, or to match a price it sells your book for in another 70% jurisdiction (to adjust for changing exchange rates, for example), then the author is paid a royalty on the selling price, not the list price that was previously set. If the author is unhappy with the arrangement their sole remedy is to switch to the optional lower 35% royalty.

Notwithstanding the above, Amazon reserves the sole right to set the customer price.

Amazon pays 60 days after the month in which a sale is made; payment is either by electronic funds transfer (EFT) or by cheque (author's choice). Sales in the three currencies can be converted to U.S. dollars; sales in euros can be converted to either U.S. dollars or pounds sterling. To summarize, this is from Amazon's website:

Receive Amazon.com payments via:

• Electronic funds transfer in USD($) to your US bank account

• Check in USD($)

Receive Amazon.co.uk payments via:

• Electronic funds transfer in USD ($) to your US bank account

• Electronic funds transfer in GBP (£) to your UK bank account

• Paper cheque in GBP (£)

Receive Amazon.de payments via:

• Electronic funds transfer in USD ($) to your US bank account

• Electronic funds transfer in GBP (£) to your UK bank account

• Electronic funds transfer in EUR (€) to your EUR denominated bank account

• Paper check in EUR(€)[36]

For EFTs, royalties due must be a minimum of $10.00/£10.00/€10,00 or more; if by cheque, there is a minimum royalty balance of $100.00/£100.00/€100,00. (At time of writing, Amazon had not yet updated its website to include information on Amazon.fr.)

On your account page, the default payment method is by cheque. If you wish to be paid by EFT, for each sale currency you must select the currency to be paid in and provide the relevant bank account details. Although some of the distributors and aggregators sell to Amazon, it is highly advised that you have your own account with Amazon and opt out of that sales channel when selling through a distributor or aggregator: not only do you not lose any royalties but your price at Amazon can act as a benchmark for how you set your price elsewhere.

To avoid needless and lengthy repetition, for details on selling directly through Amazon, I ask that you return to Chapter 1, Step 10 for instructions on the Kindle publishing interface. To this I need only add that, when uploading your book cover, this is the product image as explained in the section "Book Cover and Product Image" in Chapter 9: Cover and Interior Images; and you do not have to use an image that is between 1024 and 1200 pixels high as is recommended for novice users.

Also, note that Amazon has placed information about book lending on the Kindle publishing website under Merchandising Your Book, which is after the fact. Considering that some authors find mandatory book lending to be as contentious an issue as DRM, it behooves Amazon to put this information under the more relevant section, Publish Your Book.

Barnes & Noble's PubIt! (Nook Books)

Barnes & Noble's Nook ereaders are sold in the U.S. only, though Canadians can purchase a Nook in the U.S. and use it in Canada; both countries can also download Nook's free computer and mobile apps. Nook books are sold from the U.S. site only but can be downloaded in the U.S. and Canada. Nook books can be DRM-controlled or not (author's choice). Nook makes use of Wi-Fi for download so users do not need access to the 3G network; however, downloads outside of a Wi-Fi area are not possible. Once downloaded, books can be read without access to the Internet. Nook books currently support English, Spanish, French, German, Italian, Portuguese, Latin, and Dutch languages.

PubIt! is open only to authors who are U.S. residents and possess a U.S. tax ID, a U.S. credit card, and a U.S. bank account. The first is because Barnes & Noble must report author earnings to the IRS; the second is because if your account goes into arrears due to customer returns or fraud claims, the balance will be charged to your card; and the third is necessary because B&N pays only by EFT.

PubIt! pays a 65% royalty on ebooks priced between $2.99 and $9.99, and a 40% royalty for books published outside those figures (but they cannot be priced less than $0.99 or greater than $199.99). Again, the list price cannot be greater than a competitor's list price in any sales channel, and not greater than the print version in any sales channel. Barnes & Noble also reserves sole and complete discretion to set the customer price.

B&N pays 60 days after the month in which a sale occurs.

Please return to Chapter 2 for step-by-step instructions for uploading directly to PubIt!. I add only that you can use a differently sized image that previously recommended; the image must merely conform to B&N requirements as explained in the section "Book Cover and Product Image" in Chapter 9: Cover and Interior Images.

Apple's iBookstore

Depending on where you look on the Apple website, one can only publish directly to the iBookstore if you have a U.S Social Security Number (SSN) or an Employer Identification Number (EIN); however, once you find Apple's well-hidden account application page, it states you only require "A U.S. Tax ID. Anyone (including non-U.S. residents) can obtain a U.S. Tax ID ... If you don't have one, request one from the IRS."[37] Someone needs to explain to Apple that, while an EIN is available to any company, including sole proprietorships, whether registered in the U.S. or abroad, an Individual Taxpayer Indentification Number (ITIN) is only available to those not eligible for an SSN, and obtaining an ITIN is not quite as simple as "requesting" one from the IRS.

In addition to the tax ID, you also need a valid iTunes Store account with a credit card on file. And while the other e-retailers are cross-platform, to sell on Apple's bookstore you must use an Intel-based Mac running OS X 10.5.8 or later, with at least 1GB of RAM, and QuickTime 7.0.3 or later installed; at least 10GB of available hard drive space (more for larger catalogues), and a broadband Internet connection with an upload rate of 1MB/sec or faster is recommended. Apple sells only DRMed ePubs and they must have an ISBN assigned to them. Apple also states, "Note: Meeting these requirements and submitting an application does not guarantee that Apple will work directly with you. You may still be referred to an Apple-approved aggregator."[38]

Apple ebooks are sold in 28 countries in North America and Europe. Apple supports English, French, German, Dutch, Italian, Russian, Spanish, Danish, Finnish, Norwegian, Polish, Portuguese, and Swedish languages.

Apple takes a 30% commission on all sales and pays the remainder 45 days after the month the sale takes place, by EFT only, and in the currency designated by the publisher, subject to a minimum balance of $150.00 or equivalent thereof; if the minimum balance is not met, royalties accrue.

Kobo

Kobo devices are sold online through the Kobo store and in physical stores in the U.S., Canada, the UK, Australia and New Zealand; its computer and mobile apps are available in more than

200 countries. Books with worldwide rights are available in those same 200+ countries. Books not possessing worldwide rights are restricted as per geographical rights management.

Kobo devices are Wi-Fi only so users do not need access to a 3G network, and do not incur the expense of one. However, the mobility of the device is limited to areas with Wi-Fi service. As with other devices, once a book is downloaded the user does not need access to Wi-Fi in order to read the book.

Kobo books are priced in U.S. dollars and converted to Canadian dollars and pounds sterling; publishers who contract directly with Kobo can elect to set a fixed price in these currencies, and can also set a fourth currency. Publishers have the option to contract under agency pricing or the distributor discount model.

Kobo publishers have the option to apply Adobe DRM to their titles but the DRM is not modified to make the ePub device-specific. In this respect, Kobo has the edge over their competitors in the area of content delivery, and it is clear their decision to do so reflects a recognition that the money is in content, not hardware.

Kobo's website states: "Interested in selling your content on Kobo? If you own the digital rights to your content - be it one title, a thousand titles, or more - we can make it happen."[39] Alas, this is misleading: Kobo is not set up to deal with most indie authors. If you contact Kobo requesting an account you will be redirected to an aggregator; the reason, Kobo will give you, is that they require author/publishers have a minimum of ten titles with the appropriate ISBNs, who can provide Kobo with properly formatted ONIX code, and who can operate an FTP file system including light troubleshooting. Which begs the question, Why does it advertise it can work with a single title, and that it can "make it happen," when it is the publisher doing all the work?

Nevertheless, even if you have only a single title, if you can fulfil the other requirements Kobo may allow you to set up a direct account. For most indie publishers, however, working with an aggregator is likely your best option.

Earlier in 2011, Kobo announced it will add a direct-to-retail option for self-published authors by year's end, though a firm date has not been added. When this happens expect to see the agency model offered to indie authors.

eBook Aggregators

Authors who do not meet the criteria for working directly with a retailer, or who simply do not wish to have multiple accounts with several retailers, can buy their way out of the problem by contracting with an ebook aggregator.

To refresh your memory, an aggregator is a company that specializes in converting manuscripts into the various ebook formats, sells your ebooks through their own online bookstore, and also distributes your ebook to a selection of retail partners like Amazon, Barnes & Noble, Sony, et cetera. The retailers pay your royalties to the aggregator who then takes a percentage as their distribution fee before passing the remainder on to you.

Aggregators vary widely in the services they offer, the fees for those services, and their royalty cut. Some charge an insertion fee while others do not. Some sell and/or distribute a variety of formats while others only ePubs and PDFs. Some sell to a multiplicity of retail channels while some sell only to one. Most aggregators also sell through their own retail sites and pay a higher royalty for sales from those sites. Where the aggregator also offers print-on-demand services you will often see package deals offered to authors who choose both.

When choosing an aggregator, think critically about any claims they make about the success of their titles. For example, LuLu used to boast on their website that over 3,000 Lulu titles are available on the iBookstore, over 60,000 units have been purchased through the iBookstore, and over $130,000 in Lulu author royalties have been paid from iBookstore sales. That sounds really impressive until you do the math: what those figures reveal is that LuLu titles on iBookstore average about twenty sales per title, and pay an average royalty of $2.17 per sale.

Some aggregators offer free ISBNs; as noted in the chapter on the ISBN system, if you accept an ISBN registered to an aggregator they become your publisher.

One limitation you will run into with any aggregator is an inability to follow to the letter the rules of the ISBN agency. For example, I produced my own ePub for distribution and assigned an ISBN to it. I then signed on with eBookIt for distribution to Apple, Sony, and Barnes & Noble. Both Sony and B&N now use Adobe Digital Editions for digital rights management but one retailer, Apple, uses its own DRM and its ibooks cannot be read on competitor devices. Technically speaking, the Apple ePub should therefore have a separate ISBN, but there is not a mechanism to do this through the distributor: they distribute only the one ePub. One therefore has to rely on the consumer to know the limitations of whichever ePub they purchase.

Smashwords

One of the more popular aggregators, Smashwords accepts only Word documents, which Smashwords converts to a multiplicity of formats to sell on its own site: HTML, Javascript, mobi, ePub, PDF, RTF, LRF, and PDB. All are DRM-free and authors are not given the option to apply it. Smashwords distributes ePubs to Apple, Barnes & Noble, Kobo, Diesel, Sony Reader Store, Aldiko, and Stanza; and Smashwords has been trying to finalise a deal with Amazon's Kindle but so far without success. Authors are allowed to cherry pick which retailers they wish to do business with, which is convenient for the author who has direct accounts with the larger retailers.

Smashwords supports all languages but distributes according to the languages supported by individual retailers. For example, Smashwords will accept Japanese-, Korean- and Chinese-language books but will not distribute them to Apple or B&N since their devices do not support these languages.

Authors may assign their own ISBNs to their titles; however, they can only do so to the ePub as Smashwords does not have the option for the author to assign ISBNs to the many formats sold on the Smashwords site: the author cannot upload finished files with the relevant ISBNs assigned. Instead Smashwords converts a single file into multiple formats, so the author who wants to assign ISBNs to each format cannot do so with Smashwords. Alternatively, you can opt out of selling on the Smashwords retail site and only have Smashwords distribute the ePub format, which is the only format it assigns an ISBN to (its or yours, as applicable). Smashwords has indicated they may accept fully formatted ePubs in future but has not yet implemented this.

Smashwords pays 70.5% of net sales off affiliate sites, and 60% of the list price for most other retailers: Apple, B&N, Sony, and Diesel. This 60% is regardless of the price you set for your book, in which case your royalty through Smashwords will be higher than if you deal directly with B&N for books priced outside the $2.99 to $9.99 price range. For books within that price range, the author earns less through Smashwords: 60% of list instead of 65% of list when dealing directly with B&N. Smashwords pays 60% of list for Kobo books priced under $12.99, and only for sales denominated in U.S. dollars; sales at other price points or in other currencies earn 38%.

Apple, Kobo, and Sony automatically apply DRM to titles uploaded to their sites. Smashwords books on B&N and Diesel are not DRMed.

For sales on their own site, sales are DRM-free and non-returnable. Smashwords pays the author "up to" 85% of net for sales, with net defined as the:

> ... sales price paid and received less payment processing fees, affiliate fees, retailer discounts, costs due to erroneous or fraudulent transactions, credit card charge-backs and associated fees. Therefore, 85% of "net proceeds" does not equal 85% of the book's sales price. Payment processing fees, for example, may account for a sizable percentage of the List Price for lower cost books because they include a nominal minimum per-transaction fee ... charged to Smashwords by our payment processing service PayPal. For example, if the per-transaction fee charged by our payment processor is $.35, and a book is only priced at $1.00, then that $.35 accounts for 35 percent of the retail price.[40]

This latter charge will be mitigated if a customer buys more than one book since this is a per-transaction fee, not a per unit fee.

Smashwords pays quarterly by paper cheque (U.S. residents only) when royalties reach $75.00; until then they accrue. U.S. authors can also elect to be paid via PayPal; Smashwords will pay using this latter method when royalties reach U.S. $10.00 or more in the quarter. Foreign authors are paid via PayPal only. For authors outside the U.S. and Canada, PayPal charges a fee for the funds transfer; you need to inquire directly with PayPal as to what fees are imposed in your country and/or currency. Smashwords pays in U.S. dollars only.

BookBaby

BookBaby wholesales ePubs to Apple, Sony, and Barnes & Noble, and mobi files to Amazon; and authors can opt-out of any channel. BookBaby charges a $99.00 set-up fee per title and an annual fee of $19.00 after that but does not take a cut of royalties: authors are paid 100% of net received from retailers. However, BookBaby also charges a hefty $50.00 fee for file revisions (proofread for those typos or they will be expensive to fix). You can change the price or metadata for free only once per year; further changes are $50.00 each so promotions will be expensive to implement. You really need to do your homework before you upload to this site and to balance the loss of revenue through maintenance costs against any perceived increase in royalties: BookBaby actually pays less than Smashwords for sales to Sony and Barnes & Noble, even after taking into consideration Smashwords' cut. For sales to Apple, BookBaby will pay higher than Smashwords, but will your sales through Apple be sufficient to offset your maintenance costs?

Publishers are advised to purchase their own ISBNs though BookBaby will otherwise provide one for $19.00, and BookBaby warns that although it will be assigned to you some retailers will list BookBaby as the publisher. (This suggests to me that in the Bowker database BookBaby is perhaps listing itself as the publisher and the author as the imprint. As it is forbidden for a publisher to resell ISBNs allocated to them, this may be the workaround.)

BookBaby will convert your Word, RTF, TXT, HTML or Pages file to the mobi and/or ePub format at no charge; Adobe PDF, Quark, and InDesign files are converted for $39.00 per ebook up to 250 pages; over 250 pages, add $0.25 per page. Note, however, that BookBaby will not provide you with a copy of your final files; if you later decide you are not happy with BookBaby, you will have to start over again in your file conversion. BookBaby also offers cover design and more complex formatting services.

Files distributed to Apple and Sony are automatically DRM-managed; BookBaby files distributed to Amazon and B&N are DRMed at the author's discretion.

B&N and Sony pay 50% of the suggested list price to BookBaby authors even if B&N or Sony lower the sale price, which means they are using the distributor discount model. Amazon and Apple use the agency pricing model and pay as they do elsewhere. Since these two models conflict with each other, the author may end up in a situation where retailer competition creates a downward price spiral. For example, if you set your list price via BookBaby at $3.99,

Amazon and Apple will sell your book for $3.99 and pay a royalty of $2.79. But if B&N and Sony only have to pay a royalty of $2.00, either retailer can easily reduce the price of your book to beat the other, and BookBaby indicates these retailers usually discount 5% to 10% off list. This will likely trigger the price-match clause in the agreements with Amazon and Apple, who will then lower your book price and with it your royalty.

Using a list price of $3.99 as an example, the only way to achieve the same royalty and protect the price point is to set two separate prices: $3.99 for a list price for Amazon and Apple ($3.99 x 70% equals a royalty of $2.79), and a wholesale price of $5.50 for B&N and Sony ($5.50 x 50% equals a royalty of $2.75) and let them reduce their sale price to $3.99 if they want. But BookBaby will not let you set two different prices. So in my opinion your only real option is to contract with Amazon separately, set your target list price with them, then set a higher list price with BookBaby and let B&N, Apple, and Sony reduce their prices to match Amazon's.

BookBaby pays within seven days of your account accruing to a minimum that you set but which can be no less than U.S. $10.00. Payment is by EFT (U.S. accounts only), PayPal, or paper cheque; the latter is subject to a $1.50 fee. The currency of payment is not indicated, but one can infer it is U.S. dollars only.

eBookIt

EBookIt distributes to Apple, Sony, Barnes & Noble, Kobo, Amazon, and to a variety of smaller e-retailers via Ingram Digital; Google Books is in the works. Authors can opt out of any channel. EBookIt thus has the widest distribution of the aggregators listed here but pays the least except for Kobo, who pays eBookIt 55% regardless of the country or currency of sale. EBookIt also sells off its own site but authors have dedicated pages; eBookIt does not have a bookstore per se.

EBookIt charges a $149.00 insertion fee, no annual fee, and takes 15% of net royalties. There is no minimum threshold before you are paid, but if so it pays only by PayPal unless your royalties exceed $500.00 per month. You can opt to be paid by paper cheque, in which case royalties accrue until payment exceeds $100.00; a $5.00 processing fee applies. EBookIt pays by the fifteenth of the month after sales take place, and pays in U.S. dollars only.

EBookIt's insertion fee includes conversion from Word documents including those with the .docx extension, Pages, ODT or RTF files. EBookIt also accepts PDF files and physical books but will charge extra for the processing. Later changes are charged at $49.00 per hour. EBookIt converts to ePub, mobi, PDF, LIT, and MP3 (audiobooks). Audiobooks are sold via the eBookIt website only. The insertion fee also includes a free ISBN if you do not already have one but it will be applied to the ePub only. Note, however, that eBookIt will not provide you with a copy of your final mobi or ePub files; if you later decide you are not happy with eBookIt, you will have to start over again in your file conversion.

EBookIt gives indie authors the option to sign up as an author or a publisher. If you have your own ISBN you must sign up as a publisher; when you do the relevant metadata field will appear where you input your ISBN. If you have a fully compliant ePub you can also elect to upload it and bypass the conversion process; in this case the insertion fee is $49.00 instead of $99.00. If you later make changes to your file, you have to pay the $49.00 fee again. Price changes cost $15.00 per change.

EBookIt supports any language accepted by their retailers. You can check the eBookIt site for the latest languages supported and by which retailers.

For sales on its own site, titles are DRM-free. DRM is automatically applied by Apple, Sony, and Kobo; all others are at author's choice.

Amazon and Apple pay the same as they do directly. Sony pays eBookIt authors 40% of list. Kobo pays 55%. B&N pays 65% for ebooks priced between $2.99 and $9.99, and 40% for books priced outside that range. Ingram Digital pays 45%. All of course will be reduced by eBookIt's 15% of net. For sales from its own site, eBookIt takes 25% of list.

Note as well that Amazon, Apple, and B&N use the agency model but the rest use the wholesale discount model. As with BookBaby, then, you have this dilemma of having to set only one list price for differently modelled retailers; so, again as with BookBaby, I would advise authors to contract separately with Amazon, then set a higher list price through eBookIt and let their retailers discount down to your Amazon price.

Lulu

LuLu's website indicates it supplies only to Apple's iBookstore but a search on Amazon Kindle revealed numerous titles published by LuLu, so it is unclear whether the author is permitted to upload Lulu-published titles directly or whether LuLu's website needs updating. LuLu also sells PDFs and ePubs from its own site, both that of its own authors and as a retailer for others such as Ingram Digital.

LuLu accepts ePubs or will convert a Word document. Titles are DRMed at the discretion of the author and a fee is charged for the service though at what amount is not disclosed on its website.

Since Apple will only accept ePubs with an ISBN attached, authors must assign their own or LuLu will provide a free one; if the latter, LuLu becomes your publisher. LuLu also offers a purchase option to buy an ISBN in your own name for $99.98; this is only available to residents of the U.S., Guam or Puerto Rico. (Again, however, since resale of ISBNs is not permitted, the logistics of this transaction are unclear. Does LuLu just do the "paperwork" for you? Does it call itself the publisher and use the author's name as the imprint?)

LuLu retains 20% of net royalties from Apple and pays the remaining 80% of net to the author. For example, if your book sells for $2.99 on Apple, Apple keeps 30% and pays $2.09; LuLu then keeps $0.42 and pays the author $1.67. What royalty LuLu pays for ebooks sold through its own website I could not find listed anywhere on the website.

LuLu pays via PayPal or paper cheque. If you elect to be paid by cheque, LuLu pays 45 days after each quarter for royalties earned in the quarter provided revenues reach a minimum of $20.00; if not, they accrue. Payment is in U.S. dollars only. If you select PayPal, LuLu pays monthly as long as your royalties are $5.00 or more (or the equivalent thereof); if not they accrue. PayPal payments may be made in euros, pounds sterling, or U.S. dollars. For those outside the U.S. and Canada, PayPal charges a fee for the funds transfer; you need to inquire directly with PayPal as to what fees are imposed in your country and/or currency.

Of all the sites I tested, I found LuLu's the most difficult to find information about pricing and royalties. LuLu really makes you dig, which does not inspire trust, at least it does not for me.

eBook Wholesale Distributors

Ebook wholesalers differ from aggregators in that wholesalers do not sell ebooks directly via their own websites; they only wholesale to retailers and/or libraries. Wholesalers are further differentiated from aggregators in that the former will never offer to assign an ISBN to your title; you must provide this yourself. Wholesale services are aimed at the professional publisher in that a minimum number of titles may be required before an account can be set up, DRM is offered on all titles, files must be submitted in their final format and in working order, and in most cases ONIX code must be provided by the publisher (though some sites provide Excel templates). Smaller wholesalers willing to do business with indie authors generally do not provide the full range of distribution: you will notice in particular that the library and academic market is closed to us.

While a full services wholesale distributor like CoreSource or OverDrive will have thousands of sales channels, the ebook wholesalers available to indie publishers rarely have more than a half-dozen; in some cases, like LibreDigital, they have only one, Apple.

Wholesale distributors may charge a title set-up fee and may also charge an annual catalogue fee, and take a percentage of net sales. Except for those retailers who use agency pricing, the author sets the retail price of the ebook and the distributor discount, which means your royalties are set and also potentially higher because they are not based on the list price but the wholesale price that you set.

Two ebook wholesalers available to the indie author are Ingram Digital and LibreDigital.

Ingram Digital (Lightning Source)

Lightning Source clients can elect to sign on with Ingram Digital, which provides DRM-enabled ebooks in the following formats: ePubs and PDFs (Adobe DRM), and PDB (eReader DRM). Each format must bear a unique ISBN. Ingram Digital does not require a minimum number of titles and they produce the ONIX code for you when you upload your title and fill out information fields. Ingram Digital does not charge a title set-up fee, takes 7.5% of net, and pays monthly.

Previously, Ingram Digital also distributed LIT files but this has been discontinued: Microsoft realised they lost this one and are not developing the format any further. In August 2011 Microsoft announced that official discontinuation will take place 12 August 2012 with no new purchases allowed after 7 November 2011. I expect PDBs to go the same way as the LIT if they have not already.

Ingram Digital wholesales to several dozen retailers globally but Ingram Digital does not contract with Barnes & Noble or Sony, and Kobo only accepts PDFs (Kobo uploads ePubs only from Ingram's CoreSource). Ingram Digital also sells to Apple but under a separate agreement and publishers with less than 25 titles must bear a $250.00 account fee. These limitations I find not just a problem but incomprehensible considering Ingram's position in the industry. It leads me to wonder how much of this is pressure by CoreSource's large publishers to restrict competition from the small publishers, including indie publishers, that Ingram Digital services.

Ingram Digital uses the wholesaler's discount model, meaning you set the list price and the retailers' discount, and the retailer in turn sells your book for any amount they wish. This as you know can cause conflict with the agency pricing model so you have to set your price and discount taking into account any potential conflict with your other retailers.

One other interesting facet of Ingram Digital's distribution method is that it does not actually transfer a copy of your file to the retailer; rather, when customers order your book they are actually downloading it from Ingram Digital, even though the website interface suggests they are downloading it from the retailer. This means the retailers cannot fudge their sales reporting.

Ingram Digital pays in U.S. dollars 90 days after the month in which a sale takes place; publishers can opt for EFT or paper cheque.

LibreDigital

For the indie author, LibreDigital wholesales ePubs solely to Apple's iBookstore, does not charge a title set-up fee but offers conversion services for a fee. Titles must be assigned ISBNs. LibreDigital pays 75 days after month of sale, takes a hefty 45% of net, and pays monthly but only if royalties are $500.00 or more; if less, royalties accrue. Since all books are sold on Apple, all are DRM-managed.

eBook Distribution Strategy

As you can see from the above, distributing through only one wholesaler or aggregator, while certainly more convenient, can be problematic. Working out a pricing and distribution strategy is therefore essential for the indie author who wishes to maximize their royalties and minimize conflict between the agency and distribution pricing models.

In the case of *Baby Jane*, I elected to publish directly to Kindle, which then formed my benchmark price. I was able to publish directly to Kobo as well, and used Kobo to set my benchmark price for ePubs. I contracted with Ingram Digital because of its wider distribution channels; it uses the distributor model but as I was free to set the discount I was able to price the ebook higher than for Kindle (to protect that price point). I then contracted with eBookIt to handle distribution to Apple, Sony, and Barnes & Noble because these retailers are not covered by Ingram Digital. The price I set at eBookIt was higher than Kindle and Kobo because of the mixed pricing models, and I just let the retailers price match if they wished.

If you later decide to change your price, it is advisable to change the price with your wholesalers or aggregators *before* you make any price changes with your direct retailers like Amazon or B&N. Make a note of how long it took for your books to go from your aggregator or wholesaler to the retail channels, then structure your price changes accordingly. For example, if changes inputted through your aggregator take a month to make it onto retailer sites, make the change then monitor the sites; once you see the new price then you can change your price on Amazon, which usually only takes no more than one day to go into effect. (Do not trust your Kindle publisher dashboard; the price change will invariably take effect on the Kindle website before it shows up on your dashboard.)

eBook Returns

Most retailers do not allow refunds of electronic content. Amazon, however, does accept customer returns of digital content within seven days; refunds show up on your balance sheet as a negative transaction and are deducted from your account balance. I find this policy to be unfair to the author since seven days is more than enough time to read a book then return for a refund. Amazon claims it monitors customers for excessive returns but to what end? Granted, there are problems with fraudulent books sold on Amazon and a blanket no-return policy would be unfair to consumers; however, the consumer is allowed to download sample pages so it is not like they can claim the book was not what they expected.

Purchases made using a fraudulent credit card are also charged back to the author. Some retailers and aggregators also charge back to the author any bank charges associated with fraudulent credit card transactions. Apple even goes so far as to make the publisher responsible for Apple's commission "even if Apple is unable to collect the Customer Price for that eBook from that eBook purchaser. The 'sale' of an eBook shall occur when an eBook is first delivered to an end-user."[41] I find this practice quite cheeky considering the author has no say in payment terms accepted by the retailer; the risk should lie with the retailer as it does with print books.

Print Distribution

Print distribution is handled in a multiplicity of ways. An author can publish through a vanity publisher who will usually have both their own online bookstore and one or more wholesalers who then sell to retailers; another way is to self-publish and hire the services of a print-on-demand manufacturer who fulfils orders placed directly by large retailers such as Amazon and by smaller retailers through a network of wholesalers. Authors can also order books from the manufacturer and sell them through their own websites, direct to retailers, through online seller programs such as eBay or Amazon's Advantage, or direct to consumers.

Print on Demand

With POD, the author contracts with the manufacturer who then receives and fulfils orders directly from the retailer or via the wholesaler(s), depending upon the manufacturer's contracts. When a book is ordered at a retail site the order goes to the wholesaler who then instructs the manufacturer to print the book and send it to the retailer. If the manufacturer has a contract to supply a retailer directly, then the order goes to the manufacturer who fulfils it and ships directly to the retailer. There are also a myriad of POD companies who do not offer distribution but who can be considered as an option if you are printing for personal use or to distribute yourself.

If the author publishes through a vanity press such as iUniverse, the vanity publisher sets the list price and discount. Vanity press/POD manufacturer hybrids like CreateSpace allow the author to set the list price but the discount is fixed by CreateSpace. POD manufacturers such as Lightning Source leave the list price and distributor discount at the discretion of the author but usually have a set minimum discount. In all cases the author is paid a royalty of the wholesale price less manufacturing costs. This amount remains fixed: as with traditional printing, if the retailer wishes to discount the list price they do so out of their profits and not the author/publisher's.

Every POD contract will state that the company retains the right to subcontract to third parties in order to ensure fulfilment. This is good in that you can be assured of timely delivery but bad in that you are asked to approve a proof printed by the company you have contracted with but you cannot be certain this will be the same book delivered to your customer. Variations in quality can be quite pronounced even where each company claims to be using the same weight of cover or interior paper stock.

Some POD companies charge a per-title set-up fee while others advertise that it is free to publish. Know that nothing is ever free: if it is "free" to publish it is more expensive to manufacture or there is a fee to distribute.

Below are some of the more popular manufacturers with distribution networks. (Note: only those companies for whom author services are optional are included here; for companies where author services are mandatory, see Chapter 19: The Vanity Press Machine.)

CreateSpace

CreateSpace does not charge a set-up fee but charges a higher manufacturing fee per book unless a Pro Plan is purchased for $39.00 (and $5.00 per annum after that); since the manufacturing costs are significantly higher without the Pro Plan, and since the Expanded Distribution option is only available to those who buy the Pro Plan, you invariably do and therefore you are really paying a title set-up fee. The cost to manufacture is the total of the cost per page and a fixed per unit fee. You must also order and approve of a proof before your title can go to market; this will be charged at the manufacturing price plus delivery costs (about $25.00 for express shipping, less if you are willing to wait a few weeks). If you do not approve the proof you can make changes free of charge and you can then order and pay for a new proof or proceed to market.

With the Pro Plan, CreateSpace sets the discount for sales to its own site at 20% off list. Sales to Amazon.com are at 40% off list. Sales through Expanded Distribution are set at 60% off list. Sort of. But more on that in a minute.

CreateSpace pays the author the discounted price less the cost of manufacture. For example, *Baby Jane*'s list price is $17.95. The cost to manufacture under the Pro Plan is $3.24 (270 pages @ $0.012/page) + $0.85 fixed unit charge, for a total of $4.09. If selling directly off the CreateSpace website the discount price would be $14.36; less the manufacturing costs of $4.09, the royalty would be an impressive $10.27. However, anecdotal evidence suggests that few people order off the CreateSpace website because its shipping fees are too high. If you purchase books directly from CreateSpace, you pay the same manufacturing fee per unit plus shipping.

When a customer orders your book from Amazon.com, Amazon "buys" the book from its subsidiary CreateSpace for 40% off retail; so in the case of *Baby Jane*, Amazon pays $10.77 ($17.95 less 40%) to CreateSpace, which then pays me a royalty of $6.68 ($10.77 minus $4.09).

Under their Expanded Distribution, which includes Amazon sites outside the U.S., CreateSpace distributes solely to Ingram. CreateSpace sets the discount at 60% off list, though in reality it actually sells it to Ingram at 45% off list, pocketing the 15% as a distributor's fee (an unreasonable cut, in my opinion). Ingram then sells your book onward at anywhere between 25% off list (small, powerless bookstores) to around 40% off list (larger, more powerful players like Barnes & Noble or Chapters). You will never know what each retailer pays (unless they tell you) because those contracts are confidential. Under Expanded Distribution, I would be paid $7.18 ($17.95 less 60%) less the $4.09 manufacturing fees, for a royalty of $3.09. Titles distributed to Ingram take about six weeks to make it into retail channels.

When CreateSpace distributes globally, the books are printed in the U.S. and shipped abroad. Retailers pay for the books in U.S. dollars and then convert to their own currency and sell the book for whatever price the retailer feels is appropriate. CreateSpace royalties are thus paid only in U.S. dollars.

CreateSpace pays within 31 days after the end of the month in which a unit is sold provided your royalties are a minimum of $20.00; otherwise they accrue. Payment is by electronic funds transfer (EFT) if you have a U.S. bank account; if not, CreateSpace will pay by U.S. dollar cheque but they "may charge a per check fee and accrue and withhold payments until the total amount due meets a minimum dollar threshold."[42] What that cheque fee and minimum threshold might be is not stated anywhere.

Lightning Source

With Lightning Source, the publisher pays a fixed title set-up fee—in the case of a paperback book with a black and white interior, Lightning Source's fees are $37.50 for the cover and $37.50 for the interior—and an annual catalogue fee of $12.00. The initial proof costs a flat fee of $30.00 including express shipping. Changes are charged at $40.00 per new file (your cover and interior are separate files). However, for your money you get a wider distribution network and control over both the list price and discount, and thus a potentially higher royalty. Your titles also appear faster on retail sites, usually within one to two weeks, because Lightning Source is owned by Ingram.

Lightning Source recommends the "standard" distributor discount of 55%. I am told by Lightning Source that each wholesaler is sold the book at that discount (but I cannot confirm this), and in turn they sell it on to their retailers for a price below list; as already noted, what the terms are for each retailer you will never know because the contracts are confidential. However, since the wholesaler is buying the book at 55% off list as opposed to 45% off list as it does from CreateSpace, the wholesaler can sell it forward at a lower, more attractive price to their retailers. This increases the chances of a retailer stocking your book.

Lightning Source charges slightly higher manufacturing costs than CreateSpace: in the case of *Baby Jane*, the cost is $0.013 per page plus a fixed unit fee of $0.90, for a total of $4.41. I elected to set the discount at the recommended 55% off list. When a unit is sold, Lightning Source charges the wholesaler $8.08 ($17.95 less 55%), and pays me a "publisher's compensation" of $3.67 ($8.08 minus $4.41). So even though the cost per unit is higher my royalty is actually $0.58 higher than with CreateSpace for sales outside Amazon.com.

If the publisher buys directly from Lightning Source it charges a higher manufacturing fee of about 15%: in the case of *Baby Jane*, the fees are $0.90 fixed unit fee and $0.015 per page, for a total of $5.04. Lightning Source also charges a per shipment handling fee of $1.50 and of course shipping fees. It does, however, offer volume discounts starting at 5% for 50 books.

Lightning Source pays within 90 days after the end of the month a unit was sold provided your cumulative compensation due is $25.00 or more; if not, it accrues. Payment is by EFT into a U.S. account or by paper cheque. Clients outside the U.S. may elect to have the funds converted and paid by EFT or cheque in euros, Australian dollars, or pounds sterling depending upon which contract(s) is signed.

For sales abroad, Lightning Source sells your books in U.S. dollars and ships from the U.S. unless you contract with Lightning Source's foreign subsidiaries.

Lulu

Lulu is a U.S. company that sells print books on seven international sites: U.S., UK, France, Germany, Italy, Spain, and the Netherlands. The author sets the price in either U.S. dollars, euros, or pounds sterling and that price is used as the basis for all the other international sites: the price set by the author is converted using an exchange rate determined by LuLu.

LuLu does not charge a title set-up fee to print but only distributes for free to Amazon.com; it is a $75.00 fee to distribute through LuLu's Global Reach program, which incidentally is the only program available to authors who bear their own ISBNs. Manufacturing rates are quite high compared to CreateSpace and Lightning Source: in the case of *Baby Jane*, $6.90 compared to $4.09 and $4.41, respectively. Copies sold directly to the author are even steeper: $9.90 per unit for *Baby Jane*. Discounts are offered on bulk orders but I would have to order 1200 copies to get their lowest price of $5.94. This renders LuLu completely unfeasible for self-distribution.

The way LuLu sets the retail price is backwards: rather than you setting the retail price and from there determining your royalty, you set the royalty you want, LuLu adds a fee that is a percentage of your royalty, then adds the manufacturing cost, and doubles the total to reach the retail cost: this means LuLu offers wholesalers a 50% discount. Due to LuLu's high manufacturing costs, in order for me to achieve the same royalty as through Lightning Source—$3.67—the retail price of my novel would need to be set at $22.98 instead of $17.95; both the higher cost and the lower distributor rate makes the book less attractive to consumers and retailers. To maintain my $17.95 price my royalty would need to drop to $1.66, which is less than the 10% a legacy publisher would pay after providing me with perks.

For sales on the LuLu website, the author earns 80% of "the profit" they set on their titles. While that sounds generous, dig a bit deeper and you will discover that LuLu uses the higher direct-to-publisher manufacturing costs as the basis for its calculations. The author then adds what they want for a royalty, LuLu then adds another 25% of the royalty for its cut and arrives at a retail price. To use *Baby Jane* again as an example, the manufacturing cost would be $9.90; if I maintain my $17.95 retail price that leaves $8.05 for an 80-20 split: $6.44 to me and $1.61 to LuLu. So the same book sold by CreateSpace to Amazon.com at 60% of list actually earns me a higher royalty than when sold through LuLu at 80% of profit. (It is worth pointing out again that I had to really, really dig around LuLu's website to find these numbers.)

LuLu pays via PayPal or paper cheque. If you elect to be paid by cheque, LuLu pays 45 days after each quarter for royalties earned in the quarter provided revenues reach a minimum of $20.00; if not, they accrue. Payment is in U.S. dollars only. If you select PayPal, LuLu pays monthly as long as your royalties are $5.00 or more (or the equivalent thereof); if not they accrue. PayPal payments may be made in euros, pounds sterling, or U.S. dollars. For those outside the U.S. and Canada, PayPal charges a fee for the funds transfer; you need to inquire directly with PayPal as to what fees are imposed in your country and/or currency.

POD Printing Outside the U.S.

Lightning Source UK and Australia

Lightning Source has subsidiaries in the UK and Australia. If an author contracts with the subsidiaries and sets a price for each jurisdiction, then the printing is done locally and fulfilment times are thus shorter for the UK, Europe, and Australia/New Zealand (and possibly the other countries they supply to); books printed by Lightning Source Australia, for example, display as "In Stock" on Borders.com.au. This can increase the chance of sales of your book in these geographical areas. However, printing costs are higher in the UK and Australia: in the UK, the fee for a paperback with a B&W interior is £0.70 per unit plus £0.01/page; in euros it is €0,80 per unit plus €0,011 per page; in Australia the fees are $0.019 per page and a unit fee of $1.45. *Baby Jane*, for example, costs £3.40 in the UK, or 26.3% more to print than in the U.S. (at the posted exchange rate on the day I did the comparison); and AUD $6.58 to print in Australia, or 59.4% more. Consequently, in order to achieve the equivalent royalty you earn from your U.S. sales you will have to raise the UK (pounds sterling), Continental Europe (euro) and Australian (AUD) prices to reflect the increased costs. Customers in those areas will therefore pay more for your book than if they ordered it from the States but will get it faster. It is a trade-off for which you have to weigh the consequences of each. I have friends in both the UK and Australia who tell me they are used to paying a higher price for books, so while it is annoying it is not a deal breaker and they would rather have faster fulfillment; but this is merely anecdotal evidence for which I have no statistical data.

Depending upon your country of residence, your primary account will either be in the U.S., UK, or Australia (each services a larger geographical region); files are then shared with the subsidiaries with whom you have contracted, which means you only pay the one set-up fee to sell through all three. In the UK, the set-up fees are £21.00 each for your cover and interior, a £7.00 catalogue fee, and a paperback proof is £10.00 plus £0.07 per page (includes delivery). Corrections are £45.00 each incident. For those wishing to pay in euros, it is €24,00 each for cover and interior, €8,00 annual catalogue fee, and a paperback proof cost of €25,00 including shipping; corrections are €60,00.

In Australia, title set-up fees for a B&W interior paperback are $37.50 each for cover and interior, the annual catalogue fee is $12.00, the proof is $43.00 including delivery, and revisions are $80.00.

Lightning Source UK pays within 90 days after the end of the month a unit is sold provided your cumulative compensation due is at least £25.00 or €40,00 in a month; if not, they accrue. Lightning Source Australia pays on the same terms when compensation reaches $25.00. Payment is by EFT or paper cheque. You can elect to have your publisher's compensation converted and paid in a single currency—U.S. dollars, pounds sterling, euros, or Australian dollars—and into a single account.

Of course, POD companies are not confined to U.S. subsidiaries. An author can contract with other companies besides Lightning Source—if they can find one: an online search revealed many vanity publishing companies but I found only one POD manufacturer with automatic distribution that is truly available to the indie author (see Authors OnLine, below).

Bear in mind, however, that if you do use another POD manufacturer who also distributes to Ingram, you will run into the same problem of multiple fulfilment options disallowed by the wholesaler. You would thus have to use geographical rights management to avoid this, meaning you would need to carve up geographical areas between the two manufacturers.

Authors OnLine

Authors OnLine, based in the UK, charges a minimum set-up fee of £299.00 for their "Basic Service with Distribution"—less if you bring your own ISBN, though how much less is not indicated. Basic Service includes your initial proof, six legal deposit copies and their submission, your first year annual fee, automatic ebook distribution, and a listing on Author OnLine's sales website. It does not appear that you have the option to opt-out of ebook distribution. Authors OnLine distributes via Ingram in the U.S. and Gardners and Bertrams in the UK; it does not have distribution to bookshops outside of the UK, U.S., Canada, Mexico, and some parts of Europe.

Authors OnLine charges a manufacturing fee of £0.01 per page and a title charge of £0.70—identical to Lightning Source—but this is where the similarity ends. Authors OnLine charges a 25% premium for direct-to-publisher copies, plus shipping, and if you pay by credit card there is a further 5% surcharge. Corrections are charged at £75.00. Authors OnLine does not allow the author to set the retail price—you and Authors OnLine decide upon it "together," and it reserves the right to lower the price for promotional purposes—and the distributor's discount is fixed at 40%. This figure Authors OnLine claims is the "traditional" percentage but, as we have already learned, the modern percentage is 50 to 55%. A 40% distributor's discount means the retailer is offered your title for around 34% off retail, yet anything less than 40% off list is not an attractive acquisition for them, or at least certainly not for large retailers like Amazon.

Authors OnLine takes 40% of net proceeds as its cut. For example, *Baby Jane* sells for £12.50 in the UK. Lightning Source sells it to the wholesaler or direct to retail for £5.63. Lightning Source then deducts £3.40 for manufacturing and pays me £2.23. By comparison, Authors

OnLine would sell *Baby Jane* to the wholesaler for £7.50, deduct £3.40, then take 40% of the net £4.10, leaving me with £2.46. On the surface that seems a better deal, but will any significant retailer carry a book that costs them almost £2.00 more? Authors OnLine also pays only quarterly, with your first payment six months after your title goes live. There is no information on its website as to how Authors OnLine pays (EFT, cheque, or PayPal) or if it pays in any currency other than pounds sterling.

What really makes Authors OnLine unattractive, in my mind, is that it exercises editorial control: your manuscript is vetted and critiqued. Although it claims it "do[es] not judge your book for commercial potential," you are expected to meet its "literary standards."[43] Authors must fill out an enquiry form and email sample chapters after which you will be asked to send the manuscript if all is well. Now, this could be an excellent way to avoid scam publications and porn (two problems Amazon has encountered), and to force authors to clean up typos and poor formatting—which I wholly support—or it could be a way of soliciting further investment: though Authors OnLine offers a POD option, it is first and foremost an author services company, and what I suspect is that most if not all manuscripts will not meet its "literary standards" without some form of paid editorial assistance.

Authors OnLine also retains the right to veto editorial changes you make to your manuscript and to delete any unauthorized changes. It is also worth noting that the contract is exclusive unless you have written consent from the company.

Gardner Books

Gardner Books is a wholesale distributor based in the UK. Gardner has partnered with CPI-Anthony Rowe, a print-on-demand manufacturer, to provide POD wholesale distribution. This makes Gardner another option in the UK; however, you must have a minimum of five titles available and it does not market itself to indie authors. Thus Gardner is not an option for most of us, but might be for authors who are entering indie publishing because the rights to their back catalogue have reverted or have been relinquished by the publisher.

The terms of Gardner's POD services are not available on its website so if you are a UK-based author you will have to inquire directly with the company.

Print Returns

If you work with a distributor you will be given the option to allow returns or not. This is a contentious issue in the industry and has been the subject of considerable controversy.

As the large retail chains became more powerful they were able to demand more advantageous terms from the publishers. One of those terms is the ability to return unsold stock, usually within 90 days, and whether in saleable condition or not. Yet at the same time at least one retailer—Canada's Chapters—imposed a 110-day payment policy. What this means is that Chapters has 110 days to pay the publisher's invoice but can return unsold stock within 90 days for a refund, effectively meaning Chapters sells its stock on consignment, saddling the publisher with all the risk. Can you think of any other industry where the retailer is allowed to return unsold stock for a refund, and even if it is damaged? It is absurd.

The results have been catastrophic for many small publishers. While a large publisher expects returns of between 25 and 50% and budgets accordingly (though never happily, and it is getting harder to do), the smaller publisher cannot shoulder such a tab: not only does the publisher have to pay for the original printing but they may also have to refund the full purchase price to the retailers. For example, take that $35.00 hardcover from earlier: the publisher paid $8.75 to manufacture and ship the book to the distributor and was paid $19.25, for a net profit of $10.50. If a retailer returns any books, the distributor and wholesalers get to keep their cut yet the publisher must refund the retailer $21.70 (smaller bookstores have to pay a restocking fee, usually between 15 and 20%, but a major retailer often does not). So now instead of a profit of $10.50 the publisher has a loss of $11.20. Multiply that by a 1000 or 2000 units or even 20,000 units—a typical return for a mass market paperback—and you see how devastating returns can be.

To add further injury, if a distributor or wholesaler is involved the retailer has the option to return the books either directly to the publisher or back to the distributor or wholesaler. If the latter, the publisher then has the option to have returns destroyed by the distributor/wholesaler or to have them shipped back to the publisher at their expense, sometimes as high as $2.00 per unit. So now the publisher has to decide if they want to cut their losses and let the books be destroyed, or gamble another $2.00 per unit in the hope that these "remainders" can be resold to another retailer, usually a discount chain, thereby reducing the publisher's losses.

Print-on-Demand

POD manufacturers such as CreateSpace automatically sell books as non-returnable, meaning the retailer cannot return unsold stock except for manufacturer's defects. What this means for the indie author is that most bricks-and-mortar bookstores will not stock your book because they do not want to incur the risk. If a customer specifically orders your book the bookstore will purchase it but the customer will be told it is a special order and thus not returnable.

Having a status as non-returnable means you are automatically limiting your distribution options, mostly to online retailers who only order on demand. How they then handle returns varies. Amazon accepts all customer returns because Amazon is large enough to absorb the loss; it simply resells returns at a discount through its used book division. Other online retailers may or may not accept returns.

If your book becomes popular, bookstores may then take a gamble and stock your book but they will exercise conservatism, ordering in small numbers. Online retailers such as Amazon do the same, which is why you will often see "Only two left in stock—order soon!" under a title.

The distributor Lightning Source offers its publishers the option to accept returns or not, and I am told about 60% of publishers accept returns. For the author printing on demand, however, this is even riskier than it is with traditional publishing because you cannot control print runs and therefore manage your risk. To explain: under the traditional model, a publisher decides prior to a book's release how many copies they wish to print initially. A new author might only have a print run of a few thousand copies while the latest Stephen King will have a print run of perhaps 50,000. Once the initial print run is sold out, or near to it, the publisher orders a second printing, then a third, and so on. This is why you will often see "Now in its third printing!" as a headline on a popular title, though that really does not tell you anything because you have no idea how many were printed to begin with. (In an equally misleading practice, publishers will often advertise on a book's cover something like "Over a million copies in print!" While this is still impressive, a million copies in print does not mean a million copies sold.)

So a publisher who needs to exercise careful control over their balance sheet will print conservatively, waiting to see how the market responds before risking a larger print run. Such an option, however, is not available to the POD publisher: the POD publisher has no idea how many copies are ordered by a retailer until after the fact, and the publisher cannot place a limit on print orders; thus the POD publisher cannot manage their risk except to disallow returns.

I was told by an associate at Lightning Source that even where a publisher accepts returns, retailers tend to order conservatively, especially with an unproven author. So at the end of the day the self-published author has to decide if they are willing to gamble or not, and if they can afford to.

When print books are sold there is a transfer of ownership of the physical book from the distributor to the retailer and consequently the retailer takes responsibility for any fraudulent sales (such as with a stolen credit card) or thefts of merchandise.

One other thing you may notice when your book goes live is that almost immediately you will see "used" copies appearing for sale. How can this be possible? you ask; the book just went up. If you check those "used" copies you will find they are being sold by smaller retailers, often in other countries, and the fine print will indicate the book is actually new, printed on demand.

Fulfilment Estimates

Another factor the self-publisher has to consider is estimated fulfilment times. We live in a society with expectations of instant gratification so if a book is not in stock there is the risk the customer will move on to something that is. So with POD, what are the likely fulfilment estimates for each manufacturer?

CreateSpace

On the Amazon.com site, books published or manufactured by CreateSpace will always show as "In Stock" because it shares facilities with its parent company. When an order is placed the book is printed and shipped, usually within 12 to 24 hours. CreateSpace titles on other major U.S. sites like Barnes & Noble typically read as "Usually ships within 24 hours."

What is displayed on a foreign retailer's site depends on where it is located because the books are printed in the U.S. and shipped abroad. Thus fulfilment can be anywhere from "Usually ships in 1 to 3 weeks" (Canada) to "Usually ships in 3 to 5 weeks" (Japan) to as long as "Usually ships in 4 to 7 weeks" (UK).

Lightning Source

Since Lightning Source is owned by Ingram, if a retailer checks the Ingram catalogue all Lightning Source POD titles will always display as "100 copies available." A CreateSpace title distributed to Ingram will usually display the same, partly because CreateSpace subcontracts some of their printing to Lightning Source. Lightning Source titles on sampled U.S. retail sites ranged from "In Stock" (Books-a-Million) to "Usually ships in 24 hours" (Barnes & Noble), "Ships in 1 to 3 days" or "Available for in-store pick-up within 7 to 10 days" (Powell's).

If you contract with Lightning Source in the UK, fulfilment times range from a few days to a few weeks, and sites like Amazon.co.uk do not necessarily reflect accurate fulfilment times: Lightning Source UK titles are delivered to Amazon.co.uk within 48 hours, after which Amazon requires only another 24 to 48 hours to ship, but the website listing nevertheless states "Usually ships in 1 – 3 weeks" (unless Amazon elects to stock copies), which I find disconcerting. Titles on Amazon.de also show as "Usually ships in 1 – 3 weeks." If demand for your title is indicated—and it only takes a few sales to trigger this—Amazon will order an extra copy or two, in which case your title will display as "In Stock" until those copies are sold out, then the listing will revert to "Usually ships in 1 – 3 weeks" until more sales occur.

In Australia, Borders shows Lightning Source titles as "In Stock," and Whitcoulls in New Zealand displays as "Received in 10 – 15 working days."

Other POD Manufacturers

Some American POD manufacturers claim to use printers in other countries to speed up fulfilment times but you do not necessarily know if your book will be manufactured and shipped from the U.S. or manufactured abroad: there is not a standard for all titles.

Self-Distribution

Authors can also elect to self-distribute by purchasing POD copies then selling them directly to local bookstores and gift shops, online via the author's website, or through seller programs such as Amazon's Advantage or eBay. Some authors sell directly at book or community fairs, at author reading events, as part of a charity drive, and so on. Obviously, self-distribution is the riskiest and the most work, but many authors report that these local-level initiatives are often the most successful.

Shipping and Sales Tax

When calculating the risk and the reward of such efforts, you need to include in your calculations the cost of shipping copies to yourself and any sales tax, if applicable. Shipping rates vary considerably so you need to inquire with your manufacturer as to the fees you will incur based on your location. When contracting the services of an American POD manufacturer, sales tax is applied according to the jurisdiction the book is shipped to, not where it is manufactured. For U.S. authors, sales tax is applied to books shipped to Kansas, Kentucky, New York, North Dakota, and Washington, with rates ranging from 4% to 8.5%.

Duty and Import Fees

Foreign authors are not charged tax on books that are shipped from the U.S.; instead, you need to calculate the additional cost of duty and import fees. Import fees are usually the more significant cost because most POD manufacturers use courier companies for deliveries, and courier companies charge hefty fees to broker imports, even those at levels that would not incur similar fees if sent by post. They also charge fees for producing a Customs waybill even if no waybill is required.

For example, here in Canada commercial imports under $1600.00 do not require a Customs waybill. Instead, these are treated as personal imports: the receiver does not have to attend at Customs; the receiver merely attends at their post office where the relevant taxes and duties are paid, along with a $5.00 Canada Post administration fee, and the package is released. Books manufactured in the U.S. are duty-free and federal sales tax is 5%. So if, for example, you were to order a shipment of fifty books valued at U.S. $205.00, if sent by post the total of all duties, taxes and fees would be CAN $15.25. Add that to your shipping costs of U.S. $65.00, and your total shipping and import fees would be about $80.25 (the US and Canadian dollars are currently near par). This adds a cost of $1.61 per book.

Unfortunately, the POD manufacturer will not use the post office; they will use an international courier. The same order imported via UPS, a popular U.S. shipping company, would be U.S. $65.00 for shipping, then a CAN $44.25 customs prep fee, $5.85 bond fee, $4.25 COD tag, 12% HST on UPS fees (=$6.52), plus $10.25 federal sales tax on the books. Your total shipping and import fees would be $136.12. The added cost per book amounts to $2.72, an increase of 70% over shipping by post office.

For Canadians fortunate enough to live near the U.S. border, you have the option to have the books shipped to a commercial depot on the U.S. side where you can pick them up and import them yourself. You will pay significantly less in shipping costs (because the books are shipped within the continental U.S.), a small depot fee to accept the shipment, your federal sales tax (if Customs could be bothered to collect such a small amount; they usually are not), and of course gas money for the trip (which you can offset somewhat by buying cheaper U.S. gas while you are down there). Depending on which state the books are shipped to, there may also be a state sales tax applied to your purchase.

Using the previous example, if the shipment of fifty books were shipped to a depot in Washington State, it would cost U.S. $23.00 to ship, 8.5% Washington State sales tax on the book order (=$17.38), an average of $8.00 for the depot fee, and gas (estimated at $6.00 for the purpose of this example). Your total shipping and import fees would be $54.38, or $64.63 if Customs asks for the GST. The outside cost of shipping adds $1.29 per book compared to $2.72 when imported via courier.

How well this would work for Mexicans living near the U.S. border I cannot speak to; and of course the cost to those outside North America will be significantly greater. For those authors it might be more advantageous to contract the services of a local printer. Of course you can only do that if you have your book files, another advantage to either designing them yourself or hiring a local designer.

Useful Links

To create an Amazon Kindle account.
https://kdp.amazon.com/self-publishing/signin?ie=UTF8&Id=AZEbooksMakeM

To create a PubIt! account.
http://pubit.barnesandnoble.com/pubit_app/bn?t=pi_reg_home

Wikipedia page on DRM.
http://en.wikipedia.org/wiki/Digital_rights_management

Apple's iBookstore online application.
https://itunesconnect.apple.com/WebObjects/iTunesConnect.woa/wa/apply

Kobo's authors and publishers page.
http://kobobooks.com/companyinfo/authorsnpublishers.html

Amazon's CreateSpace.
https://www.createspace.com

Ingram's Lightning Source.
http://www.lightningsource.com/default.aspx

LuLu.
http://www.lulu.com/publish/

Authors OnLine.
http://www.authorsonline.co.uk/

Smashwords.
http://www.smashwords.com/about/how_to_publish_on_smashwords

LibreDigital.
http://marketplaces.libredigital.com/

BookBaby.
http://www.bookbaby.com/

eBookIt.
http://www.ebookit.com/

17/ Marketing Your Book

Perhaps nothing is more daunting for the indie author than marketing. What is the best use of marketing dollars, what are the best strategies, how does one engage your audience without spamming them? What is the best way to social network? Truth is, there is no one proven way. The indie market, especially ebooks, is still in its infancy and we are all stumbling in the dark, learning as we go along. And what works for one book may not work for all books. As any marketing guru can tell you, it is all about your target demographic.

The techniques outlined in this chapter are thus no more than suggestions—guidelines if you will. There is no magic formula, and any book that suggests there is, is lying to you. There is only one thing that is true of all approaches: they are hard work and time-consuming. So you have to find a balance between marketing your current book and finding time to write your next one.

Regardless of what you publish, be realistic about your sales expectations. Vanity publisher iUniverse admits 250 copies of a self-published print book is "above average." No one knows the average sales of a self-published ebook because only the very successful release their figures, but estimates put the average at below (and usually well below) 1000 paid copies for an author's debut book. So while everyone imagines having a bestseller, the odds are you will not. The odds are further stacked against you if you do not edit and proof your book or invest in a quality cover. So you have to weigh the potential cost of publishing your book with its likelihood of success. For many authors, myself included, self-publishing is a decision to invest in our careers, and we accept the financial risk that comes with any new business venture. Some authors decide beforehand upon a maximum budget, while others decide upon a timeline for the experiment, but both take a longer term approach that exceeds one book or one year.

When calculating your risks, do not compare apples and oranges. If you write literary fiction, comparing yourself to a popular genre writer like Amanda Hocking or John Locke is not appropriate. And even if you are a genre writer, still think critically about their success because their situation was very different from most indie authors: Hocking published her eight rejected novels—comprised of two series and the start of a third—over a mere ten months, so she was able to feed her audience's appetite quickly. John Locke writes dime store serial thrillers (of between 42,000 and 72,000 words), releases a book on average every three months, and sells all titles for $0.99. And it still took both Hocking and Locke over a year to achieve their now infamous success. So unless you are in a similar situation, do not compare. It will only make you feel unjustifiably inadequate or give you false expectations.

Be realistic about your goals. The typical indie author will spend six to twelve months promoting their book before they will see their efforts rewarded. Foreign authors can add another two to four months to that because of obstacles to the U.S. market. Book marketing is not like YouTube where a video can go viral in days: books require a much greater attention span of your audience and more than a three-minute or 140-character investment of their time, so do not expect the same quick results as a YouTube or Twitter phenomenon.

Do not get so caught up in marketing your book that you forget to write your next one. Of all the marketing techniques considered, the one proven technique is to write several books and let each book help sell the other, rather than to market one book to death.

Most importantly, do not get discouraged. That is a lot harder than it sounds but it is critical to your success. And it will not help that other indie writers will boast about their sales figures— "sales this month are 1800 units!"—without putting them in perspective: that the author has been at it for a year, or that this is their second or third book and they have already built a following. If you have a good product and are persistent, success will happen eventually. As the *I Ching* says, "Perseverance furthers." So allow yourself to dream big but do not forget to do the work.

Know Your Market

The first step is to get to know your market. It has been suggested that you should do that first and then write your book. While that sounds a bit cynical, it is actually done more often than you might imagine, even for fiction.

Non-fiction in a niche market is, on average, more lucrative than fiction, especially for highly specialized texts. The most expensive book on Kindle is *Selected Nuclear Materials and Engineering Systems*, at $6431.20. Fiction is the least lucrative to self-publish because it is where the most competition for readers exists, and it commands the lowest price. However, it is also more likely to result in a bestseller. Thus, non-fiction is about price over quantity; fiction is about quantity over price.

Self-published fiction sales mimic the wider industry: genre fiction sells better than literary fiction; romance sells the most of all genre fiction; series generally sell better than one-off stories.

Once you know who your market is, you can focus your efforts on those places they are most likely to be found. For example:

Genre Associations

Pretty much every genre has a long list of local, national, and even international associations. Many hold conventions, author Q&As, signings, and readings. These can be tapped to spread the word about your book.

Professional Associations and Trade Shows

Similarly, writers of non-fiction can tap into professional organizations, especially ones they may already be a member of through their own profession: you are selling to the choir. Trade shows are another possible venue.

Book Clubs and Readers' Communities

There are online sites such as Goodreads and Shelfari where you can connect with readers, create author pages, and promote your work. Offline, consider offering to attend at a book club to answer questions or read excerpts.

Book and Writing Fairs

These trade shows for the industry are likely to be too expensive to purchase a booth in but there is nothing to stop you from attending and handing out promotional materials.

Ethnic Groups and LGBT

If your writing features characters of a specific ethnicity or sexual orientation, tap into those communities for support and to grow your audience. Most ethnic groups and the lesbian/gay/bisexual/transgender community are underrepresented in literature and are hungry for new voices and stories.

Create a Web Presence

If you are going to advertise and sell on the web, you should be on the web. This means you should have a website or blog on which you can talk up your book and to which you can send your readers for more information. There are blogging sites such as Blogger and Wordpress that are simple to use and free to maintain. If you do build a blog, you should ideally post something to it no less than once per week to maintain interest and to increase traffic and with that your search engine rankings.

Blogs

One often successful strategy is to focus your blog not on your book per se but on its topic, making your blog the go-to place for information. This is obvious for non-fiction books but it can also work for fiction. For example, if you write vampire books make your blog about all things vampires. If you write police procedurals, start a blog about police procedural fiction in print and TV.

On your website or blog you should have a media section with pictures of yourself, a downloadable synopsis, a downloadable cover at print resolution, and an author's bio. This makes it easy for other bloggers or journalists to pull the info they need to write about you. You should of course also have "Buy Now" links to your books.

Author Pages

Many of the vanity publishers and aggregator's own retail sites provide author web pages. Large retailers like Amazon also have author web pages through their Author Central program. Unfortunately, these author pages are linked to a specific Amazon site and are not accessible from one Amazon site to another. This can mean the tedious job of updating several different sites.

Social Media

You can also create a presence on the general social media sites such as Facebook and the new Google+, Twitter, Tumblr, et cetera; and the book lovers' social media sites such as Goodreads, LibraryThing, and Shelfari. There are also forums such as Kindle Boards, Mobile Reads, and Amazon's Kindle Community that are devoted to ebooks.

If this all sounds like a lot of sites to keep abreast of and update, it is. So my advice is to choose the ones you already have established and build upon that, or pick ones that appeal to your interests so they can perform double duty. Do not spread yourself so thin that all you have time for is to put in another bit of advertising and run. If your connections feel they are nothing more to you than a target, they will tune out, block you, or complain to management.

With regards to taking part in social media sites, while it has long been accepted that controversy can build interest, on the social media sites I find it usually does quite the opposite. Part of the problem is that participants are often anonymous and there is a tendency to spew venom because there are no perceived personal consequences. This can be very uncomfortable for the author who cannot hide behind an avatar and who finds themselves having to defend against attacks for no other reason than they disagreed with a reader's opinion. During one Goodreads debate for which I was the target, a fellow author waded in to reveal his reluctance to take part in discussions of any kind for fear of offending anybody and losing readers. There is an interesting irony here: we finally find our literary voices only to have our personal voices silenced. And while there is some truth to the adage that "If I offend you, you're not my audience," for the indie author trying to build an audience these exchanges can be very unpleasant and upsetting. So tread carefully on these sites and perhaps save your contrary opinions for your blog.

Another word of caution is to avoid spamming the reader sites. This can be tricky because even the most casual of advertising can be perceived as spam by oversensitive members. For example, simply putting a link to your book as part of your signature was cited in one Goodread's group as "advertising"; when the reader was challenged about this characterization she went on a tirade about being "spammed" by indie authors, and was soon joined by others who echoed her beliefs. What came out of that thread was the paradox of sites such as Goodreads where authors are invited to build an author's page and told to "connect with their readers," yet so much as mention your book in a post (or add it to your signature) and you will be accused of spamming, and in some cases moderators will move your post to the section on "promotion" even if your post is not a promotion for your book. While I recognize that many indie authors do exactly that—spam people—and this has created contempt for indie authors, I also think there needs to be some common sense applied: that if authors are going to connect with readers on a site like Goodreads then we need to be able to identify ourselves, and a half-inch signature thumbnail is not commensurate with spamming. Nevertheless, we do not make the rules, so indie authors need to exercise restraint on these sites.

Create Pre-Release Hype

For the indie author on their second or third book, creating pre-release hype is easier because you might already have a following you can advertise to. But for the author on their first book, how do you create advance interest?

The first is to use social media to provide timely updates on your progress, always naming the title of your current project. Not hourly or daily updates, but when you reach actual milestones that might be of interest to your potential readers.

The second is to share bits of information from your book to pique interest. This is a lot easier to do with non-fiction than fiction, and with the latter you must always be careful not to spoil a plot point.

If you can design your book cover in advance, release it to create familiarity. Add it to your website, to your blog, to your email signature. And make sure it is a professional-looking, smart cover. A book is judged by its cover, no matter what anybody says.

Write a Great Book Description

Next to your great cover, your book description—also called a synopsis—is your second chance at creating interest. If you can write it in advance then do so because you can add it to your pre-release strategy.

A good synopsis introduces your main characters and some insight into their dilemma. It should hint at whether the ending is happy or tragic but without giving the actual ending away. The end of the synopsis may also ask a question, suggesting the outcome might be uncertain.

The synopsis should mirror the pace and tone of the book. If the book is a thriller, for example, the synopsis should be fast-paced. It should also highlight those elements of the book that most clearly identify its genre.

If your book is non-fiction, the synopsis should reveal what problem (real or perceived) the book addresses and/or promises to fix, and perhaps what it offers that others like it do not. The tone of the synopsis can either be scholarly or infomercial-like and should reflect the academic level expected of the reader. Non-fiction synopses can be longer than those for fiction but will often then break the information up into bullets or lists.

A few other common sense tips for a fiction book synopsis:

- avoid starting with "[Book title] is a [genre] about ...". This is redundant and comes off as amateurish. Start immediately with attention-grabbing, descriptive words;

- limit the introduction of characters to the principle two or three. You do not have any room here to talk about anyone else;

- if secondary characters can be identified by their group, use this instead: e.g., The Church, the FBI, the government;

- make every word count. If words or phrases can serve double-duty, all the better. You have a very limited space with which to get your message across and intrigue the reader;

- try constructing the synopsis around: a beginning, middle, and end; a want, an obstacle, a solution; a thesis, an antithesis, a synthesis. Or create a compelling situation with a cliffhanger, leaving them wanting more; and

- limit your synopsis to a reasonable length—usually 1000 characters or less; anything longer and your readers may zone out.

When writing the synopsis avoid using special characters like em dashes as many of the retail sites cannot read them, and Bowker's Books in Print database seems to be particularly sensitive. Some sites will not allow a carriage return either, so avoid multiple paragraphs. This can prove a problem with non-fiction because, as noted above, longer synopses are often broken into bullets or lists. If this is the case, then sometimes adding HTML code or using the soft return (CTRL+Enter) instead of a hard (carriage) return can solve the problem. It is also recommended that you use Courier New font and compose in a simple text editor like Notepad; this keeps Word code from infecting your text.

Also keep in mind that retailers will prohibit any product description that includes any of the following:

- pornographic, obscene, or offensive content;

- contact information for the author or publisher including websites;

- information on other places or retailers where customers can acquire your book;

- spoilers (information that reveals plot elements crucial to the suspense, mystery or surprise ending of a story);

- reviews, quotes or testimonials;

- review solicitations;

- advertisements or promotional material; and

- time sensitive information (e.g. information on author events).

Choose Your BISAC Categories Carefully

As the section on BISAC categories illustrated, this is a tricky one. With no real industry standards, choosing your categories can be a bit of a shot in the dark. Nevertheless, you can learn from my mistakes and research the larger retail sites beforehand so you will know in advance what potential problems might be lurking there.

I discovered the Amazon issue with BISAC categories the hard way. When I uploaded to Kindle I selected for my categories Fiction / Mystery & Detective / Police Procedural, and Fiction / Occult & Supernatural. The first sign that something was amiss was when I did a search for my book and it didn't come up when I searched my title and name. I contacted Amazon and it sorted that out. But then a week or so later I checked the new release mysteries and could not find my book anywhere. This is when I discovered that Amazon had apparently treated the Fiction / Occult & Supernatural category as my primary category but Kindle does not use that category and so my book was uncategorized. That was upsetting because it meant I completely missed out on anyone looking for a newly released mystery. I was instructed by Amazon to go back into my title's dashboard and change the BISAC categories to "unclassified" and then email Amazon directly with the Kindle categories I wanted. But which ones to choose? The problem with *Baby Jane* is that it is a cross-over: its skeleton is a mystery, a police procedural, but its flesh is comprised of supernatural, suspense, and romance. Adding to the confusion is that what we call supernatural my Native-Canadian characters call their religion. Thus while it was easy enough to keep Mystery Fiction / Mystery & Detective / Police Procedural as my primary category, which secondary category would be either the most accurate or the most attractive to readers, or both?

So I then looked at the various categories to see whom my bedfellows would be. I ruled out Romance as I did not want to risk alienating my male readers. Suspense was packed with competition and seemed more suited to *The Bourne* trilogy than my book. A colleague suggested Genre Fiction / Metaphysical, but that was populated with books like *The Alchemist* and *The Celestine Prophecy*; somehow my Native murder mystery didn't seem a good fit. Also, a check of the Amazon site revealed that Genre Fiction / Metaphysical did not exist in Kindle books, only in print books. I looked at Religious Fiction because, as noted, my characters call upon their Native religion to solve the mystery. Most books in this category were Christian fiction but there were one or two that were not. There were also fewer books, which meant I would score higher in the category as soon as sales began. I took the chance that my readers would not make the assumption the book was Christian fiction, and chose as my secondary category Fiction / Religious Fiction / Mystery.

However, when *Baby Jane* started to sell, I noticed that Amazon advertises as a book's category that category in which it is doing well. In Mysteries I was low with such a new book, but in Fiction / Religious Fiction / Mystery I was soon #4 and then #1. I also noticed that Amazon had put the print book into Literature & Fiction / Genre Fiction / Religious and Inspirational / Mystery: when my sales ranking there rose into the top 100 the category appeared on my book page (and *Baby Jane* eventually ranked at #22). But this meant its primary category— Mystery Fiction / Mystery & Detective / Police Procedural—got lost from view. Suspecting this might be bad for business, I casually polled mystery readers on the Goodreads site, who were unequivocal that any mention of religion would be perceived as Christian and would hurt my sales: it would suggest fundamentalism.

This was reflected by a change in *Baby Jane*'s sales. While sales were consistent, they were not growing as they had in the first few months after the book's release. I also noticed I was not receiving any new ratings or reviews. When I looked at what other books were purchased by those who had bought *Baby Jane*, I noticed this had changed from mysteries and suspense titles to religious fiction. What I suspected was that, because the book was #1 in the religious mystery category, people were buying it—only to discover it was not Christian. While they were not returning the book, neither were these readers recommending it to others or reviewing it.

Thus began the horror of trying to get the category removed: Amazon allegedly removed the category three times but it was determined to stay. Eventually Amazon figured out the glitch and corrected it. It was bittersweet: the potentially damaging category was removed but so were my excellent rankings. To make matters worse, my sales then came to a halt and I had to start all over again in my efforts to promote.

As illustrated, book categorization can be a bit of a minefield, so then how do you select the right category for your book? My advice is to check the major sites such as Amazon and Barnes & Noble first for their categories and see if there is any overlap, and then compare these to the list on the BISAC website. From there create a list of overlapping categories and prioritize them in order of preference. Be as consistent within your metadata as you can, meaning do not mix up the order from one site to the other, working your way down through your preferences depending on what is available when inputting to a retailer or registry site.

As soon as your book goes live check the sites to make sure everything is as it should be; if not, you can contact the retailer directly and ask them to remove your present categories and add ones you select from their website.

Keywords and Tagging

One other workaround to the limitations of Amazon's cataloguing system is to use its keywording system. When you upload your book to CreateSpace or Kindle you will be asked to add up to five or seven keywords, respectively, to aid in the search for your book. Then once your book has gone live you can visit its Amazon page and add a maximum of fifteen tags. Other readers and consumers can then also tag your book, confirming the existing tags or adding new ones. The more your book is tagged with a certain keyword the higher up in the search rankings you will go when a consumer searches using that keyword.

Unfortunately, this created an abuse of the system, with indie authors (and, some have claimed, legacy publishers as well), soliciting tags from their colleagues and offering the same. Amazon got so fed up it removed the tagging system but later reinstated it. Whether Amazon keeps it or removes it, what you need to take away from this is that tit-for-tat tagging or any other attempt to manipulate the system is not a substitute for a good marketing plan: all it will take for your efforts to fail is a change to the system, something you have no control over. Focus instead on reaching your audience.

Pricing Your Books

Pricing is a strategic decision, a delicate balance between remunerating yourself properly and meeting the demands of your market, and it is actually more complex than at first glance.

Firstly, you need to consider your target demographic. What can they afford? What are they willing to pay? This can actually be a chicken-and-egg question because what someone is willing to pay for a book is directly proportionate to how badly they want it. Yet you have to price your book before you have created the desire or demand. So do you price it higher and try to create demand by hyping the book's value, or do you price it low and take advantage of the impulse buyer, build your audience and then price your next book higher to reflect your acquired status?

There is no simple answer to that question, but you can increase your chances of success by looking at similar books already on the market. What is the typical price of a new release paperback or ebook in your genre, of a similar length, for a new author? Then ask yourself this: what would be your personal threshold for a book you were interested in but unsure of?

Most new authors will look to their peers for guidance, and you will find no shortage of discussions on the various forums debating the success or not of various pricing strategies. It is always good to bear in mind that, at the end of the day, what ultimately sells your book is not the price but the content. So when an author reveals that he sold the first ebook in a series for $0.99 but this did not entice his readers to pay $4.99 for the subsequent ebook, it may be because the first book is awful. Or if another author successfully sells their ebook for $5.99 this does not mean yours will sell at that level.

Fiction Writers: Price Low, Sell High

Most indie authors take the approach of pricing their ebooks low and counting on impulse buys and volume sales. Those authors that sell the best—at least those that we know about, such as Hocking and Locke—priced their ebooks at the bottom end and built a following that way. By bottom end I mean $2.99 or less. As noted, Locke prices almost all of his ebooks at $0.99. Should you do the same? Again, it depends on what you are writing. Both Hocking and Locke are producing what are intended to be short, quick reads and the price reflects that. If you are writing longer, more literary works, should you price your book on par with Hocking or Locke? And if you do, do you risk undervaluing your work in the eyes of the buying public?

My opinion is that buyers should pay for what they get. If your book is longer and more involved than a dime-store novel, then the price should reflect this, just as it does in the legacy publishing world. If the quality of the prose is better than most, the price should reflect this. If the content is good, the market will respond positively. If the content is bad, the market will respond negatively and you will have to lower your price.

When I first self-published, the buzz phrase was "impulse buy." Yet the thing to remember here is that most of the major retail sites offer sample pages; where this applies the principle of the impulse purchase falls short: the buyer is basing their decision on having read several pages and possibly becoming hooked. So if you have a good product, the sample pages may be sufficient to convince buyers to part with their money, and more money than if the book were mediocre. I liken it to buying shoes: there are the shoes that are to die for which you will pay full price, and then there are the nice-but-only-if-they're-on-sale shoes, and then there is the cheap pair you bought on impulse only to discover you hate them and off they go to charity. Where your work falls on that spectrum will determine if anyone buys your book to begin with, and, if they do, whether they become fans and buy your next.

That said, the closest I could find to a consensus is that the first-time indie author should price their fiction or creative non-fiction ebooks at no more than $4.99, a trade paperback at no more than $20.00, and a mass market paperback at no more than $10.00. This keeps you competitive against legacy published authors: regardless of how good a book you wrote, the assumption will be that you did not get the seal of approval that a publisher provides and therefore you cannot expect the same remuneration. You can prove them all wrong later, but do not go for top dollar upfront.

A very good piece of advice given to me was that, no matter what level you price your book at, remain committed to it for at least a few months. You cannot judge market response in just a few days or weeks. This is especially true if you priced your book low at first to encourage interest and then raised it to what you feel is true market value. The backlash will likely be immediate but not necessarily long-lasting.

Back Catalogues and Series

Many authors who have multiple titles price their back catalogue more cheaply than newer releases. This mirrors the legacy publisher pricing strategy. If you have a series, the first in the series can be later reduced in price once the subsequent books are published: this entices the reader and hopefully hooks them onto the series.

Non-Fiction Writers: How Valuable is Your Information?

For non-fiction writers, similar principles apply: who is your market and what will they pay? With non-fiction the costs to bring the book to market are often significantly higher—research costs, photography, travel perhaps—so when deciding upon a price you need to determine what the value is of the information you are offering (and thus whether it is feasible to bring the book to market in the first place). What would you pay for a similar book? Is it $20.00, $50.00, $100.00? Is it, like that very specialized text on nuclear energy, over $6000.00?

Pricing for Global Markets

For ebooks with worldwide distribution rights, Amazon can automatically set the price on its partner sites in the UK, Germany, and France at a converted value based on your U.S. dollar list price using the exchange rates in effect on the day that your book was initially published (or if you later change the price, at the time you did so). If the converted list price would be outside of the minimum or maximum list price Amazon accepts for the currency, the list price is adjusted to meet the requirements for that currency. You can check the list prices automatically set for your existing books by clicking the "edit rights, royalty and pricing" link under "Actions" for the title on your publisher's dashboard. You can also opt to set individual prices for each jurisdiction.

When you set your list price it is exclusive of Value Added Tax (VAT), which is the European sales tax. In some jurisdictions like the UK the price listed must be inclusive of tax; thus, Amazon adds it to your list price and pays a royalty on the list price less VAT (otherwise Amazon would be paying a royalty on the tax). In other E.U. countries the VAT is added at point of sale. The VAT applied to sales from Amazon.co.uk and Amazon.de is generally 15% but will vary depending upon where the customer is based: Ireland, for example, charges 21% on ebooks; Spain charges 18%.

In some jurisdictions, Amazon charges a 3G "Whispernet" surcharge of around U.S. $2.00. This fee covers charges to Amazon by its 3G partners. There have been complaints that Amazon is charging the 3G fee even where customers are downloading via Wi-Fi. Customers in the U.S., Canada, Australia, and Ireland are not charged 3G fees.

A lot of indie authors are quite concerned about these charges and taxes, especially the 3G charge, as it adds significantly to the cost of the ebook, especially for ebooks priced low: as a percentage of the overall cost, a $2.00 fee on a $0.99 ebook triples the cost, and then the total is taxed. The optics of this are not good. The question for the indie author, then, is do you take the sales tax and Whispernet charges into consideration when pricing your ebooks? I say you cannot, especially as these taxes and surcharges vary dramatically from country to country.

This is something you have no control over. At the end of the day, those taxes and surcharges are not just affecting your sales, they affect all sales. This is a battle for consumers and retailers, not for the content providers, though it benefits you to support consumer demands for the Whispernet charges to be dropped.

For print books, sales tax is usually applied at point of sale and varies significantly among countries. For example, in Canada print books are subject to 5% federal GST; in the UK and Ireland they are zero-rated; in New Zealand the tax is 15%; in the U.S. only the states of Kansas, Kentucky, New York, North Dakota, and Washington tax book sales, with rates ranging from 4% to 8.5%. You can really only consider tax if you intend to market to a specific jurisdiction.

Compilations and Serializations

If you have a collection of short stories, a series, or a book that can be broken down into segments, you can serialize them to maximize sales. For example, you can offer individual short stories for $0.99 while the anthology of ten stories might be $4.99. A manual (like this one) can be broken down into segments and sold individually for consumers who do not need all the information offered. A series can later be combined into an omnibus. This immediately increases your volume of titles and offers content across several price points. With the exception of the omnibus, these strategies work best only for ebooks.

The Cost of Free

Some authors—way too many in my opinion—offer their books for free in the hope of building an audience. This, to me, is counterproductive for a number of reasons. The first is that you are devaluing your work and yourself in the eyes of your readers. The second is that you will attract the bargain hunters who, like extreme coupon cutters, are in it for the bargain only and do not discriminate among brands. Also, many of those bargain hunters just fill up their Kindles or their computers with a plethora of free books they will never get around to reading. So any hope that this will result in a multitude of ratings and reviews may be shattered.

To give you an idea of what I mean, I perused the top 100 "bestselling" free books on Sony. (I selected Sony because Amazon does not allow free books, and will only mark a book down to free if it is offered free elsewhere, or will remove it from the catalogue. It is the same for Barnes & Noble's PubIt!. Kobo has partnered with Project Gutenberg, which aims to digitize all public domain content, in particular literary classics, so Kobo's top 100 free books are thus 60% Gutenbergs.) Of those 100 free books on Sony, three were samplers and eight were "user generated content via the popular eBook community Wattpad.com" (pirated?), seven were from legacy publishers (of which six were either romance or erotic fiction) and 82 were by indie writers: 81 published by Smashwords and one by the author. Of those 82 indie published free books, only five received any reviews and averaged only one to two reviews each. There was one notable exception with 21 reviews over a one-year period; it averaged a 2-star rating. So your chances of free books resulting in reviews are only about 5%.

The thing to remember as well is that a retailer like Sony will not allow those free books to affect its ratings system: free books are segregated from "bargain priced" and those in turn are segregated from the rest of the catalogue. Kobo segregates free books as well. So giving your book away in the hope of creating a "bestseller" that will show up alongside the priced bestsellers simply does not happen.

Anecdotal evidence also reveals that authors who put their books up for free can easily see 5000 copies downloaded but as soon as the author puts the price back up, sales plummet, often down to nothing. It is just those coupon cutters, who are not going to build your brand.

This marketing gimmick worked in the early days of ebook development but it does not work well anymore because of the sheer volume of free product offered. It is little more than another attempt—like tagging—to manipulate the ranking system, which, as noted, is a poor substitute for a valid marketing plan.

Book Lending

When you upload your book to Kindle, you will be asked if you consent to book lending. This allows a consumer to loan a book from their device to another consumer's device for a period of fourteen days. In my opinion this is a valid program, no different than loaning a print book, and can only help to promote your book and encourage sales.

Sample Pages

Most of the large ebook retailers like Amazon, Barnes & Noble, Sony, and Kobo offer consumers the option to download or read online a portion of your book, which will hopefully entice them to buy. The sampler is usually limited to the first 10% of the file.

With print versions, you need to upload a PDF of your book to the retailers in order to take advantage of their various sampler programs. Some POD manufacturers or vanity publishers will do this for you either automatically or as a pay-per-use option; with other POD manufacturers you have to set up sample pages with the retailers yourself.

Google Books

Google scanned hundreds of thousands of books—leading to a great deal of controversy— portions of which are made available to the public along with links to purchase options; and now publishers can voluntarily provide Google Books with PDFs of titles under your control. You open your free Google Books account online as you do other Google accounts, and then upload your files and input your metadata using the web forms provided by Google. Google will not inform you that your book sampler has gone live; you have to keep watch yourself.

When someone does a Google search on a topic covered by your book, your book comes up in the search results and pages from your book that contain the keywords in the user's search bar are made available. The number of pages made available is limited. And some retailers, Borders for example, use Google Books to provide book excerpts.

To upload to Google Books you must produce a PDF of your book content, and your front cover and back cover as separate JPEGs. All must be at 300 dpi.

Google accepts books in all languages; however, books that are not in English, French, Italian, German, Spanish, Dutch, Portuguese, Chinese (simplified), Chinese (traditional), or Japanese are currently limited in their inclusion in search results.

The other side of Google Books is the Google eBookstore, which functions as any other e-retailer, though at the moment copyrighted titles are only available in the U.S. and only U.S. publishers or aggregators can upload content.

Full details of the program can be found via this chapter's Useful Links.

Amazon's Search Inside

If you sell your book through CreateSpace it will automatically set up Search Inside but for Amazon.com only; even if you elect to use CreateSpace's Expanded Distribution your book will not feature Search Inside on global Amazon sites. To add Search Inside you have to apply to do so yourself. Likewise, for books sold on Amazon via other wholesalers, the publisher (you) have to apply for an account with Amazon and provide them with the relevant PDF files.

Books may be submitted to the Search Inside program if they have an ISBN; books with only an Amazon cataloguing number are not eligible. You may submit the covers and spine as JPEGs or separate PDFs, but ideally Amazon prefers them to be integrated with the interior content into a single PDF with the cover bookmarked; additional pages such as the copyright page and the first chapter may be bookmarked at your discretion. PDFs should be at 300 dpi. There is a 500MB limit to books submitted to the Search Inside program. (Note: bookmarks may be added to your source document then exported into the PDF when you print to PDF, or they can be added after the fact to the PDF document using Adobe Acrobat Professional.) The publisher sets the maximum viewing limit in increments of 10%; the default is 20%.

PDFs of titles not yet for sale on Amazon may be uploaded in advance of publication, and the publisher can set the date ("Minimum Onsite Date") for the Search Inside option to be made available.

If your book is English-language and is distributed worldwide by a U.S. distributor, Amazon will list your book on Amazon sites in the U.S., Canada, the UK, France, Germany, Japan, and Austria. To activate Search Inside on all sites you only need to set up one account then request that your Search Inside file be applied to your title on all the other sites. Full details of the program can be found via Useful Links.

Barnes & Noble's See Inside

Barnes & Noble will accept the front and back covers (and spine if available) as separate JPEGs but, like Amazon, prefers them to be integrated with the interior content into the PDF and bookmarked. At minimum the copyright page and the first page of each chapter must also be bookmarked; you can add bookmarks for your title page, acknowledgements, et cetera at your own discretion. PDFs should be at 300 dpi.

The publisher sets the allowable viewing limit for any 30-day period by an individual user; again the default is 20%. B&N also disallows the viewing of the entire book by making 10% or more of the book unavailable at all times (you set the percentage).

Only books already available and for sale on the B&N website are eligible for the program. For more details see Useful Links.

Promotions

Sale Pricing

Some authors have had some success with sale pricing for a limited time period to improve their rankings, then returning the book to the regular price. Bear in mind the issues raised earlier about agency pricing: you will have to extend the sale across all channels and hopefully they will all update their sites within days of each other and not weeks, which could otherwise put you into an endless price loop.

Gifting and Coupons

Amazon has a system whereby you can gift a book to a consumer; unfortunately, the recipient is not obligated to receive the book that was gifted. Huh? Precisely. Instead, the recipient receives a credit to the value of the book gifted; the credit may be applied toward the book offered or used to buy a different book. So the author is potentially burned twice: you pay full price to gift the book to a recipient who may not actually use it to receive your book and if they buy another author's book with your money the other author receives a royalty.

The result of this policy is that authors who wish to gift copies of their ebook for reviews or as promotional giveaways cannot use Amazon with any assurances. Instead, the author must send out mobi files directly to the recipient. For the author who elected to apply DRM to their titles, this defeats that purpose.

The aggregator Smashwords has a much better coupon system whereby authors can provide recipients with a coupon for a free copy; the coupon is redeemed and while the author does not record a sale they also do not have to pay any fees. EBookIt has a similar system. Note, though, that these coupons are only redeemable for downloads from the aggregator's website, not from outside retailers, and are also DRM-free.

Giveaways and Autographed Copies

Reader sites such as Goodreads and Library Thing encourage authors to give away promotional copies of their books, both ebooks and print copies. Similarly, if you approach an indie reviewer they will often ask for additional promotional copies to give away to their readers to encourage traffic to the review site. Anecdotal evidence suggests giveaways work best on the reader sites with their larger audiences, and giveaways help to build your brand though they do not necessarily result in immediate sales or reviews. A word of caution, too: as with any contest, many participants just like the thrill of entering contests and potentially winning something. One author on Goodreads remarked how the winner of her Swedish-language book did not read the language. So do not put too much stock in giveaways; see them instead as only one part of a larger, more comprehensive marketing plan.

Indie authors need to discriminate where they send free books: you want to ensure you get something in return. And do not fall for this autographed copies scam that was making its way around Goodreads: a user was messaging authors with a generic "you are my hero. I LOVE YOUR BOOKS" message that went on to gush how great the author's book(s) are without actually mentioning the author or the book(s) by name, and concluded by asking for an autographed copy. It is not certain what the recipient wanted with the books except either a free library or possibly to sell them on a site like eBay. If you are approached by a legitimate fan asking for an autographed copy, you can always offer to do so as soon as you receive a PayPal payment for the cost of the book plus shipping.

Excerpts and Ads in the Front or Back Matter

If you have a new book on the market or nearly so, you can add the book cover and synopsis, or a longer excerpt, in the front or back matter of your current titles. Some authors do this not only for their own books but also as reciprocal arrangements with other authors who work in the same genre. With ebooks you can also add a link to your other titles; however, this only works with format-specific ebooks as retailers will not allow links to competitors' sites. This means you can add to the back of your Kindle title links to your other Kindle books, but in the back of an ePub that is distributed to multiple sites you could not add links to a specific retailer. In this latter case it is better to link to your personal website where you can list participating retailers.

Collaborations

Some indie authors are also now collaborating with other writers. This potentially reduces the amount of time it takes to bring a title to market and frees up time to market one's other titles. Amanda Hocking writes with Jason Letts and J.L. Bryan, for example. Writers thus share their relative fame with each other, their fan bases, and the burden of promotion.

Collaborations can also be in the form of marketing. Renting a table together at a writers' festival or trade show, performing joint Q&As, and co-writing blog conversations are just a few things writers can band together to do.

Pen Names

Authors who enjoy writing in more than one genre will often use pen names so as to avoid alienating one fan base by courting another. Interestingly, many authors who start out using pen names often later reveal their true identity if their secondary genre is well-received: when romance novelist Nora Roberts decided to branch out into mysteries, she wrote under the pen name J. D. Robb, but when the first books did well they were repackaged to take advantage of Roberts' existing fame, and are now authored by "Nora Roberts writing as J. D. Robb."

Deluxe Editions

Taking a cue from Hollywood, authors can publish deluxe editions of popular works, adding new features such as an author interview, a bonus short story, the "writing of" biography, and anything else that might be of interest to your readership. Use sparingly, however, as fans who feel the "deluxe edition" does not offer anything new or just offers stuff they can find elsewhere on the web may be offended and the strategy will backfire.

Tie-ins

As noted earlier, series do better than stand-alone titles. However, you can create relationships between stand-alone titles by having characters "guest star" in another book. This is fun for the reader and makes the world you created more "real." Television series and movies often use this technique.

Reviews

Another element of the indie revolution is the indie review blogger. Some have become so popular even legacy publishers are now soliciting reviews of their books. The more popular a site is the longer the waiting list—up to six months—while the newer reviewers have much shorter timelines but also much smaller followings. Some reviewers will only review print books while others are devoted solely to ebooks, some do both; some are devoted solely to indie authors while others have nothing but contempt for us, and some mix it up. What all the sites have in common, however, is that they offer advertising space and/or make use of Google ads, and some are Amazon affiliates, making a commission on all sales that clicked through from the review site. In this respect they function the same as traditional print media, and so often there will be a correlation between the advertisers and that which is reviewed. However, you should never be asked to pay for a review in any media of any kind. Doing so is unethical at both ends.

Many of the review sites also invite author Q&As, interviews, and guest posts. These can be as beneficial as reviews, and are to be encouraged. Often, too, links to the author's own website, blog, author pages and such are included in the review blog post.

As with any other form of marketing, expect results to be mixed. I had a 5-star review on a UK blog but there were absolutely no sales in the UK as a result. I was promised a review on a popular U.S. blogger site; she read the book, asked for free copies for a giveaway, which I provided, and to this day has never posted a review of my book; however, I did sell a few copies that I believe were a result of the giveaway. An author Q&A on another site did not show any immediate impact on sales; a later one resulted in a few sales. Some reviewers I approached solicited me to advertise on their blog; that was a bit obvious.

If you solicit a review, you must provide a complimentary copy of your book to the reviewer with no guarantee of a review. If you do receive a review, accept it, good or bad, with grace. Not everyone will like your book.

And what of professional reviews in your local or national papers and magazines? These are possible but usually only happen once you become a bestselling author, in which case the story is not your book but that you indie published and made it big. It is highly unlikely you will convince the mainstream media to review your book because their advertisers are legacy publishers and one doesn't bite the hand that feeds you. That said, smaller local papers may be willing to review your book because they rarely get asked to by legacy publishers, and if the paper serves your area or birthplace there is the incentive of supporting local talent.

There are also reader reviews on the retail sites and on readers' sites such as Goodreads. While it is okay to ask a legitimate reader to post a review, it is not acceptable to solicit bogus reviews from friends and family who have not read your book or who will only post what you want them to. Readers are becoming savvier about this and an early, single 5-star review that is not followed by more reviews from a variety of readers often signals a bogus review.

You should be aware that there are review scams emerging that target the author. One scam consists of an indie author who downloads sample pages of competitors' books then contacts the authors to say their books are terrible and that unless the authors buy his book he will write a scathing review of their books. Another scam consists of 1-star reviews that contain a suggestion for a better book in the same genre; the reviewer turns out to be a friend or relative of the author whose book was recommended. Report such abuses if they happen but do not challenge a legitimate if disappointing review.

Blog Tours

A blog tour is the online version of a bookstore tour but instead of visiting physical bookstores the author visits blogs on scheduled stops over the course of a week or a month. The blog stops may include live interaction such as Skype or chat, a book review in advance, a Q&A, a book giveaway, or anything else the author comes up with.

Blog tours can be organized by the author but there are professional and semi-professional publicists who do this for you for a modest fee. However, the author should never be asked to pay the bloggers; this is unethical. As with any publicity service, post inquiries on author forums to find out who delivers what they promise and what is an acceptable fee to pay.

Local Indie Booksellers

If you decide to approach your local indie bookstore, keep in mind many receive a lousy discount from the various wholesalers, so offering them the same high discount you give directly to your wholesaler provides an incentive to give your book a try. To encourage this I sent out an email solicitation to several indie bookstores and offered them a 55% discount on a non-returnable basis. Four booksellers were interested enough to give the book a chance. One also offered me an author signing, which went well enough that he invited me back for a coveted pre-Christmas spot, and bought two more copies to keep in stock.

Book Signings and Readings

If you have a print version, and you are able to get it into independent bookstores, you can request to have a book signing and/or reading; you will find the signings are more popular because many indie bookstores are struggling and space is at a premium so they do not have room for a reading. If they are in a shopping mall they may place you at a table outside the front door to attract the attention of passers-by. Signings work well for both parties: they provide exposure and potential sales for the author, and increased traffic into the bookstore as consumers have to enter the store to pay for the book.

Book signings are not for the faint of heart: you will likely feel self-conscious and exposed, and you will discover you have to reach out to the consumer, invite them to look at your book, and then sell them on its merits. But if you are reasonably outgoing you can be your book's own best ambassador. And signings get easier with each one.

Readings are another option, though you will likely find that the bookstores want you to create interest in your book first, which is a bit of a chicken-and-egg situation: if you have generated interest in your book, and consumers can purchase online, do you need to do a reading at a bookstore to sell? In this situation, readings are really about connecting personally with and building your audience, not so much about selling. I also found bookstores want the author to generate the audience from their own list of friends and family, which, while I see the advantage for the bookstore, I fail to see the advantage for the author: if the bookstore does not have their own mailing list to draw upon, and you have to bring your own, then you do not need the bookstore's help to sell your book. You need the bookstore to expand your audience, not take a cut of sales to your existing one. If the bookstore does not have their own mailing list then this also limits you to one reading per city, or even one city period, because you cannot expect your friends and family to show up repeatedly at your book readings and buy multiple copies.

You can also try pairing up with a café and promote the reading yourself, or with your local library.

Marketing Campaigns

There are a multitude of new indie book marketing companies cropping up that make big promises to increase your sales but which do not necessarily deliver. Once you publish your book you will start getting their spam emails soliciting your patronage. Ironically, their solicitations often contain spelling and grammatical mistakes. One solicitation I found particularly amusing was for an email campaign in which the author must provide the email list. Seriously, you can email your contacts yourself.

Another campaign sends out a press release to media contacts nationwide. But do you really think *The New York Times* is going to review your indie book? You are better off first approaching your local press and working the local author angle, then move upward and outward as you gather steam.

Before you consider spending any money with these companies, go onto the forums and do a search of the company name and see what comes up, good or bad. If nothing comes up, put a question to forum users for feedback. You will quickly hear back whether the company's results warrant the money, or if they are scam artists best avoided.

Postcards and Bookmarks

If you invested in a cover image of sufficient quality for printing, you can have postcards and bookmarks made that advertise your book. These marketing items can be given out for free at indie bookstores or at writers festivals and other similar gatherings, or left in cafés, libraries, community centres, et cetera.

Stay Positive

More than any other marketing strategy you will come up with, none will be more successful than staying positive. It sounds flippant but it is true. There will be moments when you are exhausted, when you feel thwarted at all turns, when you feel like you are afloat at sea without a compass, and you will feel like giving up. Don't. Scale back your marketing efforts if necessary but do not stop altogether.

What you will discover, too, is that your efforts have a cumulative effect, slowing increasing reader awareness of your name and work. I have sold more books than people I know, so somehow between my blog, the forums, and the reviews, word is slowly getting out.

Useful Links

Wikipedia list of social media sites.
http://en.wikipedia.org/wiki/List_of_social_networking_websites

Facebook.
https://www.facebook.com

Wordpress.
http://wordpress.com

Blogger.
https://www.google.com/accounts/ServiceLogin?service=blogger&passive=12096
00&continue=http://www.blogger.com/home&followup=http://www.blogger.com/
home&ltmpl=start#s01

Google Books information.
http://books.google.com/googlebooks/tour/

Amazon's Search Inside program.
http://www.amazon.com/gp/help/customer/display.html/ref=hp_rel_
topic?ie=UTF8&nodeId=13685751

Amazon's Author Central.
https://authorcentral.amazon.com

Barnes & Noble's See Inside program guidelines.
https://secure.barnesandnoble.com/seeinside/Guidelines.aspx

Twitter.
http://twitter.com

Tumblr.
http://www.tumblr.com

Goodreads.
http://www.goodreads.com

Shelfari.
http://www.shelfari.com

LibraryThing.
http://www.librarything.com

Kindle Community forum.
http://forums.kindledirectpublishing.com/kdpforums/forumindex.jspa

Mobile Reads forum, a popular site for ebook authors and formatters.
http://www.mobileread.com/forums/

Kindle Boards, another popular community site.
http://www.kindleboards.com/

18/ Getting Paid

Minimum Account Balance

As discussed in Chapter 16: Distribution and Royalties, many of the companies you will be doing business with only pay in U.S. dollars. If you are paid in U.S. dollars, sales made in foreign jurisdictions may be converted to U.S. dollars, so some revenue may be lost to currency conversion. I say "may" because, in the case of the distributor discount model where the currency of sale by the wholesaler is in U.S. dollars, the currency of sale to the end consumer is irrelevant: the author is paid in U.S. dollars regardless. However, where the agency pricing model is used, the currency of sale to the end consumer is then converted to U.S. dollars, so there will be some loss of revenue to conversion. (Yet another reason why agency pricing is inferior to the distributor discount model.) Likewise, where a company offers royalty payments in pounds sterling or euros, either via PayPal or EFT, any conversion from one currency to another will result in some lost revenue.

Foreign authors who are paid in U.S. dollars can reduce their conversion losses by opening a U.S. dollar bank account at home and paying into that, then converting to your own currency at an opportune time. However, you will still suffer an expense to cash a cheque issued by a U.S. bank, and you will have to wait for the cheque to clear before you can safely access the funds.

Most of the larger retailers offer "direct deposit," which is another name for electronic funds transfer (EFT). If you are eligible for direct deposit, the retailer will then pay regardless of the balance in your account or at a significantly lower threshold. With few exceptions, EFT is available only to those authors who have a U.S. dollar bank account in the U.S. (not at a U.S.-owned foreign subsidiary). It is therefore an advantage for all authors, whether American or foreign, to have a U.S.-based bank account: you are paid more often and the funds are immediately accessible. Foreign authors with a U.S. bank account can also use it to pay for U.S. expenses, thereby avoiding currency conversion surcharges there as well (most credit card companies charge a 2.5% surcharge on top of the lousy conversion rate they give you on your cross-border purchases). This is what I do: I have a U.S. bank account, debit card, and credit card, and use my royalties to pay for further expenses, for example set-up fees for my next title or to pay for book orders. And since it is all done online, it is easy to manage the accounts: it takes no more effort to pay my U.S. credit card from my U.S. account than it takes to pay my Canadian credit card from my Canadian account.

Opening a U.S. Bank Account

So how does a non-U.S. resident go about opening a U.S. bank account? Your first option, if it exists in your country, is to open an account with a bank that has a U.S. subsidiary, or with a U.S. bank that has a subsidiary in your country; through this account you then open your

U.S. account; you do not have to attend in person at the U.S. branch. HSBC Bank, for example, has branches in 85 countries including the U.S., and clients can open a Premiere account at any HSBC Bank and, through it, open an account with HSBC in the U.S. Transfers between accounts in your country and the U.S. are as simple as a mouse click. The Premiere account is, however, not cheap: in Canada, account fees are $28.00 per month unless you carry a $100,000.00 minimum balance. Authors can also use HSBC to open accounts in the UK, the EU, and Australia, and never have to suffer the conversion of your royalties until *you* decide to make the transfer. If sales begin to take off in these other currencies, the $28.00 per month account fee may be offset by losses otherwise incurred by currency conversion.

A second option is to open a U.S. account via your bank at home, which, if you have a good relationship with them, will recommend you to a partner bank in the U.S. and help you with the paperwork. The disadvantage to this is that when you want to transfer your money home you must pay a bank-to-bank wire fee, which averages U.S. $35.00 per wire; or you can write yourself a cheque on your U.S. account, deposit it in your home bank, and wait for the cheque to clear. Although this might make the purpose of opening the U.S. account pointless, you will still save on expenses by paying them from your U.S. account, and you will still be paid your royalties more quickly.

Canadians can avail themselves of RBC Bank, the American subsidiary of RBC (Royal Bank of Canada). Royalty payments can be deposited into the RBC Bank in the U.S. and online money transfers to Canada are treated as account-to-account transfers and not bank-to-bank wires, thus saving ourselves the wire fees. These account transfers are free of charge if a minimum balance of $700.00 is maintained in the U.S. account. You will need to set up a Canadian RBC account first and then open the U.S. account through your Canadian RBC branch.

RBC sold their U.S. subsidiary and it is not clear how the accounts will function after the official transfer date of March 2012. However, the regulators have been asked that existing accounts be grandfathered in and the cross-border services maintained, and it is expected this will be granted as it was to Canadian account holders at Toronto Dominion North, the former U.S. subsidiary of TD Bank Canada, when they legally separated after the financial crash of 2008. TD is in the process of reintegrating its Canadian and U.S. banks, and will again provide to new account holders the same services currently offered by RBC, though the reintegration is not expected to be finalised until 2012.

Notwithstanding all of the above, the new indie author may wish to tests the publishing waters first and see if your revenues are sufficient to warrant the hassle of opening a U.S. account.

Withholding Tax

Americans who receive royalty payments do not have tax withheld at source; however, your earnings are reported to the IRS and failure to report them on your annual return is tax evasion.

After the end of the calendar year, any company who has paid you royalties will provide you with a Form 1099 that specifies amounts paid.

Royalties earned through Amazon's Kindle in the UK, Germany, and France are not subject to withholding tax as neither the UK nor the European Union withhold tax on royalties paid to authors.

Companies such as Lightning Source, which do not pay royalties but instead pay a "publisher's compensation," are not required to withhold tax as these transactions between Lightning Source and its publisher clients are treated by the IRS as business-to-business ("b2b"). It is all in how the IRS categorizes a company, whether as a "publisher" (who pays royalties) or as a "manufacturer" or "distributor" (who does not pay royalties).

Foreign authors who receive royalties from a U.S. company are subject to a 30% withholding tax that is remitted to the IRS. The remainder of your royalties you must then declare to your own government who will then tax you on those. This is known as "double taxation": one income taxed by two countries.

Double taxation is recognized as inherently unfair, and thus international tax treaties were developed between countries. The U.S has personal income tax treaties with 57 countries; to see if your country has a treaty with the U.S., see the link "Information on American Tax Treaties" under this chapter's Useful Links. Depending on the treaty terms, the 30% withholding tax is reduced to anywhere between zero and 15%.

After you find out whether or not your country has a tax treaty with the U.S., you will then have to find out the treaty article number that pertains to copyright royalties, as this is the treaty article number you will have to specify on your form W7 or SS4 (more on that in a minute). This will be found somewhere on the IRS website (you will have to dig as there is no one place I can send you); you can start with your country's treaty number listed in the "Information on American Tax Treaties" document. Alternatively, try typing into the search bar on the IRS website the name of your country and "tax treaty." If that fails to dig up the relevant document, you can try phoning one of the IRS International offices; see "Contact IRS Internationally" on the contact page on the IRS website (see Useful Links).

Once you know your relevant treaty article number you can apply for either a U.S. Individual Taxpayer Identification Number (ITIN) or an Employer Identification Number (EIN). Once you have either of these you can supply your publisher or distributor with a form W-8BEN and they will no longer withhold tax or will reduce the withholding tax, whichever is applicable. For any tax already submitted while you wait for your ITIN or EIN, you can apply to the IRS for a refund.

ITIN or EIN?

An Individual Taxpayer Identification Number (ITIN) is for individuals who receive income from an American company but are not eligible for a U.S. Social Security Number (SSN). An Employer Identification Number (EIN) is for companies, including sole proprietorships, doing business in the U.S. or with a U.S. company. An EIN is available to foreign companies as well as American ones.

If you are already registered as a company in your own country, the EIN is infinitely easier to obtain than the ITIN. However, if you already set up accounts with the likes of Amazon under your personal name, you may have to acquire the ITIN unless you can readily associate your personal name with your business name. This is easiest if you are a sole proprietor registered as a company under your personal name; if not, I would suggest putting down both your personal name and your business name on the form W-8BEN using the convention "[your name] dba [your company name]," which means "doing business as."

If your company is a partnership or incorporated, you may need to assign to the company the proceeds from your copyright in order for the payer (e.g., Amazon) to pay royalties arising from copyright held by an individual. You should seek legal advice before proceeding.

You will note that Amazon makes no mention of the option to acquire an EIN instead of an ITIN, although it does provide an example of a Form W-8BEN submitted with an EIN. This is probably because the vast majority of indie authors will not be registered sole proprietors or other company owners, but Amazon's failure to indicate the EIN as an option is hugely irritating for those of us who are. What is even more irritating is that if you contact Amazon and ask if it will accept an EIN you will get a form response telling you to apply for an ITIN. Yet submit your W-8BEN to Amazon with your EIN and the form will be accepted. Similarly, Smashwords briefly mentions EINs but only provides a link to the ITIN page on the IRS website. So if you have a company do not be misled into believing you need an ITIN.

Acquiring an EIN

To apply for an EIN you need to download Form SS-4 from the IRS website as well as the document "Instructions for Form SS-4." At the end of this document is a table that explains which lines in Form SS-4 need to be filled out. For the purposes outlined here, the relevant section is: "Is a foreign person needing an EIN to comply with IRS withholding regulations" who "Needs an EIN to complete a Form W-8 (other than Form W-8ECI), avoid withholding on portfolio assets, or claim tax treaty benefits." You will thus complete lines 1–5b, 7a–b (SSN or ITIN optional), 8a, 8b–c (if applicable), 9a, 9b (if applicable), 10, and 18. Once you have form SS-4 filled out, U.S. residents can apply online for an EIN; foreigners must apply only by phone, fax, or post. The contact information is in the "Instructions for Form SS-4."

You do not need to be receiving royalties prior to applying for an EIN, and you do not need to provide supporting documentation such as your company registration papers.

Once you have been approved and assigned a number, it will take up to two weeks before the number will be in the system to be verified by a third party.

U.S. Individual Taxpayer Identification Number: Form W-7

Individuals who need an ITIN must be receiving income from a U.S. source *before* you can apply for the ITIN: you must attach to your application a letter personally addressed to you, on company letterhead and signed by a representative, which indicates the company pays royalties to you and withholds tax unless you provide them with Form W-8BEN. This requirement has the effect of barring some authors from Apple and Barnes & Noble because they require a U.S. tax ID before they will allow you to open an account.

Thus, for the indie author who does not possess a U.S. tax ID, you must first have an account with Amazon, an aggregator such as Smashwords, or a POD company like CreateSpace who will allow indie authors without a US. tax ID to open an account and will provide the necessary letter in support of your ITIN application. The easiest route currently is Amazon or CreateSpace who, due to the sheer volume of their indie business, in May 2011 entered into a Memorandum of Understanding with the IRS to accept a form letter you can download off the Amazon or CreateSpace websites and submit along with a copy of your distributor account page that shows your name and address (see Useful Links).

To apply for an ITIN, you must submit to the IRS Form W-7: Application for IRS Individual Taxpayer Identification Number. The form can be downloaded from the IRS website. When filling out Form W-7, under "Reason you are submitting Form W-7," check box (a), "Nonresident alien required to get ITIN to claim tax treaty benefit." You must then also check box (h), and write in "Exception 1D – Royalty Income." On the line below write in the name of your country and the treaty article number.

Lines 1 through 5 are self-explanatory. For line 6a, if your country of citizenship is not your country of residency you will need to include in your identification your residency papers. Line 6b is the tax number you use in your own country. Line 6c is only relevant if you have a U.S. visa of some sort. Line 6d is your ID information. Sign, date and fill out your phone number.

You have the option to include in your application your original documents, which will be returned, but the IRS would prefer you send notarized copies as the IRS will not take responsibility for lost originals.

The process takes about four to six weeks (eight to ten weeks if submitted during peak tax season, January 15 through April 30).

Apostilles

Along with the completed Form W-7, you need to provide appropriate identification with your application. If you are fortunate to live near the U.S. border you can simply drive across to the nearest IRS office with your completed form and your passport and submit directly; the clerk who handles your application will copy your passport and stamp the Form W-7 indicating she or he received your ID. Similarly, if you live in or near London, Frankfurt, Paris, or Beijing you can attend at the IRS office attached to the U.S. Embassy or Consulate. You can also attend at the IRS office in Guaynabo, Puerto Rico.

If you cannot attend at an IRS office, things get a lot more complicated—and expensive—because the IRS requires copies of original documents be certified and notarized either by a U.S. notary or a foreign notary (the term "notary" as used here will mean either a lawyer or a notary public). However, as the "Instructions for Form W-7 (Rev. January 2011)" states:

> ... foreign notaries are only acceptable as outlined by the [Hague Apostille Convention Abolishing the Requirement of Legalization for Foreign Public Documents (1961)]. The Hague Convention provides for the simplified certification of public (including notarized) documents to be used in countries that have joined the Convention. A certification will be issued in the form of an "apostille," which will be attached to the copy of the document.[45]

And therein lies the rub: not every country is a signatory to this convention. To find out if yours is one of the 101 countries to have signed, you can visit the website for the Hague Conference on Private International Law where you will find the Convention and a list of contracting states and the status of their contract (see this chapter's Useful Links). However, even if your country is a signatory, how each country authenticates its documents varies. The easiest way to figure out how your documents are authenticated is to visit the website of the nearest U.S. Embassy or Consulate where, under "Citizen Services," you will find a section on "Notarial Services." There you will find a section on authentication of documents for use in the United States that will explain the requirements for documents originating in your country.

For those who live in a country that is not a signatory to the Hague Convention, "Instructions for Form W-7 (Rev. January 2011)" states that "If the document originates in a country that is not party to the Convention, applicants should have the document certified by the foreign authority that issued it."[46] Now, on the surface of things that sounds cheap and easy: you just go down to your citizenship office and ask them to certify a photocopy of the identity page in your passport or your residency papers. Unfortunately, many will not do this unless you first have a letter from the IRS requesting it. If so, what do you do?

Essentially, you need to do the following:

> 1) Have your identification—ideally the identity page of your passport—copied and the copy notarized.

2) Have the notary's signature and seal authenticated by their governing body, which will either be a law society or a society of notaries. This proves that the signature and seal is not fraudulent. (When you think about it, this makes sense: how can a clerk at the IRS know whether a signature and seal has not been faked?)

3) Have that authentication recognized by the U.S. Embassy or Consulate in the jurisdiction where the authentication took place.

This process is called "legalization and authentication" in Canada and will be called this or something similar in your country. In some jurisdictions you can bypass step (2) by hiring a notary whose signature and seal is registered with the nearest U.S. Embassy or Consulate. Unfortunately, they do not provide on their websites a list of registered notaries but, luckily, most notary societies (but, I discovered, few law societies) keep a list of their members who are registered with the U.S. Embassy or Consulate; if you call the notary society and give them your address, they can give you the names of appropriate members in your area. If such a notary is not available in your area, you can, legally speaking, courier your passport to them to be copied and the copy notarized because the notary is not certifying the authenticity of the original document, only that the copy is that of an original document. Whether the notary will do so without you in attendance is another matter; inquire as to their policy when seeking their services.

Once you have your notarized copy and, if necessary, the governing body's signature authentication document, you then need either to mail your document(s) to the U.S. Consulate or make an appointment to attend at the Consulate. To make an appointment you must do so online, but it is hidden under "U.S. Citizen Services > Notary Information" (or similar). Make your appointment and do not forget to take the relevant fee with you in U.S. dollars.

Form W-8BEN

Once you have your EIN or ITIN in hand, you must then submit to each company you do business with a Form W-8BEN: Certificate of Foreign Status of Beneficial Owner for United States Tax Withholding, signed in blue ink (I believe this is for scanning purposes). You can download Form W-8BEN from the IRS website (see Useful Links).

Under section (3) of Part I of Form W-8BEN, check the relevant box, and if you are a sole proprietor you still check "Individual." Line 6 is for your new EIN or ITIN number, while Line 7 is your national tax number. Line 8 is for the account number or reference number the company uses to identify you (for Amazon's Kindle, for example, this would be your publisher code).

Check box 9a, fill in your country name, and check box 9b. You do not need to fill out Section 10. Sign, date, indicate your capacity ("author/publisher") and submit.

Publishing Under a Pen Name

When creating a publishing account, for example with Amazon or Barnes & Noble, it is important that you do so under your real name and not your pen name as otherwise payments will be made to your pen name and you will have difficulty cashing the cheques. It will also render your EIN or ITIN useless.

Useful Links

EIN application Form SS-4.
http://www.irs.gov/pub/irs-pdf/fss4.pdf

Instructions for Form SS-4.
http://www.irs.gov/pub/irs-pdf/iss4.pdf

ITIN application Form W-7.
http://www.irs.gov/pub/irs-pdf/fw7.pdf

Instructions for Form W-7.
http://www.irs.gov/pub/irs-pdf/iw7.pdf

IRS Form W-8BEN.
http://www.irs.gov/pub/irs-pdf/fw8ben.pdf

Instructions regarding Form W-8BEN.
http://www.irs.gov/pub/irs-pdf/iw8ben.pdf

Information on American Tax Treaties.
http://www.irs.gov/pub/irs-pdf/p901.pdf

Tax Information for non-U.S. publishers selling on Amazon.com.
https://kdp.amazon.com/self-publishing/help?topicId=A1VDYJ32T5D3U4

Tax Information for non-U.S. publishers selling via CreateSpace.
https://www.createspace.com/Help/Index.jsp

List of signatories to Hague Convention on Apostilles.
http://www.hcch.net/index_en.php?act=conventions.status&cid=41

19/ The Vanity Press Machine

Nowhere is it more imperative for the indie author to think critically than when considering hiring the services of a vanity publisher; otherwise you risk falling victim to slick sales pitches that encourage you to believe that, with the right package of services, you can be the next big thing. The clue is in the name: now called "author services" companies, they are not really in the business of publishing but in selling their services to aspiring authors. Whether your book goes on to sell one copy or one million is of secondary consequence; in fact, some companies even promote their services as a stepping stone to finding a traditional publisher.

In this chapter I am going to analyze one such author services company to illustrate how dissecting their promises reveals the hidden agenda. I have selected U.S.-based iUniverse because they are the company I had personal contact with, and because any company that has a section in their FAQ headlined "iUniverse Scam Myth Buster" clearly has a problem. But the issues raised here are not confined to iUniverse; they are endemic to one degree or another across all vanity publishers, and the indie author needs to be very aware.

The Book Signing Incentive

I first came across iUniverse on the Chapters/Indigo website: at the bottom was the enticement "self-publishing: get your book published and on our shelves!"[47] A click on the "Find out how" link takes you to an ad enticing you to "Get your book published and on the shelf of your local Indigo or Chapters Store!" The subtext reads, "Through two exclusive iUniverse publishing packages you get: Guaranteed book placement in an Indigo or Chapters store [and] Guaranteed book signing in a local Indigo or Chapters store with the Indigo/Chapters booksigning package."[48]

Before we go any further, note the use of the definitive "an": this is *one* Indigo or Chapters store, not Indigo and Chapters stores. And notice it is a guaranteed book signing, not a book launch or author reading. The latter two require some investment of resources on the part of the bookstore—refreshments and nibbles, advertising—while the signing requires no more than a sign put up in the store and maybe a press release (though I would not count on a press release).

Click on the "Learn more now" button and you are taken to a sign-up page on the iUniverse website. At this point you have no idea what anything costs; instead you tell iUniverse all about your book, give it your contact information, and get your free "publishing guide," which is 71 scantily clad pages of such nebulous tripe as "The best book ever written will never sell one copy if people do not know it exists" and "There are virtually thousands of ways in which you could promote your titles, limited only by your budget and your imagination"[49]—this latter declaration proving rather portentous, as you will soon see.

You will also be treated to a video of author Lisa Dewar at her Chapters book signing, gushing about her fabulous iUniverse experience, and standing at a table covered with an iUniverse tablecloth and dwarfed by a huge sign advertising iUniverse's get-published-and-on-the-shelves-at-Chapters program.[50] So rather than promoting the author and her book, the signs are all about iUniverse, but it is the author who is paying. And how much, exactly, is the author paying?

Authors who purchase the $2999.00 "Bookstore Premier Pro" package will see eight copies of their book placed in a single Chapters, Indigo, or Coles bookstore for eight weeks but will not get a book signing. (Note how Coles is now snuck in here; Coles is Chapters/Indigo's basement brand.) The author who pays $3999.00 for the "Bookstore Signing" package gets sixteen books shipped to a single store where the book signing will be held,[51] along with a book signing package of posters, fliers and invitations that iUniverse values at $300.00.[52] Note the author is responsible for disseminating said posters, fliers and invitations, not Chapters or iUniverse. The package indicates the books available at the signing are the same sixteen copies that are to be shelved at Chapters for eight weeks; it is unclear if Chapters orders more should any of those sixteen copies sell at the signing.

I cannot tell you if Chapters advertises the book signing alongside the other events posted on its website as there were no indie author book signings when I last checked. So either Chapters does not advertise them or the program is not going so well.

When you walk into a Chapters bookstore there will be tables at front with various book selections; publishers pay to be included on these tables. Further in-store you will find the bookshelves with titles in alphabetical order (you only see the book spines), at the end of which are more prominent displays of select titles with their covers facing—and enticing—consumers. These end placements are also paid for by the publishers. So it is of interest to know that, when I queried my iUniverse point man about where my books would be placed in the Chapters store were I to purchase a publishing package, the answer was that "Chapters does not guarantee a specific location in the store. It is all case by case."

If you compare the Chapters Bookstore Premier Pro, which includes the book placement but not the signing, to iUniverse's regular Bookstore Premier Pro, which does not include book placement, the package contents are otherwise identical. The current price of the regular package is $2099.00. This means you are paying $900.00 just for the Chapters book placement, and an additional $1000.00 for the book signing. That makes for a very expensive book promotion *at a single store*.

Compare this to my book signing at indie bookseller Blackberry Books in Vancouver, at the popular tourist destination Granville Island. The bookseller advertised the event on his website and through Twitter, and was there personally to offer support and encouragement. The signing table advertised me and my book, not my manufacturer. I paid in advance for the book manufacturing and delivery but made a profit on all copies sold; I did not pay $1900.00

to the book manufacturer or bookstore. The bookseller even paid me on the day so I walked away with money in my pocket.

Lisa Dewar's book, incidentally, is "In stock" at Chapters online but not in stock in-store, and the online entry has an "image not available" place marker instead of a cover image even though a chapters.indigo.ca set-up is allegedly included in the book signing package.

The Hard Sell

Within a few days of hitting the send button with your personal information, a salesperson will call. You will be asked how close are you to publishing your manuscript because it just so happens there is a sale on (note: there is always a sale on). You will be told how publishing with them gives your book cache because the iUniverse name is synonymous with quality in the eyes of the retailers: iUniverse has a relationship with Chapters in Canada and Barnes & Noble in the U.S. that no other author services company has because of iUniverse's editorial standards. When you ask what those editorial standards could possibly be considering iUniverse does not exercise any creative discretion, the salesman will press how their authors benefit from editorial assistance. When you counter that their packages do not actually include any manuscript development and, again, is it not true that they do not exercise any editorial discretion, the salesman will admit to this but then quickly continue to press the quality of their brand.

This will be followed up by an email solicitation. Mine went like this:

> Michelle,
>
> I enjoyed talking with you today. Attached is the information I promised you.
>
> Having published over 40,000 titles in 10 years, iUniverse's unique services will help you unlock the full potential of your manuscript.
>
> No other self-publishing brand offers you these key advantages:
>
> 1. **Editorial Excellence**: iUniverse offers an unmatched Editorial Evaluation performed by editors from traditional publishing houses so you have an expert professional assessment of your manuscript.
>
> 2. **Recognition Programs**: Only iUniverse offers recognition programs such as the Star and Rising Star designations. These iUniverse-only programs give you unique marketing support like the special iUniverse Star Catalog for retailers and exclusive distribution like the Rising Star Collection on the barnesandnoble.com web site.
>
> 3. **Retail Reputation**: While it is no guarantee of how your book will sell, the fact is in a recent industry study, **iUniverse sold twice as many books in the retail channel** as other leading self-publishing brands.

4. **Greater Success**: Is it getting the attention of a Hollywood producer? Selling thousands of books at seminars and conventions? Or securing a traditional publishing contract? iUniverse can help you get there. After 12 rejection letters, Lisa Genova published with iUniverse because she knew her book had an audience. By promoting it herself and generating commercial sales and great reviews, *Still Alice* was picked up by Simon & Schuster where it debuted at #5 on the New York Times Bestseller list.

There is a reason why we are the world leader in retail channel book sales in our industry, and I would love the opportunity to work with you.

I am available for any questions you may have, and I look forward to speaking with you in the future.

As you will see, however, the professional assessment will not really amount to much, the recognition programs come with strings attached, the sales numbers are not all that impressive, and the "greater" success is not quantifiable unless you previously published the same book without success. And now that you are on the salesperson's email list, you will be spammed.

Manuscript Development

Troll through the various iUniverse packages—which range from a "low" of $599.00 to a high of $5897.00 (currently on sale, of course, for $4199.00)—and you will see all but the cheapest includes an "Editorial Evaluation" valued at $599.00. This is about the going rate for a full-length book, but all an evaluation includes is a written report on the strengths and weaknesses of a manuscript. An evaluation looks at plot and character development, at grammar and punctuation, and at the marketability to the intended demographic. It does not include fixing the problems indicated. In the case of iUniverse, it will, however, include advice on what additional iUniverse services you should consider purchasing to bring your manuscript up to saleable quality:

> [A]n Editorial Rx Referral will recommend the services of an appropriate editorial specialist—from a copyeditor or content editor to a developmental editor. You may then choose to purchase those services from iUniverse. If you do choose to purchase an editorial service, our staff will assign your book to a specialist who will address the issues raised in the Editorial Evaluation and give your manuscript the professional attention that it would receive at a traditional publishing house. You may also choose to use your own freelance editor or make the recommended changes yourself.[53]

There is a catch to that last sentence, but we will get to that later.

Now, considering that everything starts with the manuscript, one would think you would get some sort of editorial development in a package costing between $1549.00 and $4199.00, but no. What's more, iUniverse's editorial assistance is outsourced and editors are required to work under complete anonymity so you are not even offered the professional courtesy of personal contact, something every freelance editor offers their clients; and the iUniverse editors cannot be identified and accused of facilitating an agenda to sell editorial services.

What will iUniverse's editors cost you? It charges by the word for all services, but how much per word is not revealed until you request a quote. You cannot request a quote until you have already signed on and paid for a publishing package. So to get an idea of what it charges, you have to go to the complaint boards to find out. One complainant was quoted $2000.00 for a line edit, which he paid for, and the manuscript was returned with typos; he was then quoted another $300.00 to fix the typos. Another complainant was quoted $1500.00. And some of the complainants claimed that, once iUniverse flags your manuscript as in need of editorial revision, the "optional" services become mandatory or the book may not proceed to print.[54]

Moreover, if after paying thousands of dollars for editorial services you receive your proof and notice a few typos (that you paid not to be missed), you will have to, as a complainant noted above did, pay further fees to correct said typos. (As a professional editor I would *never* charge a client to fix typos that I missed.) The first fifty typos are on the house, but additional changes are charged at $100.00 per block of up to 25 corrections. These corrections "must be noted on the iUniverse Electronic Proof Form that is provided with your author proofs. The completed form must be returned via e-mail within 14 calendar days. If it is not returned within the specified time period, we reserve the right to cancel your submission without refund of the submission fee."[55]

(Note to iUniverse: if you are going to market your company as the editorial standard for self-publishers, you may wish to proof your website and learn, at the very least, how to spell "self-publish.")

Recognition Programs

There are three recognition programs at iUniverse: Editor's Choice, Star Program, and Rising Star. Eligibility for these are used as a carrot to entice you to buy one of the more expensive packages since no recognition programs are available in the $599.00 package and the Rising Star is only available at the Premier Pro level and up, currently starting at $1549.00.[56] But the key word here is "eligible" and, as the author will quickly find out, eligibility comes at an additional cost.

Editor's Choice

In order to be eligible for the Editor's Choice program you must first receive a "positive Editorial Evaluation."[57] If you click on the Editor's Choice link on the publishing packages page, you are taken to a page outlining the benefits of the Editor's Choice designation. You still do not know what the criteria are, though, so you click on the "Frequently Asked Questions about the Editor's Choice Program" link. This takes you to another page that further espouses the benefits of the designation and how it will likely increase your book sales, but you *still* do not know what the criteria are. And you will never know what the criteria are unless you scroll down to the very bottom of the iUniverse website where, in very small letters, is an "FAQ" link. From there you can click on "Editorial Services," where you will discover the carrot that may be included in your editorial evaluation:

> After carefully considering your manuscript, your evaluator will let us know whether your book has the potential to be an Editor's Choice book. As in traditional publishing, manuscripts with potential often still need the assistance of an editor, such as a copy editor or line editor. If we see Editor's Choice potential in your manuscript, we will share this information with you when you receive your completed Editorial Evaluation. If you choose to purchase the editorial service indicated in your Editorial Rx Referral and make the necessary revisions, we will work with you to bring your manuscript to the level of Editor's Choice.[58]

But what happens if you decide not to purchase iUniverse's editorial services and instead contract with an editor directly? Are you still eligible? Not unless you spend another $599.00 for a second evaluation:

> If you decide to revise your manuscript on your own and want to be considered for Editor's Choice, we require a second evaluation of your book to allow us to review the changes you have made. Keep in mind, however, that if your second evaluation still identifies the need for professional editorial assistance, we will ask that you consider working with an Editorial Specialist, as recommended, to be eligible for Editor's Choice or, if you choose, simply move to publication.[59]

What do you think the chances are you will ever qualify for the Editor's Choice designation if you do not purchase the services of an iUniverse "Editorial Specialist"? And if you do not qualify for Editor's Choice, the other two recognition programs are closed to you, rendering those parts of your expensive publishing package moot.

Star Program

Titles that make it into the Star Program "are presented to traditional publishing houses, international publishers, book clubs, large print publishers, and audio book publishers for their consideration."[60] That's the carrot. The stick is that you do not qualify for the Star Program unless you have first received an Editor's Choice designation. If by chance you manage (to afford) that, you are then eligible for the Star Program but only after selling 500 books, 250 of which must have been sold through retail channels. This figure of 250 is, as iUniverse states, "an above-average number"[61]—which gives you an idea of how many copies the average iUniverse books sells.

Editor's Choice designation and the 500-copy threshold, moreover, are still not enough to guarantee you will make it into the Star Program. First you must apply, and you must demonstrate that you are "willing and able to continue to generate customer demand for the title with support from iUniverse" and "iUniverse will invite you into the Star Program only if we believe that further investment will help you receive broader recognition and greater commercial success."[62] What is not indicated is what you must do to demonstrate your willingness, what defines "support from iUniverse," or whose "further investment" they are talking about, though I think by now we can safely read between the lines.

What is a bit confusing, too, is that "Star does not promise guaranteed placement in retail stores[;] however, we will present your title to retail buyers who will judge your commercial viability [based] on marketing plans, previous sales history success and overall genre popularity."[63] So you have to sell 250 copies through retailers at which time iUniverse will market your book ... to retailers. The Star Program includes "Returnability and a standard industry discount,"[64] which suggests to me that what is really expected is that you will sell your 250 copies through online retail channels, after which your book will be pushed to bricks-and-mortar stores.

My favourite item from the Star Program, however, is this:

> An added incentive of the Star Program, a ForeWord Clarion Review is a 400+ word (*sic*) critique created by one of the professional freelance reviewers employed by *ForeWord Magazine*. Our ForeWord Clarion Review service gives you the opportunity to have your title reviewed by one of the most prominent and respected book review publications in the publishing industry.[65]

Perhaps it's just me, but doesn't offering this service call into question the credibility of the *ForeWord Magazine* reviewers whose reviews can apparently be bought?

Rising Star Program

Only authors who sign up for a Premier Pro package ($1549.00) or higher are eligible for the Rising Star Program. As with the Star Program, you must first achieve Editor's Choice designation. "Each Rising Star title will be featured in the monthly Rising Star Special Collections section of the Barnes & Noble Web site and presented by a commissioned sales force to national, regional and local booksellers, including Barnes & Noble, Borders and Books-A-Million."[66]

It bears mentioning that wholesalers such as Ingram, with whom iUniverse contract, already distribute to the aforementioned retailers, so how this differs from the way iUniverse's sales force "presents" your title is not clear. Once again, "returnability status" for book retailers (softcover only) is included, though note that this is *already* included in "Bookstore Premier Pro" ($2099.00) and up packages.

So how many books make it into the Rising Star Program? If we take the email I received from iUniverse at face value, they have published over 40,000 titles in ten years, or about 4000 titles per year. A check of the Rising Star page on the Barnes & Noble website revealed 37 titles spanning from June 2008 to June 2011, with some significant gaps: no titles released between September 2010 and March 2011, between December 2009 and March 2010, and between June 2008 and July 2009. So, 37 titles over three years is roughly one per month, or twelve per year. That would be twelve out of an average 4000 annual titles.

Now, one could argue these are the cream of the crop and the numbers reflect this. Certainly, those that received reader reviews generally received excellent reviews: only one of the 37 received less than four or five stars. However, less than half (16) of the 37 books received reader reviews; of those that did, the average number was only one to three reviews. Only one received any editorial reviews, and while the authors of the reviews were noted the publications were not. The rest of the books did not receive any professional reviews, not even from *ForeWord Magazine*. One would think the exclusivity and alleged prestige of the Rising Star Program would have translated into more interest.

One other thing I noticed is that, despite the fact that the "See Inside" service is included in the various packages for which eligibility to the recognition programs is also included, only 19 of the 37 books featured "See Inside," though 22 books did have a sample chapter on the title's webpage (some had both See Inside and a sample chapter, some had neither). And one book did not have a cover image—inexplicable.

List Price

Authors have no say in the list price of their books published by iUniverse; instead iUniverse determines the price, which is based on the word count and other production factors; what the price will be set at "you'll only know once your manuscript has been submitted and gone through production[.]"[67]

Royalties

In the introduction to this manual we mentioned the meagre royalties paid to legacy published authors—around 15% of the cover price on hardcovers and 10% or less on paperbacks—and later we wrote about the meagre 25% of net for ebook sales. The low royalties are the trade-off for the legacy published author, for out of the publisher's cut are paid the editorial development, book design and manufacture, distribution, costly advertising, and the risk of returns. So one would think that if the author is paying for all of these things, as they are with iUniverse, then one's royalty would reflect this. You would think this but you would be wrong.

Print Books

When I spoke with the salesperson at iUniverse, I was quoted a royalty of 20-25% of the net price. When pressed to define "net," he replied that this of course varies according to the contract with the sales channel who bought the book. I asked for a typical breakdown. His response was, "You're very astute, asking all these questions, but really all you need to know is what *you* get." Which is what? I asked again. Twenty percent of the net price, was the reply.

So what does it pay? The company's website states: "Royalties are based on the payments we actually receive from the sale of printed or electronic (e-book) copies of your book, less any shipping and handling charges or sales and use taxes." It then proceeds to tell you iUniverse sells most books through Ingram, to whom iUniverse sells your book for 36% off list. An example follows of a "common sales transaction": the list price is $15.95; the book is sold to Ingram at a 36% discount, resulting in a net sale of $10.21. The royalty is $10.21 x 20%, or $2.04.[68] This amounts to 12.8% of list, or about what a legacy published author is paid—yet the legacy published author is not paying thousands of dollars to be published.

This 36% discount iUniverse calls "industry standard," but as we have already explored earlier in this manual, 50-55% is now the standard. At 36% off list, Ingram is selling forward at too low a discount—no more than 30% off list, less to small retailers—to be of interest to booksellers. And a glance among iUniverse titles on Amazon shows the retail giant selling the titles at a discount off list that is often greater than 30%. But if Ingram is buying at 36% off list and then taking its cut, how is Amazon able to sell at 30% off or more?

Amazon is able to do so because iUniverse authors quickly learn that the above pricing structure does not work for the retailers and are then enticed to enrol in iUniverse's Bookseller Discount Program. For a fee of $99.00 you can sign up to earn even less money than is already on offer: 10% of net instead of 20%. In exchange for you choosing this more modest royalty, iUniverse offers the wholesalers "up to" 50% off list.[69] So you now earn 10% of 50%, or 5% of list, which is about half of what a legacy published author is paid. (To put that in even clearer perspective, depending upon the distributor I earn between 17.9 and 36% of list for the print version of *Baby Jane*.)

This information you will not find on iUniverse's deeply buried FAQ page "Questions in Royalties & Sales"; instead it is buried on another FAQ page, "Questions in Bookseller Discount Program," a page you will likely have no idea you should be looking at until well after you have handed over your package fee and then paid even more money to have your book edited only to have it fail to show up in retail channels.

But the bad news does not stop there. You may recall from the section on distribution that books sold on a non-returnable basis are rarely stocked by bricks-and-mortar stores, and will only be stocked conservatively by the online retailers if interest is expressed in the title (your title will be offered, just not stocked). So if your goal is to get onto physical retail shelves, reducing your royalty is not going to achieve that goal. However, iUniverse has a solution: the Booksellers Return Program. Included in the Bookstore Premier Pro package and up, it can also be purchased separately for $699.00. The program acts as an insurance policy, paying the author their royalty on all books sold even if they are later returned by the bookstore.[70] Of course, inclusion in the program is still no guarantee a physical bookstore will stock your book, and the odds are they will not unless your book commands the attention of consumers: even large retailers like Chapters or Barnes & Noble only stock around 150,000 titles in store—a mere fraction of what is available on the market—and those 150,000 titles are not carried in every store.

When you sign onto this program you must sign a one- to three-year deal,[71] and each year the renewal fee is $300.00.[72]

eBook Royalties

Prior to 1 December 2010, an author had the option to grant iUniverse the licence to convert the title into an ebook and distribute it. Now that ebooks have taken the market by storm, automatic ebook rights are included in every iUniverse contract; authors cannot opt out of this arrangement.[73] Authors must submit the source file and iUniverse will convert it into the PDF format for sales on iUniverse's own website, the mobi format for Amazon, and the ePub format for Sony, Nook, Kobo, Google eBookstore, Scribd.com, iBookstore, and BooksOnBoard. The list price is set by iUniverse at its sole discretion.

The royalty paid on the sale of ebooks is 50% of net. For example, if Amazon pays 70% of list for your title, iUniverse pays you 35% of list and keeps 35% for itself. Where Amazon pays 35% of list, you get 17.5% of list.[74] Compare that to the distributor cut of 0-15% of net charged by ebook aggregators.

Your Book Files

In earlier chapters we explored the ins and outs of book design, namely the importance of owning your files and cover art, and how copyright of a work-for-hire lies with the commissioner of the artwork unless there is a contract to the contrary. With iUniverse, they assume copyright of the cover art you paid for and iUniverse will not provide you with anything more than a low-res PDF. Moreover, if you purchase a package that includes your book cover design and you later provide your own cover art, iUniverse will not discount its fees and, while you will retain ownership of the cover art, copyright of the cover itself still remains with iUniverse. If you design a mock-up for the cover and iUniverse's design team uses that mock-up, iUniverse still retains copyright.[75] Similarly, you pay iUniverse to create your internal book files yet it claims ownership of them as well, and will not provide you with a copy.[76]

Marketing

In addition to iUniverse's evaluation services, editorial services, formatting services, design services, production services, and bookselling services, iUniverse has a plethora of marketing services on offer. Among the complaints about iUniverse is the high-pressure sales calls you will receive attempting to sell you these marketing services, and one complainant noted the calls were outsourced to call centres outside the U.S.[77] The marketing services are too numerous to mention, so I will only look at a few to give you some perspective.

Author Website Setup

I chose this one because I have my own website so I know what one costs, and when I saw the iUniverse price I was flabbergasted. It charges $399.00, and for that you do not actually get the website created; instead, you use an online template system to build it yourself, with "helpful e-mail and telephone support." The site is then hosted on the American Author server (this service is offered in partnership with them), for which you pay iUniverse $29.00 per month.[78]

When I set up my first company website I used a similar service. I paid *nothing* upfront to build my site from the company's online template system, and $9.99 a month thereafter for hosting including email service. For the same package the company now charges $19.99 with email service, $9.99 without. There are many companies out there who offer similar services and the fees noted are typical. So for iUniverse to charge $399.00 just for access to the online software is outrageous.

Alternatively, you can buy website builder software, specifically designed with built-in templates for amateurs, for around $100.00 or less. Popular software includes WebPlus X5, Coffee Cup, and Web Easy; if you input "website builder software" into a search engine, several options will come up for you to explore. You can find the software at office supply shops and online at sites like Amazon or direct from the manufacturer. Many offer 30-day free trial downloads. There is also the free, open source Wordpress.org. Once you have your site built, you can then upload it to a web hosting company, to whom you will pay about $5.00 a month; and you will pay an annual web domain fee of between $10.00 and $20.00 to a domain registrar. So my website costs me $80.00 per year compared to iUniverse's $348.00 per year.

Easier still, you can use a free blogging service such as Wordpress.com or Blogger.com to build a blog. For the purpose of promoting a book, it will likely be all you need.

Email Marketing Campaign

IUniverse offers you the opportunity to reach your potential readers with an email marketing campaign. You have the choice of an individual campaign or a more "cost-effective" shared campaign, and you can choose between contacting 500,000, 2 million, 5 million, or 10 million people who have allegedly opted in to receive communications from iUniverse. Now, obviously spam works, otherwise spammers would stop, so there may very well be mileage in such a campaign, but whether the results will be worth the cost only you can decide: the individual campaign, starting with the 500K level and working up, is $1596.00, $3996.00, $7196.00, and $9996.00. If you elect to use the shared campaign, the email will feature your book and three other titles, and is priced at $399.00, $999.00, $1799.00, and $2499.00. It is important to note that you do not get access to the list; iUniverse sends the email on your behalf and only provides a report on the number of people who opened the email and the number of click-throughs to the retail site offering your book.[79]

Hollywood Book-to-Screen

I have worked in the film industry since 1995, and during this time I have written six speculative and four commissioned scripts, one optioned documentary treatment, and was the unaccredited story editor on the award-winning movie-of-the-week (MOW) *A Cooler Climate*, starring Sally Field and Judy Davis. I have also ghostwritten production notes for over thirty major motion pictures. So while I am not a big-time Hollywood writer, I can offer some insight into the services offered by iUniverse.

Three Hollywood products are offered: coverage ($799.00), treatment ($3,499.00), and screenplay ($14,999.00); but since the treatment is a prerequisite to the screenplay, the latter will really cost you $18,498.00. IUniverse has a deal with Principle Entertainment, a production company and talent agency with offices in Los Angeles and New York; the deal is "first look," meaning that any iUniverse-published author who pursues this option will have their work offered first to Principle only and not shopped around in the hope of inciting a bidding war (which are rare anyway). What this means is that Principle, if interested, will make an offer to option or buy the film rights to your book, and you, hugely flattered and not knowing any better, will likely sign whatever deal is put in front of you; or Principle may ask to represent you as talent and shop your project around.

What are the chances Principle will develop a screenplay based on your book? Principle's website advertises a partial slate of eight films that it developed and/or produced. But Principle is not listed on the Internet Movie Database (IMDB) as a production company on these eight films, meaning it was most likely an agent for the talent and/or a producer-for-hire in what is called the "service industry." In fact, one of the films, *Monster Island* (2004), was a service film shot in and around Vancouver where I live. A further search of the IMDB reveals two films accredited to Principle as the production company, *One Small Hitch* (2011) and *The Powder Puff Principle* (2006). Another eleven films are listed on Principle's website as in active development. Of these 21 films in total, only one is based on a book, *Sabriel* by Garth Nix, published by Harper Teen, not iUniverse.

Should you invest, then, in coverage of your book? To start with, authors and screenwriters do not buy coverage, producers do. If a producer has heard about your book and is interested, they will hire a writer or creative consultant to read your book and produce the coverage.

This coverage may not be complimentary, or may be complimentary but may reject your book for practical reasons. For example, a television movie is severely restricted in its number of locations, characters, shooting days, and budget; if the producer is looking for television movie projects and your book cannot be successfully adapted within the limitations of that format, the coverage will say so. By buying coverage, then, you are simply paying for a service that is rightfully the expense of the producer and which may not recommend your book for production.

"Your book has all the elements Hollywood wants – an exciting plot, well-developed characters, and fresh content – yet a Hollywood Treatment is a crucial piece you still need in order to be taken seriously by established Hollywood executives."[80] Or so says the iUniverse website. While it is true a treatment is helpful when pitching a project, it is by no means crucial or necessary in order to be taken seriously by Hollywood. A treatment is a later stage in development, an intermediary stage after a producer has optioned material but does not yet want to proceed to a script. A treatment is a cheaper way to produce a longer form document that fleshes out the plot and character development and can be used to shop the project to financiers. Treatments are also used quite often during development of documentaries, serving as an early form of the shooting script. Either way, treatments are never paid for by the book author; they are commissioned and paid for by the producer.

Similarly, a screenplay adaptation of a book is also commissioned and paid for by the producer. It is never the expense of the author. So if you were to commission a writer to produce coverage, or to adapt your book to either a treatment or screenplay, you would be acting as a producer; and if you were then to sell the treatment or script to Principle you would rightfully be entitled to be accredited as a producer on the film and to be remunerated accordingly.

Another matter of concern is that of credit and ownership of the treatment or screenplay. The iUniverse website states, "The screenwriter waives all rights to ownership of the treatment; you maintain full ownership." Two issues arise from this: the first is that waiving ownership does not mean the writer waives credit for their work: if a film is later made, and the studio is a signatory to the Writer's Guild of America, the matter of credit could be arbitrated by the writer. Principle Entertainment is not a signatory to the WGA agreement and is not bound by their rules, but if the project is later sold to a Guild signatory—and all the major studios are signatories—then the Guild can enforce their rules.

The second issue is that it is considered unethical to hire a writer and demand copyright of their work (the WGA forbids it). Just as you own the copyright to your novel, the screenwriter you hire should own the copyright to their treatment or screenplay. This copyright is the writer's only protection, the only means they have to enforce their right to be paid and accredited appropriately. Acknowledging the writer's copyright to the script in no way infringes upon your copyright to your novel, or your right to determine who options your film rights or produces any subsequent film: the writer cannot sell the treatment or screenplay you commissioned because you own the book it is based on, what is called the "underlying property," and a producer needs to secure the rights to both the screenplay and the underlying property in order to make the movie. You do not need to rob the screenwriter of their copyright to protect your own.

In the film industry there is what is known as speculative ("spec") writing; this is where a screenwriter develops their own ideas, writing treatments or screenplays at their own expense and then hoping to sell them. This is common practice, and if such a project is sold then the writer is paid the same rates as if the work had been commissioned. But it is considered unethical for a producer to ask a writer to write on spec:

> There shall be no speculative writing, nor shall the Company or the Guild condone it as a practice. Speculative writing refers to any agreement entered into between the Company and any writer:
>
> for the writer to write material, payment for which is contingent upon the acceptance or approval of the Company, or upon the occurrence of any other event, such as obtaining financing ...[81]

So what iUniverse is doing by offering this "service" to you is helping Principle Entertainment skirt the unethical practice of commissioning speculative writing by having *you* commission and pay for what it should be commissioning and paying for, and then having you submit it to Principle as "spec" material.

Lastly, about the rates paid. The current Guild minimum for a treatment is $20,554 for a low-budget film; a screenplay is $34,251 ($70,489 for a high budget film). So if you are paying iUniverse $3,499.00 for the treatment and $14,999.00 for a screenplay, out of which I assume iUniverse takes a cut before paying the screenwriter, how "professional" of a screenwriter do you think you are getting for your money? Granted, work is hard to come by these days and writers are hungry, but still.

If you look at the current trend in Hollywood, films that are based on books are usually based on bestsellers: the film then benefits from the book's success. So rather than spend money commissioning a treatment or screenplay, I would recommend you spend your time and effort turning your book into a success. If you can make that happen, Hollywood will call you.

Alternatively, learn about what are called "one-sheets": these are letter-size, poster-like adverts for a script that feature an image (you can use your book cover), the book's synopsis, review comments if available, and contact information. You can then send that to Principle Entertainment and everyone else in Hollywood and see if anyone expresses interest.

Within weeks of publishing *Baby Jane* a local producer asked if I were going to write the screenplay version. I would be happy to, I replied, if I were commissioned. Unless there is money to pay me, I know that I am better off spending my time writing another book because the odds of getting a film made are really high and not in your favour, while each book you write helps to sell the others.

And the Moral of the Story is?

There is a saying in law: "If it looks like a duck and quacks like a duck, it's a duck." A name change from "vanity publisher" to "author services company" does not change the fundamental nature of a company like iUniverse. To call what it does "self-publishing" is misleading: it mandatorily assigns its ISBN to your book, it lists itself as your publisher, it exercises editorial control (through its recognition programs), it controls the book's design, it controls pricing and distribution, it offers to market your book, and it takes a hefty cut of your royalties. Which is precisely what a legacy publisher does. What iUniverse does not do that a traditional publisher does is pay for it. Instead the author pays all costs and iUniverse reaps the rewards.

While iUniverse is one of the larger vanity publishers in the U.S., it is by no means the only one and by no means is this problem confined to the States. I found vanity publishers in every English-language jurisdiction I researched. And while they vary in the packages and services they offer, they are fundamentally the same in their objectives. Considering the sums of money at stake here, I am of the opinion that indie authors get a much better return on their investment by acting as their own publisher, taking control and reaping their own rewards.

Epilogue: Taking the Plunge

As I said in the preface, there is no one right way to self-publish but there is one wrong way: uninformed. There is no one perfect way to self-publish whether it is how you price your books or which distribution model you use, whether you forgo partial control in exchange for a free ISBN, and whether you distribute through an aggregator or set up direct-to-retailer accounts. What is important is that you now know and understand the potential consequences, good or bad, of each decision you make, so you can remain your own master.

My hope is that you will have learned enough from this manual to strategize effectively, to plan a course of action that will help you to reach your goals, goals that will be realistic and thus achievable, and which you can build upon. There are no quick riches here but you may just earn a living, which is more than most writers can boast of. And while landing a bestseller has only slightly better odds than winning the lottery, you cannot win if you do not play. Welcome to indie publishing.

Endnotes

1   In the U.S. the bricks-and-mortar powerhouse is Barnes & Noble. In the 1990s B&N opened more than 700 megastores and soon gained majority control of book retail until Amazon arrived. In Canada, the major player is Chapters Indigo who controls approximately 70% of print sales. Critics say these powerful retailers have used their position to impose hefty wholesale discounts from publishers, to force unfair payment terms, and who then over-order and return unsold stock, leaving the publishers with the bill. See, for example, Gordon Lockheed, "The book publishers' crisis," Dooney's Café, 9 November 2010, www.dooneyscafe.com/archives/2363. Smaller bookstores have also claimed some chains used their clout to force retail landlords to evict competitor tenants. See "Lichtman's files for bankruptcy protection," *CBC News*, 7 March 2000, www.cbc.ca/news/business/story/2000/03/07/lichtman000307.html.)

2   Stephen Henighan, "The BookNet Dictatorship," *GEIST*, Fall/Winter 2010, Issue 78/79, pages 121-124.

3   See, for example, William Skidelsky, "Kindle gives thriller writer a lot of success – at 71p a shot," *Guardian.co.uk*, 27 February 2011, http://www.guardian.co.uk/technology/2011/feb/27/kindle-ebooks-amazon-stephen-leather?INTCMP=SRCH%22,,0,0.

4   See, for example, Joe Konrath, "Publishers Weekly Epic Fail," A Newbie's Guide to Publishing, 24 May 2010, http://jakonrath.blogspot.com/2010/05/publishers-weekly-epic-fail.html.

5   Chuck Leddy, "A major literary agency will open its own creative writing school," *The Writer Magazine*, 25 February 2011, http://www.writermag.com/en/Articles/2011/02/A%20major%20literary%20agency%20will%20open%20its%20own%20creative%20writing%20school.aspx.

6   Marc Coté, "Why's everybody always picking on us?" *The Globe and Mail*, 14 February 2009, p. F14.

7   Grey Hoy, "Debate rages over future of Australia's book industry," *The 7.30 Report*, Australian Broadcasting Corporation, 7 July 2009, www.abc.net.au/7.30/content/2009/s2619538.htm.

8   Andi Sporkin, "E-Books Rank as #1 Format among All Trade Categories for the Month," Association of American Publishers, 14 April 2011, http://www.publishers.org/press/30/.

9   The term "aggregator" refers to a company that specializes in converting manuscripts into the various ebook formats then distributes your book to a selection of retail partners. The retailers pay your royalties to the aggregator who then takes a percentage as their distribution fee.

10 Keith Gessen, "The Book on Publishing," *Vanity Fair*, October 2011, page 265.

11 Projected, 2010. R.R. Bowker LLC, "New Book Titles and Editions: 2002-2010," Bowkerinfo.com, http://www.bowkerinfo.com/pubtrack/AnnualBookProduction2010/ISBN_Output_2002-2010.pdf.

12 For the year 2010. Publishers Association Market Research and Statistics, "UK Book Industry in Statistics 2010" (London: The Publishers Association, June 2011), page 4.

13 Association of Canadian Publishers, http://www.publishers.ca/index.php?option=com_content&view=article&id=21&Itemid=59. Accessed July 2011. Australian Bureau of Statistics, "1363.0 - Book

Publishers, Australia, 2003-04" (Canberra: Australian Bureau of Statistics, 17 August 2005), http://www.abs.gov.au/AUSSTATS/abs@.nsf/Lookup/CCAAF744A4F4F8D3CA256B3C0074D7A7?OpenDocument.

14 Tony Fisk, "The New Zealand Publishing Scene," Publishers Association of New Zealand, n.d., http://bpanz.org.nz/cms/index.php?option=com_content&view=article&id=128:the-new-zealand-publishing-scene&catid=21:introduction-to-publishing&Itemid=41. Francis Galloway & Willem Struik, "Annual Book Publishing Industry Survey Report 2008" (Pretoria: Publishing Studies, University of Pretoria, November 2009), page 74.

15 Kdp.amazon.com, "Payment information," Kindle Direct Publishing, https://kdp.amazon.com/self-publishing/help?topicId=AE24XS35AM53P. Accessed July 2011.

16 Kdp.amazon.com, "Clause 5.8, Kindle Direct Publishing Terms and Conditions," Kindle Direct Publishing, https://kdp.amazon.com/self-publishing/help?topicId=APILE934L348N. Accessed July 2011.

17 Department of Justice Canada, "Criminal Code R.S.C. 1985 c. C-46" (Ottawa: Queen's Printer, 1985), Section 298(1).

18 Ibid., Section 296(2).

19 Ibid., Section 296(3).

20 Copyright.gov, Why should I register my work if copyright protection is automatic?", U.S. Copyright Office, http://www.copyright.gov/help/faq/faq-general.html#automatic. Accessed August 2011.

21 Smashwords.com, "Smashwords Support Center FAQ," http://www.smashwords.com/about/supportfaq. Accessed 05 July 2011.

22 Authorsonline.co.uk, "Publish With Us," http://www.authorsonline.co.uk/publish_with_us/eBooks/. Accessed 14 July 2011.

23 The blog was bookyards.blogspot.com that directs you to katzforums.com. This was followed by thepiratebay.org, FilesTube, librosgratisweb (a.k.a. "free books web"), and free-ebook-download.net.

24 Betsy Reid, "Stockpiling Trouble," *British Journal of Photography*, June 2011, page 86.

25 Quoted in "Stockpiling Trouble" by Betsy Reid, *British Journal of Photography*, June 2011, page 86.

26 iUniverse.com, "Questions in Contracts and Agreements," http://www.iuniverse.com/faqs/agreements.aspx. Accessed 22 July 2011.

27 Smashwords.com, "Smashwords Support Center FAQ," http://www.smashwords.com/about/supportfaq. Accessed 05 July 2011.

28 Smashwords.com, "Smashwords Terms of Service: Updated February 20, 2010," http://www.smashwords.com/about/tos. Accessed 12 July 2011.

29 "Lightning Source Inc. CoreSource Fulfillment Agreement for Publishers," between author and Lightning Source Inc., July 2011.

30 Kdp.amazon.com, "Basic HTML Formatting Guidelines," https://kdp.amazon.com/self-publishing/help?topicId=A1KSPVAI36UUC1. Accessed 05 August 2011.

31 Ibid.

32 Ibid.

33 Kdp.amazon.com, "Types of Formats," Kindle Direct Publishing, https://kdp.amazon.com/self-publishing/help?topicId=A2GF0UFHIYG9VQ#zip. Accessed July 2011.

34 "Exhibit C, Ebook Agency/Commissionaire Distribution Agreement" (Apple Inc., n.d.), Page 17.

35 Kdp.amazon.com, "5.3.2 Customer Prices, Kindle Direct Publishing Terms and Conditions" (Kindle Direct Publishing, 8 July 2011), https://kdp.amazon.com/self-publishing/help?topicId=APILE934L348N. And Pubit.barnesandnoble.com, "eBook Publication and Distribution Agreement" (Barnesandnoble.com LLC, 2011), http://pubit.barnesandnoble.com/pubit_app/bn?t=reg_terms_print.

36 Kdp.amazon.com, "Payment information," Kindle Direct Publishing, https://kdp.amazon.com/self-publishing/help?topicId=AE24XS35AM53P. Accessed July 2011.

37 iTunesconnect.apple.com, "Requirements," iTunes Connect, https://itunesconnect.apple.com/WebObjects/iTunesConnect.woa/wo/3.0.0.9.7.3.1.1. Accessed July 2011.

38 Ibid.

39 Kobobooks.com, "Authors and Publishers," http://kobobooks.com/companyinfo/authorsnpublishers.html. Accessed August 2011.

40 Smashwords.com, "6a Royalty Rates, Smashwords Terms of Service" (Los Gatos: Smashwords, 10 February 2010), http://www.smashwords.com/about/tos.

41 "Section 5 (a), Ebook Agency/Commissionaire Distribution Agreement" (Apple Inc., n.d.), page 5. As at July 2011.

42 Createspace.com, "Section 5.1 Fees, CreateSpace Member Agreement" (On-Demand Publishing LLC, [an Amazon.com Inc. company] d/b/a CreateSpace, 6 May 2011), https://www.createspace.com/Help/Rights/MemberAgreement.jsp.

43 Authors OnLine promotional brochure, "Publishing Life's Next Chapter" (Beds, UK: Authors OnLine), Page 9.

44 iUniverse.com, "Star Program FAQ: How does my book become a STAR title?" iUniverse, http://www.iuniverse.com/WhyiUniverse/RecognitionPrograms/StarProgram/FAQ.aspx. Accessed July 2011.

45 "Instructions for Form W-7 (Rev. January 2011)" (Washington: Department of the Treasury, Internal Revenue Service), page 2.

46 Ibid.

47 Chapter.indigo.ca, http://www.chapters.indigo.ca/home/?s_campaign=goo-Corp_Chapters&. Accessed July 2011.

48 Chapter.indigo.ca, http://www.chapters.indigo.ca/iUniverse-Main-promo-page/iuniverse_main-giz.html. Accessed July 2011.

49 Brian Jud, *Get Your Word's Worth: 555 Tips for Improving Your Book Promotion* (Brian Jud, 2008), page 4.

50 iUniverse.com, http://www.iuniverse.com/chaptersindigoand_coles.aspx. Accessed July 2011. You can also view the video on YouTube at http://www.youtube.com/watch?v=tTWwodFN2AA&feature=player_embedded.

51 Chapter.indigo.ca, "Indigo Chapters Publishing Packages," http://www.iuniverse.com/Packages/Chapters.aspx. Accessed July 2011.

52 iUniverse.com, "Book Signing Kit," http://www.iuniverse.com/Servicestore/ServiceDetail.aspx?ServiceId=BS-5654. Accessed July 2011.

53 iUniverse.com, "Editorial Evaluation," http://www.iuniverse.com/Servicestore/ServiceDetail.aspx?ServiceId=BS-506. Accessed July 2011.

54 Complaintsboard.com, "iUniverse Complaints – Scam," http://www.complaintsboard.com/complaints/iuniverse-c126307.html?sor. Accessed July 2011.

55 iUniverse.com, "Proofing New Manuscripts," http://www.iuniverse.com/FAQ/FAQ.aspx?id=442. Accessed July 2011.

56 iUniverse.com, "Compare Self Publishing Packages," http://www.iuniverse.com/Packages/PackageCompare.aspx. Accessed July 2011.

57 iUniverse.com, "Editor's Choice Recognition Program," http://www.iuniverse.com/why-iuniverse/programs-awards/editors-choice.aspx. Accessed July 2011.

58 iUniverse.com, "If I buy the recommended service, does that guarantee I'll get Editor's Choice?", http://www.iuniverse.com/faqs/editorial.aspx. Accessed July 2011.

59 iUniverse.com, "If I make the Editorial Evaluator's recommended changes myself, will I still be eligible for Editor's Choice?", http://www.iuniverse.com/faqs/editorial.aspx. Accessed July 2011.

60 iUniverse.com, "The Benefits of the Star Program," http://www.iuniverse.com/why-iuniverse/programs-awards/star-program.aspx. Accessed July 2011.

61 iUniverse.com, "Star Program FAQ: How does my book become a STAR title?" http://www.iuniverse.com/WhyiUniverse/RecognitionPrograms/StarProgram/FAQ.aspx. Accessed July 2011.

62 iUniverse.com, "How You Can Qualify for the Star Program," http://www.iuniverse.com/why-iuniverse/programs-awards/star-program.aspx. Accessed July 2011.

63 iUniverse.com, "As a Star title, will I receive guaranteed placement in local bookstores?", http://www.iuniverse.com/WhyiUniverse/RecognitionPrograms/StarProgram/FAQ.aspx. Accessed July 2011.

64 iUniverse.com, "What are the benefits of the Star Program?", http://www.iuniverse.com/WhyiUniverse/RecognitionPrograms/StarProgram/FAQ.aspx. Accessed July 2011.

65 iUniverse.com, "What is a ForeWord Clarion Review?", http://www.iuniverse.com/WhyiUniverse/RecognitionPrograms/StarProgram/FAQ.aspx. Accessed July 2011.

66 iUniverse.com, "What is unique about the Rising Star designation?", http://www.iuniverse.com/why-iuniverse/programs-awards/rising-star-faq.aspx. Accessed July 2011.

67 iUniverse.com, "How does iUniverse set the price of my book?", http://www.iuniverse.com/faqs/bookproduction.aspx. Accessed July 2011.

68 iUniverse.com, "How does iUniverse calculate royalty payments?", http://www.iuniverse.com/faqs/royalties.aspx. Accessed July 2011.

69 iUniverse.com, "Questions in Bookseller Discount Program," http://www.iuniverse.com/faqs/booksellerdiscount.aspx. Accessed July 2011.

70 iUniverse.com, "Selling Your Book - Booksellers Return Program FAQs," http://www.iuniverse.com/why-iUniverse/publishing-the-iUniverse-way/selling-your-book/booksellers-return-program/FAQs.aspx. Accessed July 2011.

71 Ibid.

72 iUniverse.com, "Booksellers Return Program Renewal," http://www.iuniverse.com/Servicestore/ServiceDetail.aspx?ServiceId=BS-518. Accessed July 2011.

73 iUniverse.com, "Does this mean all books will now be ePubs?", http://www.iuniverse.com/faqs/digital_formatting_and_distribution.aspx. Accessed July 2011.

74 iUniverse.com, "What's my royalty percentage?", http://www.iuniverse.com/faqs/digital_formatting_and_distribution.aspx. Accessed July 2011.

75 iUniverse.com, "Do I own rights to the cover of my book?", http://www.iuniverse.com/faqs/agreements.aspx. Accessed July 2011.

76 iUniverse.com, "Who owns the printable (native) files?", http://www.iuniverse.com/faqs/agreements.aspx. Accessed July 2011.

77 Paul Zolbrod, complaint posted on Complaints Board.com. ~September 5, 2010. http://www.complaintsboard.com/complaints/iuniverse-c126307.html?sort=datea&page=2. Accessed July 2011.

78 iUniverse.com, "Author Web Site Setup," http://www.iuniverse.com/Servicestore/ServiceDetail.aspx?ServiceId=BS-474. Accessed July 2011.

79 iUniverse.com, "Single Book Email Campaign - 500,000," http://www.iuniverse.com/Servicestore/ServiceDetail.aspx?ServiceId=BS-3438. Accessed July 2011.

80 iUniverse.com, "Hollywood Treatment," http://www.iuniverse.com/Servicestore/ServiceDetail.aspx?ServiceId=BS-1096. Accessed July 2011.

81 "Memorandum of Agreement for the 2011 WGA Theatrical and Television Basic Agreement" (Los Angeles: Writers Guild of America, March 20, 2011), page 13.

BABY JANE

a novel by

M. A. Demers

Egghead
Books

www.eggheadbooks.com
www.mademers.com

Kindle edition published by Egghead Books, ISBN 978-0-9868914-0-3
and ePub edition, ISBN 978-0-9868914-2-7

Library and Archives Canada
Demers, Michelle A, 1964—
Baby Jane / M.A. Demers — Trade paperback edition.
ISBN 978-0-9868914-1-0

Cover design and photography by
Michelle A. Demers

ONE

The death of a child is never a good thing. A life taken before it had a chance to bloom: surely there could be no greater purpose, no divine rationale. Claire Dawson's child was dead, and nothing worthwhile could possibly arise from such a tragedy. Her child was *dead*. And it was her fault.

Yet here she was in a house paid for by that death, a house she could never have afforded otherwise, and she was perplexed and burdened by the paradox: her son was dead by the hammer of her stupidity yet that hammer would now build her a home. In what universe did that compute? "Where God closes a door, he opens a window," a well-intentioned friend had counselled, but as the friend had never suffered anything worse than disappointment the gesture had seemed hollow, a bone with all the marrow sucked out. So Claire had dismissed the advice, and despite the flutter of anticipation in her heart when she signed the purchase agreement, despite the tingling in her fingers when she began packing up her tiny, overpriced apartment, her ambivalence remained resolute. Every victory was followed by a robust certainty that she didn't deserve to be happy, that she should wear her culpability like mourning cloth, and thus she spent her days vacillating between waves of recrimination and trickles of tempered optimism.

Claire collapsed onto the sofa, kicked off her sneakers, bent one leg back and began kneading the swollen flesh beneath her toes. *The death of a child is never a good thing!* That she should consider the alternative, should let it sneak past her defences and pose itself, was troubling. Everything happens for a reason, Dr. Fitzsimmons had insisted, but while Claire had progressed sufficiently to entertain this pseudo-belief she wasn't able to wear it like her shrink did, like a second, thicker skin. Claire was still translucent, her fortifications an illusion: a heavy fog that dissipated with the mildest of winds.

She closed her eyes and wiped the sweat off her eyelids. The day had been hot for the start of summer, the movers' perspiration soaking through their thin T-shirts and onto the boxes, and she was glad she'd had the foresight to drape the sofa in plastic sheeting. The thought of rubbing against a man's scent didn't appeal to her: male company was not something Claire cared for these days, notwithstanding brief moments of carnal weakness that presented themselves as a vague discomfort along the inside of her thighs. Such moments passed quickly, and she imagined they simply moved on to a more receptive vehicle, as if thoughts could be passed on like fruit cake until they landed in the hands of the one foolish enough to take a bite. Passion: it was the candied cherries that made the messy pudding appear enticing, that suckered you in before your taste buds could register love's bitter aftertaste. No wonder it was the cake of choice for weddings.

The thought of the movers reminded Claire of her own unpleasant aroma so she pulled her unwilling carcass up off the couch with a groan and headed upstairs for a bath. She turned on the taps that curved over the end of the chipped claw foot tub, then wandered over to the window to survey the garden below. Its beauty tempered her ambivalence. Resplendent even in the shadows of a setting sun, the garden was awash in colour or the promise of it: giant hydrangea bushes waiting to flower, stunning red and purple rhododendrons already in bloom, roses and dahlias that were as yet just a promise, and a lilac tree that held court over them all. The garden had been the property's sole selling feature, beautifully maintained in stark contrast to the original 1930s condition of the house. It had been a shock to come inside, actually, the sad, faded wallpaper the first indication of a home unloved by time and ignored by its occupants. But the house had good bones, the inspector had assured Claire, and at the competitive price of $590,000 it left her money to renovate. She snickered at that last thought: "competitive" was a relative term in real estate and Vancouver had long ago dropped any pretence of affordability. For a middle-income earner—and Claire considered her teacher's salary barely even that—this was a two-wage town unless you got lucky enough to win the lottery or land an inheritance or, she thought cynically, to settle out of court.

And settled she had. Hush funds. Blood money. Seven hundred fifty thousand dollars in exchange for her silence. A silence that had proved deafening.

Claire stripped and sank into the tepid water, then leaned back to study the spider cracks that spun a haphazard web on the ceiling. *The death of a child is never a good thing.* The thought re-entered her mind again before she had the sense to stop it, and in her fatigue the tears welled up before she could stop them, too. She covered her eyes with one hand as the salty droplets trickled down her face and into the bathwater, her shoulders shaking from the small convulsions she tried to quell, and within seconds she forgot where she was, only why, and became lost in grief.

Claire's cries crept along the attic floor and echoed down the narrow stairwell, reverberating eerily in the darkening rooms below. At the back of the house a creature stirred in the gloom, its tiny ears trembling at the lamentations from above. The sound of a woman crying was frightening yet soothingly familiar, and the creature silently wondered if the house had reawakened after decades asleep. It listened, fearful yet strangely hopeful, until the sobbing slowly subsided and the house fell silent again.

TWO

Claire's eyes flickered behind their lids as sunlight poured through her bedroom window and penetrated the thin veil of skin. Without conscious thought she turned away, her soul still wandering in that indeterminate geography between sleep and wakefulness, the place where what is and what was and what might be collide in a kaleidoscope of cryptic narratives and archaic imagery. When she awoke she would remember the essence of her visions, could write it down for later scrutiny, but she didn't do that anymore, was weary of her dreams reduced to psychobabble and picked apart like scabs. She had chosen instead to put her dreams in what she believed is their rightful place: on a high shelf alongside blind hope and indiscriminate yearning.

The creature watched, curious but cautious, as the light slowly coaxed Claire awake. It had been hovering all night, slinking about at the edges of her bed, wondering if she might be its chance at freedom. But Claire seemed fragile, had whimpered often in her sleep, and the creature feared Claire might be as weak as the others whose spirits had already been broken in this house. To reveal itself would risk injury to Claire, perhaps even death; would she prove more resilient than she appeared? And even if she were, wasn't this too much to ask of a stranger who had merely wandered, unknowingly, into the den of a beast?

The creature retreated into the shadows as Claire opened her eyes and rolled out of the foetal position she'd curled herself into. She winced as sunlight burned into her retinas, a dull ache in her head. Her son had dominated her dreams as usual, though this time his face had been obscured, a curious change she would understand only later as events unfolded. But for the moment the change simply worried her: that the time was coming when she would no longer dream of him, would not be able to conjure up his face on demand, and while she knew this was progress it felt like abandonment. She fought the instinct to bury herself beneath the duvet, to indulge in a few more stolen moments with him, and after a few minutes weighing the advantages and perils of such indulgence she arrived at a verdict, throwing back the covers with a reluctant sweep of her hand and propelling herself out of bed. She stretched her back, shook the lethargy from her limbs, and headed for the bathroom.

In the tarnished mirror above the sink she scrutinized herself, a morning ritual that had begun in early adolescence when Claire had sprouted prematurely, quickly surpassing the boys who would take another three years to match her eventual five eight frame, and until they did taunted her with slurs and sexual innuendoes. She had grown up awkward in her skin, never truly believing that her gangly limbs had become shapely or that her face was worthy of lustful examination; and although she was aware men found her attractive she questioned their judgment. Admittedly, hers *was* an unorthodox beauty: ivory skin, narrow, almond-shaped eyes and dark hair that harkened back to her mix of Viking and Frankish blood, full but pale lips, a slightly upturned nose she believed made her unfairly appear standoffish, and a sprinkling of embarrassing freckles that Claire took pains to diminish with makeup and a compensatory rise of her chin. Her beauty attracted suitors, her insecurity predators, and to her shame she'd mistaken the latter for the former with tragic results.

She pushed that last thought away and forced a smile. "Today is a new day and every day is a new promise," Claire reminded the doppelganger in the mirror, the one who counted on these daily mantras to transform themselves into genuine confidence. It was a technique Dr. Fitzsimmons had taught Claire, had stressed repeatedly in their weekly sessions: the power of positive thinking. The phrase had irritated Claire at first, had sounded like one of the many late-night infomercials she'd come to depend upon when insomnia had been her only companion, but over time she'd come to accept there was truth to the idea. "Life is about attitude," she declared, mimicking Dr. Fitzsimmons' confident, authoritative tone. Besides, she reminded herself as she pressed a toothbrush into her molars, every cloud has a silver lining. Was it possible that the darker the cloud the shinier the lining?

She finished brushing her teeth, plunged her head beneath the bathtub tap and scrubbed herself awake, then dressed and grabbed her purse: nearby Commercial Drive was awash in coffee shops, and maybe if she also bought a bran muffin she could convince herself she'd eaten a legitimate breakfast. *You can't just drink coffee, Claire; now sit.* Her mother setting a plate of poached eggs and toast on the table then hovering about, cloaking her anguish in a stream of maternal nattering. *Come back to Calgary; your family is there. What's for you here? Nothing but trouble. Come home. We'll help you through this.* But Claire had refused, determined not to return to the bosom of a mother whom Claire adored but had struggled to separate from, and unwilling to submit herself to the disappointment of a father whose standards exceeded those of compassion and common sense. The move to Vancouver had been a deliberate accident: deliberate in that Claire had applied for the teaching position posted online, accidental because she never believed she would be chosen. But chosen she was, and she found in that affirmation an unexpected courage. It was that same courage that kept her here despite the fallout from her lapse in judgment, that persuaded her to stand her ground despite its ever-shifting sway.

She locked the door and headed west. Lakewood Road was quiet this late morning except for the *click-click* of hedge trimmers coming from behind a tall screen of green velvet boxwood four doors down, while across the street two older Italian women were in the midst of an animated conversation in their native tongue. Both women had thick ankles, dark moustaches and heavy breasts, with a cheap black handbag over one arm and the other dragging a metal shopping basket. One basket was full, the other empty. One finished, one not yet started, and neither going anywhere in a hurry.

It was this slower pace of life that attracted Claire to the neighbourhood. It possessed a tranquility that suggested peace lay behind closed doors, that no dark secrets lurked in shadows threatening to explode with an unexpected violence. It screamed, yes, but of barbecues and swing sets and a fierce competition for prize rose bushes. It was the classic suburban illusion, a brilliant visage that masked loneliness here, battery there, and neglect behind that green door of envy on the corner. Every street has it skeletons. Lakewood Road was no different.

The morning rush was over when Claire reached Audrey's Coffee House but most of the tables were still occupied. Commercial Drive was a hub for artists and film types mixed in with blue collar shift workers, and so The Drive (as the locals called it) seemed to follow a different schedule altogether from the rest of the city. It buzzed this day or that night without any apparent logic, the jumbled noise in perfect juxtaposition to the quiet streets it bordered. It was as if one minute you were in your garden and the next you were falling through the rabbit hole. And Claire loved it. She loved its beatnik flavour, its multiethnic hue, its cheap restaurants, artisan shops, and used furniture stores. It was vibrant and chaotic and schizophrenic and far removed from the posh private Eaton Academy where Claire had taught spoiled rich kids whose fathers thought nothing of seducing their sons' English teacher—

Stop it! Claire gave herself a mental kick in the shin. She had no one to blame but herself for that. Dr. Eric Mellor, esteemed cardiologist, devoted husband and father, had seduced her, but she had let him. She had let him ply her with flowers and champagne, with passionate, stolen nights, with diamond earrings on her birthday. Blinded by superb credentials, intoxicated by charm, Claire had willingly believed Eric's false professions of a future together, had been complicit in lust masquerading as love. She had no one to blame but herself, she confirmed. Still, her complicity had not prepared her for the brutality of his derision when she told him she was pregnant. "You stupid girl," he had sighed with exasperation, as if their baby had been conceived with no participation on his part. "I thought an English teacher would be smarter than that."

"Well," he'd added after his words were met with a stunned silence, "I assume you'll be discreet and get rid—"

A high-pitched wail broke Claire's reverie and sent a dose of adrenalin coursing through her nervous system. She jumped in her seat and spun around to find nothing more than a new mother settling in at the next table. Claire smiled awkwardly, trying to regain her composure, and hoped her face read surprise, not terror. "Somebody's hungry."

"No, not hungry," the woman replied with what Claire guessed was a Mexican accent, "just unhappy. He didn't sleep well last night." The woman looked to be about twenty-five years old, with a youthful if fatigued round face and large eyes. She wore casual grey slacks and a white cotton twinset with a small beige stain on one shoulder. At her knees was a baby stroller that seemed altogether too big for the tiny cherub nestled within. "He's teething. Hungry is a different sound altogether."

Her last comment intrigued Claire. "There's a difference?"

"Sí." The woman dipped the baby's soother in her coffee and put it back in his mouth. "At first I couldn't tell the difference, but I found if I listened closely enough I could hear a change in pitch." She paused, then shrugged. "Now it's automatic. You don't have children?"

"No," Claire said a little too abruptly, as if the question had been a judgment. She stood up, her faced taut with indignation. "I have to go. It was nice to meet you."

The woman smiled anxiously. "I'm sorry. Forgive me. I come looking for adult conversation and what do I do? I start talking about babies."

"It's okay. I understand. I'm just ..." Claire looked helplessly at the woman and her son. "I'm just late for a meeting with my contractor," Claire lied, and shot out of the café, leaving her muffin behind.

The walk home was riddled with self-reproach. It wasn't like Claire to be rude or unkind and yet in a single gesture she'd managed both. The journey back to herself seemed plagued with U-turns. She thought of the woman who had loved Eric, who witnessed a monster masquerading as a prince and looked the other way. She became adept at compensating, at leaving extra tips for mistreated wait staff or steering conversations toward the frivolous so as to avoid the inevitable verbal slaps Eric administered to dissenting opinions. She learned to feign pleasure, sold her self-respect for his approval, accommodated his caprice until she inevitably mistook the chameleon she became with the woman she had been. Friends who voiced their concerns had been vehemently repudiated until only the most loving and tolerant remained, and those she did not lose to her duplicity she later lost to despair.

It hadn't begun like that, of course; these things never do. It had begun with a need, hers to find an emotional anchor to replace the ones she'd left behind in Calgary, his to exercise a pathological narcissism. She would later discover how carefully he chose his victims: she needed to be vulnerable, so his attentions would feel extraordinary; kind and maternal, so she would pity his marital unhappiness and refuse to abandon him to his condition; incurably romantic, so she would naively believe the fairy tale he fabricated with every loving word and amorous gesture. He was a master storyteller, a skilled weaver of plausible fictions, so capable a manipulator that when he eventually dropped the pretence even that was expertly calculated, perfectly timed to coincide with the final surrender of her heart. Unable to free itself, the heart had remained committed while the mind adapted. It would take a year of therapy to untangle the mess.

Still, she reminded herself, something good *had* come of her stupidity and misfortune. The house on Lakewood Road was no Shangri-la but it was hers. She would make it a home, a sanctuary, a shelter from the storm. How it had come about was not important. The past was done and buried; all that remained was the future and the now, and the now was looking better every day.

She maintained that positive endnote until self-flagellation was replaced with optimism, and despite the latter's minor but perceptible false note Claire managed nonetheless to push the incident at Audrey's out of her mind as she organized her new space, and by late afternoon she was able to turn her attention to the start of renovations. She taped thick plastic sheets over the dining room floor and doorway then stood before the wall it shared with the kitchen, tapping her fingers on her arm as she contemplated the best approach to tearing it down. The heavy sledgehammer hanging from her hand felt surprisingly light, a contradiction she chalked up to excitement, and when she looked in the mirror after donning safety goggles and a dust mask she found herself giggling. Claire picked the best spot, she figured, for the first blow, took a fat felt pen from her pocket and drew a cartoon of Eric's face onto the pale beige wall, then swung the sledgehammer like a bat. It crashed into the wall with a leaden crack, thick veins snaking through Eric's cheek. A self-satisfied grin crept across Claire's lips as she paused to appreciate the moment, and remained there as she took another swing then another and another until Dr. Eric Mellor, esteemed cardiologist, devoted husband and father, was reduced to rubble at Claire's feet. *This is better than therapy*, she thought, laughing inside. Could have saved herself *a lot* of money had she simply crushed his head months ago.

The creature watched as Claire dismantled the wall with an intriguing ferocity. With each blow its own resolve was building, too, spurred on by an inexplicable sense of connection to this delicate yet curiously determined woman. But it didn't have a plan, only hope; would hope be enough to pierce the veil?

After about an hour of demolition Claire's euphoria gave way to pain from the shockwaves that reverberated through her body with each swing of the sledgehammer. She surveyed the pile of broken lathe and plaster and figured she was done for the day. A fine, silky dust hung everywhere, coating her hair and permeating every exposed pore, and when she pulled off her goggles the ring of clean skin around her eyes gave her a ghoulish appearance made all the scarier by its reflection in the small antique mirror that hung on the back of the closet door. Claire stripped down to her underwear, left her filthy jeans and T-shirt where they lay, and headed upstairs for a bath.

She sank her aching body in the steaming water then took a breath and submerged her head to loosen up her hair. One thorough shampoo and body scrub later, Claire was beginning to feel human again. An anti-inflammatory would sort out her muscles she reckoned as she stepped into her pyjamas and dried her hair with a towel. She took two ibuprofens then collapsed onto her bed, tired but pleased with her efforts.

She was just starting to drift off when she heard it. It was faint, muffled, like the sounds from the other side of an apartment wall. Claire's eyes opened wide with alarm and darted about the room. *No, it can't be. Not again!* A weight fell upon her chest; she could hear her pulse swishing against her eardrums. The corners of the room, slung low with shadows, began to fold in upon themselves, rapidly closing in and shrouding Claire in a claustrophobic caul. The sound slowly crawled up the stairs, becoming more and more audible until it became exactly what she feared most: the unmistakeable cry of a baby.

Claire's stomach did a somersault. She sprang from her bed and into the bathroom, heaving up the Chinese delivery she'd eaten earlier. *God damn it! Not again!* For months after her son's death Claire had suffered similar hallucinations, hallucinations she'd eventually eradicated with the dispassionate knife of analysis. Their return smothered her in a dark, cold panic—until something made her stop and sit at attention. There was something new, something odd about this now. *A different sound altogether.* A chill ran along Claire's spine as she leaned motionless against the toilet, straining to hear, trying to ascertain the nature of the change when—

BANG!

Claire screamed and bolted upright, her heart a bullet train. She pressed her back against the wall, frightened and alert, but everything had gone quiet again. And then she remembered she'd left a window open in the dining room to let out the dust from the demolition, and breathed a heavy, welcomed sigh of relief: the window had simply fallen shut, nothing more. And the baby must belong to a neighbour.

Her overreaction made her feel silly, and she quietly admonished herself as she padded down the stairs to reopen the window. She slipped into the shoes she'd left beside the doorway and entered the dining room, the air still heavy with dust that floated hazily in the waning shafts of light. She covered her mouth and nose with her hand as she crossed over to open the window—when the glass suddenly shattered! Claire gasped as an unseen force slammed into her back and hurled her toward the razor-sharp shards that clung to the window frame. A strangled cry escaped Claire's throat; her feet scraped helplessly against the plastic-covered floor as she tried to find her footing. She raised her arms in a desperate attempt to protect her body from the inevitable mutilation—when another unseen force spun her around and pulled her back to the center of the room. A dark shape appeared in the mirror but before Claire could see what it was the mirror shattered and fell to the floor, the shards exploding into a silver galaxy as they collided with the hardwood. And then it started again: the frightened, bewildered cry of a baby. And it was coming from the closet.

Claire stood paralyzed as the crying pounded in her ears and reverberated off the walls that closed in on her. The cries became momentarily muffled, as if someone were trying to smother them, before intensifying again and pressing down upon Claire. She could feel the tension of opposing forces, struggled to stay upright as the room spun around her. The caterwauling continued, incessant and demanding, bouncing off the walls and crashing into Claire in waves. "Stop ... this ... please," she stammered between waves of nausea. "I ... I'm sorry. I'm sorry. Isn't that enough?"

It wasn't. The wailing continued unabated. Claire sobbed as the wallpaper began to stretch then recede, stretch then recede, as if a heart were trapped behind it, pressing against the embossed roses. Claire began to hyperventilate at the same rapid rate as the wall—when a bear-like growl pierced the air and the closet doors began to vibrate! Claire screamed and backed away, beads of glass cracking beneath her shoes. The closet doors trembled violently as if someone were shaking them, demanding to be let out. The crying was eerily distant now, as if the closet were a door that led to other, far off rooms, rooms that Claire knew didn't exist. "What do you want from me?" she begged her tormentor. "I can't bring you back."

The closet didn't answer. The crying simply became louder and more insistent again, like a colicky baby who remains inconsolable no matter how long you rock it. The child's lament intensified until it filled every molecule of air in the room, until Claire could feel the tears filling her lungs, suffocating her. The doors were shaking violently, the hinges straining against the weight—then with an angry roar the doors flew open and an energy flooded the room that pushed Claire back and she fell, tripping over the sledgehammer and crashing down on her hip. She cried out as a sharp pain shot up through her spine and caused an explosion of fury within her! She grabbed the sledgehammer and came up swinging, landing a heavy blow into the back of the closet. Bits of lathe and plaster sprayed out as she attacked the wall over and over and over again, tears of pain and anger mixing with the dust to form grey veins beneath her eyes. She lowered her head to shield her face from the flying debris—then stopped cold.

Two tiny eyes, frozen in time, peered out from between what appeared to be decaying strips of linen. Claire fell to her knees and feverishly began pulling away the wall with her bare hands, praying this were anything but what she imagined.

The crying had ceased. Claire, her hands raw and bleeding, pulled off the last bit of plaster. There was no mistaking it now. "Oh, God," she sobbed, then pulled herself up onto unsteady legs and staggered toward the phone.

THREE

Detective Dylan Lewis squatted down in front of the closet and stared at what appeared to be infant remains, then surveyed the room: wall debris and glass scattered about, the broken window, a large sledgehammer cast into the rubble. "Has anything been moved?"

"No sir," one of the responding officers replied. "As soon as we ascertained the situation we contained the complainant in the living room and called you. She's pretty shaken up but coherent."

"I'll need to talk to her. Keep her around and keep her calm. Anybody hear yet from Anil?"

"He's on his way. Was at the obstetrician's with the wife when we called. Hear she's expecting their third. So a dead baby should really complete his day."

Dylan shook his head and pinched the bridge of his nose. He'd been working Homicide for five years now, seen things most people would lose their lunch over without ever tossing his, but a dead child always gnawed away at his insides. And he knew it was the same for Anil. Dylan had seen the pathologist walk out of a field carrying the decapitated head of an accident victim then take a sip of coffee, all without missing a beat, but a child on his slab turned Anil's stomach into knots. For those who worked with the dead, for those whose job it was to apprehend criminals and comfort victims, emotional distance was a trick of the trade. There was a certain cynicism reserved for violence between adults but a child victim, especially a baby, changed all the rules: distance was impossible, cynicism unforgiveable. A dead child encapsulated everything that was wrong with the world, with the universe, with the idea of an omnipotent god. No one was in charge, it seemed, when something like this happened.

"Hey doc," the attending officer greeted Anil.

"Hey. You the one that called it in?"

"Yeah. Lewis is inside," the officer gestured over his shoulder. "There appears to be a baby in the wall."

Dylan looked up as Dr. Sanjit Anil, his clothes covered by a forensics suit, entered the room and carefully walked over the rubble to squat down beside Lewis. At five foot eleven the two men were equals but whereas Sanjit was slender with delicate features, Dylan was stocky and sturdier. It was the same with their personalities. Sanjit carried himself with an elegance that belied the gruesomeness of his profession while Dylan's composure said cop at first sight: purposeful, authoritative, intimidating. The men said nothing to each other, their relationship cemented by years working cases together; it was enough for Lewis to nod his head in the direction of the remains.

"Jesus," Sanjit whistled between his teeth when he caught sight of the baby. "Mummified. That's unusual."

"Does it tell you anything?"

"Likely stillborn, I'd guess, then placed in the wall soon after. And probably in the heat of summer: the area would've had to be sufficiently hot and dry to allow for mummification. And there couldn't have been insect or rodent activity until after mummification took place. Other than that, not much until we get it to the lab."

"Why stillborn?"

"Babies are born without any bacteria in their gut and it's intestinal bacteria that triggers decomp. Without it the process is delayed until external bacteria can penetrate the body. So if the climate is right mummification can take place before the bacteria have a chance to do their thing."

"How long before you'll know for certain?"

"A day for the autopsy, but then tox and trace will take another few days. DNA is backed up something awful but I'll see what I can do. Dental's our best bet: the baby's teeth will tell us how long it lived, if at all."

"How long's it been in there, do you think?"

Sanjit shook his head. "No idea. I'll call the university first thing in the morning, get the bones dated. It might take awhile, though." Sanjit glanced over and saw the disappointment on Dylan's face. "I'll ask them to rush the results."

Dylan nodded his appreciation and rose to leave. He pulled back the plastic that sealed off the doorway and signalled to the forensics team the room was theirs. "So, where's the caller?" he asked the constable.

Claire was curled up on the couch, staring at the floor, a cup of tea held tightly between clenched fingers someone—she couldn't remember who exactly—had been kind enough to treat with antibiotic cream and bandages. A policewoman sat beside her making small talk. Lewis signalled from the doorway and the officer walked over to give a whispered account. "She's quite distraught. Just bought the house and moved in yesterday. Claims she was knocking out the wall for a kitchen renovation when she discovered the remains. Name's Claire Dawson. Teaches grade six at Eastside." The officer paused and raised a flirtatious eye at Dylan. "By the way, you going to Miller's retirement party Friday?"

Dylan recognized the invitation and chose to ignore it: Becky Wilson was a good cop and a good woman but Dylan didn't like to date within the force and he didn't like redheads. "Nah," he shrugged, "Miller's a prick," then pretended not to see the disappointment on Wilson's face as he left her to join Claire at the couch. "Ms. Dawson?"

She looked up, her face a roadmap of confusion and despair. Her hair, mousy brown from the dust, fell in clumps around her face, diminishing her prominent cheekbones; and red circles had formed around feline eyes the colour of seafoam. Beneath the dust Dylan could see Claire's face was well-proportioned, and she possessed a nose one might call regal if not for the smattering of freckles that reminded Dylan of Pippy Longstocking and made him nostalgic for a childhood when adults were, at their worst, clumsy fools easily outwitted by a precocious orphan. Dylan succeeded only partially to suppress a smile, an indiscretion he regretted immediately and which would later prove portentous. He straightened his mouth back into a grim line. "I'm Detective Dylan Lewis. Mind if I sit down? I'd like to ask you a few questions." Claire nodded but her eyes fell away as he sat down beside her and opened up his notebook. "Can you give me your full name and date of birth, please?"

"Claire Cynthia Dawson. July 8th, 1981." She kept her head lowered but raised her eyes over her teacup to watch him as he wrote down her details. He had clean, well-manicured hands and his fingers were long like a piano player's. Claire followed the lines of his hands to his wrists where fine black hairs peaked out from behind the cuffs of his black leather car coat. Underneath he wore a crisp sky blue shirt, a navy striped tie, black chinos and black leather shoes. His skin appeared lightly tanned, his hair jet black and cut short, and when he looked over at her again she noticed his eyes were so dark there was little distinction between iris and pupil. "Are you Native?" she asked impassively.

"Excuse me?" Dylan replied, his annoyance evident. What the hell did his heritage have to do with the situation? What the hell did it have to do with anything? No one was surprised that an East Indian was a pathologist, so why did everyone find it so damn interesting that a *Native* Indian was a cop?

"Your eyes, they're almost black," Claire explained, oblivious to his umbrage. "They remind me of the Native children I teach in East Van. They always have the darkest eyes." Her voice trailed off as she wandered into the black depths believing, perhaps, that she might find in his eyes answers to the mystery that now preoccupied her, answers that would free her mind from the morass of questions that sucked into its stranglehold all other thoughts—including the realization that the silence and intensity of her gaze had shrouded the two strangers in an ambiguity that was unnerving Dylan: she had breached his defences, and that she'd done so without apparent intent or even, he suspected, conscious thought made her doubly dangerous. His muscles contracted involuntarily in a primal fight-or-flight response, and he responded by mentally pushing her back so he could regroup.

"Ms. Dawson," he said, raising an eyebrow, "I understand this has been a traumatic discovery but I need you to stay focused."

The strategy worked, wrenching Claire out of her reverie with an embarrassing snap. "I-I'm sorry. I'll try to do better." She found a spot on the floor and stared at it, a flush of crimson in her cheeks.

Dylan kicked himself. He needed to keep Dawson on his side, to gain her trust, and he was letting personal issues mar his technique. *Focus!* he ordered himself as he reassured Claire with a smile. "No offence taken," he lied. "But perhaps we should stick to the matter at hand." He shifted back to his practiced, professional tone. "I understand you were taking out the wall to renovate the kitchen when you found the remains?"

"Yes."

"You hurt your hands," he said gently, eyeing the bandages.

Claire glanced down at her damaged fingers. The image of her frantic hands clawing at the wall came flooding back and she struggled to contain her despair. She nodded: yes.

"Did you tear out the closet wall?"

She nodded again.

"I'll have to ask you to provide fingerprints so we can separate you from possible suspects," he said in the same gentle voice. "Are you okay with this?" It was a courtesy question, really, since Dylan had a warrant, but it was always best to create the illusion of cooperation.

"Yes, I understand."

"I'll have Officer Wilson attend to that later." Dylan paused, then slyly shifted his approach. "I'm curious, why were you punching out the closet? It's not on the shared wall."

Dylan registered the startled look that swept across Claire's eyes and the paling of her skin. "Oh, um, well ..." Panic was paralyzing her tongue. What could she possibly say that wouldn't sound insane? She opted instead for evasion, staring into her teacup in the hope he'd forget the question and move on.

He didn't. "Ms. Dawson, there's a dead baby in your wall."

Claire scrambled for a plausible response. "There was a scratching noise. I thought maybe it was a rat's nest. I overreacted."

Dylan looked at her sharply. He'd been a cop long enough to know when he was being lied to but he couldn't pinpoint a reason why she was holding back. After all, it was Dawson who'd called police, who opened the door to the investigation. He chose another avenue. "Who did you buy the house from?"

"Whom" thought Claire to herself, and almost corrected him before remembering she wasn't talking to one of her students. The paralysis had ceased and she was able to look him in the eye again, his grammatical error having rendered him less threatening. It was petty, really, that an inconsequential error could make her feel stronger—a little superior even—and yet she didn't want to lose that feeling, didn't wish to cower again beneath his gaze. "It was a court ordered sale. Power of attorney or something like that. I never met the owners, or even the seller. Just their agent. He said his client was a lawyer. I can get the purchase agreement for you, if you like."

"Where is it?"

"Upstairs."

"I'll need to accompany you, if you don't mind."

The request caught Claire off guard and she became acutely aware she was losing ground again. "Is that really necessary?" she asked, uncomfortable. "My bedroom is upstairs."

"I understand," Dylan replied, and though his smile was meant to reassure she knew he was evaluating her. It was nothing more than a cop's professional mistrust and yet she felt crushed under the weight of suspicion. The sensation was so intense she wasn't even aware she had stopped breathing until Dylan glanced over her shoulder and hollered "Hey Wilson" and Claire's breath returned with a gasp. The female officer appeared in the doorway. "Could you please accompany Ms. Dawson upstairs. She needs to retrieve a document."

Claire smiled awkwardly at Officer Wilson as the two women headed upstairs. "I need to use the bathroom," Claire said to what felt like her captor. "May I have my privacy or do you need to accompany me there, too?"

"Relax, Ms. Dawson, it's just procedure. I'll wait outside the door."

Claire disappeared into the bathroom, sat down on the toilet and used the moment to collect herself. That Detective Lewis had, even fleetingly, considered her suspect rankled her: if he knew what she had suffered, if he saw her scarred body and wounded heart he would understand the crime he was investigating was beyond her comprehension, that she was incapable of anything so hideously inhuman. Did he know about her past? But even if he did, how could he equate carelessness with murder?! How could he be so quick to judge her?

She was shaking now, terrified to face him again yet knowing she had no choice. She flushed the toilet and washed her hands then splashed cold water on her face until she felt her calm return sufficiently, opened the bathroom door and addressed Wilson. "The document is over here," Claire gestured toward the second bedroom where she had dumped all her office boxes. She grabbed the purchase agreement then the two women headed back downstairs. Wilson gave Lewis a surreptitious "nothing unusual" signal as she and Claire re-entered the living room then Wilson disappeared back into the kitchen.

"The seller was Benjamin Keller," Claire read as she crossed back over to the couch. "The registered owners were Therese and Armin Keller."

Shit! thought Dylan, hoping it wasn't the Benjamin Keller he knew. "Was there anything in the property disclosure to indicate past renovations?"

"No," Claire answered, handing the agreement to Dylan and picking up her teacup. "The house is in original condition. That's why I was able to afford it." She watched him intently as his dark eyes skimmed over the purchase agreement and his slender fingers wrote down the particulars in his notebook. He was aware of her eyes on him but he didn't let on, reading through the document as if it might hold something of use beyond the names and addresses of the sellers. He knew it wouldn't, of course, but in the moments that elapsed he also knew Claire's anxiety was increasing again, ensuring he retained the upper hand he was certain he'd regained.

"Speaking of which, how does a single teacher afford her own home?" He asked the question as if he were simply curious, glancing up from the papers only briefly to register her reaction. In truth he *was* curious: he was always curious when single people bought property: had they resigned themselves to remaining that way? Houses were for families, in his book. A place to raise your kids, give them security and stability. Until he committed to that he'd never commit to a mortgage: he didn't see the point.

Claire's face paled at the question. That was twice now. "I bought it with the proceeds of a lawsuit," she replied, and in her voice Dylan detected a minute tremor, like the subtle shaking of the floor just before an earthquake hits. What was she hiding from him?

"May I ask the nature of the lawsuit?"

"I don't see how that's relevant," she replied cautiously, her fingers tightening around her teacup.

"*I* decide what's relevant, Ms. Dawson," Dylan snapped before he could catch himself. It was a substantial error: Claire's face was suddenly ablaze and she struggled to contain her indignation.

"I'm bound by a confidentiality agreement," she explained as evenly as she could manage, "so unless you get a court order I can't reveal the details."

"Fair enough," shrugged Dylan. And I just might do that, he added in his head.

"Do you have anything else for me, detective?" Claire asked, still clearly irritated.

"Not at the moment. But I may have to question you again as the investigation proceeds. I'd appreciate it if you stayed in town or provided me with notice if you go away." The moment he spoke Dylan regretted his tone: he'd been aiming for respectfully authoritative but what came out was surly and imperious.

Claire felt the hackles on her neck stand. "Fine," she lobbied back. "And how much longer will your investigators be in my house?"

"Until they're done," came the brusque reply. "It would be best if you stayed elsewhere tonight. Is there someone you can call?"

The question knocked the hauteur out of Claire. She looked stunned, as if she'd been slapped. She stared at the floor and bit her lip as the ground swallowed her whole. When she finally spoke again her voice was small and quiet. "No one I wish to impose upon."

Dylan's brow furrowed. The woman was all over the map; he couldn't keep up. One minute she was testing his patience and the next she was like an injured child he wanted to shield from harm. She had him off-kilter, shy of his game. And he didn't like it one bit. But what to do with her? He had the authority to kick her out of the house until Forensics were finished but he didn't want to create an adversary, especially so early in the game: he might need her later. And he had already antagonized her; any more and he might lose a potential asset. Dylan sized her up, calculated the risk and decided it would be advantageous not to burn any more bridges. Still, he would need to set firm boundaries. "I can allow you to stay here," he said with counterfeit contrition, "as long as you provide me with assurances you will not interfere with my team or attempt entry into the back room until I've released the scene." Claire nodded her agreement without looking at him. "And I need a number where you can be reached."

Her voice still a whisper, Claire gave him the number to the house and her cellphone. Finished for now, Dylan rose to leave. He called out again for Officer Wilson, who appeared so quickly Dylan wondered if she'd been lurking behind the doorway. "I need you to fingerprint Ms. Dawson for a comparison set and help her write up an official statement. And she'll require company until Forensics are done." Wilson nodded and Dylan turned his attention back to Claire. "Ms. Dawson?" Claire looked up and he saw in her eyes a sorrow he hadn't expected and which made him swallow his words. "We'll talk again," was all he managed to say. She nodded and went back to staring at the floor. Dylan felt like a bully.

He almost made it outside before a sense of shame stopped him just shy of the front door. He turned his head to face Claire. "I'm half," he offered, by way of apology.

She looked up, puzzled. "Half what?"

"Half Native," he admitted with a conciliatory gesture. "I'm half Native."

Claire smiled. "What's the other half?"

Dylan shrugged, "Dunno," then walked out the door.

Dylan got into his unmarked cruiser, put the key in the ignition then changed his mind. He leaned back in his seat, rested his elbow on the door and began an internal review. How could that have gone so awkwardly awry? He was trained to stay even-tempered, to keep his emotions in check, and yet the woman had managed to crawl under his skin without even trying, had upset his equilibrium and left him scrambling to maintain his artfully crafted composure. He felt outwitted, trumped. And it was pissing him off.

He tried to cast off the shackles of discomfort by forcing a shift in thought to more practical issues. The baby in the wall wasn't Dawson's—both experience and gut instinct told him so—and yet he couldn't officially rule that out until any connection between her and the previous owners had been disproved. And she was definitely hiding something.

But then aren't we all? he contemplated next. He hadn't lied when he said he didn't know his father's heritage but he did know his father had been white. White and drunk. His mother had been drunk, too, when Dylan had been conceived, had sobered up only long enough to have him before abandoning him to his grandmother. He'd been lucky in that respect, though, and he knew it: his *ta'ah* was a strong, proud and affectionate woman who raised him to respect himself, his elders, and the world around him. She never tired of telling him he could be whatever he wanted to be, never judged his dreams or squashed his imagination, not even when he was five and announced he wanted to grow up to be an eagle. Ta'ah had just smiled and said chances are he already was one, he just didn't know it yet.

Dylan smiled at the memory then made a promise to himself to visit her on Sunday, maybe take her out for lunch after church. That was another thing about his *ta'ah*: she was a woman who deeply loved the Creator. Her faith was an odd mix of Catholicism and traditional Coast Salish spirituality; and when he'd asked Ta'ah how could she still attend church after the horror of residential school, she had simply shrugged and said she thought Jesus would've made a good Indian.

Dylan started the car and headed for the station. He'd get his preliminary report written then head home. Tomorrow was going to be a long day.

FOUR

On the outskirts of a forest, at the edge of a river, a lioness gazed upon her reflection in the water but saw only a common domesticated tabby. The image troubled her for she recalled having been born a lioness, yet clearly the river did not lie. "You seem confused, my Lady," mused a large female bear as it ambled over to the riverbank and sat down beside the feline.

"What do you see, Bear, there, in the water?" asked the lioness.

"I see a lioness who thinks she's a cat," replied Bear.

"Hmmm, yes," murmured the lioness. "Most curious, don't you think?"

"Not curious," shrugged Bear. "Unfortunate. Your power, your pride: these were your birthright. You should reclaim them."

"But how does one reclaim what the king has taken?"

"The king's authority is not absolute," pronounced Bear. "And conditional love is not love."

"I was expected to do better," the lioness said sadly. "I failed. Should there not be a price for my shortcomings?"

"Perhaps it is the king who suffers shortcomings," Bear said dismissively.

The lioness laughed lightly. "I envy your certainty, my friend."

"Reclaim your power, my Lady. You will need it." And with that Bear took her leave of the lioness. And Claire awoke from her dream.

Most curious, was her first semi-conscious thought, but the dream was quickly lost as the events of the night before slipped stealthily into her consciousness and pushed aside all images except those of the baby. In its mummified state it had looked almost simian, its skin blackened and shrunken tautly over its skull. From her perch on the sofa Claire had watched as the small body bag was carried out to the waiting van, and hours later, when the door had closed behind the last of the officers, Claire had sat in the dining room on the dusty pine chair and finally let flow the tears she had fearfully kept in check.

She glanced down at her bandaged fingers, the black ink on their tips still evident despite her best efforts with a fresh lemon and vigorous scrubbing. The act of being fingerprinted had felt invasive, the air thick with imagined accusation made all the more pervasive by Officer Wilson's barely concealed irritation, which Claire, not having witnessed the awkward exchange earlier between Wilson and Lewis, had interpreted as suspicion and contempt. The repressive atmosphere had made Claire nervous, and she had strained to hear the chatter of the police over the din of the television she'd pretended to watch, terrified they would find evidence of the guilt she carried about her person and believe it relevant to the case.

But now, as the morning light banished the shadows that had given form to her fears, the trauma of finding the baby was yielding to a curiosity that perplexed Claire: she felt oddly detached, and she wondered if her distance were a coping mechanism or something more disturbing, like relief. Relief that this hadn't been all in her mind; that she wasn't descending into madness or even over-imagination. That her house was haunted seemed strangely concrete, not preposterous as a sceptic would insist but a rational explanation, though one which now raised its own disturbing questions: Why now? Why Claire? Was there a relationship between her dead child and this one, some cosmic connection Claire didn't yet understand? Or was the relationship illusory, merely the kind of synchronicity that beguiles the gullible into seeing patterns in the universe where none exist?

And yet the former owners had lived here for decades, Claire reminded herself as she rolled out of bed and headed for the bathroom; surely they wouldn't have stayed had they suffered the same haunting on a daily basis. So then now what? What more did the spirit expect beyond discovery? What if it returned, demanding more?

And there had been something else in that room, something sinister. It had tried to maim Claire, had tried to smother the child's cries. What if it came back, too? The thought made the hair on Claire's arms rise, and her first instinct was to call back the movers and run; but something else was rising in her too, an unexpected fortitude that rapidly swelled while she scrubbed her hair and face, and by the time she rinsed out the last of her toothpaste she was in a fighting spirit: something had tried to harm her and something had caused a child to suffer, and damn it if Claire were not going to get to the bottom of both offenses!

But how? And where to begin?

Reclaim your power. What? thought Claire, and then fragments of her dream came floating back: a lioness gazing into the river, a bear, a conversation about ... what was it again?

Lost in thought, Claire tromped down the stairs only to be surprised by the smell of fresh coffee and cinnamon. Puzzled, she followed her nose to the living room and found a plump, grey-haired woman transferring a coffee pot and a Bundt cake from a tray to Claire's small pine table.

"Hello?" Claire asked.

The elderly woman spun around and clutched at her chest. "Oh, dear, you startled me," she gasped. Her accent was German, faded but still noticeable. She was wearing a lace-collared floral print dress, gathered at the waist, and flat, thick leather sandals over sagging stockings. Her face, wrinkled with age and framed by wispy grey hair pinned back in a bun, was bright and gentle.

Claire figured the surprise should be the other way around. "Who are you and what are you doing in my house?" she asked, polite but confused.

The woman chuckled and nodded earnestly. She struck Claire as the animated type, the kind who spoke with the grand gestures and exaggerated expressions of one who believes all of life is entitled to the exuberance of a thespian. "Of course, forgive me. I thought you might appreciate some sustenance after all the excitement of last night. I knocked on the back door but you mustn't have heard. It was unlocked so I thought I would just leave this for you with a note. Though I'd think you'd be more careful after a break-in."

"Break-in?"

"Yes, the police, they came and asked me questions. I asked them if the house had been burgled and they said"—she paused and raised a finger to pursed lips—"well, actually they didn't say anything, now that I think about it. But you really should lock your door."

"Thank you but who are you?"

"Oh, forgive me again," she said, clasping her hands together. "Yes, yes, of course you wouldn't remember me from a passing wave. I'm Frau Müller. I live next door."

The image of the elderly woman glancing up from her flowerbeds and waving as Claire had walked past with the home inspector came back to her. "Oh, yes, I remember now. You were gardening."

Frau Müller nodded enthusiastically. "Getting my spring bulbs in. A bit late this year, I'm afraid. My arthritis was acting up."

There was a moment of awkward silence before Claire remembered her manners, and sensed a possible opportunity. "I'm sorry. Would you like to join me for some of your cake and coffee? They both smell wonderful."

Frau Müller's face lit up at the invitation. She'd been hoping for just that: it's not often one sees so many police cars and men in funny white suits poking about and loading heavy black bags into a van. Her weekly ladies' Rumoli game had been abandoned for the window and they were all expecting an update at bridge on Friday. What would they think of her if she attended empty-handed?

Claire rummaged about in a box and pulled out two dessert plates and forks, coffee mugs, and a knife. "Would you like cream? I have some in the fridge. Sugar might be a tad more difficult. I haven't unpacked all my staples yet."

"Don't fret. Black is fine for me." Frau Müller cut two large slices of Bundt cake as Claire poured the coffee and set the cups down on the table.

"How long have you lived next door?" she asked, settling into a chair.

"Oh, a very long time. Since 1939. My parents fled Hitler's Germany. We were liberals, and," she added weightily, "we were Jews. In 1950 I became engaged and my parents gave me the house as a gift. They moved nearer to the university. My father was a professor."

Claire perked up. If Frau Müller has been living next door for seventy years she must know almost everything about this house. Maybe even something about the baby. "What can you tell me about this house?" Claire asked, managing to conceal her anticipation. "I'd love to know its history."

"Oh, let me see now. It was built in the early thirties, if I remember correctly. I was told there was a smaller house before, a shack really, and the owners tore it down when they started to do well. They were also German. Everybody stuck together in those days, Germans in these few blocks, Ukrainians over there, Russians a few blocks north. It wasn't until after the war that the Italians took over."

"The original owners, then, was that the Kellers?"

"No, that was the Zimmermanns. The Kellers moved in the year before I got married. Came after the war. Elsi and Franz Keller and their two boys, Armin and Randolf. Armin was the eldest, at twenty-two. Randolf was a year or two younger. They were only here for a few years when Armin got married. He bought the house from his parents. I don't know where they and Randolf went. Our two families didn't talk much." Her face puckered as if she'd bitten into a lemon. "Armin had been a member of *Hitler-Jurgend*, the youth wing of the party."

"Did Armin have any children?"

"Two. A boy and then a girl. The boy was the reason for the marriage, though it wasn't polite to talk about that in those days. Karl was born about five months after the wedding. Elisabeth came a few years later. Such a beautiful little girl. So different from her mother. At least at the beginning."

"What do you mean?"

"Oh," Frau Müller replied, lowering her voice and leaning across the table as if someone might be listening, "Therese was such a *Mauerblümchen*—"

"A what?"

"A wallflower. She always looked like she wanted to disappear. There was a brief period when I thought I should at least try to be friends but any time I said hello she would just tuck her head down and keep walking."

"And Elisabeth?"

"Oh, Elisabeth," Frau Müller sat back up and smiled, "she was such a charmer." The image of the little girl, her brown hair falling about her smiling face as she turned cartwheels on the grass, filled the elderly woman's memory. "So full of life and energy. She had a cousin—Benjamin was his name—they were about the same age and they would play for hours in the garden together, always laughing. So much laughter. I used to give them apples from my tree." Frau Müller paused, the smile fading from her lips. "It was so sad what happened to her." She shook her head and sipped her coffee.

Claire's curiosity piqued. "What happened?"

"She went crazy. I think the family was touched that way. Therese certainly wasn't right." Frau Müller feigned discomfort. "I don't wish to disparage them; it's just the truth."

"Of course," Claire said reassuringly. "When was this?"

"Well now, Elisabeth must have been about thirteen, I guess, when things went wrong." The sparkle of anticipation in Claire's eyes made Frau Müller smile inside: she loved a captive audience. She intentionally took a sip of her coffee to create more drama before continuing. "They had to take her out of school: she was becoming disruptive. Poor thing. Benjamin stopped coming to the house to play. The whole family stopped visiting, actually. Elisabeth never left the house again. Not until Armin had his stroke."

The wheels in Claire's head were turning. Was it possible Therese had had another baby, one she didn't want, one that also "wasn't right"? "Did Therese ever have any more children?" Claire asked.

"No, just the two."

"Are you *sure*?"

"Yes. Why?" Claire saw the expectant look in Frau Müller's eyes, knew she was hungry for some reciprocation, a little insider information about the "excitement of last night," the mention of which had not passed by Claire. She paused, debating in her head whether to tell Frau Müller about the infant remains, then concluded it would only be a matter of time before it reached the media, so why not?

"Last night I found the remains of a baby in the wall of the dining room." Frau Müller gasped and clutched at her chest. "Are you sure you never saw Therese pregnant again?"

Frau Müller nodded. "Yes, but I suppose I *could* have missed something." Her face was flushed with shock but it was shock tempered with a good dose of excitement. She couldn't wait for Friday's bridge game.

And Claire couldn't wait to talk to Detective Lewis again.

§

Dylan was contemplating a late lunch. He'd had a productive day so far but now he was on hold, waiting to hear from Anil and the university's Department of Forensic Anthropology. Anil had done as promised and by nine a.m. a section of the baby's femur was in an accelerator mass spectrometer. He'd already determined sex—a girl—but age was the domain of the forensic dental specialist and the man for the job was at a conference in Boston until Monday. There would be a DNA profile in a week but until Dylan found a relative to match it to the profile wouldn't be much help in identifying the remains. As for cause of death, Anil wouldn't even be able to guess until later in the day.

Dylan hated this part of investigating, this lull between questions and answers. He wasn't a particularly patient man, a fact obscured by what appeared to be a precise and methodical approach to solving whatever mystery was presented to him. He considered all angles, contemplated all motives, and even when he'd ruled out a possibility he kept his mind open to the unexpected twist that sometimes sprang from nowhere to land a swift uppercut to the jaw. Those were especially painful: the ones he didn't see coming just when he thought he had it all figured out.

Dylan drummed his fingers on his desk and glanced over the property search he had procured first thing that morning. Prior to Dawson the house had had only three owners, the Zimmermanns and then two generations of Kellers. This certainly narrowed the search for possible perpetrators or at least accomplices after the fact, assuming the house or its rooms had never been rented out. Dylan prayed this was the case: up until the war Commercial Drive had been a hub for migrant workers and if that house had known any of them it could make identifying Baby Jane essentially impossible. On the upside, Dylan considered, all the Zimmermanns who had lived there were deceased, as were Elsi and Franz Keller, so that narrowed the list a little bit more, though if the remains dated that far back Dylan would likely have nothing but dead suspects and a lot of unanswered questions.

The younger Kellers were a more interesting lot. Randolf was charming widows in a retirement community in Orlando. Therese and Armin were both in assisted living facilities, but not the same one Dylan had noted with curiosity, while daughter Elisabeth was in Bellevue Home for Psychiatric Care. Karl was dead: Bosnia, 1993. Then there was Benjamin Keller, star criminal defence attorney. Dylan bristled. He'd probably need a warrant just to *talk* to Ben. No, Dylan would start with the old folks first, he calculated, maybe get lucky and get some info before Benjamin got wind of the situation. The daughter was another story: Dylan would have to dance around hospital staff for her, and then it all depended on just how nuts she was.

As for Dawson, so far Dylan couldn't see any connection between her and the Kellers beyond buying their house. She hadn't even lived in Vancouver until four years ago when she'd left substitute teaching in Calgary for a part-time position at the private Eaton Academy over in Shaughnessy. She now taught full-time at the inner city Eastside Elementary—a demotion despite the pay raise, Dylan thought with a cynical chuckle. She was popular with the children, a "dynamic educator who inspired her students to dream big" the principal of Eastside proclaimed; they'd been fortunate to find her. Dylan had run Dawson's name through all the crime databases but none had spit out anything more interesting than a minor speeding ticket, which had been promptly paid he'd noted with a snort. His contact in Calgary had nothing to add on her. The only blotch on an otherwise immaculate sheet seemed to be "a personal indiscretion which had resolved itself" the headmaster at Eaton had volunteered before thinking otherwise and refusing to elaborate, citing privacy concerns.

Dylan put the property search aside and picked up the preliminary forensics report, hoping by some miracle something new had been added in the ten minutes since he last looked at it. There hadn't, of course, and so he dwelled instead on the one bit of good news the report contained: no evidence of further victims in the Dawson home or its grounds had been found: a cadaver dog had scoured the house from the attic eaves to the darkest recesses of the crawl space without pause, and the garden had yielded up nothing more than a few old chicken bones. So if Baby Jane had been murdered—and Dylan didn't know yet if she had—at least it seemed unlikely her death had been at the hands of a serial killer.

Dylan's musings were interrupted by the phone. He snapped up the receiver, hopeful for test results, and was disappointed when he heard the voice of the front desk clerk. "Detective Lewis, there's a Claire Dawson here to see you." There was a momentary pause for effect before she added, "She says it's about last night."

Dylan rolled his eyes at the accusation in the clerk's voice. Stupid old bat assumed this was a personal visit and was, as usual, jumping to conclusions. She was a constant irritation to everyone in the department but that didn't seem to be sufficient grounds for dismissal. There were some, Dylan knew, who secretly counted the days until her retirement, and when she'd had emergency gallbladder surgery last spring there had been a private betting pool on her prognosis. Dylan had put a fiver on fatal septicaemia.

"Tell her I'll be right down."

His mood soured by the clerk, Dylan found himself anticipating further irritation as the elevator descended to the main floor. The last thing he needed was Dawson poking her nose in his investigation so unless she had something pertinent to tell him this was going to be a short visit.

He found Claire pacing in the lobby under the accusing eye of the desk clerk. "Ms. Dawson?"

She turned around to face him and Dylan felt a rush of air hit his lungs like the sticky, portentous wind that heralds a storm. Her beauty was seductive in its simplicity: eyes that in the greyed light of trauma had been the colour of seafoam were a striking peridot in the sun; and her face, all dewy skin and rosé lips, was framed by cinnamon-sprinkled chestnut hair that shimmered and tumbled down onto the shoulders of a crisp white shirt opened to her breasts. His gaze fell to her cleavage then followed the lines of her body down, past the waist of low-rise jeans to curved hips and shapely legs until it came to rest on unpainted toenails that peeked out from a pair of strappy flats Dylan judged to be expensive. His eyes longed to make a slow assent but he corrected himself and quickly raised them to her face, which to their shared embarrassment had flushed beneath his unabashed inspection.

Claire swallowed nervously. "Detective Lewis, I'm sorry to come unannounced like this. You didn't leave me a number and I have some new information I thought you might find useful."

"Have a seat." Dylan gestured to the nearby deck of chairs and watched her as she moved ahead of him. Her hips swayed tantalizingly and the temptation to flirt caught him before he could smother it. "Where were you when I was in school? I would have paid more attention to Hemingway." Claire smiled uneasily as she sank into a chair, and Dylan immediately regretted his aloofness. "Sorry." He paused to underscore the sincerity of his apology, then pulled out his notebook. "You said you have new information?"

The question offered a hasty exit from the awkwardness that had developed between them, and Claire launched into a spirited recounting of her conversation with Frau Müller, eager to be helpful. Her information was nothing new, however: the canvass team had already blanketed the neighbourhood and the whole of the morning had been spent confirming facts and tossing out fictions. Still, Dylan didn't have the heart to tell Claire he was way ahead of her: he was enjoying the sparkle in her eyes and the way her breasts bulged slightly upwards when she clasped her hands in front of her for emphasis. So much so he was a little saddened when she reached her conclusion. "So you think Therese Keller had an unwanted child," Dylan said, more a statement than a question.

"It's a possibility, don't you think?"

"Anything's a possibility at this stage," Dylan shrugged, putting his notebook away.

"But it should be easy enough to prove," Claire replied with a wave of her hand. "You just get Therese's DNA and compare it to the child's."

Dylan smiled privately at Claire's naïveté. "I wish it were that simple, Ms. Dawson. Unfortunately, I have to show a direct link between Therese and the baby before I can get a DNA warrant, and at this point we don't even have a timeframe for the remains. Also, Therese was neither the only female occupant of the home nor its only owner. I don't have grounds yet for a warrant."

"Why do you need a warrant? Can't you just take DNA off her juice box or something? You see it all the time on television."

This time the smile was public. Such misconceptions usually annoyed Dylan but in Claire Dawson he found them endearing. Had he paused to ask himself why he might have inwardly acknowledged the unflattering fact that his libido was making allowances for her, his tolerance exchanged for the opportunity to educate her, to appear erudite in her eyes. But he didn't ask, he simply indulged, leaning inward just a little when he answered her. "Well, yes, that's true. It's called castaway. But the police can only collect castaway in places where there isn't an expectation of privacy. Therese Keller is in a private hospital, which might be construed by the courts as no different than if she were in her own home. And she's mentally incompetent so I can't get a voluntary sample. I have to tread carefully here. As much as it might frustrate me to operate within the boundaries of the law, I have no choice if I want to secure a conviction. And it's also important not to get ahead of oneself. It's possible this may not even be a homicide."

"But even if it isn't a homicide, don't you want to *know* what happened to it?" Claire asked, her eyes suddenly ablaze. "Don't you care to give it a *name*?" She regretted the question even before she asked it but the words spilled forth anyway, unfettered and raw, the implied accusation hanging heavily in the silence that followed.

"*It* is a she, Ms. Dawson," Dylan declared, rising to leave, "but thank you for your information. It's interesting and may prove useful."

Claire felt a crimson flush in her cheeks. She kept her eyes on his face but struggled to hold his gaze, for it seemed as if he were growing taller or she smaller; and so she quickly rose in the hope of regaining some semblance of equality and salvaging what was left of her good intentions. "I'm sorry, I didn't mean—"

Dylan's cellphone rang. Saved by the bell, he thought as he fished the phone out of his pocket. He glanced at the text message from Anil: *Prelims in. Bad news.* Dylan tensed, and his annoyance at Claire's insult was pushed aside by expedience: he had bigger worries now. "I'm sorry, Ms. Dawson, but I have to address this. I appreciate you coming in. And please don't hesitate to call if you have anything further." He pulled out a card from his breast pocket. "This has my direct line and cellphone numbers."

Flustered by the abrupt dismissal, Claire nervously smoothed back her hair behind one ear. "Of course. I'm sorry to have bothered you."

"It was no bother," Dylan smiled, but the smile was tense. He held out his hand.

Claire shook his hand then raised her own to her chin. "There's just, um, one other thing."

"Yes?" he replied, impatient to move on to Anil.

"Shortly after I started at Eastside, a woman—a prostitute actually—died on the school steps one day. The children were traumatized and so a Native medicine man came in and cleansed the school. It seemed to work. The whole atmosphere changed for the better. I was thinking," she paused, anxious, "I was thinking it might be good to have my house cleansed the same way. I was hoping that since you're Native—"

"Half Native," he corrected her.

"Since you're half Native that you might know someone."

"I'm sorry, I don't," Dylan lied. "Have you thought to call your colleagues?"

Claire nodded. "I called this morning. The medicine man, he died six months ago and they don't know of anyone else."

"I'm sorry, I can't help you there."

Claire smiled but her disappointment was evident. "Right. Well, um, thank you anyway." She turned to walk away when an inexplicable urge made her stop. "Detective," she asked over her shoulder, "do you believe in ghosts?"

"Excuse me?"

"It wasn't a rat's nest. I heard the baby crying." She said this matter-of-factly, in a voice not entirely her own, and the confession caught them both by surprise. Her expression read shock then confusion, then she turned her face away and fled the station.

Through the lobby windows Dylan watched Claire sprint furtively up the street, then he dialled Anil. "Hey, it's me," Dylan said into the phone, too distracted by Claire's admission to pay attention to his tone. "Tell me something useful."

"I'm fine, thanks for asking," Sanjit answered with obvious sarcasm. "Been here since six dissecting a baby so I'm a bit wiped. And you?"

Dylan winced under the weight of the reproach. "Jesus, Sanjit" was all Dylan managed to say before Anil cut him short: "My first guess was wrong. The baby was full-term and born alive, at least in theory: lung floated, liver sank. Mind you, won't stop a good defence attorney claiming she was stillborn and there was an attempt to resuscitate but at least you'll have reasonable doubt."

"Anything on race?" Dylan asked, hoping for more.

"Caucasian, brown hair and green eyes. That's useful: the combination is statistically small. Most often found in North America in those of Icelandic or Germanic descent."

"Age?"

"Can't tell for certain without dental. There's no fat left on the body to give us an accurate weight but I can tell you the length: 19.5 inches. Statistically that puts her between newborn and one month old."

Dylan sighed and pinched the bridge of his nose. "Cause of death?"

"So far indeterminate. Tox and trace will tell me more. But there's no obvious physical trauma to the body, no hematomas or broken bones. Spinal cord and brain are intact. Babies are difficult, Dylan, you know that. All it takes is a light pillow over the face and even the gods couldn't prove murder, assuming it was murder. You might have to settle for concealment."

"Fuck that. A baby in the wall deserves more than two years."

"I hear ya," Anil agreed, then paused. "There's something else."

"Yeah?"

"It's off the record."

"Go on."

"Was having a chat with a friend over breakfast. Emergency room doc. Your homeowner was brought in about seven months ago hallucinating about a dead baby. Doc remembered her because she was ranting about a married colleague in cardiology. The guy claimed she was some nut job who'd been stalking him."

Dylan's head shot up. He bolted outside the entrance and surveyed the street but Claire was long gone. "Shit!" he muttered into the phone.

"I know. And you didn't hear it from me," Anil said, then hung up the phone.

About the Author

M. A. Demers is a freelance writer, editor, and fine art photographer based near Vancouver, British Columbia.

Prior to publishing her first novel, *Baby Jane*, Demers wrote almost exclusively for the film industry, including the ghostwriting of production notes for over thirty major motion pictures. She is a screenwriter with, to date, six spec and four commissioned scripts, one optioned documentary project, and was the unaccredited story editor on the award-winning MOW *A Cooler Climate*, starring Sally Field and Judy Davis. Demers has many published editorials and articles in print or online, and is a featured essayist in *Writing About Literature: A Guide for the Student Critic*. She also blogs regularly on a variety of cultural issues at www.mademers.com/bad_egg.

On the photography side, Demers began her career in the late 1980s in Edmonton where she exhibited in several solo and group shows including at the Fringe Festival, The Works art festival, and with Celebration of Women in the Arts; she also took on small commercial assignments and acted as a creative consultant on other artists' projects. In 1992 she moved to London, England, where out of necessity she abandoned her photography career though she remained attached to the industry. In 1995 she returned to Canada and in 2007 turned her attention again to fine art photography but without forsaking her writing. You can see her fine art at www.mademers.com/fine_art_photography.html.

Made in the USA
Charleston, SC
11 November 2011